BEHAVIOURAL ECONOMICS IN CONSUMER POLICY

BEHAVIOURAL ECONOMICS IN CONSUMER POLICY

The Economic Analysis of Standard Terms in Consumer Contracts Revisited

Hanneke LUTH

intersentia
Antwerp – Oxford – Portland

Distribution for the UK:
Hart Publishing Ltd.
16C Worcester Place
Oxford OX1 2JW
UK
Tel.: +44 1865 51 75 30
Email: mail@hartpub.co.uk

Distribution for the USA and Canada:
International Specialized Book Services
920 NE 58th Ave Suite 300
Portland, OR 97213
USA
Tel.: +1 800 944 6190 (toll free)
Tel.: +1 503 287 3093
Email: info@isbs.com

Distribution for Austria:
Neuer Wissenschaftlicher Verlag
Argentinierstraße 42/6
1040 Vienna
Austria
Tel.: +43 1 535 61 03 24
Email: office@nwv.at

Distribution for other countries:
Intersentia Publishers
Groenstraat 31
2640 Mortsel
Belgium
Tel.: +32 3 680 15 50
Email: mail@intersentia.be

Behavioural Economics in Consumer Policy
Hanneke Luth

ISBN 978-94-000-0086-5
D/2010/7849/77
NUR 827

ACKNOWLEDGEMENTS

One of the final stages in a PhD project will often be writing the acknowledgements, even though it is the first part of the dissertation that you as a reader will turn to (except for the most adamant scholars, who might have browsed through the contents pages first; praise to you). This book represents a lot to me personally, and not only, and probably not even most importantly, as a means to get conferred the title of doctor. During these four and a half years of being immersed in academia, the scientific community has challenged me more than ever before. I've met the most wonderful people, I've had extremely stimulating discussions, travelling, flexibility, and pressure, all and all I am enormously happy that I have embarked upon the PhD path.

First and foremost, I would like to acknowledge the supervision of Roger Van den Bergh, my first supervisor. Roger, you have allowed me the opportunity to shape this PhD project, and my path all the way to the end result, in the way that I saw fit. I see myself as a person who needs to be allowed to do her own thing; that is the way in which I bring projects to a higher level. This research could not have developed the way it did without your gentle support, your belief in me, you allowing me to choose the focus and methodology that I wanted to apply even when you would never have opted for those yourself, and your aiding me in defining structure and scope. That being said, I do also appreciate the gentle nudges, and even the more harsh ones, towards writing it all down, mainly applied by Michael Faure. Michael, where I acknowledge Roger's help regarding the content of this thesis, you have been a tremendous support in making me finish. As you so rightly put it, I need a little pressure. Your understanding of that fact, and your acting upon it, allowed me to finish in a respectable timeframe. I am not sure when I would be writing these acknowledgements if it would not have been for you, but let's say it would probably have taken longer than volcanic ash clouds to disappear.[1]

Further acknowledgements are due to both of my paranymphs, Elaine and Margreet. The two of you have stood by me, endured my highs and lows, supported me at times with advice, and at times just by listening. Jeroen, mijn piefde, I do

[1] These acknowledgements have been written while enjoying an extended stay in Oxford, visiting my twin sister and future member of Parliament, Margreet. The extension was due to a misunderstanding involving the country of Iceland. Following the collapse of Landesbanki, the Netherlands and the UK had requested cash from this icy nation, but somehow the letter 'C' was lost in translation, which unfortunately resulted in the cancellation of flights, including but certainly not limited to my own.

love you and I hope we will spend the rest of our lives together. Ilja, I'll be forever happy you kicked out your boyfriend and asked me to move in; I could not have found a more compatable flatmate. Mom and dad, you have always supported me, even when I took ten years to complete my economics degree; it really means a lot to know that you are proud of me. Sonja, my fellow guinea pig, it has been great to have someone who can perfectly relate, as she is in exactly the same situation. L5-117 rules! Thanks for continuing to run when I slowed down. Hilda, thank you for being so empathic with my joys and troubles, and getting my mind off them by pressing me to take up sports again. When K is born, we will continue running! Michelle, thanks for always being there for me, especially when I need you.

Furthermore, I have tremendously enjoyed and benefitted from the support of all my colleagues in the RILE, EDLE, JAR, EPAR, BACT and ESL.[2] The best thing about the RILE is that you are treated as a full member of the team from the moment you step in; if I had wanted to stay in academia, the RILE would be the place for me. Special thanks to Wicher, without whom the RILE would have been lost, Louis, my mentor since many years, and Marianne for all her help and support. Dear Claudia, Stefano, Rosa, Ilan, Gwendoline, Sharon, Franzi, Katka, Vania, Weiqiang, Vera and the rest of the EDLE gang, it has been an honour to be part of this group. Thanks for providing the necessary distractions. Ulla, Marjolein, Monika, Betina, Aleks, Türkan, Jacob, Niels, Maarten, Pascal, JAR, EPAR and the rest of you: sometimes I wished you guys were as boring as I had imagined PhDs to be, but no, you had to be great fun and distract me from my job...

The last group of people, who have had a tremendous influence on my PhD project, but not always in a dissertation stimulating way, is the Erasmus Mundus Students and Alumni Association (EMA). Dear Rikke, Jenni, Pelicano, Sandra, Ross, Taghi, Chunyu, Manuel, Matt, Sebastian, Natalya, Koen, Vito, William, and everybody else that I have cooperated with during those three years: I have never enjoyed any position as much as I have enjoyed being an active member of EMA. EMA really brings the best people together: active, positive, intelligent, socially involved, with so much energy that you just cannot do anything but give yourself fully to the cause of improving European Higher Education, the Erasmus Mundus programme and the EMA itself. It has been an honour to serve on the Steering Committee as Jobs Team Coordinator and President, supporting the excellent work all of you did; it has been an amazing ride.

Egbert, Leonoor, Karst-Jan, Marleen, Cees Jan, Eveline and Lennard, I love you very much. Opa, er is maar een reden waarom ik het jammer vind dat dit

2 Acronyms seem to be as useful and popular in academic communities as they are annoying for outsiders. Therefore, some clarifications are due. RILE: Rotterdam Institute of Law and Economics; EDLE: European Doctorate in Law and Economics; JAR: Legal PhD Association Rotterdam; EPAR: Erasmus PhD Association Rotterdam; BACT: Behavioural Approaches to Contract and Tort, the research programme in ESL that this PhD project is a part of; ESL: Erasmus School of Law.

proefschrift in het Engels geschreven diende te worden: ik weet dat jij het graag had willen lezen. Opa en oma's, bedankt voor alle goede zorgen, gedurende mijn hele leven. Clubje Circuit, it's been almost twelve years and we are still going strong! Then of course there are so many others that have left their footprints somewhere along my PhD path. Sometimes with aid and advice, or inviting me for a conference or presentation, sometimes just by going out for a coffee, dinner or drink, and providing me with the necessary perspective on life that there is more than the PhD. Or maybe, just by reading the end result! My sincere gratitude goes out to all of you. I hope you will enjoy reading this book.

Oxford, 19th April 2010

CONTENTS

LIST OF ABBREVIATIONS AND ACRONYMS

B2B; B2C; C2C	Business-to-business; business-to-consumer; consumer-to-consumer; referring to contracts
CLAB	European Database on Case Law about Unfair Contractual Terms
DCFR	Draft Common Frame of Reference: Principles, Definitions and Model Rules of European Private Law
DG SANCO	Directorate General for Health and Consumers, part of European Commission
ECC	European Consumer Centres
ECJ	European Court of Justice
EC / EEC	European Community / European Economic Community
EU	European Union
FTC	Federal Trade Commission (US)
NMa	Dutch Competition Authority
OECD	Organisation for Economic Co-operation and Development
OFT	Office of Fair Trading (UK)
RECAP	Record, evaluate and compare alternative prices, a method for giving people feedback on their choices
RCT	Rational Choice Theory
RIA	Regulatory Impact Analysis
SER	Social Economic Council (the Netherlands)
UK	United Kingdom
US	United States of America
WRR	Scientific Council for Government Policy (the Netherlands)

CHAPTER 1
INTRODUCTION

1.1. INTRODUCTION

Before the credit crisis swept across global economies, affecting all nations and almost all individuals, rational choice was quite well established as the main paradigm to inform policy making. While occasionally criticism did occur, on the whole this paradigm continued to be regarded as the most helpful in predicting human behaviour, partly because it is a lean and simple theory that can be used to make very general predictions. In the real world, people were thought not to behave irrationally. According to rational choice theory, people will weigh their options more carefully when decisions really matter; when decisions have considerable consequences. Irrational behaviour may be found in some experiments, but it tends to disappear when things really matter, or so it was argued.[3] Recent developments however, most significantly the credit crisis but also other factors such as issues pertaining to deregulated markets, have created an understanding in policy discussion and economic theory not only that people are not that rational after all, but more importantly that public policy should account for that. Several commentators argue that perhaps economic theory should be based upon another paradigm, at least when regarding some contexts in which individuals are prone to suffer from biased decision making.[4] These new insights suggested that policy making based upon classic economic theory should also be adjusted in certain cases, and be based upon a more realistic view of individual behaviour. The unconditional belief in the rational behaviour of mankind and the predictive value of traditional economic insights is waning.

Behavioural economics is seen in economic theory as a possible contender for this more realistic view in the recent decades. The insights that have been developed in behavioural literature have enhanced the understanding of individual behaviour and the accuracy of predictions made regarding individual behaviour. The insights of behavioural economics focus on the decision making process of individuals. In for instance consumer protection policy, the idea that

3 See Ariely (2009: xii-xv) discussing these arguments brought against his research.

4 Several contributions have been made to literature that argue extensively against the unconditional belief in the value of the rational choice paradigm for theory and policy, see for instance: Thaler and Sunstein (2008), Ariely (2009), Velthuis and Noordegraaf-Eelens (2009), and Akerlof and Shiller (2009).

as long as consumers are adequately informed they are competent to discipline the market and push sellers to draft well-balanced contract terms was prevalent. The idea runs as follows: as long as consumers are adequately informed, they are competent to discipline the market and push sellers to draft well-balanced contract terms. If competition is sufficiently present, sellers have to compete for consumers. If consumers shop for the best deals and are vigilant market parties, they can themselves assure that they will not be taken advantage of. Recently however, this position has been more and more criticised. Various authors have pointed out that the above described process will not work quite so smoothly without certain information. If consumers are to profit from the internal market and competition, they have to be able to receive and process this information and they have to be able to take welfare-enhancing decisions on the basis of it. And that is where behavioural insights come in. Behavioural notions suggest that consumers are constraint by several cognitive factors, emotions, preferences for fairness and so on. Due to these constraints, consumers are not able to optimise their decision making as is suggested by conventional economic theory. The enhancement of the understanding of consumer decision making processes sheds a new light upon the effectiveness of information duties and the reliance on consumer vigilance to discipline market.

The literature on behavioural economics however, even though it was once regarded as extremely promising, has of yet failed to influence policies to a very significant extent (Amir et al., 2005). Behavioural insights raise numerous points of critique to for instance consumer policies, some of which indeed pose valid concerns. Opponents point to the context-dependent nature of behavioural insights and argue that they are therefore insufficiently valid to inform general consumer policies. Another point that has been made against translating behavioural insights to policy is that the market mechanism itself may correct biased consumer behaviour, rendering policy based upon behavioural insight unnecessary. Even if we grant, for now, that these points of criticism have some merit, behavioural insights can still improve the explanations and predictions regarding consumer behaviour to a certain extent. The question becomes therefore whether behavioural insights can be translated into consumer policy in a way that enhances social welfare but that at the same time takes due notice of any valid cautions and considerations that might be raised against a policy based upon behavioural economics. This research aims at providing an answer to that question.

1.2. AIM OF RESEARCH

1.2.1. RESEARCH QUESTIONS

The research that is presented in this dissertation has the dual aim of assessing two main and interrelated research questions. The first discussion focuses upon the addition of behavioural insights to the economic insights regarding consumer policy. In behavioural literature, it is argued that especially in the realm of consumer protection the insights derived from behavioural economics can have far-reaching implications. However, behavioural literature in its aim to influence theory and policy literature has also evoked some valid points of critique. This research therefore first aims to answer the following research question:

1. To what extent can the application of insights from behavioural economics and empirical research to economic analysis be relied upon to improve consumer policy from a social welfare perspective?

To answer this question, an introduction to both economic rationales of consumer protection and behavioural insights to the issue will be presented. It will be concluded that behavioural economics is able to provide recommendations to consumer policy that can be justified from a social welfare perspective beyond the traditional rationales provided by economic theory. After that, the debate regarding the desirability of relying upon behavioural insights to improve consumer policy is reviewed, highlighting and discussing the most important concerns. It will be concluded that even though the application of behavioural insight can be relied upon to enhance consumer policy from a social welfare perspective, several cautions and considerations should be taken into account. Guidelines to counteract several concerns are presented, among which the recommendation that behavioural insights should be used to inform consumer policy in specific rather than general policy issues.

Therefore, and to further assess the extent to which behavioural insights inform consumer policy in a welfare-enhancing way, the discussion turns to the issue of policy interventions in standardised terms in consumer contracts. This issue has been extensively discussed in conventional economic theory, and was by many regarded to be sufficiently explored. It was argued that as long as information asymmetry problems were properly counteracted, the consumer would discipline the market and bring about efficient terms in standardised consumer contracts. Applying behavioural insights to this issue however changes the assessment. Behavioural insights into the consumer decision making process challenge the conclusion that consumer vigilance, aided by information remedies, can sufficiently discipline sellers into drafting fair contract terms. The second research question assessed in this dissertation is therefore the following:

2. To what extent can consumer policy regarding standardised consumer contract terms be improved by re-assessing policy on the basis of behavioural economic insights and proposing corresponding interventions from a social welfare perspective?

The answer to this research question comprises three different analyses. First, it is analysed to what extent behavioural insights can improve traditional economic *policy recommendations* concerning standardised consumer contract terms. Based upon this analysis and empirical studies, it will be concluded that behavioural insights can improve policy recommendations in cautioning against overly relying upon information duties and consumer vigilance to overcome the market failure of information asymmetry. The second analysis turns to the legal debate, reviewing the *common core of European unfair terms regimes*. It will be explained that these regimes do depend upon information asymmetry and consumer vigilance to a large extent. Therefore, the third analysis reviews *policy strategies* to enhance unfair terms regimes. Based upon this last assessment, it will be argued that an often mentioned policy strategy, namely solving the signing-without-reading problem, will not be efficient or effective. The most promising proposals aiming to enhance consumer policy on standardised contract terms are pre-approval of standardised contract terms through administrative control and negotiating a model form of standard terms through business and consumer representatives.

1.2.2. RELEVANCE

This research is highly relevant from both a theoretical and a policy making perspective. One of the main questions pertaining to policy interventions in consumer policy nowadays is: what to do with behavioural insights? Recent developments related to mainly the credit crisis and deregulation of markets seem to have left policy makers somewhat reluctant to once again place their trust in traditional policy recommendations based upon rational choice. Policy institutions such as the OECD, the FTC, the OFT and ministries in European Member States are aware of the upcoming behavioural economic literature;[5] the suggestions that stem from this literature have however not been used extensively in policy as of yet. This is mainly because it is not yet clear how and to what extent exactly behavioural insights can and should inform (consumer) policy. It is this question that this research aims to answer. It points out which cautions and considerations are relevant in both the theoretical and policy making debate. Moreover, the research devises guidelines to account for some of these concerns in a cautious way. Whereas these cautions and considerations have frequently

---

5 See below, chapter 3, section 3.3.2a.

been discussed in several publications, guidelines providing a way of dealing with (some of) the concerns have not been offered often.[6] The guidelines developed in this research can be used to form a basis for devising policy procedures that cautiously implement the insights of behavioural economics into policies and policy recommendations, while accounting for the cautions and considerations regarding behaviourally informed consumer policy that have been identified. This research takes a stance in the academic debate between behavioural scholars and conventional economists regarding the added value of behavioural insights to economic theory. It presents the crucial aspects of this debate and argues how behavioural insights can successfully inform both economic theory and policy.

Furthermore, this research exemplifies how behavioural insights can improve consumer policy by focusing upon the issue of standardised consumer contract terms. This research applies the insights from behavioural economics to the issue of standard terms in consumer contracts. Previous publications on the economic analysis of standard terms have only limitedly involved behavioural insights.[7] In this research, not only behavioural notions are applied to the issue of standard terms in consumer contracts, but also results from empirical research are added to the analysis. These empirical studies provide further insights to critical questions in the debate, such as how many consumers read standard terms, factors that are given by consumers for failing to read, whether standard form contracts contain onerous terms, and so on. Economic policy recommendations regarding standardised consumer contract terms are thus enhanced by the improved analysis that is presented in this research.

Continuingly, the common core in European legal systems regarding standard terms consumer policies is reviewed, and several suggestions to improve these policies are assessed using insights derived in the improved analytical framework. The desirability of government interventions in standard terms in consumer contracts is therefore reassessed by adding insights from behavioural literature and empirical studies to the analysis.

Moreover, in this research a systematic research method for assessing policy questions from an economic and a behavioural economic perspective is presented. The proposed method first focuses upon the economic and behavioural insights and then turns to actual policy, followed by an assessment of proposed interventions. The analytical method, that is used to assess standard terms policy in this research, can also be used to assess other policy questions, especially in the field of consumer protection policy. By systematically reviewing the different perspectives to the debate, and including empirical insights to the analysis,

6 See for some of many publications discussing relevant concerns pertaining to behaviour economics and relying upon behavioural economics to inform the policy debate: Posner (1998a), Sunstein and Thaler (2003), Camerer et al. (2003), Camerer and Loewenstein (2004), Epstein (2006; 2008) and Bar-Gill (2008).

7 Notable exceptions are: Becher (2007; 2008), Ben-Shahar (2009), Stark and Choplin (2009) and White (2009).

policy questions can be evaluated more extensively than merely relying upon one discipline.

1.2.3. METHODOLOGY

This research takes a multidimensional approach. Combining different kinds of sources and several (scientific) perspectives on the same issue will result in a translation of all these insights to provide an answer to relevant policy questions (Van Boom, Giesen and Verheij, 2008: 35). The analysis of consumer policy includes both traditional economic insights and behavioural insights. The more specific analysis of standardised consumer contract terms is approached from a multitude of perspectives. First, the issue is approached by *traditional* or *neoclassical* economic method, followed by an assessment focusing upon the *information economic* aspects. Then the analysis turns to *behavioural* insights, and compares the explanations and hypotheses stemming from neoclassical, information and behavioural economics based upon results from *empirical studies*. Finally, a *legal perspective* is presented, analysing actual consumer policy that addresses the issue of standardised consumer terms.

This research distinguishes between the *neoclassical* or *traditional economic* approach, the *information economic* approach, and the *behavioural economic* approach. The boundaries of these, especially the first two approaches, are not clearly drawn in literature. Economics of information can also be seen to be a part of the neoclassical approach, even though the insights stemming from a focus on information change the previous insights derived in earlier neoclassical economic discussions. The importance of information to consumer protection issues was clearly established only in later stages of neoclassical economic thinking. The impact of insights from psychology and other social sciences on consumer protection theory and policy followed only in behavioural economics. The distinction between the views in economics before information issues were deeply considered, the economic views that do consider the impact of information on consumer protection, and the economic views that regard insights from psychology and other social sciences is made clear in this research through distinguishing the different economic approaches as mentioned.

The economic analyses of laws, policies and other government interventions, that are present in this research, are conducted on the basis of the assumption that the primary goal of laws, policies and government interventions is the enhancement or ideally the maximisation of social welfare. This type of assessment does not negate the possibility that other valid policy goals could be envisaged and are indeed adhered to by government, such as a (more) equal distribution of resources, justice or fairness. It will however evaluate government interventions only on the basis of social welfare enhancement or maximisation. Even though issues such as a (more) equal distribution of resources are highly relevant in policy discussions, they will not or only to a very limited extent be included in the analysis. Both positive and normative economic analysis of law will be employed in this research.[8]

Reviewing the legal debate, this research aims to present the common core (or *ius commune*) of unfair terms regimes, instead of presenting a comprehensive comparative analysis of several legal systems. This approach is commonly used in comparative law and economics.[9] It allows for a description of the possible use of economic and behavioural insights in actual policy without having to account for all the specific details that are a part of respective legal systems. The analysis of the common core can be used in further research to assess specific legal systems and, where possible, provide recommendations to enhance the legal system while taking the specificities of that legal system into account.

1.2.4. SCOPE OF RESEARCH

As stated above, this research focuses on the economic and behavioural analysis of consumer policy in general, and on the analysis of consumer standard contract terms more specifically. Economic analysis of consumer contracts is mainly concerned with information asymmetry problems. In this research, these issues are considered to be the primary concern of consumer protection policy. To the extent that competition issues are a problem in the relevant consumer markets, competition policy should cure these particular market failures. Competition issues will therefore be outside the focus of this research; the analysis will assume markets to be competitive. This assumption will allow a focus on the issue that is considered to be most problematic in the economic analysis of consumer protection: information asymmetries.

Furthermore, this research assesses transactions conducted between commercial parties and consumers, also known as business-to-consumer (or B2C) contracts. Business-to-business (B2B) or consumer-to-consumer (C2C) contracts will also fall outside the scope of the analysis. As will be discussed in chapter 6, most consumer protection legislation applies to B2C contracts. Moreover, it is these types of contracts in which the market failure of information

8 In *positive economic analysis* of the law, the effects of laws, regulations and policies are looked into. The questions which are focus of the analysis concern the likely effects of the law, whether these effects have actually occurred, and whether the objectives of the law have been arrived at. *Normative economics* centers on the concept of allocative efficiency (see below, chapter 2, section 2.2.1). Allocative efficiency is an ideal type notion describing the situation in which all goods are possessed by the parties that value those most. In that situation, social welfare would be at the highest level possible. Normative economics assesses whether allocative efficiency is attained, and suggests how improvements can be made from an efficiency point of view. See for a more extensive description of both positive and normative economics: Burrows and Veljanovski (1981: 5–13).

9 See for an introduction to this approach: Bussani and Mattei (1997: 340 mainly).

asymmetry is most likely to exist, even though it can also occur in B2B or C2C contracts; this will be more extensively discussed in chapter 2. Finally, the focus in this research will be on exchange contracts; employment contracts or other contracts that might be conducted between individuals and commercial parties are therefore outside of the scope of this research as well.

The analysis of consumer standardised terms takes a general approach, in the sense that it discusses the general issue of standard terms in consumer contracts. By taking this approach, this research is able to re-assess the insights developed in the conventional economic debate towards standard terms in consumer contracts, which also takes a general perspective. The desirability of specific terms that can be found in standard terms contracts is not reviewed in this research. In addition, specific standard term contracts such as for instance software licences or consumer financial products are not taken up in the analysis either, although the discussion might touch upon these specific topics when they are the focus of empirical studies that are relevant for this dissertation. The insights developed on the general issue of standard terms in consumer contracts might be used in further research to assess specific consumer contracts, such as mortgage contracts, online vending or time-share agreements, and specific contract terms such as certain risk allocations, late payment fees, terms that specify procedural specifications for terminating contracts or requesting refunds, terms that specify the legal regime that governs the contract, caps on damages, and so on.

When discussing interventions into the market by the government, this thesis will focus on regulation. Other types of government intervention, such as enforcement, will be mentioned, but will mainly fall outside the scope of this research. Limiting the scope will enable an in-depth discussion of regulatory issues, focusing on standard terms in consumer contracts. Considering the interplay between regulation and enforcement, it is important to first address the desirability in terms of costs and benefits of specific regulation and possible improvements to it. Before delving deeper into issues of improving the enforcement of certain regulations, the desirability of those regulations itself should first be evaluated.

While this thesis combines the insights of neoclassical economics, information economics, behavioural economics and empirical research by applying all these approaches to the single issue of regulating standard terms in consumer contracts, this research does not aim to extend or improve upon existing theories. Neither will empirical studies be undertaken to enlarge empirical insights into the research questions that are relevant to this topic. The aim of this research is to translate the insights that have been developed in the respective scientific approaches to policy. This step in the scientific analysis of laws and policy is often lacking. This project aims to fill that gap in the discussion of how consumer policy, on the basis of these insights, can deal with issues related to the regulation of standard terms in consumer contracts. Extending theories and performing empirical studies would go beyond the scope of the research project.

When translating the insights from neoclassical, information and behavioural economics to consumer standard term policy, a general approach will be taken with respect the implementation of the lessons learnt for policy. The common core of legal approaches employed in European legal systems will be used as a basis for interpreting the insights derived. Specific legal systems should be assessed on the basis of the insights derived in this research project to examine the need for adjusting these legal systems. Furthermore, when suggesting strategies that could be followed when improving legal policies regarding consumer standard terms, a general approach will again be followed. The discussion of several strategies that seek to improve current standard term policies intends to suggest approaches that could constitute an enhancement of current policies. These suggestions, and their costs and effects, should be examined in more detail before it can be concluded that they will indeed provide a welfare enhancing improvement of European legal systems. In addition, the approaches that have been distinguished in this research as promising would need to be better adapted to the specificities of respective legal systems before they can be operationalised. This thesis consequently aims at providing a starting point for further discussions on implementable improvements to consumer policy on standard contract terms.

1.3. STRUCTURE OF RESEARCH

This research aims to find out whether, and if so how, behavioural insights can improve economic policy recommendations that target consumer policy in general and standard terms regimes more specifically. Chapter 2 of this research will therefore first introduce the conventional economic approach towards interventions in consumer markets. A rationale for government intervention in consumer contracts from a social welfare perspective will be found in the correction of market failures and the limitation of transaction costs. The most important market failures in consumer markets are competition issues, transactions costs and information asymmetry. Of these, information asymmetry is the main concern of consumer policy.

Behavioural economics will be introduced in chapter 3. Insights into the decision making process of individuals show that the predictions stemming from traditional economics often do not hold.[10] Consumer decision making is shown to be affected by several biases and heuristics, which is argued by behavioural economics to have serious and potentially detrimental consequences for consumer and social welfare. This welfare loss might justify government interventions from a social welfare perspective. Chapter 3 will establish that behavioural insights can give implications for policy, especially consumer policy, which go beyond conventional economic insights.

10 See below, chapter 3, most notably 3.2.3.

However, even when behavioural insights are shown to enhance the understanding and predictions of consumer decision making, the conclusion that it would be desirable to account for behavioural insights in consumer policy does not automatically follow. Chapter 4 discusses various concerns that are raised with respect to the role of behavioural insights in informing welfare-enhancing consumer policy. Methodological concerns refer to issues such as the context-specificity of behavioural insights, fear of overly generalising behavioural results and the parsimonious advantages of economic theory. The policy debate focuses upon issues such as consumers learning to overcome biased decision making, whether sellers are able and in fact do abuse consumer biases, policy makers' errors in deciding what is best for consumers and the enhanced risk of manipulation that could result from behaviourally informed consumer policy. It will be concluded that as long as several considerations are sufficiently taken into account, behavioural insights can and should be used in theory and policy recommendations aimed at enhancing social welfare. In addition, guidelines to account for some of the cautions and considerations that have been identified will be provided.

To further assess the extent to which behavioural insights can be used to inform consumer policy in a welfare-enhancing way, chapter 5 turns to the issue of the desirability of policy interventions in standardised terms in consumer contracts. This assessment constitutes a re-assessment of the extensive review of that has been portrayed in economic literature discussing how to regulate standard terms in consumer contracts on the basis of new insights developed in behavioural literature. Two main conclusions are arrived at in this chapter. First, when the aim is to enhance the quality of standard terms in consumer contracts from a social welfare perspective, government interventions beyond providing information remedies can be beneficial. These policy interventions should limit the dependence on consumer vigilance to discipline the market in providing efficient standardised terms. Secondly, as the shift in policy focus away from relying upon consumer vigilance and information remedies stems from behavioural notions and empirical research, behavioural notions and empirical research provide an improvement to the policy recommendations stemming from mainstream economics in the context of standardised consumer contract terms.

Chapter 6 reviews the issue of standard terms in consumer contracts from a legal perspective by assessing the common core in European legal approaches to consumer standard terms. The common core will be explained to correspond mainly to the insights of information economics. Information remedies form the main intervention method in standard terms policy; intervention to improve the quality of these terms often relies greatly on consumer vigilance. The effectiveness of these intervention methods is discussed based upon the behavioural insights derived.

In chapter 7, several strategies to enhance standard term consumer policy will be assessed. The aim of this assessment is to provide a starting point for discussions on how to improve current legal approaches towards regulating consumer standard terms by identifying approaches that are likely well able to improve the quality of standard terms in consumer contracts. In this research, it will be argued that solving the signing-without-reading problem will not bring the ultimate solution; pre-approval of standard terms through administrative monitoring, and a model form of standard terms that results from negotiations between business and consumer interest groups, are more promising proposals when the aim is to enhance the quality of consumer standardised terms.

Chapter 8 concludes by providing an answer to the research questions that have been presented in this introduction. It will be concluded that at least theoretically, it is possible to enhance consumer policy through the application of behavioural economic insights in a social welfare enhancing way. This will however require the cautions and considerations identified regarding the translation of behavioural insights to policy to be taken into account, possibly through the guidelines that have been devised. Second, this research concludes that behavioural insights are able to enhance economic policy recommendations regarding standard terms in consumer contracts by arguing for a limited dependence upon information disclosure and consumer vigilance. This shift in policy focus is a clear addition to the economic analysis of standard terms, constituting insights that would not have resulted but for the application of behavioural insights to the issue of standard terms in consumer contracts. It will be argued that implementation of these enhanced policy recommendations will improve the common core of unfair terms regimes. The main focus of policy should not be on solving signing-without-reading, but on enhancing the content of standard term contracts. Recommendations for further research will conclude this dissertation, pointing to the necessity to further explore specific legal systems, specific standard terms and specific business sectors when behavioural insights are to inform and improve consumer policy regarding standardised contract terms.

CHAPTER 2
ECONOMIC RATIONALES FOR CONSUMER PROTECTION

2.1. INTRODUCTION

As has been explained in the introduction, this research aims to find out whether, and if so how, behavioural insights can add to conventional economic theory and change consumer policy recommendations. The answer to this question will start with a discussion of the conventional economic approach towards interventions in consumer markets and the implications that behavioural insights will have on consumer protection. In this chapter the conditions under which government interventions in consumer markets are desirable from an economic point of view will be assessed. The next chapter focuses on behavioural insights to consumer decision making.

Many strands in economic theory focus on the actions and interventions of government institutions into the market. Law and Economics is one of these strands; using economic theories to analyse laws, regulations, policies and other legal instruments and actions. This chapter will start with an outline of some concepts used in the economic analysis of law. The economic rationale for government interventions in markets is provided by the need to reduce transaction costs and correct market failures such as incomplete competition, public goods, externalities and information asymmetry. Government interventions are costly however, and besides that, market solutions to counteract market failures and decrease transaction costs are also provided within the market itself. The costs and benefits of government interventions should therefore be carefully assessed, taking the subsidiarity with market solutions into account.

Regarding consumer contracts, issues resulting in welfare decreases relate mainly to transaction costs, information asymmetries and competition. This research focuses on the first two. Transaction costs in consumer contracts consist of many types. Contracting costs can be decreased by the instrument of contract law itself, through the setting of default terms. To overcome rational apathy, the government might provide or stimulate the provision of simple and comparable information, written in plain language, by sellers. Information asymmetries, resulting in adverse selection, might be counteracted by disclosure duties or mandatory quality standards. To overcome market failures, government intervention is not always necessary. Market solutions can also correct the market mechanism. Reputation, brands and warranties signal information; the market for market information will decrease information asymmetries and transaction costs. Other considerations regarding government interventions in consumer contracts include the costs of intervening, consumer moral hazard, decreased choice options, and the provision of optimal information instead of full information.

2.2. ECONOMIC RATIONALES FOR GOVERNMENT INTERVENTION

The economic analysis of law provides several justifications for government intervention in the market, but also prescribes certain conditions for those interventions. After briefly portraying some of the main concepts of the methodology of economic analysis of law, such as welfare, efficiency and the several forms of market failure, the economic rationales for government intervention will be discussed.

2.2.1. METHODOLOGY OF ECONOMIC ANALYSIS OF LAW

Law and economics is a scientific approach used to describe and predict the effects of rules, laws, regulations, policies and other legal instruments on the behaviour of people.[11] The desirability of these effects is analysed, and potentially more efficient alternative solutions are formulated. Legal rules are seen as instruments to influence the behaviour of people, whether they are individual actors, civil servants or whether they act on behalf of a (private business) company. Legal rules affect people to make a different decision than they would have done in absence of the legal rule. An example can be found in liability law: people are deterred from certain actions if and because they would have to pay damages for engaging in these actions. The economic analysis of law typically involves one or all of three fundamental questions:

1. Which goal is achieved by a certain legal rule, what is the rationale behind it?
2. Which effects are caused by this legal rule?
3. Is the legal rule desirable from a social welfare point of view?

---

[11] In this chapter, a brief introduction to the economic analysis of law is provided. More extensive introductions to the scientific approach of law and economics can be found in several publications, such as Posner (1998b), Cooter and Ulen (2003), Kanning and Kerkmeester (2004), Schäfer and Ott (2004), Weterings (2007). The introduction presented in this chapter draws mainly from these publications.

The first two questions are referred to as *positive law and economics*: using economic analysis to predict the effects of various legal rules. Positive law and economics also offers descriptions of the goals that are achieved by legal rules, and why these legal rules are in place. *Normative law and economics* makes policy recommendations based on the economic consequences of various policies.

a. *The concept of welfare*

An important current within the economic analysis is focused on maximisation of *welfare*, which may refer to either *individual* or *social welfare*. Welfare or *utility* is the extent to which the preferences of individuals can be fulfilled with the means and goods that are available to them. The further the preferences of an individual are met, the more individual welfare is obtained by this person. Also, as her welfare is part of social welfare, the more her position contributes to the welfare of society as a whole. The notion of *social welfare* refers to the commonly obtained welfare by all individuals together. A raise in individual welfare does not necessarily have the same effect on social welfare: where an individual increases his own welfare and by doing so 'hurts' the welfare of other people, social welfare might diminish as a result of this action. When economic assessments refer to welfare in general, usually social welfare is implied.

b. *Rational Choice Theory*

In conventional law and economics, the choices people make to increase their welfare are predicted using *Rational Choice Theory* (RCT).[12] When several choices are available, individuals are assumed or hypothesised to opt for the alternative that yields the most expected welfare.[13] When someone decides to buy a new car, he will buy the car that conforms best to his preferences. Also, buying the car implies that this person attaches more welfare to the car than to the money itself, or to other objects he could buy for this money. RCT tries to conceptualise the way in which individuals make decisions. RCT states that people make decisions based upon stable and consistent preferences. In their decisions they try to best accommodate their preferences, thereby maximising their utility. People are also assumed to be able to optimally assess and acquire information, including information about the risks and possible outcomes of the decisions involved. Lastly most economic reasoning assumes economic man to be a self-interested, mostly

12 Rational Choice Theory is similar to Expected Utility Theory. There are minor differences, of which the main one is that RCT is slightly more general than Expected Utility Theory. Although this dissertation will usually refer to RCT, for the purpose of this research both terms are interchangeable.

13 The individual and the individual decision making process are focal points in this analysis, a method known as methodological *individualism*.

financially motivated actor, with utter disregard for the wellbeing of other people.[14] RCT is not concerned with the actual decision making process of individuals; it merely addresses the outcome of the decision making. To summarise, Issacharoff distinguishes five characteristics of the law and economics approach concerning individual behaviour (Issacharoff, 1998: 1732):

1. People respond to costs and benefits (the incentives) of options before them
2. They evaluate their options accounting for different time settings
3. They invest in acquiring information to an optimal level
4. Evaluations are accurate, any mistakes are random and non-systematic
5. When incentives change, behaviour changes correspondingly

Different versions of RCT have been developed over time, but often scholars do not make explicit which version of RCT they adhere to in their research. Korobkin and Ulen provide a categorisation of the different versions of RCT, visualising the different conceptions of RCT in a spectrum (Korobkin and Ulen, 2000: 1060–7, see figure 1). The dominant conceptions of RCT are the expected utility version and the self-interest version (captured in bold in figure 1). In the definitional version of RCT, an individual is simply supposed to rationally maximise his ends. This version of RCT does not take any normative stance on either the means or the ends of this individual. People are assumed to rationally maximise their ends, therefore any behaviour can be justified as rational, since it is assumed that any behaviour serves the ends (or utility) of the individual. Because people act, their act must necessarily be rational and welfare-enhancing; if the act would not be rational and welfare-enhancing, people would not engage in the action. This is the 'thinnest' version of RCT, meaning that it is non-falsifiable.

Figure 1. Rational Choice Theory Spectrum

"Thin" Conceptions			"Thick" Conceptions
◄			►
Definitional Version	**Expected Utility Version**	**Self-Interest Version**	Wealth Maximising Version

Source: Korobkin and Ulen (2000: 1061).

The expected utility version does specify some of the means by which the decision maker will try to maximise his ends, and is therefore 'thicker' than the definitional version. Namely, the decision maker is assumed to attach values of utility to each available option, and assess the risks that are concerned with each option. Discounting the utility with the related risk, the option that yields the highest expected benefit is revealed and will be opted for. This version is however also thin in the sense that it does not specify the goals or preferences

[14] This last issue is not always part of the RCT framework, even though it is often implicitly assumed; see for a more extensive description of RCT, Kelman (2003: 1352–60).

that the individual will try to achieve, making the expected utility model to some extent testable, even though it does not lead to the creation of directly falsifiable behavioural predictions.

The self-interest version is a thicker version of RCT from which these directly falsifiable behavioural predictions can be derived. Besides making assumptions about the means through which the individual will try to assume his ends, the self-interest version predicts also which goals or ends the individual will try to achieve, namely that what is in their self-interest. It assumes individuals are not concerned about the disutility their courses of action cause to other people. The fourth version of RCT, the wealth maximisation version, goes even further in predicting the ends that decision makers will try to achieve and is therefore the 'thickest' of the four versions. This version predicts that individuals will try to maximise their financial well-being or monetary situation. These last two thick versions of RCT dominate economic literature.

c. *Efficiency and optimal allocation of goods*

Efficiency is the central criterion in law and economics used to assess legal rules and policies. The extent to which a certain rule can enhance (social) welfare determines whether or not it is efficient. A shift from one law or policy to another is efficient when the proposed alternative yields a better cost-benefit ratio (more benefits than costs). In literature, several definitions and concepts of efficiency can be found. They all however share one central idea: that nothing more can be achieved with the same amount of resources. When the cost-benefit ratio of a certain proposed solution is positive (more benefits than costs), it is said to be *cost-effective.*

Two well-known concepts of efficiency are *Pareto* and *Kaldor-Hicks efficiency.* The former relates to a situation in which nobody can be made better off without making another person worse off. A *Pareto improvement* is a change in the current situation which leaves at least one party better off, whereas all other parties involved at least not worse off compared to the status-quo. An example would be a rule prescribing all traffic participants to drive on the right side of the road. This rule serves a coordination purpose; it is impossible for interested parties to come together and agree on it in some sort of contract. This rule is Pareto efficient, as everyone is better off knowing how the other parties will behave on the road.

The second concept, Kaldor-Hicks efficiency, refers to situations in which social welfare is optimised. This means that all parties are as well off as they can get. This concept of efficiency is used to describe a certain ideal state of a market.[15] When in a certain market all goods are distributed in such a way that the end users (consumers) are able to accommodate their preferences optimally, this

[15] 'A market' refers to the sum of all supply and demand of related goods and services. 'The market' refers to the aggregation of supply and demand in general.

market it said to display *allocative efficiency*, which corresponds to Kaldor-Hicks efficiency. The market is producing the right goods for the right people at the right price. When all goods are in the hands of those individuals that value them most the optimal allocation of goods is reached. Goods are produced up to the level where production costs equal the proceeds of these goods.[16] In the ideal market, whenever someone values a good at a level which is higher than the production costs of this good, the good is produced and supplied to this person. To illustrate, when someone owns a painting which his neighbour values higher than him, the market has not reached allocative efficiency. Selling the painting from the one individual to the other would increase welfare. When all transactions that would increase welfare have taken place and no other transactions can occur that would increase welfare, allocative efficiency has been achieved in the market. To reach this ideal-type situation, the initial allocation of rights (to goods and services) is irrelevant; through transactions a more efficient allocation of rights can be established. This is called the *Coase theorem* (Coase, 1960).[17] The Coase theorem however does not account for transaction costs, which might prevent individuals from entering into a welfare-enhancing transaction.

A *Kaldor-Hicks improvement* then is a change in the current situation in which social welfare is increased, even if in some cases individual welfare is not. If the parties that are better off could *in theory* compensate those that are made worse off, so that a Pareto improving outcome would result, a Kaldor-Hicks improvement is established. For instance, when someone builds a garden shed, his welfare is increased (presumably, otherwise his decision to build it would not be rational). His neighbour however might suffer from the shade this garden shed produces in his garden. The tan-loving neighbour's welfare might be decreased by the building of the garden shed. If the welfare increase of the shed-building neighbour outweighs the welfare of the tan-loving neighbour, the building of the shed is Kaldor-Hicks improvement, even though it is not a Pareto improvement. The shed-building neighbour could compensate the tan-loving neighbour for his loss, in which case a Pareto improvement would result, which is also Kaldor-Hicks improvement. However, even if the compensation does not take place, a Kaldor-Hicks improvement is still the outcome of the change in situation.[18] Pareto improvements are by definition Kaldor-Hicks improvements; the opposite is not the case.

16 The marginal costs of production, which refers to the increase in total production costs when one more unit of the good is produced, is in the optimal level of production equal to the price that can be attained for this good.

17 This is also related to the Adam Smith (1904) that individual pursuit of self-interest will lead to the optimal operation of the free market, which will result in the maximisation of social welfare.

18 See for a discussion: Arrow (1950).

2.2.2. TRANSACTION COSTS AND MARKET FAILURES

Allocative efficiency can only be achieved in a perfect market: a market without market failures or transactions costs. When market imperfections such as market failures and transaction costs exist and social welfare is decreased because of it, government intervention might be efficient. *Transaction costs* are any costs connected with the creation of transactions themselves, apart from the price of the good that is the object of the transaction. Transaction costs can thwart welfare enhancing transactions. Different types of market failure can also hinder welfare enhancements. Every impediment to perfect competition is seen as a market failure. Different forms of market failure are: *imperfect competition, public goods, externalities* and *asymmetry information*, leading to *adverse selection* and possible *moral hazard* on the side of sellers and of consumers.

a. Transaction costs

By means of transactions welfare can be increased. Transaction costs can be defined as funds, effort and time spent on a transaction that do not (directly) benefit the counterparty (Sovern, 2006: 1644–45). Transaction costs include search and information costs, negotiation costs, contracting costs and monitoring and enforcement costs. These transaction costs might prevent welfare enhancing transactions from taking place. When someone wishes to buy a house, but is only able to pay the mortgage itself and cannot afford the legal expenses attached to buying this house, he might not be able to enter into the contract. This contract would have been welfare enhancing, but cannot be established due to contracting costs.

b. Imperfect competition

Under *perfect competition*, an ideal-type situation, all goods are offered at the level where production costs equal the prices at which those products are sold, and no profits are incurred in the market. Every market participant, who values the good above cost price level, is able to buy the good. All welfare enhancing transactions are entered into, and the optimal allocation of goods is achieved. When competition is hindered in a market, a situation knows as *imperfect competition,* welfare losses can occur. Under perfect competition, suppliers have to offer goods at the level of marginal costs.[19] If they charge higher prices, a competitor will outprice them and sellers will not sell their goods. Under imperfect competition, suppliers are able to limit supply, and charge a higher price for their goods or services than marginal costs. As competition is imperfect, they do not have to be worried that their prices will be undercut by a competitor. Alternatively, sellers

[19] See above, note 16.

could collude and agree upon a price that is higher than marginal costs, thereby also increasing price and decreasing supply.

If goods are produced whenever individuals would like to pay more than it costs to produce the good, social welfare is increased. However, if sellers are able to limit supply, the product becomes more scarce.[20] Through the interplay of supply and demand under scarcity, prices for goods rise. There is not enough competition to stimulate production of this good up to the efficient level, leading to under-supply in the market. For a lower price, still above production costs, goods could have been produced which would have increased welfare. As these goods are no longer being produced or sold, potential welfare enhancing transactions are not concluded, resulting in a welfare loss. Suppliers that have *market power* or a *dominant position* on the market are able to offer their goods above marginal costs by limiting supply. Several factors can result in one or more suppliers holding a dominant position on the market:

- Heterogeneity of goods
- Low market transparency
- Low number of suppliers
- Entry barriers
- Unclear definition and allocation of rights
- Transaction costs

c. *Public goods*

The second type of market failure relates to situations where property rights are not clearly defined, or when it is difficult to exclude people from the usage of certain goods or services. These goods are called *public goods* or *collective goods*. Welfare losses occur when people are unable to reap the benefits or their investments in this good. Public goods have two characteristics: *non-rivalry* and *non-excludability*. A non-rival good is a good of which the consumption does not impede other people using the good. Non-excludability refers to the issue that people cannot be excluded from using the product. Examples can be found in the common fields, military forces defending a country, fire-brigades and protection from flooding.[21] When a dyke is built, all houses behind it are protected. Leaving a gap in the dyke wherever one house owner does not want to contribute to the building of the dyke makes little sense. But as this person cannot be excluded from

---

20 The concept of scarcity implies that the goods are not abundantly available; all products, services, capital, labour et cetera are scarce, as they are not abundant, also in economic equilibria.

21 Non-rivalry and non-excludability are conceptual notions that are not often found in their totality in the real world. Even though some goods, such as the examples mentioned above, are seen as public goods, these goods are not always fully non-rival and fully non-excludable. When the fire brigade is extinguishing a fire somewhere, the same brigade cannot put out another fire at the same time in another part of town; in that sense, the service provided by the fire brigade is a rival good.

the common benefit of the dyke, he has no incentive to pay for the building of the dyke. This however holds for all inhabitants of housed that are protected by the dyke. Every individual has an incentive to free ride on the efforts and investment of other people in flood protection. Therefore, even though building a dyke could (greatly) improve social welfare, the market mechanism is struggling to provide this good. This is called a *collective action problem*. Similarly, fire-brigades could only possibly exclude free-standing houses in remote areas from protection, and then still the fire, ashes and fumes could cause damage to the surroundings. Again, it is hardly possible to exclude individuals from this service.

Another example is taking down trees in a public forest. Waiting for the tree to grow to optimal height before harvesting would be the most beneficial strategy to individuals, and thus to society. However, trees are then in danger of being chopped too early. To reap any benefit at all, individuals need to be the first to harvest the tree, otherwise their neighbour might do it and they end up with nothing. Planting new trees might not be worthwhile for individuals, since they cannot be sure they will be the ones to benefit from the wood. Abstract social values, such as legal security or public health, can also be seen as public goods. As the incentive to invest in public goods is lacking or at least less than optimal, under-investment in these goods occurs.

d. *Externalities*

An action of an individual party or a transaction between two to or more parties can have consequences for a third party; consequences which are not taken into account in the transaction. These consequences are called *externalities* and can either be positive or negative. In both cases, a potential welfare loss occurs. This is a third type of market failure. An example of negative externality is environmental pollution. A factory which pollutes a river can thereby deteriorate fishing grounds which results in a negative externality for fishermen. When the factory is not held responsible for the costs of the externality, it will overproduce. Not all the actual costs (including the externality) are then accounted for in the alleged costs connected to the production of the good, which includes productions costs but also other social costs that are a result of the production of this good. As price is lower than equilibrium level, demand will be higher than equilibrium. In this situation, the product is less expensive than it should actually be to cover all production and social costs. Neither the factory itself nor the buyers of the factory's products are confronted with the costs of the externality, resulting in too many goods being produced and demanded by the market. The excess production and consumption lead to excess environmental pollution. At equilibrium, environmental pollution would also exist, but the total benefits of production (welfare for the factory and buyers) would outweigh the costs (pollution and other production costs). Overproduction and excess pollution give rise to welfare decreases.

Medical shots against diseases display a positive externality. When a person gets a vaccination, he not only protects himself, but also everyone he gets in contact with. Medical shots could therefore be considered 'too expensive': people getting vaccinations yield a greater welfare to society than only to themselves (or their direct family), but they only take the latter into account. Therefore, from a social welfare perspective, too little vaccinations might be requested by individuals.

e. Asymmetry of information

Some goods have quality characteristics that are quite easy to appraise; for other goods an accurate quality assessment is more problematic. A classification of the consumer's ability to determine quality is provided by the distinction between search goods, experience goods, and credence goods (Nelson, 1970; Darby and Karni, 1973). The quality of search goods quality is easily evaluated before acquiring the good, the quality of experience goods can only be evaluated after the product or service is purchased, and the quality of credence goods will not be fully clear even after buying the product. The classification is not clear-cut: some goods possess more search features, some more experience features and some more credence features. The more experience and credence features a certain good has, the more difficult it is to assess the quality of the good before acquiring it. This can lead to information asymmetry problems, which refers to a situation where one party possesses information about a certain product characteristic and the other party does not. Information asymmetries can occur with respect to every aspect of a good, such as safety aspects, whether or not hygienic procedures were adhered to, production errors et cetera. Through *adverse selection* and *moral hazard*, information asymmetry can lead to decreases in welfare, and it therefore constitutes the fourth type of market failure.

Adverse selection

As a consequence of information asymmetry, high quality products can be driven out of the market, a process known as adverse selection (Akerlof, 1970). All product characteristics such as quality, service, return-of-good modalities, et cetera can be subject to adverse selection. Adverse selection occurs when a buyer cannot make a sufficient assessment of the attributes of the product, which holds for all products in this specific market. The buyer does know however that in the market, this product is offered in varieties of different qualities. The risk of buying a product that is low in quality is therefore discounted in the price. The buyer is not willing to pay the same price for this item including a chance of getting an inferior product, as the price he would have been willing to pay if he knew for sure this item is of excellent quality. The lower price however does not enable suppliers of high quality goods to stay in the market. Presumably, offering a higher quality will also entail higher production costs. The higher costs cannot be recuperated through the lower price that can be obtained in the market. The superior quality producers leave the market, and only inferior producers continue offering their products. The consumers know that quality is decreased, but as they are unable to distinguish higher quality, they cannot credibly demand it. This cycle continues until only the products of most inferior quality are offered in the market, a process which is known as a *race to the bottom*. A decrease in (potential) welfare is the result. Welfare enhancing transactions between suppliers of high quality goods and consumers willing to buy these goods for a price higher than production costs could be concluded if trustworthy information about quality would have been available.[22] As it is not, these transactions do not occur in the market, resulting in a market failure and welfare loss.

Moral hazard

Another problem that can result from information asymmetries in the market is *moral hazard*. Moral hazard describes the situation in which the interests of different parties to a transaction do not correspond to each other. This leads one party to have an incentive to act in a different way or display information differently than the other party would like him to act or would like the information to be. The other party cannot monitor nor correct the actions or information of the first party. The most frequently mentioned example is the conflict of interest between employers and employees, where the employee has an interest in shirking and the employer would like the employee to concentrate fully on doing his job. Social welfare would also benefit more from the employee creating more benefit to the company, as long as that extra benefit would outweigh the benefit of shirking. When the employee shirks, but insists to his employer that is has been giving it all to the job, how is the employer to find out? Moral hazard could therefore lead to welfare losses.

Moral hazard can also occur in the consumer market, and not only on the side of sellers. Sellers might have an incentive to portray information about their product more advantageous than is in reality. Consumer moral hazard can however also occur, for example when a consumer buys an expense dress, wears it to a party and returns it (for a full refund) afterwards. Another example would be when a consumer carelessly writes down his debit card pin codes on a sticker on his debit card, making it easier for him (and thieves!) to take out money from ATM machines. The consumer can however still opt to write down his pin numbers because he can expect his bank to cover his losses in case of theft. The consumer here is the *cheapest cost avoider*, the one who can most efficiently

22 Sellers offering high quality goods can inform buyers that these products are in fact high in quality; this information however will not be trusted by buyers, nor can they verify the information.

prevent this welfare loss. As the consumer does not have sufficient incentives to take sufficient care, a welfare loss is lurking.

2.2.3. WELFARE ENHANCING CORRECTIONS OF MARKET FAILURES AND TRANSACTION COSTS

Market failures can be counteracted and transaction costs can be decreased by government intervention. The costs and benefits of government interventions should however be carefully assessed, taking market solutions into account.

a. Corrections of market failures and cutting transaction costs

There are several ways in which the government can intervene in the market to correct market failures or decrease transaction costs. Several examples will follow to illustrate the various ways of intervention. Transaction costs can for example be decreased by providing default rules in legislation. Market participants can save on contracting costs by referring to the already formulated terms.[23] Correction of imperfect competition by government intervention should correspond with the market situation. If obscurity of prices hinders competition, the government can opt to regulate price disclosure. When the market is too concentrated, the government can force companies to split up, or prohibit mergers from taking place. Government institutions can correct the market failure of public goods by providing in these goods or stimulating production by providing subsidies for example. When the government commissions and pays for flood protection through dykes or otherwise, the costs can be divided over everyone who benefits and free riding is avoided. Externalities can be corrected by either taxing or subsidising the behaviour that causes externalities, thereby internalising the external effects. Pollution should be taxed, while getting vaccinations should be subsidised to create a positive effect on social welfare. Finally, asymmetry of information can be counteracted by information provided by the government, or by measures such as forcing sellers to disclose relevant information, monitoring of quality and setting standards for hygienic or environmentally friendly production procedures.

b. Costs and benefits of government interventions

The government can interfere in the market to correct for market failures or decrease transaction costs. Government interventions however always come at a cost, such as administrative costs, monitoring and enforcement costs. The implementation of rules, regulations and other kinds of government intervention

[23] See below, chapter 5, section 5.3.4, for a discussion on the efficient provision of default terms.

are also costly. Government decision making procedures constitute more costs, not only in connection to deliberation, representation, and decision making, but also error costs and lobbying. Before a certain intervention is designed, information about these costs needs to be collected and a proper cost-benefit analysis has to be executed. For the enforcement of certain laws, enforcers need to be employed and trained; sometimes an entire enforcement institution has to be set up. Monitoring and enforcing regulation itself also brings about costs. Once new regulation is in place, it is difficult to do away with it, thus creating a type of path dependency.[24] Furthermore, negative consequences of government interventions could also be envisaged, such as the creation of a market failure due to intervention. Regulating the quality of legal services will constitute a barrier of entry on the market, decreasing competition and increasing prices.

Costs of correcting market failures should be outweighed by the benefits of doing so. Also, the negative effects of market failures and transaction costs might also be counteracted by market solutions such as reputation, provision of warranties and price-comparison websites.[25] As government intervention is a costly measure in itself, the efficiency of government intervention depends on more than just being able to correct the market failure or decrease transaction costs. In the assessment of the costs and benefits of the intervention, the subsidiarity between market solutions and the government intervention and their respective impact should be considered. The relative benefit of government interventions might then turn out to be less than previously thought.

2.3.4. SUMMARY: ECONOMIC RATIONALES FOR GOVERNMENT INTERVENTION

To correct for market failures and decrease transaction costs, government intervention in markets can be justified from a social welfare perspective. Market failures that can occur are imperfect competition, public goods, externalities and information asymmetry. Even though these market failures can be counteracted by market solutions, there might still be a potential increase in social welfare to be achieved through government interventions. As government interventions are costly however, it needs to be carefully assessed whether the benefits of the intervention actually outweigh the costs. Also, the subsidiarity between market solutions and government intervention should be taken into account. In the

---

24 Klick and Mitchell (2006) state that a choice for a specific type of intervention would increase the costs of returning to a situation without (that) government intervention. The chosen path therefore becomes more desirable than other alternatives, including the option of no intervention. The authors therefore call for a social cost benefit analysis of interventions versus a laissez faire approach, granting that these effects are hard to quantify.

25 Market solutions will be discussed more in detail in the section on consumer contracts, section 2.3.2b.

following section, the discussion will turn to the specific issue of the desirability of government interventions in consumer contracts.

2.3. ECONOMIC RATIONALES FOR INTERVENING IN CONSUMER MARKETS

The economic justifications for government interventions in consumer contracts are founded in the improvement of social welfare by counteracting market failures and transaction costs. Market failures in consumer contracts can primarily be ascribed to imperfect competition and information asymmetries. This research focuses mainly on the second market failure, information asymmetry, as competition issues are dealt with in competition policy. Consumer protection policy, the subject of this research, focuses on information issues and transaction costs.[26] Consumer sovereignty is seen in traditional economic viewpoints as a crucial instrument to allow welfare maximising decisions to be taken by consumers, as consumers have an incentive to promote their own welfare. When consumers are in a less informed position than the contracting counterpart, quality in consumer markets can decrease due to adverse selection (Van den Bergh, 2003: 19–20). Consumer protection legislation can then be justified from an economic perspective in order to enhance allocative efficiency and consumer welfare by supporting the functioning of competitive markets and correcting market failures (Van den Bergh, 2003: 2).

2.3.1. MARKET FAILURES IN CONSUMER CONTRACTS

In a situation of perfect competition, market equilibrium and an optimal functioning of the market, consumers are well protected (Van den Bergh, 2003). This is however an ideal-type state of the world. Several market failures can arise, and in fact, all possible types of market failure can be found to occur in relation to consumer contracts.[27] The most important types of market failure concerning consumer protection are however the restriction of competition, transaction costs and information asymmetries (Grundmann, 2002: 277–80). As Shapiro states, "the economics of consumer protection is the economics of information" (Shapiro, 1983: 528). Competition policy focuses on the supply-side of the market, whereas transaction costs (especially related to information costs) and information asymmetry issues are more relevant for the demand-side. Economic

[26] See below, chapter 6, section 6.2.1.

[27] Reasons for intervening in consumer contracts are discussed by several authors. See for instance: Ramsay (1984: 15–35), Haupt (2003), Van den Bergh (2003), Levitin (2007) and Rischkowsky and Döring (2008).

theory sees a clear role for government intervention in cases of market failure such as information asymmetry or a possible reduction in transaction costs.

a. Transaction costs

Transaction costs in consumer contracts can consist of many types other than mere information costs. Costs might be related to transaction initiation and bargaining, such as search costs, processing and storing information, conclusion of the contract, and costs might also be related to the monitoring and enforcement of the contract. Modalities to end the contract can also be regarded as transaction costs. Transaction costs can be reduced for instance by guaranteeing access to justice. Contract law in itself decreases transaction costs, as it provides an alternative for trust in market parties. Uncertainty concerning the completion of the contract is reduced, as are monitoring and enforcement costs. Also, opportunistic behaviour is sanctioned through contract law provisions.

Consumers suffer from *rational apathy.*[28] At a certain point, the costs of gathering and evaluating more information to improve a decision about buying a product or hiring a service, comparing different providers outweigh the benefits of that added information to improve the decision (Hadfield, Howse and Trebilcock, 1998: 145). Hence, consumer costs related to acquiring and utilising more information in the transaction outweigh the benefits. Government interventions that simplify the task of receiving and understanding information might improve consumer decision making (Sovern, 2006: 1688). Examples include mandatory comparable overviews in consumer financial products (written in plain language, not legalese), and the disclosure requirement for standard terms, which makes the form of standard contract terms available before the transaction occurs or at least provides easy access to these standard terms. Another example of a government intervention that reduces transaction costs for standard terms in consumer contracts is the fairness test. The fairness test constitutes a standard for consumer contract terms. When a contract term is considered to be overly harsh, allowing a disproportionate advantage to the seller vis-à-vis the consumer, the contract term will not pass the fairness test. As a result of this test, consumers do not need to worry about overly harsh terms being included in their contracts, as these terms cannot be legally invoked against consumers.[29]

---

28 Rational apathy is a term originating from political science literature explaining why people do not vote. See for a seminal treatment of the issue of rational voting behaviour: Downs (1957).

29 Terms that will not pass the fairness test can be drafted into contracts by sellers; in this case, the unfair terms will be void and have no legal meaning. The problem is of course whether the consumer is aware of the fact that this particular term will not pass the fairness test. If she is not, an unfair term might still be used against the consumer by the seller, irrespective of this term being void. Standard terms in consumer contracts will be discussed in more detail in chapter 5.

Government interventions aimed at reducing transaction costs to consumers and addressing the transaction costs caused by complex or demanding modalities on how to end the contract, might do so by prescribing easier modalities, or by prohibiting automatic renewal of contracts. Automatic renewal of contracts decreases transactions costs when the consumer had wished to stay with the current supplier anyway. However, it increases the costs of switching to another supplier and increase the costs of ending the contract, resulting in extended services being requested by the consumer, which might result in welfare decreases. The problem is however that firms can nearly always offer some justification for increasing transaction costs to consumers (Sovern, 2006: 1702).[30] It is pivotal to establish which situations call for government intervention aimed at the reduction of consumer transaction costs to increase social welfare.

b. Information asymmetry

Information asymmetry is a particular problem in consumer protection. Due to the disparity of both parties to the contract (seller vs. consumer), asymmetry of information is very likely to arise. As most consumer protection issues stem from the asymmetry of information between sellers and consumers, this thesis will focus on the market failure of asymmetric information in consumer transactions and how the government should and does in fact intervene in this market failure. The economics of information concerning consumer decision making focus on the ability of individuals to assess the quality of product characteristics.[31] If consumers cannot easily assess the quality of a certain product, other product characteristics like price will dominate the decision making process (Goldberg, 1974). This leads to high quality products being driven out of the market, a situation of adverse selection. The more difficult it is to determine the quality of a product, the more difficult it will be to provide a consumer with the information necessary to make an informed decision. The market failure of information asymmetry and subsequent adverse selection will be the result. If information about a certain product characteristic is hard to obtain for consumers, government intervention may be justified to prevent adverse selection from occurring, for instance by disclosure duties or mandatory quality standards.[32]

---

30 There is an overlap between transaction costs and information asymmetry as causes of welfare decrease, and also in government solutions addressing these issues. There is no clear distinction between both causes of non-optimal social welfare: information asymmetries could refer to information that is or can be attained by the seller, whereas information costs as transaction costs could also comprise other costs. See Rischkowsky and Döring (2008: 293) for a discussion on how information economics unjustly neglects or insufficiently assesses transaction costs as a source of diminishing social and consumer welfare.

31 See Stigler (1961) for and influential publication on economics of information; see also Goldberg (1974).

32 See Schwartz and Wilde (1979) for an early but very informative discussion of the potential legal implications of information economics.

To address information asymmetry, economic literature argues consumer protection policy should resort to an information based approach (Hadfield et al., 1998). Consumer protection legislation can improve social and consumer welfare by prohibiting fraud, the distribution of false information and imposing duties to inform (Van den Bergh, 2003: 1). Another possible measure is the prescription of mandatory quality standards such as the monitoring of hygienic procedures in restaurants and licensing of services. Even if the license can be obtained without an entry test, this measure allows for the license to be revoked in case of inferior quality of service, thus providing the seller with an incentive to maintain a proper standard of quality. The strict liability doctrine is another example of an instrument to protect the less informed party (Schwartz and Wilde, 1983).

c. *Other market failures*

When the market failure concerns the supply-side of the market and pertains to incomplete competition between sellers, competition policy should address the issue. Failure of competition could be addressed by interventions against price abuse and monopoly pricing, or by inhibiting mergers to take place.[33] A point which is very relevant to consumer contracts is that the government could provide in public goods such as consumer education. Governments can also provide service information.[34] A possible externality in consumer contracts is the risk that the use of a certain product might cause to third parties. Product safety regulation could be set up to increase the safety of products beyond the point that would result from market transactions that have not internalised the safety externality.

2.3.2. MARKET SOLUTIONS OF INFORMATION ISSUES

As mentioned above, information issues and transaction costs are key topics in consumer protection. Therefore, this section will assess the correction of these issues in more detail. Next to government correction of information issues, market solutions can counteract the effect of market failures as well. The typical market solutions to information asymmetry, such as warranties, reputation and brands, aid consumers in their decision making process. Product comparison modalities like reviews on the internet have severely decreased costs in searching for information and enable increased competition with benefits to consumers. Market solutions should be incorporated in the cost-benefit assessment of

33 For a discussion on the interplay between competition and consumer policy, see Van den Bergh (2003), Cseres (2005), Van den Bergh and Camesasca (2006) and Armstrong (2008).

34 European Consumer Centres (ECCs) are an example of the provision of consumer education in Europe, focusing on consumer redress modalities and corresponding legislation. See for more information: ec.europa.eu/consumers/redress_cons/webcenters_en.htm.

government interventions, as well as other relevant considerations such as the provision of optimal information and consumer moral hazard.

a. *Market corrections of information issues and other transaction costs*

Corrections by the government are not the only instrument able to counteract information asymmetries. Market solutions such as signalling and screening, long term relationships, learning, market provision of information through comparison instruments and the unravelling of information can also correct information asymmetries.

Signalling and screening

Through reputation, brands and warranties, sellers can *signal* the quality of their products to consumers. *Signalling* is a market solution for adverse selection where the initiative to provide information about superior quality comes from the informed party. A quality certificate, investment in the brand name, an ethical code, luxury offices and showrooms can signal quality and the desire to stay in the market. A seller can also offer a warranty on the quality of the product. Fly-by-night sellers, who offer inferior quality products, reap benefits quickly and then leave the market, do not have an incentive to invest in these quality signals. Quality signals therefore have to be both *trustworthy* and *costly* to convey the required message. The signal should correspond to the higher quality provided by the seller; the signal also has to be a reliable instrument to consumers. Furthermore, when the signal is cheap to obtain, low-quality competitors can invest in acquiring the signal. This would diminish the value of the signal for consumers. Reputation and brands as signals of quality can however act as barriers of entry for new competitors, decreasing competition and resulting in a different welfare loss.

Warranties on the quality of the product provide certainty that if the good is found to be of inferior quality, the transaction can be annulled or compensation for the inferior quality can be awarded. The incentive to supply inferior quality therefore decreases significantly through warranties. The conditions of the warranty could be problematic however. Even after the transaction, the quality of the good might not be evident until after the warranty has expired. Also, it might be difficult to prove a defect was caused by a production flaw instead of misuse on the side of the consumer.

The market solution of *screening* can also overcome the market failure. Screening refers to the uninformed party taking the initiative to offer a menu of options to the informed parties. From the choices sellers make, the uninformed party can then screen for quality. This market solution is however not commonly used by consumers in consumer markets. Sellers do screen for consumers, for instance in offering different goods to different consumer types.

Long term relationships and learning

When several transactions take place between the same parties, they both have an incentive to maintain a good relationship, in order to secure future profits from future transactions. Sellers are then more inclined to deliver the quality-type goods at the buyers' requests, and the buyer will pay on time. In situations of repeated buying and long term relationships, the adverse selection problem is less likely to be an issue. Consumers learn from their mistakes, and will only transact with trustworthy parties. Next to this *intrapersonal learning*, consumers can also learn from each other, a process which is referred to as *interpersonal learning*. Consumers are known to ask each other for advice, and to tell others about their experiences with other contracting parties especially when quality is a concern. The information and communication networks of the digital era have greatly improved and increased the possibilities of interpersonal learning.[35]

Market provision of information

There are also market solutions that can mitigate some of the costs consumers face in their search for information. Price-comparison websites and other information intermediaries form a market for market information.[36] If the information is deemed valuable enough, it can be purchased through intermediaries or otherwise obtained in the market. Information however has characteristics of a public good and therefore risks being underprovided if the provision is solely left up to the market (Rischkowsky and Döring, 2008: 290–1). Market parties will have an incentive to decrease consumer transaction costs only when this will enable more consumers to conclude a transaction with them. Communication between consumers and sellers can be facilitated, by for instance a toll free number, an e-mail address or other contact information that is easy to obtain. Competition between parties cannot be relied upon to sufficiently decrease transaction costs in the market. Not all contract terms are salient to the consumer and these will understandably not be a relevant issue in consumer choice (Korobkin, 2003). In such a case, no competition will result and these particular transaction costs will not be decreased by the market. If markets are not performing correctly with respect to some product attributes, sellers have an incentive to behave monopolistically (Sovern, 2006: 1673). Sellers do not have any incentive to decrease transaction costs when doing so will not help them to attract consumers.

Unravelling is an important principle of information economics. This principle relates to the argument that a seller has an incentive to provide all

35 See Epstein (2006) for a general discussion of consumer learning. See Repo, Timonen and Zilliacus (2009) for a discussion and overview of how consumers who are active in social networks can aid each other in sharing information regarding product features.

36 See for a general discussion, Armstrong (2008: 109–12).

information he privately holds, if that information can be verified at no costs (Grossman, 1981). The seller has an incentive to be open about information that can be verified, for instance the amount of chocolates in a box. If the seller does not reveal the amount of chocolates, consumers will infer from his silence that his box contains fewer chocolates than the similar box to be purchased from other sellers. The information will therefore be unravelled by the market, and disclosed without government intervention. High-value sellers will distinguish themselves by communicating their (verifiable) quality; low-value sellers who keep silent will be driven out of the market (Baird, Gertner and Picker, 1998). Unravelling however will not always take place in the market. Information is less likely to become unravelled when information is not verifiable, sellers do not possess the information, or consumers do not regard the same information as relevant and therefore do not know how to interpret sellers' silence. Also a significant number of consumers needs to understand the information that is provided (Van den Bergh, 2003: 26–8).

b. Market solutions versus government interventions

Usually, market solutions can be preferred over government solutions. Market solutions aimed at counteracting market failures, as privately set-up activities, are likely to bring more benefits than costs to the parties involved, otherwise they would not exist in the market. The same is not always true for government interventions. Also, private parties have an incentive to cater for the needs of the consumers who receive the information, and are more informed about the specific needs of the consumers. Government institutions face bureaucracy problems and are less flexible than private parties. Furthermore, costs and benefits of the market solutions are likely to fall with the parties involved, whereas government action is financed through taxes. This implies that everyone bears the costs of the enhancement of the market through government intervention, not only the beneficiaries of the intervention. Therefore, when there are market solutions available to correct market failures, they can be expected to outperform government interventions. Before information regulations are set up, market solutions such as signalling, consumer learning and seller's interests at decreasing transaction costs and unravelling information should be assessed as possible counteractions to the information asymmetries that the regulation is supposed to target.

In some situations however, government intervention which addresses the market failure can still increase social welfare. The costs of market solutions might fall with third parties who do not benefit from the market solution; this would constitute an externality. These external costs might even cause the market solution to no longer be enhancing social welfare, even if it does bring sufficient benefits to the market parties who devised and set up the market solution.

In addition, even in the case of a competitive market, a market-based solution is sometimes unlikely to emerge (Hadfield et al., 1998: 155–6). This might occur when repeat transactions are rare, which makes the flow of information more difficult. When entry and exit costs are low, fly-by-night sellers might be active in the market, decreasing the reputation of the market as a whole. If the consequences of a 'bad' transaction will only become known after a long time, consumers are less likely to file suit against sellers even if their actions have given rise to liability. Consumers are also unlikely to take sellers to court if sellers do not have many assets or the size of the transaction is relatively small. Many consumer markets can be considered to have these characteristics.

Also, there might be circumstances in which governments are more efficient information providers than the market (Hadfield et al., 1998: 157–8). If the government possesses the information already, it might be more efficient for the government to provide it. This is also the case when private parties have difficulties gathering the information or if the government can provide the information more easily than private parties. Furthermore, the market for information may be uncompetitive as only one party possesses the information. Providing the information to consumers might fail even when there is a demand, since information has the characteristics of a public good. In these situations, it could be more efficient if the government assumes the role of information provider.

In some situations, the outcome of the decision making process is potentially detrimental. Consumers, before being able to learn from mistakes, can be severely hurt by bad decisions. Therefore, banning a hazardous item can be more effective and even efficient from a social welfare perspective than providing information about the risks it may have. In addition, with regard to the quality of intermediaries, consumers can be unable to assess information regarding quality, in this case the quality of the service. Signals of information are crude mechanisms, which could stimulate sellers to invest more in the signal itself than in enhancing actual quality. Information is a public good and therefore suffers from free riding problems; it might be underprovided when provided solely by private parties. This can also make market provision of information more difficult. Market mechanisms cannot always be relied upon to sufficiently counteract information asymmetries. In some situations, government intervention in information issues might be justified.

2.3.3. POLICY BASED UPON INFORMATION ECONOMICS

If policies are designed to counteract information asymmetry, these policies should consider specific issues connected to the particular issue of information provision. Hadfield et al. distinguish three steps in designing policy that is based upon the insights of information economics (Hadfield et al., 1998: 152–62): first, the problem should be clearly defined, assessing the situation at hand. Second, it should be established whether government intervention is justified, taking costs and benefits including adverse effects of interventions into account. Third, a regulatory instrument should be carefully chosen. Even though information asymmetries are preferably counteracted with the provision of information and disclosure duties, these instruments might not always be the most efficient. These three stages in the assessment will now be discussed in more detail.

a. *Defining the problem*

First, the information problem should be clearly defined. When certain information is available to sellers and not to consumers, constituting a possible information asymmetry problem, the value and cost of this information should be assessed. When the value of information that is currently not available to consumers is low and the costs of gathering the information are high, the information asymmetry is less likely to be sufficiently counteracted by market mechanisms. The market characteristics are also important; whether the market is competitive, imperfectly competitive, or a monopoly. Special consideration should be given to the fact that when consumers expect no problems, they will take less care. Such a situation should however be a concern to regulators. When the problem already receives much attention, consumers are likely to take more care, and consumer problems are less likely. In cases of highly publicised scams or certain unfair trade practices (recent examples of these include time-share contracts or hidden fees), consumers will be on the lookout. The cases where consumers expect no danger are more likely to cause consumer problems.

b. *Is government intervention justified?*

Secondly, it should be decided whether an intervention by the government is a feasible and necessary response. The identification of a problem does not automatically result in the conclusion that the government should regulate the information flow or otherwise intervene. As any market intervention, government interventions in consumer contracts to correct market failures come at a cost. As sellers will be confronted with costs due to for instance mandatory information duties, these costs will be passed on to consumers where possible.[37] Price increases due to consumer protection might even cause the product to no longer be obtainable in the market for lower income groups (Leff, 1970b: 156; Van den Bergh, 1997: 94–5). Adverse effects of consumer protection policies include

[37] See Hartlief (2004: 258–60) for an overview of economic and distributive effects of increased consumer protection, claiming lawyers "often seem to overlook that it is the consumer him- or herself who will ultimately pay for this increased protection" (at 259). See also Howells and Weatherill (2005: 39–41) for a discussion.

industry protection measures that act as a barrier to new entrants, for instance by prescribing certain production methods that only the incumbents can fulfil.[38]

Another costly effect could be restricting consumer choice by mandating a certain quality. This would protect consumers who prefer the higher quality, but do not pay sufficient attention, but hurts other consumers who genuinely prefer the lower quality as it can be obtained at a lower price.[39]

Furthermore, government interventions in consumer contracts can result in moral hazard problems. The seller is not the only party in consumer contracts that could display moral hazard. *Consumer moral hazard* can be instigated by removing consumers' individual responsibility through government intervention, stressing the responsibility of the seller. Consumers have no incentive to take care, and careless behaviour from the side of consumers might be the result (Van den Bergh, 1990). Also, it is important to distinguish the distributional effects that might occur from government interventions, as some consumers could suffer due to the protective measures while others benefit.[40] As has been described above, market solutions might be available to correct the information failure. The market characteristics should be considered to determine whether market solutions are likely to emerge. Market parties cannot always be expected to sufficiently counteract information failures. Governments might be more efficient information providers as has been shown that signals are a rather crude mechanism and do not necessarily reflect quality. Since information is a public good, it might not be efficiently provided by the market. The costs and benefits of government intervention should be carefully evaluated, taking the possibility of market solutions into account.

c. *Choosing a regulatory instrument*

The third step is the choice of regulatory instrument to counteract the asymmetry in information or to compensate for adverse selection problems through enhancing quality. Possible options for regulatory instruments are: information disclosure, bans on products, warnings, mandatory quality standards and the use of information intermediaries. Regulatory interventions in consumer contracts can be *outcome-based* (also known as *substantive) interventions*, which impose legal rights and duties regarding the substantive part of the agreement, or *process-based* (or *procedural) interventions*, which aim to affect the way parties communicate and interact (De Hoon, 2007: 6–9). Interventions to prohibit fraud,

---

38 See generally Van den Bergh (1997) on the adverse effects of consumer protection regulation; see also Hadfield, Howse and Trebilcock (1998: 159–62).

39 A possible example is European legislation which mandates compensation for flight delays (EC No. 261/2004). Some consumers might prefer to run the risk of a delay for a decrease in price, a choice that is no longer possible in the market.

40 See Haupt (2003: 1162–4) for a discussion.

false information and unfair clauses in standard terms would fall under the first category, whereas information duties would be an example of the second.

Information disclosure

Information can be disclosed in two ways: either the government provides the information herself, or sellers can be obliged to provide consumers with the information through *disclosure duties.* A clear benefit of information provision as a governmental intervention as opposed to for instance mandatory quality standards is that the first will not lead to a decrease in choice and will stimulate the individual responsibility of the consumer. Process-based interventions interfere to a lesser extent with party autonomy, as consumers are still allowed a choice from all provided options. Mandatory quality standards reduce choice. Mandatory allocation of risk, mandatory disclosure duties and other obligations will create additional costs to producers and sellers, who will pass these costs on to consumers where possible (Van den Bergh, 2003: 22).[41] A price increase, as well as mandatory quality standards, could then lead to a decrease in choice. Not all consumers prefer the same product characteristics; some might prefer a lower quality if the price is sufficiently lowered to balance the decrease in quality.

Information duties should be allocated to the party that is the cheapest information provider. The party that is able to disclose relevant information most efficiently, encompassing for instance the costs of acquiring that information and the costs of effectively disclosing it to other parties involved, should be allocated the duty to disclose.[42] A further important aspect that should be addressed in the regulation of information is that aim should be the *optimal amount of information*, not complete information. Not only will more information duties result in more administrative and compliance costs, they will also make the consumer decision process more lengthy and complex. As evaluation of information is costly, instruments that aim to provide more information should take the costs of information assessment into account. Also, a *crowding out* effect of disclosure should be considered. When information about certain aspects is disclosed, this disclosure might distract consumers from other important pieces of information. Disclosure therefore leads to *opportunity costs of attention* for consumers. As described above regarding the equilibrium in production, information should be produced (mandatory if necessary) up to the point where marginal costs of information outweigh the benefits of p{{}}roviding information. Even though the provision of information is often preferable to other instruments as it does

41 The extent to which this is possible depends on the price-elasticity of the demand for this particular product or service, which is the rate in which demand fluctuates with price changes.

42 See Cooter and Ulen (2003: 273–84) for a discussion on how disclosure duties influence the incentives to gather information: the seller should have an incentive to acquire and use the discovered knowledge to their benefit.

not diminish the range of available options, the costs of information assessment should be taken into account.

Other instruments

These considerations could imply that information disclosure should not always be preferred as a means to overcome adverse selection problems. While crude instruments like bans have the negative effect of restricting consumer choice, they are also likely to lower information costs. When products are particularly hazardous, a ban could be preferred over the provision of information regarding risks. There is thus a trade-off between information costs and decreasing the range of available options. A trade-off also exists with respect to simple instruments and more effective ones. Simple warnings that are sufficiently effective in informing people can thus be more efficient and effective than sophisticated information devices that are possibly more accurate, but also connected to higher information costs. When properly warned, consumers can choose whether or not to buy the product, and are more inclined to use it with care. A ban would no longer provide the opportunity of using the product at all.

By introducing mandatory quality standards for products or for professional services (doctors, lawyers), low quality options are taken out of the market. Effectively, there is a ban on low quality. Prices of products and services are increased, as competition between providers decreases. These interventions however could be justified when the potential adverse selection problem caused by low quality services is too costly. Consumers are less able to evaluate the quality of these professional services: they are credence goods. As a result, reputation mechanisms are less likely to work effectively. Merely providing information about bad risks and bad services would not be sufficient to overcome the severe consequences of these particular adverse selection problems. Furthermore, when the use of an information intermediary such as a pharmacist is made mandatory, a clear signal is sent that these products require the search and assessment of information. Information will then be considered more extensively by consumers.

2.3.4. SUMMARY: ECONOMIC RATIONALES FOR INTERVENING IN CONSUMER MARKETS

In the case of consumer contracts, to the main market failures are transaction costs, information asymmetries and competition. This research focuses on the first two. Transaction costs in consumer contracts consist of many types. Monitoring and enforcement costs can be decreased by the instrument of contract law itself, through the setting of default terms. To overcome rational apathy, a government might provide or stimulate simple and comparable information, written in plain language. Information asymmetries leading to adverse selection might be counteracted by disclosure duties or mandatory quality standards.

Market solutions however might also contribute in overcoming these issues. Reputation, brands and warranties signal information; the market for market information will decrease information asymmetries and transaction costs, rendering additional government intervention less beneficial. Information that is verified at no costs will unravel, leaving information disclosure duties concerning this information without added benefit and as a result inefficient. Market solutions are usually to be preferred over government interventions. Other considerations regarding government interventions in consumer contracts include the costs of intervening, consumer moral hazard, decreased choice options, the provision of optimal information instead of full information and distinguishing the party which is the cheapest information provider.

2.4. CONCLUSION: ECONOMIC RATIONALES FOR CONSUMER PROTECTION POLICY

This chapter has introduced the conventional economic approach towards interventions in markets in general, and more specifically in consumer markets. It aimed at establishing the economic rationales for intervening in consumer protection policy from a social welfare perspective. The conditions under which government interventions in (consumer) markets are socially desirable from an economic point of view can be concluded to be the following: interventions to correct for market failures, being imperfect competition, public goods, externalities and information asymmetry, and to decrease transaction costs can be justified from a social welfare perspective. The costs and benefits of the intervention should be considered, a well as the subsidiarity between market solutions and government interventions. Regarding consumer contracts, issues connected to transaction costs, information asymmetries and competition can result in justifiable government interventions, where this research focuses on the first two. Transaction costs such as contracting, monitoring and enforcement costs can be decreased through providing enforcement mechanisms and setting of default terms in contract law. To address the market failure of information asymmetry, interventions can consist of providing or stimulating simple and comparable information, written in plain language, disclosure duties or mandatory quality standards. Even though market solutions exist to counteract these market failures, there might still be a potential increase in social welfare to be achieved through government interventions. As these interventions are costly, the benefits of the intervention should outweigh the costs, and market solutions that render government intervention superfluous should be regarded.

The following chapter will introduce a new stream of thought in economic theory, namely behavioural economics. The insights developed in behavioural economics might provide reasons for intervening in consumer contracts beyond the rationales stipulated in conventional economic theory. Whether behavioural insights can indeed offer implications for policy that are not brought forward in standard economic theory will be the focus of the next chapter.

CHAPTER 3

BEHAVIOURAL ECONOMICS OF CONSUMER PROTECTION

3.1. INTRODUCTION

In the previous chapter, the economic rationales for government intervention and the specific rationales for consumer protection have been discussed. These rationales are based upon conventional economic theory. Economists conventionally rely on the *invisible hand* of markets when making policy recommendations, using rational choice models to predict consumer and seller behaviour. With regard to consumer policy, people would be best off with an abundance of options to choose from. People are then able to choose that specific contract that corresponds best to their preferences, regardless of the actual content of those preferences. Homo economicus "knows it all": he knows all his preferences and is able to assess both the full set of options and corresponding risks and probabilities. Furthermore, he is able to solve the resulting optimisation task, no matter how difficult. Therefore according to rational choice, contracts that are voluntarily entered into, are necessarily welfare enhancing. When none of the conventional market failures exist in the market, individuals themselves are best able to decide which options correspond best to their preferences and promote their own welfare by doing so. RCT thus dictates that governments' focus should be to enable consumers to choose, and not to paternalistically make decisions for individuals.

In recent years however, a new strand of economic literature has surfaced: behavioural economics. The insights developed in behavioural literature have spurred knowledge about how individuals make decisions and respond to law and policy. These insights into the decision making process of individuals show that the predictions based on traditional economics often do not hold. Behavioural economics shows that consumer decision making is affected by several biases and heuristics, and argues that this has possibly detrimental consequences for consumer and social welfare. This welfare loss could potentially make government interventions justified from a social welfare perspective even beyond the economic rationales provided in the previous chapter. This chapter will aim to answer the question of whether behavioural insights can have implications for consumer protection beyond conventional economic rationales for government intervention.

To answer this question, first the approach of behavioural (law and) economics will be introduced. Several biases and heuristics, causing individuals to deviate from rational choice, will be explained: bounded rationality and information overload, risk perception biases, self-serving biases, status quo biases, time related biases, contexts and framing, anchoring and adjustment, and bounded will-power. Then the aim of the behavioural research project is discussed, which can be either to update economic theory, or to devise a new paradigm for individual choice. When rational choice and behavioural insights are empirically tested, neither theory is proven to hold in all circumstances. In some situations, people can be shown to behave as is predicted by RCT. In other situations, predictions based upon behavioural insights are more accurate. Distinguishing the contexts in which either theory (or set of insights) is better able to predict behaviour is therefore argued to be one of the main challenges for the behavioural research project.

After the introduction of behavioural economics, the implications of behavioural literature for policy are discussed, with a focus on consumer protection. Examples of situations in which consumers are inhibited from rational decision making by biases and heuristics will be provided to clarify the theory. Arguably, it is these situations in which sellers are able to take advantage of consumers to consumers' detriment. Behavioural insights imply that government interventions might be justified even in competitive markets without market failures. To aid consumers in their decision making, behavioural insights provide grounds for decreasing available options. Information disclosure, one of the most preferred government interventions in consumer protection policy, also needs reassessment in the light of behavioural biases.

The intervention in individual decisions is viewed critically in economic literature, as individuals are argued to be the most able to know their own preferences and act accordingly. Therefore, in behavioural literature a regulatory approach is developed that leaves free choice uninhibited: soft paternalism. Soft paternalism nudges individuals into welfare enhancing decisions without imposing a particular choice. Even though this might seem intrusive, it should be kept in mind that there are hardly any conceivable situations without so-called "choice architectures". This is to say that there is no such thing as (or hardly any) completely neutral choice; all choices are affected by for instance presentation, the range of alternatives provided, and the contexts of the decisions. When biases, heuristics and non-rational influences on behaviour render individual decision making suboptimal, intervention strategies can be designed to enhance these decisions. Individuals can be debiased, nudged into rational decisions by for instance providing less and better information. In other circumstances, nudging consumers to rely on other biases to counteract the effects of the first bias is a more effective intervention. Also, the default that results from an inactive decision making process can be changed to a more socially beneficial default. The choice for a particular intervention strategy should take several relevant factors into account such as the costs and benefits of the approach, the level of intrusiveness, the effectiveness and the predictability of the intervention.

This chapter aims to establish whether behavioural insights provide helpful implications for policy, especially consumer policy, which go beyond conventional economic insights. Further issues to discuss would be concerns that arise when behavioural insights are used to improve economic theory and predictions, both from a methodological and a policy making perspective. These concerns include the robustness of the theory, and difficulties related to the lack of an overarching theoretical paradigm in behavioural economics. Other issues could be that consumers can learn to overcome their biased decision making, that sellers are biased themselves and not able to take abuse of consumer biases, and that behavioural economics arguably can provide a justification for all policy options, thereby increasing policy makers' discretion. These and other concerns will be discussed in the next chapter, chapter 4.

3.2. BEHAVIOURAL LAW AND ECONOMICS

This section will provide an introduction into the current of literature known as *behavioural economics*, and its application to legal issues, *behavioural law and economics*. The focus of this research programme will be elaborated through the discussion of several behavioural insights. After this introduction, the aim of the behavioural research programme will be reviewed in the light of new insights in social sciences: it seems that people employ two main decision making systems: an intuitive/automatic system, and a cognitive/reflective system. With this consideration in mind, a likely direction for behavioural research could be to sort out in which situations and circumstances individuals are more likely to employ the first system of decision making, or the second.

3.2.1. AN INTRODUCTION TO BEHAVIOURAL (LAW AND) ECONOMICS

The field of literature that focuses on incorporating insights from other social sciences, and most notably psychology, into economics is called *behavioural economics*. Below, this research field will be outlined, as well as some of its main findings regarding individual decision making and behaviour.

a. What is behavioural law and economics?

Behavioural economics is a current of literature that incorporates insights from other social sciences than economics into economic theory.[43] It has been used to describe all sorts of non-economic insights to explain and predict behaviour. Sometimes it is referred to as *Economics and Psychology* in acknowledgment of the social science from which most behavioural insights to economic theory are derived, namely psychology. Other insights such as social norms, group behaviour, ethics, preferences for fairness and so on are also part of the analysis. Behavioural economics tries to infuse insights on *actual* behaviour, not just *predicted* or *hypothesised* behaviour, into economic assessments (Jolls, Sunstein and Thaler, 1998a: 1476–9). It argues that in many situations a set of consistent biases is found that results in individuals displaying behaviour different from the behaviour that would be predicted by rational choice models. These biases are generally based on heuristics – simple rules of thumb which people use in day-to-day decision making. By introducing these insights into economic theory, scholars attempt to increase the predictive value of theories by making the underlying assumptions more realistic (Jolls, 1998: 1654). Chaudhuri provides a graphical illustration which can be used to demonstrate the way behavioural economics extends conventional economic methodology (Chaudhuri, 2006: 2, see figure 2). Referring to the figure below, standard economic theory only considers *stimulus, rational response,* and *behaviour.* Not all stimuli are included, only the ones that should have an impact on decisions: the stimuli that change the expected costs and benefits of options. Emotional responses and the "black box" of consumer psychology and sociology have been neglected by economists for reasons of simplicity and *tractability* of the theory.[44] As individual characteristics and their impact on choice are considered too difficult and too random to take into account, behaviour is predicted according to the rational choice model.[45] However, behavioural scholars have pointed out that this reliance upon rational choice to predict behaviour has undermined the accuracy of the resulting predictions. Behavioural research tries to extract information from the black box which is systematic, thus improving these predictions. Figure 2 is primarily concerned with perceptions and attitudes, such as risk perceptions and fairness preferences. Stimuli that should not have any influence on behaviour according to the rational choice model, but that are shown to have an impact empirically, are included in the assessment as well. Also, the responses consumers portray are

[43] As economics also focuses upon behaviour of individuals and collective institutions, as is pointed out by Jolls, Sunstein and Thaler (1998a: 1476), the term behavioural economics is in fact a pleonasm.

[44] Tractability of theory refers to the ease with which a theory can be used to generate predictions Wilkinson (2008: 8–9).

[45] The methodological issues regarding economic theory and behavioural insights will be more thoroughly discussed in the next chapter, section 4.2.

not all rational; they can be influenced by emotions. Even these responses can to some extent be predicted, which is also one of the attempts of the behavioural research programme.

Figure 2. Individual decision making model

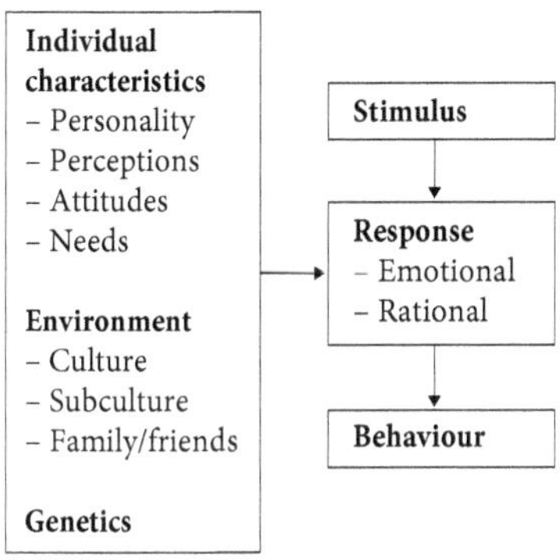

Source: Chaudhuri (2006: 2).

Behavioural law and economics focuses on the consequences of these insights for economic analysis of law. Understanding and predicting the consequences of laws, policies and other legal rules should include a proper understanding and prediction of the choices that will be made by the people who are subject to these legal instruments. The main thesis of behavioural law and economics is that economic analysis of law can be improved through applying behavioural insights, in the same way that economics can. Both behavioural economics and behavioural law and economics rely upon traditional economic theories to set the basic framework, which is then adjusted by introducing insights from behavioural theory. This approach combines economic with behavioural (non-economic) insights to improve predictions and theory in general. Behavioural economics has become a large sub-discipline in economics and provides valuable insights for law and policy (Ramsay, 2007: 72).

b. Focusing on deviations from rational choice

The behavioural insights that are collected in behavioural economics have one main focus: to explain how, when and why individual choices and preferences differ from what has been hypothesised in standard economic theory relying upon rational choice assumptions. As has been explained in the previous chapter, RCT assumes that people make consistent choices based upon the costs and benefits of options, maximising their own benefit, optimally using and searching for information, and neglecting information that does not influence the costs and benefits of the options. *Rational man* or *homo economicus* is a person who knows what he wants, or what he aims to achieve; he carefully balances the expected costs and benefits of options, and decides accordingly; he is responsive to incentives and changes his behaviour when costs and benefits are altered; he promotes his own welfare and is effective in achieving his goals.[46] It is acknowledged in economic theory that these assumptions will not always hold. However, conventional law and economics asserts that deviations from this behaviour will not be systematic, and thus may cancel each other out or are only small deviations anyway, and can thus be left out of consideration. Therefore, RCT is considered to be the best approximation of human behaviour, relying upon relatively simple assumptions that enable fairly accurate predictions (Arlen, 1998: 1766).

Behavioural insights on the other hand claim that individuals systematically deviate from rational choice, and that predictions of human behaviour can be improved by taking these systematic deviations into account. Empirically, people are found to make decisions under the influence of several biases and heuristics, failing to maximise their own welfare. A heuristic can be defined as a strategy for making decisions that simplifies the problem through elimination of possible options (Dowling and Chin-Fang, 2007: 38). A bias refers to a decision outcome that is systematically different from rational choice predictions. Individuals can for instance be biased by the presentation of information and the availability of that information. Behavioural research has identified certain errors in decision making that may lead consumers to act in a way that would deviate from the rational choice prediction, even when they are fully informed or have the possibility to obtain the information at low cost.[47] When incentives are altered people fail to respond accordingly. They are influenced by the context of the problem at hand, even when this context should not influence decision making according to standard economic insights. Furthermore, individuals are concerned with more than just maximising their personal self-interest. Through heuristics and biases, people often fail to maximise their utility, contrary to the predictions from RCT. Behavioural scholars claim that as a consequence of the importance of behavioural insights, "rational man" should not be used as a basis in economic theory, and as it does not accurately reflect human decision making it should neither be used as a benchmark for making policies. A more accurate description of human choice would enable an improvement of both positive and normative legal analysis, behavioural law and economics asserts (Rachlinski, 2000: 740–1).

46 See for instance Rachlinski (2000: 746) and Jolls, Sunstein and Thaler (1998a: 1488) for a description.

47 OECD (2007).

3.2.2. INTRODUCTION TO BEHAVIOURAL INSIGHTS

Where behavioural literature used to focus on cognitive processes, currently all research studying behaviour that is inconsistent with standard economic theory is grouped under the denominator behavioural economics.[48] This refers for instance to bounded rationality, but also to altruism and charity, to cooperation instead of competition in prisoners' dilemma type situations, to social influences on choice such as behaviour of other people and social norms, to ethics, trust, happiness, fairness and emotions. In this section, some biases and heuristics that are frequently commented upon in behavioural literature will be introduced. These insights are said to contest rational choice models. The overview aims to provide an introduction to some cognitive biases and heuristics, without the intention of presenting a full and comprehensive overview.[49]

The selection portrayed follows from the focus of this research: in the area of consumer decision making, cognitive biases and heuristics are deemed to be most relevant for theory and policy. Issues such as altruism, charity and happiness research will not be discussed here, as these are less relevant for consumer decision making and consumer protection policy. Behavioural insights regarding cognitive decision making and bounded will-power are most relevant for this analysis.[50] The biases described can almost all be categorised under cognitive biases and heuristics, involving choice strategies that can lead to suboptimal decision making, which are inconsistent with the rational choice assumptions. Bounded will-power is the only exception, as this is not considered a behavioural

---

48 See for a discussion of how behavioural economics, or economics and psychology, evolved: Langevoort (1998: 1499–502), Camerer and Loewenstein (2004: 5–7) and Wilkinson (2008: 10–3).

49 The overview presented in this chapter is mainly based upon Hillman (2000: 720–35) and Langevoort (1998: 1503–5). Hanson and Kysar (1999a) and Korobkin and Ulen (2000) also provide valuable overviews of the literature, as well as Jolls, Sunstein and Thaler (1998a: 1548–50) in the appendix of their seminal article. See furthermore Bernheim and Whinston (2008: 453–87) for an overview of several biases and heuristics, with applications. This research focuses on cognitive decision making, combined with bounded willpower.

50 Besides cognitive biases and heuristics, other categories of biases can be shown to influence behaviour. For instance, Jolls, Sunstein and Thaler (1998a: 1476–9) describe three 'bounds' on human behaviour, which represent systematic deviations from rational behaviour: bounded rationality, bounded willpower, bounded self-interest. Benjamin and Laibson point to four sources of bad decision making: bounded rationality, (slow) learning, framing, and lack of self-control (Benjamin and Laibson, 2003: 7). On happiness studies focusing on which issues can empirically be shown to add to the subjective wellbeing of individuals, see for instance Lane (2000), Frey and Stutzer (2002), Easterlin (2003) and Layard (2005). See for happiness and public policy: Helliwell (2006), Layard (2006) and Frey and Stutzer (2009). On evolutionary psychology explaining why non-optimal decision strategies might survive in the market, see Zywicki (2007). See for an overview of varieties of the ultimatum game empirically tested, Fehr and Gächter (2000) and Bowles (2004: 114).

decision making strategy. It is however relevant for the consumer decision making process.[51]

a. *Bounded rationality and information overload*

People are limited in their computational capacities, understanding, memory and other capabilities: they are *boundedly rational*.[52] When choices become more difficult, when they have to evaluate more options and consider multiple issues, people are less able to arrive at optimal decisions. For instance, when consumers wish to assess which product scores best when it comes to product attributes they deem important, according to rational choice they should assess all options and calculate the expected benefits of each of the options.[53] Higher quantities of information decrease the extent to which consumers are able to do so. Too much information confuses consumers in their decisions (Keller and Staelin, 1987). A quantity of information that is so great that it provides difficulties for individuals to evaluate the information accurately is called *information overload*.[54] This effect can even be created by information disclosure regimes as disclosure will result in more information that needs to be assessed.

To deal with their bounded rationality when confronted with huge quantities of information, behavioural theory claims that individuals will *satisfice* on options, rather than optimising them. Satisficing is a search strategy linked to bounded rationality (Simon, 1957). The strategy of satisficing entails looking for

---

51 An application of these biases to the consumer decision making process will follow below in section 3.3.1. In that section situations will be described in which sellers are argued to abuse consumers' biased decision making.

52 Bounded rationality was introduced by Simon (1957: 196–206). See Simon (1978) for further discussions on the issue. There has been some debate whether this view belongs to behavioural economics or conventional economic theory. Simon himself mentions that satisficing behaviour should be distinguished from irrationality. See also Williamson (1981: 553). Nowadays satisficing is seen as a part of behavioural economics, being an example of a decision strategy which makes choice easier, even though it might lead to suboptimal decision making.

53 As will be more thoroughly discussed below, the economic concept of *rational apathy* also describes how people are less able to arrive at the most efficient choice when information is abundant; in this case, it would be rational for people to calculate costs and benefits of options until the costs of calculating and weighing options become larger than the benefits of doing so (see chapter 5, most notably section 5.3.1c). The concept of rational apathy overlaps with information overload to some extent; however, whereas economic theory merely points out that some information will rationally be disregarded, behavioural insights shed some light on which information is more likely to be disregarded, and how the information that is regarded will be interpreted. For a discussion on this particular issue, see below, chapter 5, most notably sections 5.4.1a and 5.4.3.

54 A famous example of information overload is provided by Iyengar and Lepper (2000): people are more likely to purchase gourmet jams or chocolates when offered 6 choices rather than 24 choices (30% of consumers bought jam when offered 6 options, whereas only 3% decided to purchase when confronted with 24 different jams). Moreover, the participants reported who had been confronted with 6 options reported being more satisfied with their choice than those who had been confronted with more options. See also Schwartz (2004) for several examples of how more information might actually be less informing.

product characteristics that are satisfying, rather than optimal. By choosing some product characteristics, and screening products to see whether they correspond to acceptable levels of quality regarding those characteristics, several products can be eliminated from the choice set. Thus, the choice set is reduced, and the choice becomes easier to make. Rather than evaluating and 'grading' each product on every product characteristic, satisficing enables consumers to deal with large choice sets.[55] When a decision comprises many dimensions, some issues will be considered more important than others. These *salient* issues are then taken into account; other issues will be neglected.

Issues can be made salient by sellers or by other parties, for instance by a greater amount of publicity over certain decision dimensions than over others. This is referred to as *priming*. The issues that are neglected could however have been important enough to tip the scales in favour of a decision different than the one that is arrived at. Lacko and Pappalardo, reporting on a study done by the FTC, identify a situation in which information distorted rather than benefited consumers' ability to enhance their welfare by using available information (Lacko and Pappalardo, 2004).[56] In this study, it was found that information on broker compensation rates confused consumers, rendering them less able to identify the less expensive loan and less likely to choose the less expensive broker loan. Disclosing the broker compensation rates apparently created an "anti-broker bias", priming the consumer towards this piece of information. As a consequence, the quality of decisions taken by consumers was lowered.

Satisficing is not the only decision making strategy that is employed. As a response to information overload, individuals can also refuse to take any decision at all, which is called *decision paralysis*, also referred to as *inertia* (Jacoby, 1984; Malhotra, 1984). There is thus a clear risk of suboptimal decision making when consumers are faced with more information they can handle. An example of information that is likely to be ignored is information about death or dreaded events; behavioural insights show that this information is frequently left out in decision making by individuals, even when this information can easily be argued to be relevant for the decision making party.[57] In economic theory, consumers are not expected to neglect relevant information, at least not when the costs of considering this information would be lower than the benefits of doing so. Furthermore, economic theory does not distinguish between types of information, and can therefore not predict which information is more likely to be ignored. Behavioural economics could help out here, as it might be able to points out which information is more likely to be neglected, and which risks might occur as a result of this neglect (Fudenberg, 2006: 704–5).

---

55 See also Eisenberg (1995: 214–6) for a discussion of bounded rationality and decision strategies to deal with large quantities of information.

56 See also Lacko and Pappalardo (2007) and Mulholland (2008) for a discussion of these results.

57 See also below, chapter 5, sections 5.4.1d and 5.4.3.

b. *Risk perception biases*

Another difference between behavioural insights and RCT is the way in which *risks* are interpreted.[58] According to behavioural insights, people account for risks in a different way than is assumed by RCT.[59] Instead of 'rationally' discounting contingencies using the appropriate risk factor, people are *overoptimistic* about future contingencies. People underestimate the risk that natural disasters such as earthquakes or flooding will cause any damage to themselves, which is known as *low probability neglect*. However, small probabilities, such as chances of a disaster such as airplane accident, are sometimes *over*estimated. It seems that unlikely events are underestimated unless they are highly salient, such as when they have just occurred (Camerer and Kunreuther, 1989: 570). This is sometimes attributed to the *focusing effect*. Events that spring to mind easily are also considered to be quite likely to occur. Their *availability*, however, might be entirely unrelated to the rate in which they actually occur in reality. Events that are highly publicised, particularly gruesome or happen to have occurred lately are often estimated to occur frequently. The frequency of these events however does not automatically follow from the fact that information on these events is very available, and these events might therefore be less likely to take place than is commonly thought. A related yet opposite effect is the so-called *dread factor*. When choosing which aspects to take into account, people are shown to have particular difficulties with risk assessment when issues such as death, pain, suffering and other gruesome connotations are concerned. People do not like being confronted with these situations, and therefore block them from their minds. They will opt for not making any decision, disregard the risk when it is small or overestimate the risks when they are salient enough. In any of these situations, the overall estimation of risk does not portray a correct risk assessment.

The *certainty* effect describes how people have a strong preference for things that are certain. There is a large gap between 100% probability and 99%, whereas the difference between 99% and 98% probability is not interpreted to be that large. Apparently, even the smallest probabilities are considered very different from knowing for sure. This is related to the behavioural finding that people discount

---

[58] As is famously described by Knight (1921: 233), '*risk*' refers to situations where the decision maker can assign mathematical probabilities to the 'randomness' which he is faced with. '*Uncertainty*' on the other hand refers to situations when this randomness cannot be expressed in terms of specific mathematical probabilities. This distinction has been the subject of a longstanding debate, which will not be explored in-depth here. See for instance: Arrow (1951) and Ellsberg (1961), who make a similar claim that even though there might be a distinction between the two concepts in theory, individuals might respond to both risk and uncertainty in the same way. Individuals do not 'know' probabilities, but have 'beliefs' about the occurrence of events, whether these are considered risks or uncertainties.

[59] See Eisenberg (1995: 223–5) for a discussion and references to empirical literature to provide evidence of risk related biases.

for risks in a non-linear way, also known as *hyperbolic discounting* (Samuelson, 1963).

Hindsight bias is another well-known risk perception bias, which is frequently discussed in relation to judge and jury assessment of risks. Hindsight bias describes how events seem much more likely in retrospect than they were assessed to be before or at the time of the occurrence of the event (Fischhoff, 1975). Looking back, a certain event taking place, such as a machine malfunctioning during a certain dangerous procedure causing injuries to employees, seems almost inevitable. However, at the time, the risk may have been well looked into and well understood by experts who designed the production line, and it may have been a freak accident.

c. *Self-serving biases*

When people have to assess risks such as the risk of mortgage interest rates increasing, salaries decreasing, or products failing, people tend to make assessments in their own favour. This is referred to as *self-serving bias* (Babcock and Loewenstein, 1997). The future is looking bright, chances of something going wrong are slim, and pay checks will forever increase. Furthermore, people display *overconfidence* regarding their own capabilities (Weinstein, 1980). When asking groups of individuals, usually 70–80 percent of individuals claim to be better than average drivers (Svenson, 1981).[60] Even though this could be true, depending on the composition of the group, it is unlikely that all groups that were surveyed consisted of a high percentage of skilled drivers. The percentage found therefore indicates that the persons participating in the survey displayed overconfidence regarding their own driving skills. Overconfidence regarding risks especially occurs when people feel in control of the risk, even though their own behaviour has not much influence on the contingency occurring.

Self-serving biases however not only concern the interpretation of risks. In general, when interpreting information, people tend to take information that is in line with their previously held thoughts into account, and neglect information that is contrary to their beliefs. This is known as *ambiguity aversion* or *confirmation bias*. A well known example is discussed by Babcock et al. They explain how, when the same information is provided to individuals assigned the role of plaintiff and individuals assigned the role of defendant, information is interpreted in a self-serving way (Babcock et al., 1995). Both parties assess the information in the way that is most favourable to them, or at least more favourable than disinterested parties assessing the same information would.

60 Svenson (1981) also finds regional differences in perceptions of risk and skill. In the study undertaken, Svenson reports that 93% of the US survey participants believed themselves to be more skillful drivers than the median driver; 'only' 69% of the Swedish drivers shared this belief.

d. *Status quo biases*

People have a preference for the status quo, for leaving things as they are. This preference has been attributed to different factors, resulting in related biases. The *endowment effect* describes how people attribute higher values to things they own than to things that are not (yet) in their possession. The famous 'mug-experiment' carried out by Kahneman, Knetsch and Thaler confirmed a gap between willingness-to-pay and willingness-to-accept prices between students who were allotted a mug, and the ones who were not. Owning the mug apparently immediately raised the value this item portrayed for the students (Kahneman, Knetsch and Thaler, 1990). *Regret aversion* describes how people try to avoid the negative emotion of regret by justifying their behaviour in retrospect, even if the decision did not turn out so well. This is also referred to as *cognitive dissonance*. Again, the status quo is preferred over alternative options. Another reason for residing with the status quo is the *omission-commission bias* (Ritoy and Baron, 2000). People generally feel less bad over inactions that proved to be the wrong, than active choices that turned out to the chooser's detriment. Not doing anything and thereby losing out is apparently not as bad as actively choosing your own demise.

e. *Time related biases*

When having to compare options, people prefer present states of the world over states that will occur in the future. In behavioural literature, this observation is called *present bias*, or *myopia* (O'Donoghue and Rabin, 1999). Relatedly, people search for immediate gratification instead of patiently awaiting future benefits. Receiving one euro today is seen as more preferably than receiving one euro fifty tomorrow, even when the respective interest rate is extremely high. The implicit discount rate that people employ cannot be explained through standard economic views on the devaluation of money; this observation, related to present bias, is named *hyperbolic discounting* (Laibson, 1997). A relation between this bias and the certainty effect can be pointed out, as present situations are certain, and the future is not. Also, people exaggerate how long sensations of pleasure and of discomfort will last, making choices inconsistent with the actual experience. Individuals are prone to isolate particular instances, feelings and consequences of certain actions, and then fail to see or feel the whole picture of events (this is also part of the *focusing effect*).

Another time related bias is linked to procrastination (O'Donoghue and Rabin, 2006). People can be shown to be inactive, preferring to enjoy the leisurely present and to postpone taking actions. Especially when these actions are considered cumbersome or boring, action is postponed, and might eventually never be engaged in, even when this action would yield people significant benefits. Not engaging in a beneficial action, putting it off to a later time which may never come, is called *inertia*. Economic theory would suggest that the benefit that can be obtained is apparently not worth the hassle; however, in cases where the forgone benefits are considerable and the required action relatively easy, cheap and effortless, the rational prediction does not seem to hold up. The behavioural account can thus be claimed to more accurately predict the observed behaviour. Inertia is shown to increase when a longer time frame is allowed for the action to take place. For instance, when a rebate requires a certain form to be sent in, and the period in which this form can be sent is longer rather than shorter, people are less likely to actually perform.[61] Counter-intuitively, if people have a longer period and thus more opportunities for claiming the rebate, they are less likely to send it in.

f. Contexts and framing

Even though RCT indicates that contexts of a certain decision should not matter for the end result, behavioural insights suggest that frequently other factors than the costs and benefits of options are taken into account. People tend to go for middle options; medium sizes are most frequently picked, and extreme options in the range are avoided (Smith and Park, 1992). This would indicate that preferences depend on contexts and available alternatives, contrary to what can be hypothesised on the basis of RCT.

The *affect heuristic* describes how people attach positive perceptions to certain goods or products as a result of advertising for instance, where these perceptions have nothing to do with the good itself. For example, when a beautiful woman stands next to a car, this will on average increase the attractiveness of that car to men. Such choices and perceptions cannot be explained by rational choice models, as preferences should not depend on either unrelated issues or which other options are shown.

Furthermore, the way in which the various options are framed can be shown to have an impact on individual decision making. People strongly prefer avoiding losses to acquiring gains. Therefore, when options are framed as a *loss*, people become more prone to take risks. When options are framed as *gains*, people become more risk averse. This behavioural insight is known as *loss aversion* (Kahneman and Tversky, 1979).[62]

---

[61] See below, section 3.3.1, for some examples of consumers' biased decision making, including regarding rebates. See also Edwards (2007) for an extensive discussion of consumer behaviour regarding rebates.

[62] An example based upon the test conducted by Tversky and Kahneman (1981) is the following: people are told to imagine that they are doctors, preparing for outbreak of a disease which is expected to kill 600 people. Medicine A will save 200 people, whereas medicine B will save all 600 individuals with probability 1/3. Given the choice between medication A and B, most people (73%) choose Program A. However, the question has also been posed differently, framed as a choice between medicine C, which will allow 400 people to die, medicine D which will let no one die with probability 1/3 and all 600 will die with probability 2/3. When confronted

Mental accounting is another bias that emphasises the importance of contexts. It shows that money is not fungible in the way prescribed by conventional economics. Money that is allocated to a specific purpose is not easily interchangeable with other purposes. To exemplify, consider an experiment in which people are asked to think of the following situation: you have decided to go to theatre. The ticket for a show is 10 euro. Upon going to the theatre, you find out that you: (A) have lost the 10 euro bill; (B) have lost your ticket, which you bought in advance. The question is, would you buy another ticket? The authors show that in situation (A), 88% of individuals report they would buy the ticket, but upon having already bought and then losing the ticket (B), only 46% would buy another ticket (Tversky and Kahneman, 1981: 457).

g. *Anchoring and adjustment*

Behavioural research furthermore indicates that in early stages of the decision making process consumers make an estimation which serves as an *anchor* for the ultimate decision. These anchors are insufficiently adjusted later on in the decision making process. When new information comes up which is relevant to the estimation, the arrived-at value is not updated in the way described through RCT.[63] To give an example: a car might be shown to travel through rough terrain, combating snow and icy roads, the driver calm and at ease, never losing control of the car. When consumers see this ad, they might have an anchor for this car that it is safe and easy to drive for everyone. When later a warning is shown that the performance of the car in rough circumstances in fact depends on capabilities of the driver, the anchor people have set might not be adjusted accordingly.[64]

In connection to anchoring and status quo, current situations provide an anchor for valuation. Changes are not valuated in absolute numbers, but in relation to the status quo. Steady increases in salary, for instance, yield a higher benefit in subjective well-being than a large raise followed by a decrease in salary, even when the first process results in a slightly lower end-salary than the second (Layard, 2005). The anchor does not have to be related to the actual object of estimation. When people are shown a high number (say 10.000), and then asked to estimate some value (such as how many countries are comprised in the continent Africa), they arrive at higher values than when a low anchor (such as 3) is shown before making an estimation. Anchors can thus also be provided in the context of decisions, and do not have to be related to the actual issue at stake.

---

with these two options, most people (78%) choose option D. Notice that the two situations are identical in quantitative terms, but in the second one the decision maker is losing instead of saving lives. When losing lives, people are willing to take risks to lose fewer lives, but when people are saving lives they are less willing to take any chances.

63 Economic theory assumes Bayesian updating; see Bernheim and Whinston (2008).

64 The example is based upon Korobkin and Ulen (2000: 1102).

h. Bounded will-power

Besides all these cognitive quirks, people can be shown to have difficulties making decisions that would accrue benefits only in the long term; especially when in the short term some cost will have to be paid. *Bounded will-power* describes the actions people take that are in conflict with their own long term interest (Jolls et al., 1998a: 1479). Dieting, smoking, addictions and going to the gym are all examples of instances where in order for long terms benefits to be accrued, something will have to be given up in the present. Frequently, the present wins the battle. Even though people report wanting to quit with the detrimental behaviour, they seem not able to behave accordingly and take the necessary steps. This is of course inconsistent with RCT; when people have a preference for quitting, they should go for that option. Psychological constraints, not considered by economic theory, might restrain people from attaining their highest welfare possibilities.

3.2.3. THE BEHAVIOURAL RESEARCH PROJECT

As has been shown in the previous section, behavioural insights can point out many causes of suboptimal decision making. These insights are an accumulation of notions rather than stemming from one behavioural paradigm. Whereas most scholars accept that behavioural insights will be most useful as updates to economic theory and modelling, others scholars argue that the aim of the behavioural research project should be to establish a whole new behavioural paradigm, which, a point about which there is consensus at least, has up to now not yet been developed. Both rational choice and behavioural insights are supported and negated by empirical theory. This might provide foundation for dual process theories which indicate that individuals employ two (or more) different decision making processes. According to these theories, which are supported by neuro-economics and social psychology, one decision theory would be more intuitive and affective, while the other is more rational and reflective. The second decision process would correspond to rational choice, where the first corresponds more largely to behavioural insights. A fruitful direction for behavioural research might then be to point out which decision strategy prevails under which circumstances. The subject of dual process theories will be explored in more detail later.

a. The behavioural aim

Behavioural economics tries to better understand the motivations of 'economic actors', to improve economic predictions through more realistic economic foundations (Camerer and Loewenstein, 2004: 3). Camerer states that "(b)ecause economics is the science of how resources are allocated by individuals and by collective institutions like firms and markets, the psychology of individual behaviour should underlie and inform economics…" (Camerer, 1999: 10575).[65] This view, which would have been considered exotic in the earlier days of behavioural economics, is now held by many economic scholars. The traditional views on rationality as the prime model to use in theory may even no longer represent a majority position (Loewenstein and Haisley, 2008: 211).

Behavioural insights gain credibility in the experiments that repeatedly show the existence of these biases and heuristics, but suffer from the lack of a unifying alternative theory.[66] One notable exception however does aim to provide this alternative theory, namely Prospect Theory (Tversky and Kahneman, 1974; Kahneman and Tversky, 1979).[67] Prospect Theory holds that people evaluate losses and gains in a different way. It notes the importance of the reference point, which is used as a basis from which results are assessed as being losses or gains. When predicting behaviour, arguments should therefore be based upon changes in states or events rather than in states themselves.[68] Also, small and large probabilities are interpreted subjectively; causing a tendency to overvalue a small likelihood of gains and losses is overvalued and to undervalue a large likelihood. Thirdly, Prospect Theory points out how individuals portray dynamic inconsistencies by excessively discounting future gains or losses against current or short-term payoffs. Prospect Theory thus combines the biases of framing, endowment effect and status quo bias, loss aversion and hyperbolic discounting. As of yet, this theory has however not been able to replace rational choice as the paradigm for economic theory and policy.

Whether the aim is, or should be, to develop a systematic framework of behavioural (law and) economics, is a debated topic in literature. Some scholars argue that a behavioural framework should be the aim of the behavioural research programme. Rachlinski, and Kahneman and Tversky, for instance, argue that the goal of the behavioural programme is to construct an accurate model of human judgement and decision making, and that researchers in the field are working to accomplish that aim (Kahneman and Tversky, 1996: 582; Rachlinski,

---

65 Behavioural economics is thus a "reunification of psychology and economics", as stated by Camerer (1999: 10575). Early scholars such as Adam Smith (1790) in his Theory of Moral Sentiments were much more involved in psychological thinking than modern day economists.

66 This is also frequently pointed out by economists in favour of adhering to RCT. This point will be more thoroughly discussed below in chapter 4, section 4.2.1b.

67 See Dowling and Chin-Fang (2007: 62–83) for a comprehensive introduction to Prospect Theory.

68 Where RCT assumes utility functions to be concave, Prospect Theory posits that utility functions are convex below a reference point, being the point the subject interprets to be the status-quo. Above that reference point, utility functions are concave.

2000: 752).[69] This framework has however not yet been established.[70] Camerer and Loewenstein on the other hand claim that behavioural (law and) economics does not aim at constructing an entirely new paradigm. It extends the insights that have been developed within economics, aiming to advance economics "on its own terms" (Camerer and Loewenstein, 2004: 3). Behavioural law and economics does not aim to abandon rational choice models, but to extend them (Ho, Lin and Camerer, 2006: 308). Far from being a critique of law and economics, behavioural law and economics is argued to aim at improving its predictions by infusing insights about actual behaviour into the assessment (Jolls, 1998: 1654). Arlen argues that behavioural analysis of law cannot supplant economic analysis of law. She adds that the research programme is more likely to produce a set of suggestions through which conventional law and economics can be updated. That being said, she notes that law and economics should not ignore the insights derived from other social sciences; it should take advantage of these behavioural insights (Arlen, 1998: 1787–8).[71] By accounting for behavioural insights in theory and policy, predictions, models and legal rules can be improved from a social welfare perspective. Behavioural scholars such as Jolls, Sunstein and Thaler have expressed a hope that behavioural insights will come to enhance economic theory as a whole and that the term 'behavioural' economics will no longer be used (Jolls et al., 1998a: 1547).[72]

b. *Confronting rational and behavioural decision making strategies*

Whether behavioural insights are able to improve traditional economic analysis with respect to explaining and predicting the behaviour of consumers and sellers is in the end an empirical question. Technological advances have enabled various experiments testing RCT, Prospect Theory and behavioural insights in general.[73] The results of these studies are not yet revealing a clear winner. In fact, both approaches have been falsified in various experiments, but have not been rejected in other ones.[74] White for example claims finding that behavioural theory is

[69] See also Korobkin and Ulen (2000: esp. 1075) arguing that especially in the realm of law and behavioural science the rational choice assumption should be abandoned.

[70] Nearly all authors agree that this systematic behavioural framework has not been construed yet, see for example Kelman (1998), Posner (1998a), Camerer and Loewenstein (2004), Armstrong (2008), Bar-Gill (2008), Epstein (2008) and Shafir (2008).

[71] Similarly, Korobkin and Ulen (2000: 1075) claim that the end point of the behavioural research agenda will likely not be a single unified theory designed to explain or predict the full realm of human decision making behaviour. It is more likely to be a "pragmatic collection of situation-specific insights that can be accessed by policymakers dealing with relevant problems".

[72] In response, Kahneman (2003: 166) remain of the opinion that economics and behavioural theory sharing a common methodology is unlikely to happen (soon).

[73] Due to technological advancements, most notably in the area of information technology, researchers are enabled to conduct larger experiments and perform more elaborate statistical testing.

[74] See for instance Abdellaoui, Barrios and Wakker (2007), Wakker, Timmermans and Machielse (2007) for experimental results consistent with Prospect Theory. See also the overview of

proven right by empirical analysis (White, 2009); Wright on the other hand states that conventional price theory is more accurate in predictions than behavioural theory, and provides empirical evidence to make his claim (Wright, 2007).[75] The results from experiments and empirical studies have not been able to identify one methodology, either rational choice or Prospect Theory, to be more supported by their findings than the other. Both rational choice assumptions and behavioural insights can be shown to have merit; the 'truth' might lie somewhere in between (Dowling and Chin-Fang, 2007: 1). As has been stated above, these findings correspond with a current of thought in social psychology and also in neuro-economics, namely dual processes theory: the position that individuals utilise two (or more) different cognitive processes. Dual process theories could provide an answer to the empirical finding that in some situations people apparently behave more rational than in others.

c. *Dual processes*

Both RCT and Prospect Theory are unitary process theories, asserting that human behaviour can be best explained and/or predicted by one solitary theory. People however might be employing not one single decision making process, but at least two and possibly more, in different situations (Arlen and Talley, 2008). *Dual process theories*, or even *multiple process theories*, claim that people employ different processes of human decision making, and not merely one. People might not always be thinking rationally, but sometimes make decisions on the basis of intuitions and affection. One mode of thinking could be employed by a person in one situation, and another mode of thinking could be employed by the same person in another situation. Both modes of thinking could even both be used at the same time, regarding different aspects of the same decision. The outcome of the decision could differ significantly on the basis of the used method of thinking and decision making. Dual processes of thinking are described by several authors. For instance, Slovic et al. assert that humans employ an experiential mode of thinking and an analytical mode of thinking, both being continuously active and interacting (Slovic et al., 2002: 330–2).[76] They argue that positive and negative affective feelings are connected to images, words, and circumstances, like tags.

---

empirical evidence of rational choice, Prospect Theory and neuro-economics in Arlen and Talley (2008), and Shafir (2008) for a discussion of empirical findings regarding human behaviour.

[75] Similarly, see the exchange between Bar-Gill (2008) and Epstein (2008) on behavioural and neoclassical economics in consumer contracts.

[76] These two modes of thinking are also often referred to as System 1 and System 2; Thaler and Sunstein (2008: 20), in *Nudge*, refer to it as Automatic System and Reflective System respectively. See Lee, Amir and Ariely (2009: 174) for a description of several dual system models, all describing a similar distinction between two decision making systems: one automatic, reflexive, affective, and passive, while the cognitive system is relatively more analytic, logical, abstract, and active.

Rather than rational thinking, these tags guide judgement and decision making in the experiential system (see figure 3).

Figure 3. Two Modes of Thinking. Comparison of Experiential and Rational Systems

	Experiential System		Rational System
1.	Holistic	1.	Analytic
2.	Affective: Pleasure-pain oriented	2.	Logical: Reason oriented (what is sensible)
3.	Connections by association	3.	Logical connections
4.	Behaviour mediated by 'vibes' from past experiences	4.	Behaviour mediated by conscious appraisal of events
5.	Encodes reality in concrete images, metaphors, and narratives	5.	Encodes reality in abstract symbols, words, and numbers
6.	More rapid processing: Oriented toward immediate action	6.	Slower processing: Oriented toward delayed action
7.	Self-evidently valid: "experiencing is believing"	7.	Requires justification via logic and evidence

Source: Slovic et al (2002: 330).

People who do not have well constructed preferences and think more intuitively than deliberately might thus experience positive and negative associations with certain items that might not be rational but that influences decision making nonetheless. There is a clear link between dual process theories and common complaints found in behavioural literature against the use of *homo economicus* in economic thinking of consumer behaviour. When people employ the intuitive or experiential system to make decisions, these decisions might better be understood and predicted through the use of a paradigm other than RCT.

In the field of neuro-economics, Klucharev and Smidts report that arguments can be found for the existence of dual process theories.[77] Neuro-economics tries to see which part of the brain is active in making decisions. Parts of the brain can be connected to either intuitive or more deliberative decision making. Decision making is not always based upon conscious deliberation; intuition and other non-conscious decision making is utilised in various contexts as well. As dual process decision systems can be supported by neuro-economics, neuro-economic research suggests that automatic decision making should be accounted for in policy. Rational decision making, Klucharev and Smidts claim on the basis of neuro-economic findings, should not be the standard for all policy (Klucharev and Smidts, 2009: 234). The outcomes of decision making could differ significantly

[77] Neuroscience can be used to further insights in decision making theory as well, as is suggested by Shiv et al. (2005). On neuro-economics and policy, see for instance Zak (2004). For a more specific defence of the claim that the law can be structured to take advantage of our neural mechanisms to improve social welfare, see Chorvat and McCabe (2004).

on the basis of the used method of decision making. Policy should account for different modes of thinking, instead of only RCT, when RCT cannot be expected to predict decision making most accurately.

The apparent existence of dual (or even multiple) cognitive processes sheds a whole new light on the rational choice - behavioural insights debate. It seems to argue against the existence of one methodology that has more predictive power, instead providing foundation for the claim that scholars should aim at identifying which cognitive process is employed under which circumstances, and how individuals can be triggered to switch from one to the other. The issue of defining the conditions under which rational, experiential or other thinking respectively is utilised becomes very relevant. When (consumer) biases or automatic decision making can be shown to prevail in certain situations, decision making could be more accurately predicted using other models than rational choice, such as behaviourally informed economic theory. Future research in behavioural insights will be extremely useful in determining which circumstances trigger the effects caused by certain biases and heuristics (Kahneman and Tversky, 1996: 589).

3.2.4. SUMMARY: BEHAVIOURAL LAW AND ECONOMICS

Recent insights gained in behavioural research have shed a different light on the abilities of individuals to assess information and have provided insights that differ from economic analysis. Behavioural research has identified certain biases and heuristics in decision making that may lead consumers to act in a way not predicted by the rational model of decision making even when they are fully informed or have the possibility to obtain the information at low cost. Behavioural insights that have been discussed in this section are: bounded rationality and information overload, risk perception biases, self-serving biases, status quo biases, time related biases, contexts and framing, anchoring and adjustment, and bounded will-power. Individuals are thereby shown not to behave rationally under all circumstances. Whether this should lead to a fully new framework of economic theory and policy based on behavioural insights remains unclear. It is however commonly accepted in behavioural literature that through implementing behavioural insights in economic theory and policy, predictions and policy can be improved. Whether a new behavioural framework will ever be developed, and whether such a framework will compete with, add to or merge with economic theory will most likely become clearer in the future. For the present, this research will posit that, based upon current findings and discussions, the potential added value of behavioural insights to economic theory is that these insights can improve predictions by increasing the reality of the assumptions, and that a new behavioural paradigm has not, at least not yet, been provided.

When competing hypotheses based upon rational choice and behavioural sciences are tested, no clear winner is revealed. This would correspond to the theorem of dual processes in cognitive decision making. According to dual processes theory, one cognitive system would be more rational, analytical, and logical as well as based upon evidence, whereas the other would be more experiential, affective, intuitive and oriented towards immediate action. Defining the situations where the one or the other cognitive system is utilised will become one of the major issues in future discussions in behavioural literature. To cite Sunstein, "(t)he future of economic analysis of law lies in new and better understanding of decision and choice" (Sunstein, 1997: 1175).

After this introduction into behavioural economics and behavioural law and economics, the relevance of these insights to policy will be discussed in the next section. This section will focus upon consumer decision making and the biases and heuristics that affect it, potentially enabling sellers to take advantage of consumers. The behavioural literature has devised a specific regulatory approach to counteract biased decision making: soft paternalism. The intervention strategies combined in this approach will also be discussed in detail.

3.3. BEHAVIOURAL INSIGHT TO (CONSUMER) POLICY

Now that the approach of behavioural (law and) economics has been introduced, this section aims at establishing which implications the behavioural approach can have for consumer protection policy. First some examples of situations in which consumer biases enable sellers to take advantage of consumers' decision making will be laid out. Secondly, the possibility of using behavioural insights in policy will be discussed. Behavioural notions can have several implications for policy, especially for the policy instrument of information disclosure. Paternalistically interfering with individuals' free will is however severely criticised. Therefore, in behavioural literature, the regulatory approach of soft paternalism is developed, that nudges individuals to beneficial decisions while still allowing them sufficient freedom of choice.

When discussing how behavioural insights can be used to amend consumer policy, many concerns are brought up that caution against the use of behavioural insights in policy. These methodological and normative concerns will be discussed in the next chapter. This section focuses on the implications behavioural insights could have for policy, the next chapter will discuss which cautions and considerations should be taken into account when implementing behaviourally informed consumer policy.

3.3.1. CONSUMERS' BIASED DECISION MAKING

Many situations can be pointed out in which consumers are said to rely upon biases and heuristics which are exploited by sellers. Whereas standard economic theory would deem consumer decision making in these cases efficient, behavioural insights indicate that consumers might not be able to maximise their own welfare. This could provide arguments for governments to intervene on behalf of consumers, thereby also aiming to increase social welfare.

a. *Examples of consumers' biased decision making*

In behavioural literature, many consumer biases and heuristics are identified that could lead consumers to take sub-optimal decisions regarding their own welfare.[78] These biases and heuristics thereby also provide opportunities for sellers to take advantage of consumers. Examples of such advantage-taking are:

- Consumer credit contracts, fitness club subscriptions and price plans for mobile phone subscriptions. On entering into these contracts, consumers have great difficulties in assessing prices and gains before and sometimes even during the contract. In such contracts the price that consumers have to pay for the product or service and the benefit consumers expect to gain from contracts depend on use patterns (Bar-Gill, 2007). When consumers can make a realistic assessment of their own expected use, they will opt for the contract that is most beneficial to them in the light of their personal use pattern. Consumers however might err in the assessment of the extent to which they will make use of the respective product or service. Biases like overoptimism and overconfidence influence the assessment of prices and gains to contracts, and enable sellers to exploit consumer biases. Often, the payment schedule and subscription plans in these contracts can also abuse the imperfect self-control of consumers. Consumers are lured into credit structures and subscription plans that are not cost-effective for them. Della Vigna and Malmendier find that consumers choose subscription types that, in hindsight, were not the ones that maximised their utility based upon their use patterns. Their research establishes that overestimations of future self-control and of future efficiency are the main reasons for these sup-optimal choices (Della Vigna and Malmendier, 2006: 716).

---

[78] See for instance: Korobkin and Ulen (2000), Becher (2007), Wright (2007), Bar-Gill (2008), Rischkowsky and Döring (2008: 301–305) and White (2009). In a collection of articles, Hanson and Kysar discuss sellers' manipulation of consumer biases. In the first article, Hanson and Kysar (1999a) give an overview of behavioural biases that might be exploited by sellers, and explain why sellers can be expected to do so; in the second article Hanson and Kysar (1999b) aim to provide evidence of this market manipulation focusing on the tobacco industry; in the third article Hanson and Kysar (2000) describe how liability for sellers exploiting consumers could be a solution to the problem of market manipulation of consumer biases.

- Consumer credit contracts such as mortgages and credit card debts similarly enable sellers to take advantage of consumers' present biases and overoptimism. Consumers agree to take on certain risks without a realistic assessment of the consequences of that decision. They are overoptimistic about their personal abilities, and concerning future developments such as salary raises. In reality, repayment of loans and debt might be more difficult than anticipated (Bar-Gill, 2004; Bar-Gill, 2008: 763).
- Rebate coupons lure consumers into more expensive options, as consumers base their decision on discounted prices. They are overoptimistic about their propensity to send in rebate coupons, and tend to postpone actions through inertia. Sellers are well aware that rebate coupons increase sales, as consumers expect they will take advantage of coupons; sellers also know that not all rebate coupons will be sent in. Gift vouchers as compensation for some damage, such as a delay or lost item, can increase the reputation of the seller. In fact, sellers know large quantities of gift vouchers are never used; the gift is thus less beneficial to them than consumers expect (Edwards, 2007: 384–7, 393–5).
- When people buy medicine on sale, they report worse medical outcomes for this cheaper product; the same medicine, bought for a regular price, receives a higher evaluation. Consumers therefore seem to induce quality from higher prices. A placebo effect is apparently affecting consumers in their evaluation of prices (Ariely, 2009: 181–4). This gives adverse incentives to companies in terms of pricing their products.
- Consumers have difficulties assessing product warnings, which make them less able to accurately respond to the information provided. Information overload and overoptimism can cause consumers to disregard product warnings (Pape, 2008).
- Taking a test drive entices consumers into a projection bias. They expect to enjoy the positive sensations of the new car for a long time. However, they are overly projecting present preferences into the future, and find that they benefit less from the car than they had expected (Loewenstein, O'Donoghue and Rabin, 2003).
- Standard contract terms cause information overload and are therefore not fully assessed (Korobkin, 1998). Even the salient items that are assessed can be interpreted self-servingly, especially when the formulation is ambiguous. Suffering from various forms of status quo bias, consumers are likely to accept the terms as they are, even though their preferences would be better served with other terms than the default provided by the seller. Generally, terms in consumer contracts allocate risks between consumers and sellers. As the assessment of information might provide difficulties to consumers especially where the assessment of risks is concerned, consumers might not fully realise the consequences of agreeing to take on certain risks. Furthermore, decision

paralysis might cause consumers to refrain from regarding the standard terms at all.

- Hyperbolic discounting, where individuals overvalue short term consequences in comparison to long term consequences, has its implications especially for contracts where gains are immediate, but costs follow later. Payday lending is an example of contracts that take advantage of this bias (Edwards, 2008).
- With respect to insurance, consumers are argued to underestimate certain risks, causing them to underinsure. However, when risks are highly salient, consumers might over-insure (Camerer and Kunreuther, 1989: 570). The conventional economic claim is that individuals, when insured, will take more risks than not being insured as they will no longer face the consequences of their careless behaviour. The empirical support for *moral hazard* on the side of consumers is however inconclusive, and does not seem to appear as regularly as hypothesised by rational choice models (Faure and Van Boom, 2008; Van Boom, 2008).
- Framing through shelf spaces in supermarkets induces consumers to opt certain products (Hanson and Kysar, 1999b: 1444). The options provided to consumers induce them to go for more expensive options or larger quantities. Consumers can be shown to opt for middle sizes. Adding a highly priced good to the mix induces the medium range (which was before the higher range) to be chosen more frequently (Simonson and Tversky, 1992: 286–7). Also, impulse buying is stimulated through store layout (Edwards, 2008).
- Money-back guarantees, thirty-day no-risk trial periods, free samples, and so on, create in the consumer a sense of ownership. These strategies take advantage of the endowment effect (Hanson and Kysar, 1999a: 734). Once having acquired the good, the consumer values the contract more than he would have beforehand. The consumer will thus keep the good instead of returning it as he thought he would do. Inertia is a related problem, causing consumers to not return goods that they would have wanted to return. Interest rates on savings accounts which are depressed once the consumer is hooked are another way of abusing status quo bias and inertia in consumer decision making.
- A related issue is that consumers have difficulty switching from one provider to another, which is especially problematic in deregulated markets. Consumers tend to stay with the provider they had already contracted with, even when competitors could provide better options now the market has been opened up. Faced with the hurdle of having to go through all different aspects of several options, consumers opt not to choose, and fail to adjust their contract to a more beneficial one (Brennan, 2005).[79]

[79] See also NMa (2009) for a report of the Dutch Competition Authority on the Dutch energy market, also concluding consumers fail to switch suppliers after the market has been opened up, to their financial detriment.

- Advertisements are also criticised for unduly influencing decisions. An example frequently made is how perceptions of products such as cars are positively influenced through advertisements featuring physically attractive human models, conveying no product information, and who are unrelated to the advertised product (Julander and Söderlund, 2005). Feel-good advertising is used to create a positive affect with the product, neglecting negative aspects. A frequently referred to example of this affect heuristic is Marlboro's Tobacco Man advertising and the neglected negative aspects of smoking (Epstein, 1994: 712).

In the situations described above, consumer decision making might be suboptimal leading to situations that are undesirable from a social welfare viewpoint. Behavioural insights could thus provide reasons to interfere in the market by means of behaviourally informed consumer protection. In fact, policy makers are becoming more and more interested in using the insights uncovered by behavioural sciences to enhance consumer protection legislation.

3.3.2. USING BEHAVIOURAL INSIGHTS IN POLICY

Behavioural insights are more and more frequently used in policy, even though the interest of policy makers in behavioural economics is quite a recent development. Some general implications that behavioural economics will have for policy will be discussed below. Of these implications, the relevance of behavioural insights for information disclosure will be discussed in detail, as this instrument is highly relevant in consumer policy. Behavioural economics is often criticised for intervening with people's choices, thereby obstructing free will. In behavioural literature, the policy strategy of soft paternalism is developed precisely counter this critique. The approaches combined in soft paternalism all include one key aspect, namely that individual choice is guided to welfare enhancing options while still allowing consumers the opportunity to decide as they please. Free will is therefore not obstructed in soft paternalism. Some examples of soft paternalism will be provided to clarify the concept.

a. *Policy interest in behavioural insights*

Ramsay claims that behavioural economics has become an influential source for consumer policy (Ramsay, 2007: 71). Actually, in various countries and organisations, policy makers have taken up an interest in behavioural insights for policy. Conferences, reports, working groups and so on are being organised by the OECD, the Productivity Commission in Australia, the FTC in the United States and the Ministry of Economic Affairs in the Netherlands, to name just a few.[80] Economics has been much more influential in informing public policy than other social sciences, such as psychology or sociology (Ross and Shestowsky, 2003: 1081; Amir et al., 2005: 444). As a result of the flourishing behavioural economic research project Benjamin and Laibson expect many behaviourally inspired policies to be proposed in the next decades (Benjamin and Laibson, 2003: 32).[81] The decision tree of consumer policy, as it is developed by the OECD, can serve as an illustration for policy interest in behavioural approaches (OECD, 2007: 13, see figure 4). It is interesting to see the extent to which this decision model corresponds to the conditions for desirable government interventions from an economic viewpoint, as described in chapter 2.

First the decision tree focuses on the demand-side of the market, compatible with the view that issues of imperfect competition are better dealt with by competition policy.

Secondly, the model focuses on two different failures with respect to consumer decision making, namely information failures and behavioural biases. The tools that are distinguished in this model (referred to as informational, behavioural and other instruments) are unfortunately not very well defined in the report. Traditional economic analysis focuses mostly on information failures in consumer protection, but also grants that externalities and public goods could form a basis for government intervention. Of course, consumer policy is not the only vehicle for these interventions. Externalities can be addressed via tort law; public goods could be provided by either stimulating production in the market or by government institutions producing the public good themselves. The decision model focuses on information asymmetries and behavioural aspects in consumer decision making.

---

80 See for instance: OECD (2006; 2007); see Edwards (2008) on how the FTC deals with behavioural insights in the US, and Productivity Commission (2008) regarding Australia. Several conferences have been organised by governmental institutions and consumer authorities about the consequences of behavioural insights for policy, such as: FTC Conference April 20th, 2007: *Behavioral economics and consumer policy*, www.ftc.gov/be/consumerbehavior; Dutch Ministry of Economic Affairs, Conference June 2nd, 2008: *Competition and Consumer Protection*, cpb.nl/nl/activ/workshop/consumer_protection, EC Conference November 28th, 2008: *How Can Behavioural Economics Improve Policies Affecting Consumers?*, ec.europa.eu/consumers/dyna/conference/index_en.htm. The Dutch Scientific Council for Government Policy (Wetenschappelijke Raad voor Regeringsbeleid, WRR) has also embraced behavioural insights into choice and behaviour as highly relevant for government policy, and will advise the Dutch government on how to include behavioural insights in public policy: see Tiemeijer, Thomas and Prast (2009) and wrr.nl/content.jsp?objectid=4795.

81 Amir et al. (2005: 451) suggest to behavioural scholars and psychologists that they should make policy a focus of their research. They claim that would be the most promising approach to help psychological insights to get through to politicians. These research projects should aim to formulate theoretical and empirical answers to questions that are relevant for policy makers, using behavioural insights. Policy pilot studies, which are hardly undertaken, would be obvious examples where behavioural scholars could help out and through which the psychological and behavioural influence on policy can be increased.

Figure 4. Decision tree – Demand-side market analysis by consumer regulators

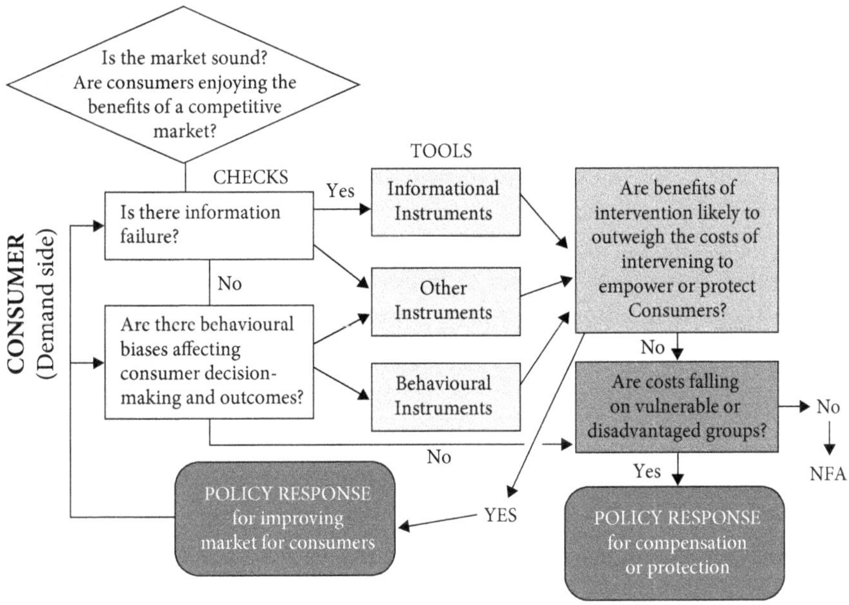

NFA = no further action

Source: OECD (2007: 13).

Thirdly, the decision tree pays explicit attention to the question of whether the costs of government intervention outweigh the benefits of the intervention on behalf of the consumer. Which costs could be attached to the government intervention is a topic to be addressed below. When the benefits of the intervention outweigh the costs, policy response is warranted to counteract the market failure.

As a fourth point of interest, policy response is also warranted according to the OECD decision tree when distributional issues are a concern. Following the decision tree, when costs are falling to vulnerable or disadvantaged groups, policy response for compensation or protection is justified. This argument does not correspond with standard economic justification for government intervention. This is an equity argument, not an efficiency argument: protecting disadvantaged parties through the use of consumer protection law could be inefficient, and counterproductive from a social welfare point of view.[82] In general, the decision tree attempts to combine the classical economic view on consumer protection with new insights developed by behavioural sciences and the aim to address distributional concerns. This illustrates how behavioural insights are becoming

[82] Distributional concerns and fairness issues in policy have been topic of many debates, which will not be further explored here. For some interesting arguments in the discussion, see Kennedy (1982), Swygert and Yanes (1998), Kaplow and Shavell (2002; see Kaplow and Shavell (2003) for a summarising restatement of the main arguments of the previous article) and Craswell (2003).

more important for policy makers, while traditional economic views also remain valid.

b. *Behavioural implications for consumer policy*

While there might be a case for government interventions in consumer decision making based on behavioural insights, the extent of that intervention is still a debated topic. Behavioural insights are said to call for *paternalism*, which can be defined as actions interfering with the liberty of another person, without the consent of that other person, to improve the welfare of that subject or in other ways promote his or her interests (Dworkin, 2005). Insights from cognitive psychology can be argued to justify constraints on individual choice by policy institutions (Rachlinski, 2003: 1166). Paternalism is regarded quite negatively from an economic perspective. Individuals can best decide for themselves, as they themselves are in the best position to know what they prefer. Governments should therefore allow individuals optimal choice, and not intervene with the options available to them.

Behavioural insights could give alternative reasons, other than economic arguments, for government intervention. Ramsey discusses five main implications that behavioural insights have for policy (Ramsay, 2007: 77–8): firstly, behavioural insights indicate that a more careful analysis of the potential effects of disclosure programmes is necessary. Disclosure should not be rejected as an important regulatory tool, but it should be reassessed. Consumers interpret and assess information differently than predicted by rational choice models, especially where risks are concerned; issues such as presentation and framing of information are more relevant than previously thought.[83] Secondly, even when markets are competitive, when there is no excess profit being made by sellers, markets might still be suboptimal from a welfare point of view due to consumer biases. As Hanson and Kysar argue, competition might even force businesses take advantage of consumer biases, as their competitors are taking advantage as well (Hanson and Kysar, 1999b: 1424–5). Thirdly, as consumers have difficulties in accurate risk assessments, it might be socially optimal to provide rules that remove such a risk from the market entirely. Regarding for instance product safety, a mandatory and intrusive intervention on behalf of consumers might thus be justified, even when this limits options to consumers. Fourthly, consumer sovereignty has in the past been seen to trump government intervention, as consumers know their preferences best. According to this view, governments should allow people to make their own choices. Behavioural insights suggest however that consumers benefit from intervention that helps them to improve their choices, and maybe even protect them from foolish choices. Consumer sovereignty might therefore

[83] The implications of behavioural insights for the policy instrument of information disclosure will be more thoroughly discussed below, in section c.

have to lose its trump status in issues of consumer protection.[84] Finally, the distinction between rational and 'vulnerable' consumers needs to be re-assessed. In some policies, this distinction is made to allow protection for people who are less able to make rational decisions. Children and mentally challenged individuals are considered to be vulnerable, whereas mentally capable adults are usually considered rational. Whether in policies the standard of 'rational' or 'credulous' consumer should remain to be adhered to is a topic of continuous discussion.[85] Behavioural economics, especially insights about framing and contexts, make it clear that distinguishing which types of consumers will be more vulnerable is complicated. In some situations, nearly all consumers can be expected to err in their decision making.

Among these implications, the reassessment of information disclosure is especially relevant in the context of consumer protection policy. Information economics points to the provisions of information as the primary and most desirable tool in consumer protection policy.[86] Behavioural insights however show that the interpretation of information can be biased and therefore does not always correspond with traditional insights from economic theory. Using the policy instrument of information disclosure should therefore take behavioural insights into account as well.

c. *Focus: information disclosure in the behavioural light*

As has been discussed in the previous chapter, consumer protection is in economics regarded to be mainly an issue of information. The other market failures notwithstanding, information asymmetry is the market failure that is most relevant in consumer markets. This market failure occurs frequently in consumer markets as the parties to the contracts are of different types, namely commercial sellers and private consumers. Whereas the other market failures are dealt with by specific interventions such as competition issues by competition policy, consumer protection is seen as mostly aiming at decreasing information asymmetry problems. As information asymmetry can lead to adverse selection and thus decrease quality, information disclosure is often the instrument of choice to correct the asymmetry of information. Behavioural insights however show that this policy prescription is prone to suffer from several issues. Information disclosure focuses upon providing information to consumers, often without providing any advice about in what way or how much information is to be disclosed (Jolls et al., 1998a: 1533).

84 The regulatory approach of *soft paternalism* will be explored below in section e. This is the regulatory approach that behavioural literature often calls for, especially since the issue of consumer sovereignty and free choice is regarded as an important point in this literature as well.

85 See for instance Incardona and Poncibò (2007).

86 See above, chapter 2, section 2.3.3c.

As indicated by behavioural literature, acquiring and assessing information might be more troublesome for consumers than is implied by information economics. Due to information overload, the quality of the consumer decisions can actually decrease. Korobkin and Ulen point to two aspects of decision making that are most important in causing people to make decisions that fail to maximise their expected utility. These are the complexity of the problem at hand (too many options and aspects of those options) and possible ambiguity in the content of the options (Korobkin and Ulen, 2000: 28–32).

As argued by Jolls, Sunstein and Thaler, providing information to consumers without paying any attention to the format, quantity and effectiveness of the disclosure can be inefficient or have adverse effects (Jolls et al., 1998a: 1533–5). Huge quantities of information will be complex to apprehend and might even paralyse consumers into not making any decision at all or neglecting the information altogether. When given highly technical or excessive information, consumers "switch off" and do not reap the benefits of being informed. Risks might not be accurately taken into account by consumers, even when they are disclosed. The information that is to be disclosed can also prime consumers' attention towards a particular product aspect, even resulting in decisions of lesser quality (Lacko and Pappalardo, 2004). Through priming, attention is focused on what is disclosed. This distracts the attention from other elements in the decision making process, and can thus lead to suboptimal decision making.[87] Risks are interpreted differently than rational choice models would predict. Merely providing information about a certain risk therefore does not automatically imply that consumers will account for this risk in their decision in the way predicted by RCT.[88] Product attributes or other contextual items that should according to economic theory be irrelevant to the decision are shown in empirical tests to have an effect after all. The effectiveness of information disclosure can thus (willingly) be altered through framing of information.[89]

When information disclosure is prescribed however, the presentation is often not regarded in the prescription. Presentation is very important in framing choices, and influences the decision to a large extent (Jolls et al., 1998a: 1533–5). Brooker and Cullum caution that information regulation often does not have the desired outcome. Information requirements seem to be a first remedy of choice for regulators, but this remedy is often applied without carefully construing the effectiveness of the policy instrument. Regulators should therefore pay more attention to the design of regulation and its effectiveness in achieving the desired regulatory goals. Information requirements should be prescribed only when and in such a way that they will aid consumers and businesses in overcoming information problems (Brooker and Cullum, 2008: 6). When information disclosure is relied

87 See above, section 3.2.2a.
88 See above, section 3.2.2b.
89 See above, section 3.2.2f.

upon to cure information asymmetry, the effectiveness of that instrument should be assessed. Prescribing certain formats or procedures to disclose the information might increase the effectiveness of information disclosure.

Rachlinski points to another behavioural insight to information disclosure: cognitive errors can undermine the benefits of information disclosure (Rachlinski, 2003: 1177). Consumers are only aided by information disclosure if it helps them to make better choices. Disclosure can however also lead to people being worse off. Sellers who have disclosed the information in a way that concurs with policy prescriptions are often no longer liable for mistakes made by a consumer not taking that information into account. As information disclosure prescriptions do not account for behavioural biases, the information disclosure might be legitimate though ineffective: the consumer, suffering from information overload and biased interpretation of information, fails to accurately take the information into account. As a result, while consumers have not benefitted from the information disclosure, they are suddenly confronted with the fact that they no longer have an action against the seller for not informing them. This adverse effect should be weighed against positive effects of information disclosure, such as a decrease in fees or prices and a general increase in quality of the item subjected to disclosure. The mere fact that a certain term, price, hygienic procedure et cetera has to be disclosed makes this product aspect salient to consumers and sellers. Notably, this can have also have a positive impact on the quality of this product aspect, as sellers know that it will be regarded extra carefully by consumers.

In the information economics discussion, Schwartz and Wilde already claimed that information costs might lead to insufficient search, which in turn leads to supra-competitive prices, which was not taken into account sufficiently by economic models relying upon rational expectations. They argue for a more realistic model which allows more insights about consumer behaviour to enter the assessment (Schwartz and Wilde, 1982). Rather than allowing the fact that consumers have difficulty interpreting information to cause a rejection of disclosure regimes entirely, the notions in behavioural sciences can be used to highlight the scope and limitations of these regimes and to point out problems in certain markets and situations that might warrant further intervention (Ramsay, 2005: 57). The impact of available information on the outcome of the decision making process is subtle and often hard to predict, which calls for more sophisticated approaches to the information problems (Hadfield et al., 1998: 141). In light of behavioural findings, the government would be wise not to rely entirely on information disclosure to overcome biased or uninformed consumer decision making and to be aware of the effects of the disclosure regimes (Tiemeijer, 2009: 302).

d. *Behavioural policy approach: soft paternalism*

Behavioural literature has often been criticised for being paternalistic.[90] In response to that critique a specific kind of regulatory approach has been developed in behavioural literature: *soft paternalism*. Since not all consumers decide sub-optimally, and in the situations and conditions that are connected to sub-optimal decisions have not been properly identified yet, behavioural literature often opts for government interventions that do guide consumer behaviour but that still allow free choice if consumers would rather decide for themselves. These interventions are commonly referred to as soft paternalism but are also known as the *lighter hand approach* or *light paternalism*.[91] Soft paternalism is a strand of regulatory approaches that share a common perspective: responding to insights from behavioural sciences, they aim to change the outcome of biased decisions but they do so without coercion and at low cost to people who would rather opt differently. This element of free choice is what sets soft paternalism apart from 'hard' paternalism. The approaches that are combined in soft paternalism are compatible with the free will of individuals. They assist people in enhancing their welfare by improving their choices without coercing them to opt for a particular outcome. As argued by Amir and Lobel, soft paternalism corresponds to the approach of *new governance*, which is a form of government intervention that is situated between command and control on one hand, and *laissez-faire* politics on the other (Lobel, 2004; Amir and Lobel, 2008).

Several versions of the soft paternalism approach might be suggested to account for behavioural insights. *Asymmetric paternalism*, a term coined by Camerer et al., refers to regulation that creates large benefits for those who are affected by the bias or heuristic at hand, at very low or no costs to those who act fully rational (Camerer et al., 2003). It is explicitly mentioned that some costs could be incurred by the rational parties. This implies that asymmetric paternalism might have some distributional effect. Sunstein and Thaler dub their approach *libertarian paternalism*, referring to a soft form of paternalism that does not block choices and is therefore non-intrusive (Sunstein and Thaler, 2003). Libertarian paternalism is the best known version of soft paternalism and aims to be compatible with libertarian views by protecting the freedom of choice within these regulatory proposals.[92] This paternalistic approach claims to respect the

---

90 For a more extensive discussion of the criticism of paternalism in behavioural literature, see chapter 4, especially section 4.3.3.

91 The *lighter hand approach* is mentioned in OECD (2006: 18). *Light paternalism* is mentioned by Loewenstein and Haisley (2008).

92 Several authors criticise the denomination of libertarian for the policy suggestions made by Sunstein and Thaler. The terms *libertarian paternalism* has been criticised as being neither libertarian, nor paternalistic. As interventions cannot be value-neutral, Amir and Lobel (2008: 2120) claim these interventions cannot be called truly paternalistic. Libertarian value freedom above all, which includes the freedom to make mistakes and not have any architecture intentionally directing choice. See Grüne-Yanoff (2008) for a similar claim.

autonomy of individuals by setting non-mandatory defaults or opt-outs. Thaler and Sunstein argue that when biases lead people to make undesirable decisions, 'nudges' based on behavioural theory can gently steer them into a more desirable direction (Thaler and Sunstein, 2008).[93] *Optimal paternalism*, as described by O'Donoghue and Rabin, recognises costs and benefits of paternalism, including distributional issues, and argues for interventions that aim at optimal welfare from society's point of view (O'Donoghue and Rabin, 2003).

These approaches all aim to address the *internalities:* costs that people impose on themselves but due to biases and heuristics fail to internalise in their decision (Herrnstein et al., 1993). Traditional externalities, non-internalised costs imposed on other parties, are dealt with by several forms of existing regulation such as liability and tort law. To further address the consequences of negative or positive externalities, Korobkin proposes to use the malfunctions in people's decision making and steer them towards social welfare enhancing options that might not be rational from the perspective of their individual welfare (Korobkin, 2009). Externalities can thus also be corrected by nudging people in socially beneficial behaviour. This *welfarist paternalism* is different from asymmetric or libertarian paternalism as it does not necessarily aim to increase individual welfare but does intend to improve social welfare.

While behavioural literature makes a distinction between these different versions of soft paternalism, the approaches are actually quite similar. The non-intrusive nature, in line with individual sovereignty and free choice, are a focal point in all types of soft paternalism. Also, the types of problems and respective solutions that the approaches are concerned with are comparable. In this research, the term *soft paternalism* will be used to refer to the collection of various approaches described in this paragraph.

e. *Some examples of soft paternalism*

Soft paternalism focuses mainly on non-optimal decisions caused by either heuristic shortcuts or on the apparent use of the intuitive and automatic system. If the result of this decision making strategy is undesirable, policy makers could try to change this result with a nudge that induces a different decision outcome without imposing it. This nudge could for example provide certain information that might make people arrive at a more rational decision. It could also change a default so that the outcome of the same decision is altered, or utilise another bias that could influence the decision. Again, *nudging it* crucially entails nothing more than a hint towards a certain decision; if people prefer to do something else, they should remain free to do so. Any intervention that encourages, but not mandates,

[93] 'Nudges' is an acronym which stands for six subtle methods for improving choice, devising a good choice architecture: iNcentives, Understanding mappings, Defaults, Giving feedback, Expecting errors, and Structuring complex choices Thaler and Sunstein (2008: 81–100).

people to switch from their current decision to another one that is preferred by the party instigating the intervention can be seen as a nudge. To clarify the concept of soft paternalism, some examples of softly paternalistic interventions will be now discussed in more detail. Note that these interventions are not exclusively implemented by governments; entities such as businesses can also enact softly paternalistic business policies.

The best known example of soft paternalism is the Save More Tomorrow Savings Plan, or the Tomorrow Savings Plan as it was originally called. Policy makers were concerned about the low rate of saving in employees' pension plans. The status quo in this respect turned out beset at not saving: without any action on the part of the employee he or she would not save or be enrolled in any pension plan. To overcome present biases, hyperbolic discounting, or just plain and simple status quo bias, Thaler and Benartzi developed the Tomorrow Savings Plan, in which an employee agrees to save a larger amount for every increase in wage he receives (Thaler and Benartzi, 2007). The default of non-saving has been changed to a default of saving, taking advantage of status quo biases to cure present biases and hyperbolic discounting. This policy has been implemented in several firms in the United States, and has proven to greatly increase employee savings. Another example is provided by Sunstein, who suggest conferring entitlements to the employees instead of to employers, and to let those entitlements be waivable (Sunstein, 2001). This might be a solution for certain difficulties that employees have when entering into a labour contract. As Sunstein explains, most employees in the United States are under the impression they can only be fired 'for cause', but the majority of labour contracts actually specifies the ending of the contract 'at will'. He argues that many employees would apparently prefer to have a 'for cause' term in their contract, but are somehow unable to establish these term in the labour contract. This could be partly due to status quo bias, or bounded rationality, meaning that the employees fail to assess the contract accurately. Sunstein argues that the default should privilege employees, as they are less knowledgeable about their rights. If they want to contract around the privileges, and to get a higher salary instead, they are welcome to do so. Employees are thus nudged towards contracts that supposedly are the better choice, without this contract being imposed on them.

Sunstein and Thaler also suggest giving people feedback on their choices through the *RECAP* method: record, evaluate and compare alternative prices (Thaler and Sunstein, 2008: 93–4). This instrument entails disclosure by the seller to the consumer of the individual costs of the services rendered to him. An example of a feedback based intervention is provided by Bar-Gill. When a use pattern can be established concerning a certain good, especially when the relevant decision factors are complex, it is likely that the seller of the good has more information about the use pattern of the consumer than the consumer himself. This kind of situation might arise in fitness club or phone subscriptions, or credit card applications for instance. Biases such as overconfidence and self-serving bias are likely to influence decision making in these contracts. When the consumer has been using the good or service for some time, the seller has acquired information on the specific use pattern of the individual. Bar-Gill suggests requiring the seller to disclose use pattern information to the consumer. With this information, the consumer can be enabled to opt for a more welfare enhancing choice should the current option be sub-optimal (Bar-Gill, 2007). Such a scheme could even provide new business opportunities, such as websites that calculate the best price plan or credit card option for your established use pattern.[94] Even before the consumer enters into the contract, the seller could disclose information about the average use pattern, which would also be likely to benefit consumers as it provides them with an anchor that could well make their personal assessment more accurate.

Several other examples of providing better information and thus correcting bounded rationality are suggested by Thaler and Sunstein (2008), for instance concerning school choice. People often prefer the 'easy option' of the local community college than other schools that might provide better alternatives, arguably because they feel overwhelmed by the options available and have no access to relevant information. Providing a selection of information for instance on pass and fail rates, ranking, and positions adhered by alumni of the respective schools might enable people to make more informed choices. In order to help people to realise that they are driving too fast, Thaler and Sunstein suggest painting horizontal stripes on roads for instance near dangerous intersections. The nearer the dangerous point, the closer these stripes should be to each other, so that people get a sense of speed. Even when people realise the stripes are a nudging instrument, their automatic system will still send a signal of speed when the stripes on the road are noticed. It helps people slow down, which benefits everyone including the driver (Thaler and Sunstein, 2008: 38).

The best-known example of a Dutch nudge, also mentioned by Thaler and Sunstein (2008), is the Urinal Fly.[95] This nudge in the form of a sticker image of a fly placed in urinals, famously introduced at Amsterdam International Airport Schiphol, has reduced spillage of men's urine by 85%. By providing them something to aim at, men are nudged to spill less urine.[96] Other examples of soft paternalism are putting up signs in parks that remind people to bin their litter, signs that ask people to make an effort to conserve energy, or setting the printer standards in offices to double-sided print. Governments could enlarge the percentage of organ donations by either changing the default from opt-out to opt-in, so that people have to consciously opt out of donating their organs, or

94 Suggested by Richard Thaler, in keynote lecture at the Dutch Scientific Council for Government Policy (WRR) lecture 2009, November 26th 2009, The Hague. See also Thaler and Sunstein (2008: 142–4).

95 See www.urinalfly.com.

96 These last examples correct for externalities and thus improve social welfare without improving individual welfare per se.

by making any conscious choice mandatory.[97] Conscious choice could be made mandatory for instance by obliging people to fill in a donor form when they come to pick up or renew their drivers licence.[98]

3.3.3. INTERVENTION STRATEGIES BASED UPON SOFT PATERNALISM

When policy makers suspect certain intuitions are causing consumers to make decisions that are not in their best interest, policy makers can opt to intervene in the decision making process. Choice is influenced by context, the range of options provided, the presentation of these options and so on; choice architectures are always in place, nudging decisions into certain directions. Three intervention strategies will be distinguished, namely switching defaults, debiasing and rebiasing.

a. Choice architectures

As has been mentioned above and frequently pointed out by Sunstein and Thaler in their research, choices are usually already nudged in a certain direction, whether that is intentional or not. Choices are hardly ever, or never, made in a neutral environment. As Sunstein and Thaler posit, neutral choice is impossible. Choice always depends on context, the alternatives that are provided, the presentation of the various options, et cetera. This *choice architecture* is always present in some way; either through government or business action, wilfully or unintentionally, individuals are nudged towards certain decisions. Businesses are well aware of this fact; government institutions may be less aware, but their actions and interventions have consequences for choices nonetheless. Choice architectures will influence choice even if they are unintentional; it is the responsibility of the government to consider the effect of the choice architectures that are put in place by government action or policy. The choice architecture that is in place must be evaluated on whether it is appropriate, beneficial, or even optimal (Thaler and Sunstein, 2008: 3).

An example of such a choice architecture can be found in empirical literature. Cialdini describes how persuasive communications can also produce

[97] Suggested by Richard Thaler, in keynote lecture at the Dutch Scientific Council for Government Policy (WRR) lecture 2009, November 26th 2009, The Hague, based upon the current policies in the state of Illinois, USA; see nudges.wordpress.com/2009/09/27/richard-thaler-on-organ-donation.

[98] For more behavioural insights into individual decision making, advice to individuals on how to overcome biases and softly paternalistic interventions, see the books *Nudges* by Thaler and Sunstein (2008) and *Predictably Irrational*, by Ariely (2009), and the Nudges website: nudges.wordpress.com. See for an evaluation of both Ariely's and Thaler and Sunstein's books: Amir and Lobel (2008).

counterproductive effects in his study of theft of petrified wood (Cialdini, 2003). This study explored the effectiveness of different signs that aimed to discourage visitors of Arizona's Petrified Forest National Park from stealing pieces of petrified wood. The first sign read as follows: "Many past visitors have removed wood from the Park, changing the natural state of the Petrified Forest". The second sign read: "Please don't remove the petrified wood from the Park, in order to preserve the natural state of the Petrified Forest." This sign was accompanied by a picture of a lone visitor stealing a piece of wood, with a red circle-and-bar symbol over his hand. When the effectiveness of these signs was tested, the first sign was shown to be much less effective in deterring people from taking pieces of petrified wood. In fact, more people were taking petrified wood from the forest when the first sign was displayed than when no sign was displayed at all. The second sign was able to reduce petrified wood theft in comparison to the situation when no sign was displayed. As Cialdini explains, the first sign is interpreted by individuals as: "Many people employ this behaviour, so I would just be doing what a lot of other people are doing too." Cialdini refers to this type of statement as *descriptive norms*, involving perceptions of which behaviours are typically performed. The second sign on the other hand is an *injunctive norm*, involving perceptions of which behaviours are typically approved or disapproved. This type of statement, when negative, ostracises the few individuals who violate the norm. Instead of portraying thievery as a behaviour that is pervasive, the second message portrayed thieves as a tiny minority. People apparently do not like to follow a tiny ostracised minority in their behaviour. This example shows how communicative statements, even though aiming for the same result, can have very different consequences due to how they are interpreted by the target audience. Some statements can even have counterproductive effects, nudging people towards the undesirable behaviour instead of preventing it.

b. Switching defaults, debiasing or rebiasing

When a certain choice architecture is suspected to lead individuals make decisions that go against their own and/or social welfare, several instruments can be used to correct or account for biased decision making on behalf of the policy target group. Consumers can be nudged into rational decision making or beneficially biased decision making, or the default-decision might be altered. Policy suggestions based upon softly paternalistic approaches therefore often involve one of these three intervention strategies:

- Switching the default rule so that the outcome of the decision will change, whereas the decision making strategy of individuals is not altered;
- Encouraging people to switch their thinking-system from an intuitive to more rational one by providing a specific selection of information, or by correcting for other kinds of biases in order to *debias* the decision making strategy;

- Encouraging people to switch from one bias to another to arrive at more beneficial outcomes; this change in decision making strategy could be described as *rebiasing*.[99]

Switching defaults

The first type of intervention strategy that addresses sub-optimal decision making due to biases and heuristics is to switch the default rule. In this way the outcome of the decision is changed while the decision making strategy itself can remain intact. When people used to employ the intuitive system to make the decision, they can and probably will continue to do so after the regulatory intervention. The majority of cases addressed by soft paternalism involve problems arising from a combination of too much, complex or contradicting information and too little expertise. Other complicating factors are a lack of time to invest into the decision process or unwillingness to invest the necessary effort. Furthermore, severe worries about the potential outcome of the situation might cause consumers to block the decision from their mind. Individuals in these cases often opt for relying on the default, or refrain from making a decision at all. Default rules have been shown in several occasions to be 'sticky': even if a switch from the default rule would involve negligible transaction costs and substantial gains, people still stick to the default.

Policy suggestions described above that involve switching the default rule regularly involve switching from an opt-in to an opt-out default, for example in savings and pension plans, including the Save More Tomorrow plan. Another example of this policy intervention is a change from the default terms in contracts from 'at will' to 'for cause', as are business strategies making use of switching defaults by for instance changing the printer settings to double sided print.

Debiasing

In the second type of intervention strategy, individuals are nudged into more conscious and rational decisions instead of intuitive ones. A switch from the automatic system to the reflective system can be invoked by information designed to enable people to choose rationally instead of intuitively or in line with heuristics or the default position. Providing clearer, better and preferably less information

---

99 Jolls and Sunstein (2006) combine debiasing and rebiasing under one denominator, *debiasing through law*. In some of the policy suggestions offered policy would deliberately use the interaction between compensating biases. Through aiming to replace one intuitive type of thinking for another one consumer heuristics are used to consumers' advantage. This would fall under the regulatory strategy of rebiasing in the typology mentioned above. Korobkin (2006: 14–6) does distinguish between interventions that aim to push consumers into deliberation instead of relying upon intuition, or interventions that use heuristics to their advantage.

could allow individuals to switch to a decision strategy that implies weighing options more carefully than they would have done before.

Of the above mentioned examples, interventions correspond to debiasing are providing use patterns in credit card statements and fitness clubs, and providing information about schools to enable informed choice. Mandated choice, such as requiring people to choose whether they wish to donate their organs, can also be employed to debias individuals. Failing to make a choice could in this case be due to inertia and the dread factor, which cause individuals to postpone and refrain from choice as they do not want to confront the issue. Mandated choice addresses these biases by forcing individuals to make a choice. Self-interested interpretation can be tackled by specifically asking the individuals to consider which aspects of the issue might work against them; in the discussed example of plaintiffs and defendants, individuals who were asked if the judges might find reasons to not rule in their favour made more accurate assessments of their chances of winning the case (Babcock, Issacharoff and Loewenstein, 1997).[100]

Rebiasing

Policy makers can also use biases instead of eliminating them, or take advantage of another heuristic that could influence decision making. In the third intervention strategy, the countervailing effects that some biases might have are taken advantage of. To overcome the negative effects of one heuristic, another bias might be employed to compensate for these effects and thus nudge individuals towards welfare enhancing decisions. Certain biases might lead to better decisions than others; nudging consumers into employing these more beneficial biases might be more effective than aiming for a rational decision (Amir and Lobel, 2008: 2116).

An example of such a detrimental bias that could be counteracted by another more beneficial one is overconfidence in drivers. When safety belt regulation was introduced, the consequences were twofold: on the one hand, the mortality rates of people who were driving a car decreased, showing a positive impact of the newly instituted mandatory rule. On the other hand however, the mortality rate of cyclists and pedestrians went up (Peltzman, 1975). Apparently, people feel safer while driving buckled up and therefore decrease the amount of care they take on the road. The overconfidence bias could play a role here, especially since this effect is stronger when individuals feel they are in control of the risks, as is usually the case with driving. Furthermore, people fail to fully appreciate the damage they might cause other traffic participants. In response to this externality aspect usually liability rules are set up to incentivise internalising the external effects of careless behaviour. The above-mentioned example of painting stripes on the road could nudge people into driving more slowly when approaching a dangerous traffic point. To further encourage people to drive carefully, policy makers could

100 See above, section 3.2.2c.

use the availability bias to counteract the overoptimism effect (Schwartz and Wilde, 1983: 1437–8). When persons themselves or others in their close vicinity have recently been in an accident, they change their actions. Policy makers could stimulate the dissemination of information concerning the effects of being in a car accident, pointing not only to the damage done to pedestrians but also to other passengers and relatives left behind. This approach could furthermore be used to address cases in which individuals underinsure personal risks, or to counteract health damaging behaviour such as smoking.

Nudges to invoke a change in a social norm also have links with this intervention strategy. Following a social norm is likely to be an intuitive rather than a rational decision. Signs in a park asking the public to bin their litter remind people of the social norm concerning littering and thus encourages people to follow the social norm.[101]

c. *Which intervention strategy to use?*

When deciding which intervention strategy to employ, several aspects are worth bearing in mind. As with any policy intervention, these include of course the costs and benefits of government actions. When it comes to behavioural intervention strategies and the choice between debaising, rebiasing and switching defaults however, some issues are worth special consideration.

For a start, the level of *intrusiveness* of the intervention is very important. The intervention strategy of debiasing could be regarded as less intrusive as it encourages a more rational decision and thereby still allows consumers a range of options instead of nudging them towards a certain specific decision that is deemed by the intervener to be the most beneficial. However, debiasing often entails providing (better and less) information, thus enabling individuals to make an informed choice instead of merely following certain biases or accepting the status quo due to information overload. The crucial point here is of course the selection of this information. Inevitably, the issues that are highlighted by the nudging institution will become salient in the decision making process, causing other issues to be are neglected. The policy maker would necessarily decide for the consumer in this respect. One could however argue that this decision would still be a more informed and argument-based decision than the decision that would have been taken in the absence of any intervention. The intervention strategy of switching defaults has the explicit aim of the default setting the standard for the decision more often. This implies that governments choose a particular preferred end-result of the individual decision making process, which will not be any more informed and argument-based than the end-result without the government

---

101 Litter on the streets however reduces this effect, as people no longer believe that picking up litter is what everybody does. See Sunstein (19962021) and Cooter (1998) for discussions of the expressive function of laws, rules and notices.

intervention. The default switching intervention strategy is therefore quite intrusive, even when consumers can opt out with relative ease. The fact that this intervention itself relies on the default bias, expecting people not to deviate from the default option makes the intervention intrusive. This does not necessarily have detrimental consequences; it does however complicate the position of the policy maker and necessitates a large degree of discretion.[102] Another issue to keep in mind regarding discretion in setting defaults is that most often some choice of default will have to be made anyway. Printers need to have a default setting; donation policies will have a default option in case people do not state any preference; pension plans have to be designed as either opt-in or opt-out procedures. There has to be a default setting, and the way in which the default is set has consequences. The awareness that individuals will probably stick to the defaults justifies and urges to take considerable effort in making a well-balanced decision about the consequences of a particular formulation of the default even though it might be intrusive. The choice of the default rule thereby becomes very important; the default should be set in a way that optimises social welfare.

Another issue to consider is that the effectiveness of interventions strategies will be influenced by the specific circumstances of the case. Consumers can not always be nudged into rational decision making; they might already be overwhelmed by is the range of options. In that case the debiasing process could be complicated by the fact that a switch to rational decision making is unlikely to occur.[103] Changing the default might then be a better option. In cases like the social norms example described above, where governments would like individuals to show behaviour that is efficient from a social welfare point of view but not strictly speaking in the interest of the individual per se, decisions based on rational choice might not produce the desired effect. Rebiasing might then be most effective and efficient option from society's perspective.

Furthermore, the *predictability* of the outcome of an intervention is important to consider. Changing the default rule has the benefit of having a predictable outcome. Once in a certain choice architecture a preference for the status quo has been established, the end-results of decision making can be changed with relative easy. The only thing governments have to do is switch the default to a more socially beneficial option. Debiasing might not always have the effects it was set out for, but this procedural intervention strategy does allow for freedom of choice by not intrusively and directly stimulating the outcome of the targeted decision process. As has been pointed out by Amir and Lobel, not all biases are linked to intuition. Sometimes, people do think more consciously about their options, but

[102] See for a discussion of policy makers' discretion resulting from behaviourally informed policy making, chapter 4, section 4.3.3.d.

[103] An example of how a strategy of debiasing, trying to get consumers to decide rationally, making use of relevant information, might not always be effective, can be given with respect to trying to enhance consumer reading of standard terms. This example will be thoroughly discussed in chapters 5, 6 and 7.

they are still inhibited by certain biases. These biases, as Amir and Lobel argue, are much harder to correct than biases based on faulty intuition (Amir and Lobel, 2008: 2110–5).[104] The effect of rebiasing, using biases to overcome other ones, can also be quite unpredictable. This intervention strategy, which is arguably the most difficult one to implement, would require testing before it is implemented. Still, as has been argued above, there might be circumstances in which rebiasing is the most effective and efficient intervention strategy.

3.3.4. SUMMARY: BEHAVIOURAL INSIGHTS TO (CONSUMER) POLICY

Behavioural insights can have many implications for policy, especially consumer policy. Consumer policy aims to benefit consumer interests. Consumers can suffer from many biases and heuristics, which enable sellers to take advantage of their biased decision making. Behavioural insights that have been introduced in this research are: bounded rationality and information overload, risk perception biases, self-serving biases, status quo biases, time related biases, contexts and framing, anchoring and adjustment and bounded will-power. Governmental institutions and policy makers have recently taken an interest in behavioural insights and are devising ways of implementing these insights into policy. Behavioural insights can have several implications for consumer policy. Biased decision making might provide a justification for paternalistically protecting consumers from their own errors. This could even imply that consumer interests are served by limiting choice instead of allowing consumers all possible options. Even in competitive markets where according to traditional economic views market failures are absent, consumer interests might still be harmed. Behavioural insight has several implications for market instruments, especially the instrument of information disclosure. This policy instrument might be less effective than has been previously thought, as consumers are not able to take full advantage of the information provided. Information disclosure can therefore even have counterproductive effects, as sellers can no longer be found liable for uninformed decision making on the part of consumers, even though the disclosure has not served consumers any benefit.

Policy making that aims to enhance consumer choice has been criticised for being paternalistic and interfering with the free will of individuals. To counteract this criticism, a regulatory approach has been developed within behavioural literature that does not obstruct free will: soft paternalism. Some examples of soft paternalism have been discussed. Interventions in individual decision making

[104] Amir and Lobel (2008: 2110–5) refer to these different biases as 'type 1 biases', biases that are linked to intuition and reflexive thinking, and 'type 2 biases' that exist even when people contemplate their actions.

can follow several strategies. Consumers can for example be debiased, which means they are nudged into more rational decision making. Another strategy is to change the default option of the decision, which might be the most effective strategy especially when people have been shown to usually opt for the default and debiasing is not an option. In other cases, consumers can be nudged into using other biases to counteract the effects of the first one, which can be referred to as rebiasing. Also, some issues have been discussed that should be considered when deciding which intervention strategy to use. These include the intrusiveness of the intervention, the effectiveness of it and the ease with which the effects of the intervention can be predicted.

3.4. CONCLUSIONS

This chapter aimed at establishing whether or not behavioural insights can give implications for consumer policy that go beyond the rationales for intervention provided by classic economic theory that were discussed in the previous chapter. In behavioural literature, several biases and heuristics have been identified that might affect consumer decision making. These insights do not correspond to standard economic theory and the rational choice model of (consumer) behaviour. Following these new insights, biases and heuristics evidently influencing consumer behaviour might provide additional rationales for intervention in consumer protection. Conventional economics does not account for biases and heuristics which can be abused by sellers or otherwise detrimental to individual and social welfare. However, whether behavioural insights can predict consumer behaviour more accurately than rational choice depends on the specifics of the case. There is some evidence for dual processes in cognitive decision making, which would imply the use of two systems of thinking; one more rational and analytical, the other more affective and intuitive. Specific contexts should be assessed to see which decision making process will be employed by consumers under which circumstances.

Behavioural insights can have several implications for consumer policy such the requirement to protect consumers from their own errors, possibly even by limiting their options. Consumer interests might be harmed even in markets where no traditional market failures are present and the market is sufficiently competitive. The effectiveness of information disclosure in aiding consumers in their decision making processes is challenged by behavioural insights. Soft paternalism has been developed as a regulatory approach that arguably does not impose specific decisions on consumers. Interventions in individual decision making can aim to debias consumers; nudging them into more rational decision making. Also, the default position of the decision can be changed to alter the outcome of the decision without changing the decision making process itself. Alternatively, heuristics can be employed to enhance the end-result of the decision. Which intervention strategy is preferable should be carefully assessed, and depends on factors such as the intrusiveness and effectiveness of the intervention combined with the ease with which the effects of the intervention can be predicted.

In behavioural literature, it is commonly accepted that predictions and policy can be improved by the implementation of behavioural insights in economic theory and policy. However, the extent to which behavioural insight can be used to inform consumer policy and interventions in a social welfare enhancing way is debated. The methodological concerns connected to behavioural research and the normative issues that might arise when behavioural insights are implemented in policy will be discussed in the next chapter. Also, some guidelines will be developed to address these cautions and considerations.

CHAPTER 4

CAUTIONS AND CONSIDERATIONS FOR BEHAVIOURALLY INFORMED CONSUMER POLICY

4.1. INTRODUCTION

The goal of behavioural economics, as has been discussed in the previous chapter, is to improve the predictions of economic theory, whether or not this includes bringing about a consistent new theoretical paradigm. Behavioural law and economics aims to extend this improvement of predictions to policy making and economic assessment of laws and policies. However, the question of whether and how to implement behavioural insight into public policy has been left unanswered until this point in the dissertation. This chapter will therefore examine to what extent behavioural insights should influence theory and policy recommendations. This dissertation will conclude that behavioural insights can be used to inform theory and policy recommendations aimed at enhancing social welfare, provided that certain cautions and considerations are taken into account.

There are two types of criticism concerning behavioural insights' influence on consumer policy: methodological versus more policy related concerns. The methodological debate focuses on questions such as whether behavioural insight actually has anything substantial to add to rational explanations and whether psychological findings in economic theory can be generalised. The contextual dependency of behavioural insight and the extent to which behavioural insight can serve as a basis for tractable hypotheses will be discussed. Other topics in this section include conflicting biases, the advantages of a simple theory and the empirical accuracy and reality of theoretical assumptions.

The policy debate focuses on the specific concerns that might arise once behavioural insights are used in policy making. Normative cautions and considerations related to the possibility of biases being both beneficial and detrimental to consumer welfare are discussed, as well as the possibility and likelihood of sellers taking advantage of consumer biased decision making. This section will analyse the chances of policy makers actually improving consumers' biased decision making and the costs and potential abuse of behaviourally informed consumer policy, including adverse distributional effects.

Subsequently the discussion will turn to explaining how the described cautions and considerations can be addressed through enhanced policy design and decision making procedures. A scientifically sound basis, an extensive market-based assessment of consumer behaviour, interventions that are efficient and context-specific and heuristics savvy combined with transparent and rigorous decision making procedures for policy should enable behaviourally informed interventions in consumer policy to be devised in a welfare-enhancing way. This chapter will conclude that behavioural insight can inform welfare-enhancing consumer policy provided that the cautions, considerations and guidelines that have been discussed in this chapter are taken into account.

4.2. METHODOLOGICAL CONCERNS TO BEHAVIOURAL ECONOMICS

Implementing behavioural research insight in theory or policy raises several methodological concerns as well as certain issues that are more directly related to policy. This sections aims to provide an overview of the methodological debate. It will also determine the validity of the methodological critique, and then develop some cautions and considerations that address this criticism. The next part of this chapter reviews the 'normative' discussion and discusses policy issues that arise when behavioural insights are implemented in policy discussions and design.

The methodological issues of behavioural economics have been widely debated. Any research that embarks onto new paths and aims to become part of the scientific paradigm will have to pass the methodological test (Rabin, 2002: 659). The methodological debate in light of the discussion on behavioural insights and their influence on economic theory and policy has focused on several issues. This dissertation will discuss most important ones, including:[105] the *innovativeness* of behavioural insights, *generalisability* and *contextual dependency*, *tractability* of behavioural insights and conflicting biases, *parsimony*, *empirical accuracy*, and the extent to which research based upon behavioural insights is able to make policy prescriptions.

After discussing the normative cautions and considerations connected to behaviourally informed consumer policy in the next section, the fourth section of this chapter will devise guidelines for policy to address these concerns and to steer consumer policy interventions into a welfare enhancing direction.

---

[105] For a discussion of these issues, see for instance: Arlen (1998: 1768–70), Issacharoff (1998: 1734), Posner (1998a), Rachlinski (2000), Rabin (2002) and Wilkinson (2008: 8–9).

4.2.1. METHODOLOGICAL CONCERNS

The behavioural research project has evoked considerable critique regarding its methodology, mostly from traditional economists. An overview of that debate will follow here.

a. Innovativeness of behavioural insights

A first question point of critique raised against behavioural insight is whether it adds anything new to the debate. This critique claims that both the theory and policy observations that are discussed in behavioural literature can well be covered within the rational choice paradigm. If the rational choice paradigm would also explain the observed behaviour, there would be no need for behavioural theories in order to explain these observations.

Explaining and predicting behavioural anomalies

When in behavioural literature a certain behavioural anomaly is pointed out, conventional economic scholars typically respond by finding a rational explanation for the observed behaviour (Jolls, Sunstein and Thaler, 1998b: 1595). For example, Posner argues that issues such as hyperbolic discounting can be explained within the rational paradigm by the notion of 'multiple selves'; the present self having different preferences than the future one. Also, there is a sound rational explanation for the question why people would initially like to eat lobster, but lose their appetite once they have to choose a live one from an aquarium. From a conventional economic viewpoint, one could argue that these are two different goods; having different preferences for two different goods is not surprising. Conventional economic scholars thus argue that the rational choice paradigm is too easily dismissed (Posner, 1998a: 1553–6). Epstein finds several traditional economic explanations that account for anomalous behaviour in a number of cases that are contended by behavioural economics, such as teaser rates, hyperbolic discounting and health clubs (Epstein, 2008: 821–31). Wright, discussing observations regarding credit card debts, shelf space purchases in retail stores and standard terms, argues there are sound standard explanations for the proposed behavioural anomalies and that the behavioural insights are therefore irrelevant (Wright, 2007). Another argument put forward by traditional economists is that the supposedly influential biases and heuristics have in fact only a minimal effect on behaviour. A better understanding of these biases and heuristics will therefore not (greatly) improve predictions of behaviour.

As has been stated in the previous chapter, there are however many behavioural observations that are less easily reconciled with the rational economic framework.[106] Behavioural scholars maintain that decision theory and predicting behaviour can be improved by behavioural insight. Differences in risk perception, inertia that cannot be contributed to transactions costs and the framing of options that should not have any effect on decisions are examples of situations that do not correspond to RCT. Understanding the influence of present biases informs the understanding of behaviour concerning savings, credit cards, advertising, procrastination, costly self-commitment strategies to fight procrastination and so forth (Rabin, 2002: 671–2). These insights are *robust*, which refers to the fact that they have resulted from several similar experiments. Also behavioural insights can be shown to be significant enough to have a distinctive effect on behaviour, and should be used to improve predictions (Fudenberg, 2006: 708).

Behavioural literature is quite critical of these attempts to provide a rational explanation to behavioural observations, as this is deemed to stretch the applicability of rational choice as a paradigm beyond acceptable limits.[107] Furthermore, behavioural literature argues that even when thinner versions of rational choice can retrospectively *explain* certain behavioural effects as rational behaviour, rational choice would have had a harder time *predicting* those effects. A thin version of rational choice for instance assumes that when a person acts, this act must be in accordance with his preferences and therefore his self-interest, otherwise this person would not engage in the action. Choice is thus necessarily welfare enhancing and rational.[108] Thin versions of RCT can explain most to all phenomena pointed out by behavioural theory, but they lack predictive powers as they are non-falsifiable.

Behavioural notions try to provide insights into why certain acts are engaged in or omitted. These insights can help to explain and predict behaviour, and would not have been developed when the paradigm of rational choice was exclusively used in economic theory (Rachlinski, 2000: 765). Behavioural law and economics asks different questions about law and policy than law and economics scholars or lawyers do. It exposes influences on choice and judgement that would have never come up in either law and economics scholarship or in traditional legal analysis. These insights, such as regret aversion or the endowment effect, can be very relevant to law and policy. Behavioural insights have furthered the discussions and ability of scholars to explain observed behaviour, and the ability to predict behaviour in certain cases.

---

[106] See above, chapter 3, section 3.2.3.

[107] For critical views, see for instance Rabin (2002: 683) who argues that scholars go out of their way to find an alternative 'standard' explanation for behavioural phenomena whenever they can find one, even if this would make the prediction counterintuitive and complicating. Kreps (1998: 170) argues that some of the economic models developed to provide a rational explanation for behavioural observations are "too bizarre to take seriously, … too complex to be of any analytical use whatsoever, or do not apply to all cases".

[108] For thinner and thicker versions of RCT, see above, chapter 2, section 2.2.1b and Korobkin and Ulen (2000: 1060–7).

Alternative theories explaining one observation

In economics, some scholars still claim that rational choice as a theory should be adhered to as long as it is not absolutely falsified. According to this view, the standard explanations in line with rational choice should be favoured as long as the standard explanations hold. Behavioural insight in general has not been proven to be more valid than rational choice at explaining or predicting behaviour, and thus conventional economic theory will be preferred by these scholars as the theory to predict human behaviour.[109] In response, Jolls et al. claim that the existence of two competing explanations for one theory does not automatically imply that RCT should triumph (Jolls et al., 1998b: 1595). Both sets of explanations and predictions should be carefully assessed. The question should not be which paradigm is more valid in general, but which set of insights is more valid in specific situations. After all, neither the predictions based upon rational choice nor the ones based upon behavioural insights are shown to hold under all circumstances.[110] Economists who hold on to rationality and who deny that behavioural insights have any value, are claimed by the defenders of behavioural theory to suffer from "*theory induced blindness*".[111] These scholars are unwilling to review their theoretical paradigm, even though compelling insights that are contrary to their beliefs have been brought to their attention. Behavioural scholars argue that behavioural insight does not need to be proven correct in all circumstances in order to be a valid alternative to RCT in some situations.

Still, theory induced blindness can also work in the opposite direction: Rabin argues that the growing acceptance of behavioural economics has made some economists overly receptive to alternative assumptions. The rational choice paradigm has always been criticised as being counterintuitive and overly simplifying. Even though behavioural economics offers explanations for behaviour that are more intuitive, they are not necessarily or automatically more accurate. In some situations, rational choice models are shown to provide more accurate predictions. Scholars of either current of literature should be aware of their possible blindness. The existence of a 'rational' explanation should not necessarily tip the scales in favour of one literature current, but neither should the existence of a 'psychological' explanation (Rabin, 2002: 674).

---

109 See for this claim for example: Klick (2005: 555–9)

110 See above, chapter 3, section 3.2.3.

111 The term *theory induced blindness* was mentioned by Prof. Daniel Kahneman during his inaugural lecture when receiving an honorary doctorate from the Erasmus University Rotterdam, November 6th, 2009; see also in interview with Haaretz, by Guy Rolnik, published online April 19th, 2009. Available at: www.haaretz.com/hasen/spages/1077151. Similarly, Korobkin (2005) argues against the "*standard theory*" bias that exists among economic scholars. He furthermore claims that because decisive evidence is still lacking and research efforts are necessarily limited by time and money, the more plausible explanations and predictions should be the ones that are investigated; not just any possible theory.

b. *Overarching paradigm: generalisability and contextual dependency*

A common concern that is raised against on the influence of behavioural insight on theory or policy recommendations is that behavioural law and economics lacks an *overarching paradigm*. It offers explanations for observations, but encounters some difficulty in predicting the outcome of the biases under even slightly altered circumstances. The *contextual dependency* of these insights is high; they cannot easily be generalised. The strength of the bias is hard to estimate. In some instances, biases run in opposite directions, making the outcome uncertain. Behavioural insights are therefore said to fail to generate testable hypotheses. The *generality* or *generalisability* of behavioural insights, which refers to the extent to which the insights can be applied to a wide set of phenomena, is called into question (Wilkinson, 2008: 8–9). Experiments that are argued to provide evidence of behavioural anomalies are conducted in laboratory settings, mainly using students. Critics of behavioural theory therefore doubt the *external validity*, which can be described as the extent to which observations and causal inferences from studies be generalised to other subjects and conditions. Therefore, in the view of this critique, again the standard explanations should be favoured and rational choice models should continue to be adhered to until a behavioural paradigm is developed, upon which more theories and predictions can be built.

Creating a behavioural overarching paradigm

As has been described in the previous chapter, there is some debate about the question whether the aim of behavioural research should be to develop an overarching paradigm. It is doubtful whether a comprehensive paradigm based upon social psychology can ever be constructed in a way that can compete with RCT. This issue is tied to the nature of the science of psychology, as opposed to economics (Brennan, 2008: 32). Economists like to explain the world using a few axioms. Economic theory is general and comprehensive. Traditionally, it uses deduction to come to theoretical premises and predictions. Economists try to find general theorems, and from those theorems deduct predictions. Psychology on the other hand is a more inductive science and (hesitantly) uses observations to come to generalisations. Empirical findings are very specific and context related, and can therefore not easily be generalised into one social theory that explains it all. Psychologists often refrain from generalising their results, fearing over-generalisation. Findings are done within their specific contexts, and results will be accumulated only when this is methodologically possible. As Rabin explains, psychology probes the details of human nature, and is not as devoted to generality as conventional economics (Rabin, 2002: 672). Psychological insights are therefore less suited to provide a theoretical basis for one comprehensive paradigm such as rational choice, or to encompass the same generalisability. Therefore, a generalised theory of decision making which accounts for behavioural insights might never be developed. Behavioural economics does strive for generality, which could be accomplished through updating economic theory with behaviour insights (Camerer and Loewenstein, 2004: 7). The generalisability of behavioural notions will however remain a limitation of the behavioural research project.

Contextual dependency

Behavioural notions are often context specific, and apply to the situation in which they were observed; as they are (psychological) observations, they do not stem from one overarching theory (Korobkin, 2006: 11). Contextual dependency complicates the formulation of general predictions.[112] A bias found in one context is not automatically relevant to another context. Behavioural insights do not allow for an overly extensive generalisation of observations. Another concern points to the standard methods of behavioural research. Behavioural research is usually based upon laboratory and experimental research, and often uses students at universities as subjects. The findings in these studies might not be so easily generalised to situations involving non-student individuals. Furthermore, the laboratory settings have little in common with real life.[113] Empirical studies that review choices that people have made in their daily life are more able to make valid generalisations than experimental or laboratory studies.[114]

Scott argues that it is important to realise the limitations of behavioural science, as social data is often too easily generalised. Data should be more cautiously interpreted, especially when it is used for policy. This caution is even more important when social data is interpreted by people who are not accustomed to interpreting statistics, such as most legal researchers and policy makers (Scott, 2000: 1639, 43).[115] The difficulty of understanding the significance of statistical studies is a further complication to a cautious interpretation of the social data used in behavioural research. Statistical research is often misinterpreted, even by expert researchers themselves (Hoekstra, 2009). Any statistical study should be interpreted with caution; not all studies are sound; biases found might not apply

112 Methodological concerns about the contextual dependency of behavioural insights are mentioned by many scholars. See for instance: Arlen (1998: 1768–70), Issacharoff (1998: 1734), Rachlinski (2000: 743–4), Scott (2000: 1639) and Kelman (2003: 1363–4).

113 See Korobkin (1998: 661) and Levitt and List (2007) for discussions on generalising problems in laboratory and experimental research. Della Vigna (2009) provides an overview of empirical literature on psychology and economics that explicitly does not rely on laboratory tests.

114 Bernheim and Whinston (2008: 452–3) provide several considerations for the interpretation of social data for policy or theory, such as robustness, whether it is a sound study, whether the findings are based on laboratory or real world observations, and which other explanations for the observation can be explored.

115 Scott (2000: 1639, 43–5) argues that especially legal analysts are prone to making unjustified generalisations from social data. Legal scholarship, he claims, uses a generalising methodology. If A is sufficiently similar to B, than A and B should be regulated in the same way. A is then either sufficiently similar or it is not. The behavioural insights are more nuanced than the legal 'black or white' view.

to all circumstances; a single study showing some behavioural effect cannot be a valid ground for far-reaching policy decisions.

However, behavioural insight can improve the accuracy of predictions within certain contexts. Observations made in behavioural research that are not easily generalisable can still be relevant. Sorting out which biases affect behaviour in which contexts is important when trying to implement behavioural insights in theory and policy. Psychology has a tradition of researching how contexts influence behaviour. Context thus affects behavioural research in two ways: on one hand, it poses a concern as behavioural findings are not easily generalised and depend on context. On the other hand, behaviour and decisions can be shown to be influenced by contexts, not only in the laboratory, but also in real life. Behaviour is shown to be context-dependent, just as behavioural insights. Context as an aspect of decision making should not be overly generalised, but included as a variable or otherwise accounted for in behaviour research.

c. *Tractability and conflicting biases*

A related concern points to the *tractability* of behavioural notions, which refers to the ease with which the theoretical models can be applied to different situations in terms of making testable predictions (Wilkinson, 2008: 8–9). Explaining in retrospect why an individual apparently came to a certain decision is not the same as predicting beforehand how people will decide in certain situations. When biases can go either way, or when the impacts and contexts of biases are unknown, it will be difficult for behavioural theory provide valid predictions (Posner, 1998a: 1559). Tractability was especially considered to be an issue when the behavioural research programme came into existence. Behavioural research however is progressing and creating more and more testable hypotheses. The tractability of the behavioural research programme is considered less of an issue, now that the modelling of behavioural insights has advanced. Numerous scholars have included insights from behavioural sciences into their models.[116] Behavioural insights are being used to create testable hypotheses, which are then tested empirically (Della Vigna, 2009). In some situations however, conflicting behavioural biases might be argued to have an effect on behaviour, which is a concern for tractability (Hillman, 2000: 731–3). In these situations, it might be harder to pinpoint the causes of the observed behaviour. As Rachlinski argues, conflicting biases still pose a real issue in behavioural theory; they also however reflect the reality of human judgement. For example, people do both underestimate and overreact to small probabilities of unfortunate events.[117] Therefore, more behavioural research is needed; research

[116] See for instance Munier et al. (1999), Rubinstein (1998) and Arlen and Talley (2008) on bounded rationality modelling in general; see for examples of modelling behavioural insights, Bernheim and Rangel (2005), Abdellaoui, Barrios and Wakker (2007) and Wakker, Timmermans and Machielse (2007).

[117] See above, chapter 3, section 3.2.2b.

takes into account the contexts in which decisions are taken. Reconciliation of conflicting biases can require extensive empirical research (Rachlinski, 2000: 746). To improve the predictions of human decision making, an indication should be made of which biases will have a stronger effect than other ones and of how different circumstances may influence the dominance of one bias over the other.

d. Parsimony

Precise and testable hypotheses cannot possibly take all aspects of human nature into account. A lean and simple theory that uses fewer assumptions, thereby allowing for a relatively easy formulation of hypotheses is a valuable tool for predicting behaviour. *Parsimony* is thus better than complicated and complex theories. Rational choice can be argued to be more parsimonious than theories based upon behavioural insights; behavioural insights complicate the story.

In conventional economic theory, how individuals exactly construe their choices is considered to be irrelevant. The decision making process can be seen as a "black box". What is inside is not what economics is concerned with; economics is concerned with the outcome of the black box. As long as the predictions by rational choice models hold, the inside of the black box is irrelevant for theory and would only complicate the analysis.[118] In order to create precise and testable hypotheses, some elements of human nature are to be ignored. How individuals actually construe their decisions is not of interest, the choice that they arrive at in the end is what matters to economists (Rabin, 2002: 672).

Behavioural literature criticises the standard economic model for being overly parsimonious, which actually results in low empirical accuracy (Wilkinson, 2008: 9). Korobkin argues that the assertion regarding rational choice being leaner, simpler and less complicated, is not always true (Korobkin, 2005: 782, 89–90). Rational choice has already incorporated several assumptions that have complicated the analysis greatly, such as the transaction costs, availability of information (or lack thereof), or whether bargaining is costless or of a high cost.[119] In some situations, Korobkin claims, a theoretical approach based upon behavioural insights might therefore be more parsimonious. An example of how assumptions are simplified in order to allow conventional economics to provide predictions based on a simple and lean theory is the *doctrine of revealed preferences*. The doctrine of revealed preferences enables economists to assume that choices people make will benefit their well-being, instead of having to assess whether choices actually improve welfare (Bernheim and Rangel, 2005). One of the main insights from behavioural literature is that people in some situations

118 See above, chapter 3, section 3.2.1.

119 Rabin (2002: 673) questions the parsimony of economic theory, positing that looking at one copy from Econometrica would suggest economists to be very able to deal with complicated theories; behavioural insights would add to the realism of theory, while not complicating economic theory much further.

make choices that are inconsistent with their own welfare. Behavioural insights, especially those related to the issues of saving and addictions, have claimed that the choices that people make should not automatically be trusted to reveal their true preferences. Preferences are shown to depend on contexts and defaults; they can therefore be endogenous. Preferences also differ over time, an observation known as time-inconsistent preferences. To illustrate this point: even if people would like to lose weight in the long run, they prefer to eat chocolate now. The fact that the choices that people make cannot automatically be assumed to correspond to their preferences, and therefore to increase their welfare, is an important argument against the revealed preferences doctrine.

Choices do not always reveal true preferences; that realisation however indeed complicates the analysis. When choices can no longer be relied upon to reveal preferences, scholars and policy makers will have to develop some other way of distinguishing what it is people really want, and what therefore should be maximised through decisions and policies. Assessing the true preferences of individuals is very difficult. As Hill states: "Often, we just do not have a clue" (Hill, 2007: 448).[120] Theories based upon behavioural insights are likely to result in a more complicated analysis than the rational choice paradigm would have provided. Rejecting the doctrine of revealed preferences for instance results in questions that are very hard to answer. However, parsimony could be traded off with empirical accuracy, as more facets of human decision making can then be taken into account (Wilkinson, 2008: 8–9).

e. *Empirical accuracy and the reality of assumptions*

The accuracy of predictions is what the behavioural research project aims to enhance (Rabin, 2002: 674).[121] Behavioural scholars assert that increasing the reality of the assumptions of theoretical models will improve the resulting predictions. The standard assumptions of economic analysis, which for example claim individuals to have exogenous and self-regarding preferences, a capacity for dealing with tremendous amounts of information, rational expectations and instantly and correctly updating beliefs about the occurrence of a certain event, are argued to be rather unrealistic.[122] According to behavioural literature, the predictions of economic theory stand to be improved by the use of more realistic assumptions. In economic theory it is well established that RCT often

[120] See Loewenstein and Haisley (2008: 216–23) for a discussion on which welfare criterion to use when revealed preferences can no longer be depended upon. See also Jolls, Sunstein and Thaler (1998b: 1604) stressing that they do not mean to imply government should find out what people's true preferences are.

[121] See above, chapter 3, section 3.2.1.

[122] These standard assumptions have been developed mostly by Stigler and Becker, see most notably: Stigler and Becker (1977). Critique to the unreality of standard economic assumptions has been given by many scholars throughout the years, especially when economic theory should serve as a basis for public policy. See for instance Schwartz and Wilde (1982).

cannot provide a fully accurate description of human decision making. RCT is not intended to be an accurate description of human decision making; it is constructed to be an aid in predicting behaviour. As this instrument is lean and simple, many economists prefer to adhere to standard economic assumptions in economic analysis instead of accounting for behavioural insights. As has been put forward famously by Friedman, economic theories are evaluated on the accuracy of predictions, not on the reality of assumptions (Friedman, 1953). The simplicity and clarity of the analysis is aided by making these assumptions, even if they are inaccurate descriptions of the human decision making process. A theory can be contradicted only when its predictions are proven to be flawed, or when another theory proves to be more accurate in its predictions. RCT is by many economists considered the best way of predicting behaviour; best being a combination of generality, parsimony and accuracy.

Concerning rational choice and behavioural economics, there is thus a struggle and a trade-off between different features of theory: for a theory to be effective in its application, it has to be simple enough to generate predictions, yet also subtle enough to take the difficulties faced in real world situations into account (Issacharoff, 1998: 1733). Economics has the benefit of being a relatively simple theory, but it (arguably) lacks in predictive power. That very problem is addressed by behavioural insights, as it can be shown to provide more accurate predictions in some situations (Jolls et al., 1998a: 1487–8). Policy analysis can benefit from the methodological rigor of economics, while incorporating a more realistic view of the errors people make by using behavioural insights (O'Donoghue and Rabin, 2003: 191). The use of behavioural insights to improve predictions could however render the model and research method more costly, less parsimonious and less general. The question is whether the extra cost is justified by the benefit of an improvement in the accuracy of predictions. A point to take into account in addition to enhanced predictive power is that as behaviour research progresses, behavioural research will be applied to economic theory and policy more and more. Due to experience, learning effects, and being able to apply insights from other studies to similar but different fields, it will become easier and less costly for behavioural scholars to apply their insights to economics and policy.

When the aim is to develop insights for laws and policies, other considerations come into play. Choosing an instrument or paradigm to use in analysing the consequences of law and policies is a cost-benefit analysis in itself. Increasing the complexity of the analytical framework will increase its analytical costs; a simpler theory that is slightly less accurate could then be preferred over a costly extensive method that delivers more accurate results. What the behavioural approach gives up in parsimony and generality, relative to RCT, could be traded off with enhanced accuracy in the development of context-specific legal policy (Korobkin and Ulen, 2000: 1075). Again, as behavioural law and economics becomes more developed as a research field, behavioural policy research will become easier and less costly. A flawed policy prediction can also have costly consequences;

extending the research paradigm to include behavioural insights might therefore very well be justified.

f. Normative implications

A last comment related to the methodology of behavioural economics is that it has been criticised for not taking a normative stance. As long as behavioural economics merely criticises RCT and does not come up with a positive theory that can serve as a foundation, the research programme is doomed (Posner, 1998a: 1559; 1998c: 565). Behavioural scholars agree that behavioural economics should do more than just provide critique to law and economics and the rational choice paradigm. Behavioural insights must be capable of being operationalised for specific legal regulations (Issacharoff, 1998: 1734). As the research programme has progressed, the normative implications of behavioural biases have become clearer. Behavioural insights frequently support a normative position, a position however that should incorporate the context of the legal issue (Rachlinski, 2000: 741–2). Behavioural economics has evolved beyond a research program that merely points out problems with current economic assumptions and has moved on to systematically exploring behavioural alternatives to policy solutions provided by economics (Rabin, 2002: 658).

As has been discussed in the previous chapter, several consequences for policy result from behavioural insight (Ramsay, 2007: 77–8).[123] Government interventions based upon consumer biases might be justifiably paternalistic (limiting consumer sovereignty), even when they restrict choice options; they should reassess information disclosure, and consider competitive markets as well. A strict distinction between vulnerable and rational consumers is deemed less relevant by behavioural theory as consumers might all be vulnerable, or vulnerable in one context while rational in the other. A main source for normative stances and policy prescriptions based upon behavioural insights is the work of Sunstein and Thaler, most notably their book *Nudge* (Thaler and Sunstein, 2008). Sunstein and Thaler provide recommendations for policy interventions according to soft paternalism, which leaves the free will of the individual intact. These recommendations are not general prescriptions for government interventions in the market as a whole, but, corresponding to behavioural insights, are focused on specific circumstances.[124] Besides the methodological concerns reviewed above, several normative issues have been raised concerning the consequences

---

[123] See above, chapter 3, section 3.3.2b.

[124] See above, chapter 3, section 3.3.1. To illustrate, an analysis will follow in the next chapter regarding the desirable policy interventions in standardised terms in consumer contracts. This assessment will consider conventional economic theory as well as information economics, behavioural insights regarding this issue, and results from relevant empirical research, concluding that normative predictions can result from behavioural insights in that specific policy issue.

and effects of implementing behavioural insights into laws, policies and policy recommendations. The cautions and considerations for behaviourally informed policy that can be derived from this critique are the topic of the next section.

4.2.2. CONCLUSIONS

In the methodological debate, concerns are raised in relation with the incorporation of behavioural insights into economic theory and policy. A summary of this debate will be given below, followed by a conclusion.

a. Summary: the methodological debate

The first frequent critique of behavioural insights is that they do not add anything new to the debate. RCT is argued to be able to explain nearly all of the anomalies pointed out be behavioural theory. In response to this critique, behavioural literature contends that even when RCT can be stretched to explain behavioural insights, it would not have been able to predict them. Behavioural research has developed new and important notions that are incompatible with rational choice, or that would not have come up in the mere (or combined) contexts of rational choice and legal scholarship. Behavioural research has therefore expanded scholarly knowledge about behaviour by being able to generate more accurate predictions in certain specific cases. As rational choice is more accurate in other cases, neither set of insights should be regarded as triumphant or disproving the other. The predictions should be tested in specific situations to determine the value of the both currents of insight.

Behavioural (law and) economics today lacks an overarching paradigm to compete with rational choice as a theoretic base for predictions on the outcome of human decision making. Economics and psychology are very diverse sciences. Where economics is traditionally more deductive, general and comprehensive, psychology focuses on observations within specific contexts and makes inductions from these observations. Psychology is therefore hesitant to overly generalise these results. An overarching paradigm like (micro-)economic theory, which relies upon a general decision making model provided by RCT, might never be developed within the behavioural research project. This however does not automatically imply that behavioural insights cannot be used in economic theory or policy making. Economic predictions could be updated with behavioural insights, thereby increasing accuracy in specific contexts.

Psychological research, as well as behavioural economic research, relies heavily on laboratory and experimental research. The extent to which these data can be accurately generalised to fit real life situations can be limited. Any statistical study should therefore be interpreted cautiously, and consideration should be given to the possibility of overgeneralisation of behavioural data. Behaviour can be shown to be dependent upon contexts. The tractability of the behavioural research programme is less of an issue because behavioural (law and) economics has progressed and is now providing testable hypotheses, and also testing them. Conflicting biases do reduce the tractability of behaviour research; the compound effect of conflicting biases should be sorted out with extensive empirical research. Economics has the benefit of being a parsimonious theory: lean and simple, with few assumptions. Behavioural insights complicate the story. Looking into the black box of decision making makes the assessment more murky; it could however also improve its accuracy. Parsimony could then in those cases be traded off for empirical accuracy.

The most criticised aspect of RCT is the perceived unreality of its assumptions. In defence of rational choice it is argued that the reality of assumptions is irrelevant, as only the accuracy of predictions matters. Behavioural scholars are not the first ones to argue that increased reality in the assumptions would increase the accuracy of predictions, but they are the first to actually provide corroborating experimental and empirical proof to substantiate their criticism. However, the implementation of behavioural insights in economic theory would be likely to make the theory less general and parsimonious and the assessment more complex and costly. Whether these disadvantages are outweighed by the benefits of increased accuracy is a disputed question that can only be clarified by doing context-specific research. The normative implications that stem from behavioural research have also become clearer over the years. In behavioural literature, ample evidence can be found of behavioural insights providing a normative stance. Strong indications can be found to support the view that behavioural insights could be used, and are being used, for generating testable hypotheses and policy recommendations.

b. Conclusions: methodological cautions and considerations for behavioural public policy

In methodological discussions, several concerns have been raised with regard to the implementation of behavioural insight in economic theory and policy. Some of these issues have already been (partly) resolved by the developing behavioural research project, other concerns are still valid. Therefore, certain considerations should be taken into account when implementing behavioural insights into theory and policy:

- Social data should be interpreted cautiously. There is an evident danger of over-generalising results from behavioural studies. A bias found in one study conducted in a laboratory setting involving students should not automatically be implied to give rise to concerns in real-life situations. Empirical studies should be undertaken as results from this kind of study are more easily generalised.

- As behavioural insight and individual decision making are shown to be dependent upon context, context should be accounted for in behavioural studies. Even though psychological insights are less suited as a basis for one general paradigm, through behavioural research the accuracy of predictions can be enhanced in specific contexts. Behavioural theory thus calls for context-specific research, theory and policy
- Conflicting biases can decrease the tractability of behavioural research. In cases where conflicting biases can be argued to affect decision making, empirical research (as opposed to experimental studies) should be used to clarify matters.
- Accounting for behavioural insight could increase the complexity and analytical cost of the assessment and render the results more context-dependent. This loss in generality and parsimony could however be traded off against increased accuracy in the cases where behavioural insights are shown to enhance predictions. As behavioural economics progresses, the analytical costs of behavioural research will also decrease.

Even though behavioural insights are by now well accounted for in behavioural economic literature, their impact on public policy is remains largely underdeveloped. The relevance of a specific finding for policy is not always immediately clear. Several behavioural considerations have however been brought up that should be taken into account in policy and policy proscriptions. These considerations apply to issues such as costs and (arguably) adverse effects of behaviourally informed policy, the ability of policy makers to decide what is in the best interest of individuals, whether biases are harming consumers or are actually beneficial, whether consumers learn from their mistakes, whether sellers are actually able to abuse consumer biases (a common claim of behavioural literature), and so on. These and other policy related issues will be discussed in the next section of this chapter. The following section will focus on the effects and consequences of translating behavioural insights into policy. The aim of this section is to derive normative cautions and considerations for behaviourally informed consumer policy.

4.3. NORMATIVE CAUTIONS: USING BEHAVIOURAL INSIGHTS IN CONSUMER POLICY

Behavioural researchers and policy makers should realise that policy on the basis of RCT, when inaccurate, could have very costly consequences as well. Behavioural theory, when included in policy recommendations, might improve the accuracy of policy. This section will review the policy discussion concerning the introduction of behavioural insights into consumer policy from a social welfare perspective. The aim is to derive normative cautions and considerations that should be taken into account when behavioural notions are translated to consumer policy. The detrimental and beneficial effects of consumer biases will be addressed, as well as consumer learning and the strategic responses of sellers to consumers' biased decision making. The capabilities of policy makers to 'correct' biases of consumers will be discussed, including the biases that might be affecting policy makers themselves. Furthermore, this chapter will analyse the increased discretion of policy makers that might result from the far-reaching interventions that are justified by the various biases and heuristics. The approach of soft paternalism, which entails nudging individuals into decisions, can be criticised for being manipulative, which is a serious concern for behaviourally informed consumer policy. The costs of government interventions will be reviewed, focusing on the costs that are mainly argued to be related to behavioural interventions: distributional effects, decreased learning and increased dependency of consumers.

This section concludes with normative cautions and considerations for translating behavioural notions to consumer policy. These concerns should be addressed, or at least accounted for, when deciding to what extent and how behavioural insights can and should be implemented into (consumer) policy. The section that follows next will therefore discuss how some of the cautions and considerations can be addressed in policy making processes.

4.3.1. THE IMPLICATIONS OF CONSUMERS' BIASED DECISION MAKING

As has been argued in the previous chapter, consumers' decision making is influenced by several biases and heuristics which possibly lead to welfare-decreasing choices. However, even when behavioural insight can show that behaviour is affected by these biases and heuristics, government intervention is thereby not necessarily warranted. Biases and heuristics can be very helpful and efficient in simplifying personal decision making processes. Also, consumers can learn from their mistakes, or be educated to improve their faulty decision making. Allowing people to make their own mistakes could therefore be a valuable and very efficient consumer protection policy strategy.

a. Biased consumers acting against their own welfare

Even when behavioural insight can show that consumers are under the influence of biases, it does not automatically follow that this biased consumer decision making is welfare decreasing. Heuristics simplify decisions by requiring a limited amount of time and effort. Every individual utilises heuristics and biases to make decisions on a daily basis. Behavioural shortcuts help people to reach a decision which is relatively beneficial without having to weigh the consequences of every option. The decision reached might not be optimal considering the overall choice-set, but including the costs and benefits of the decision making process itself it might be quite close. Relying upon heuristics can be a welfare enhancing choice strategy in the light of information and deliberation costs (Kelman, 1998: 1583). Heuristics help when important decisions need to be made fast, such as in life-threatening situations (Gigerenzer, Todd and ABC Research Group, 1999). Individuals can also employ biases and heuristics themselves, making behaviour seem irrational when it is not. For instance, paying high yearly fees for gym subscriptions might seem irrational when the consumer actually does not use the gym very often. However, the subscription might be specifically employed by the consumer as a self-commitment device, without which he knows he would never attend the gym. The advance payment makes people want to get some benefit out of their 'loss', and makes them feel guilty for not attending the gym after they have paid a high subscription fee.

Biases may have other beneficial effects. Self-serving biases are one of the prime examples of cognitive quirks that, even though they impede optimal decision making, have beneficial effects nonetheless. Being positive about one's own abilities is considered to be very healthy in social and clinical psychology. People are shown to have overly optimistic views of themselves. Only people that have been diagnosed with a clinical depression are shown to make accurate predictions about their likelihood of success. Positive illusions serve people very well, and promote their psychological well-being (Taylor and Brown, 1988; 1994). Also, people sometimes feel the need to help other people out, thereby abiding to social norms. Other regarding preferences, even though not necessarily rational from the perspective of self-interested individual rationality, can be argued to be highly efficient from a social welfare point of view (Stout, 2006: 27–35).

Problems arise though, when heuristics fail and render consumers vulnerable and easy to be taken advantage off, making 'rational fools' out of consumers instead of rational actors (Slovic et al., 2002: 339–40).[125] When choice is complex, or when the consequences of a choice lie mainly in the (distant) future, consumers can easily be deceived by their own biases and heuristics. Other examples include irregular decisions and choices that are so dreaded (or complex) that they cause inertia and consumers end up not making any decisions at all (Camerer et al., 2003: 108). Loewenstein and O'Donoghue criticise pre-commitment devices, claiming that these instruments of altering behaviour through self-imposed feelings of loss or guilt are a crude and insufficiently effective way of controlling one's own behaviour (Loewenstein and O'Donoghue, 2006). These are situations which therefore should be assessed by policy makers to see whether social welfare could be improved.

[125] See for a discussion of how sellers might be abusing consumer biases: below, section 4.3.2.

b. *Consumer learning and education*

Another point of critique often offered by economists against behavioural insight is that consumer error does not by itself warrant a change in policy recommendations, as consumer error will be corrected by the market. Competition, learning by consumers and the education of sellers by consumers will drive out consumer errors (Epstein, 2006). The traditional economist's argument proceeds as follows: people learn from their mistakes. Confronted with the detrimental consequences of their previous decision, they improve their biased decision making and are then able to choose a more beneficial option when a similar situation arises. Learning effects will cause irrational behaviour to disappear over time; people should therefore be allowed to make their own mistakes (Kelman, 1998: 1583). Relying on consumer learning could be a very effective and efficient instrument to support consumer welfare.[126]

Whether or not consumers are able to learn from their mistakes or can be educated to employ improved decision making strategies, depends on several factors such as feedback, spill-over effects, the cost of education and ability to improve the decision based upon the mistake. Also, the size of consequences might prevent learning and correcting mistakes.

- *Feedback*: for consumers to know that decision making could be improved, they have to be aware of the flaw in their strategy. Feedback will only be taken into account when the consumer has an incentive to do so. When the consequences of the malfunctioning decision are small, consumers might not feel that improving their decision strategy is worth the trouble. Empirical evidence suggests that learning does not occur in every context and/or situation. Even highly experienced experts rely on misleading heuristics (Guthrie, Rachlinski and Wistrich, 2001: 782–3).
- *Spill-over effects*: learning by one consumer can have spill-over effects on the decision strategies employed by other consumers, thus increasing social welfare. The information strategies that are employed by sellers can also be improved when the learning process of consumers can provide feedback to sellers. However, one person learning does not necessarily make other people learn the same lesson; this implies that the external effects of learning might cause not enough learning in the market (Bar-Gill, 2007: 8–9).
- *Cost of education*: sellers have an incentive to educate consumers when they are better able to fulfil consumers' true preferences than their competitor. They can thus be a valuable source of information. However, it might be more

126 Some evidence of consumer learning is discussed by Epstein (2008: 811–3). Agarwal et al. (2007) discuss how consumers are found to be best able to reach decisions about financial products when they are about 53 years of age. This would indicate that younger consumers have yet to learn, and older consumers have forgotten what they had learnt before.

beneficial for sellers to rely upon consumer biases than correcting them.[127] This holds especially when the bias is hard to correct, such as in the case of information overload concerning highly complex information.[128] When sellers put new innovations in the market, consumers need to be educated about the advantages of this new product. Scepticism about new developments, cheaper products, high savings rates, low mortgage interest rates or other benefits and relying on incumbent firms stifles competition. The balancing act between knowing when a product is too good to be true or a great new innovation might be quite difficult for consumers. Even when consumers can nowadays disseminate information amongst each other, the risks remain that new innovations are mistrusted and are not at all or only after a long time picked up by consumers (Hviid, 2009). Consumers can also opt for 'education' through information intermediaries, delegating individual decision making to privately employed experts with better judgement. Delegation to privately employed experts can however be prohibitively costly (Bar-Gill, 2007: 10).

- *Ability to improve*: consumers should be able to correct their decision making strategy. As has been mentioned above, some mistakes might be irreparable or too costly to repair; relying on consumers to employ improved decision making might be ineffective in these situations. In order to correct decision making strategies, a similar situation needs to arise in which the improved strategy can be employed, preferably with a relatively short time span between both situations. People do learn from their mistakes but if the mistake is remote, the lesson might be forgotten. Even when a person receives a lesson in one situation, he might not apply that lesson in a slightly different context, because he fails to recognise the similarities. Some decisions are taken for a lifetime, or are very seldom. It is hard to learn from these mistakes.
- *Size of the mistake*: a mistake that has huge detrimental consequences could very well stimulate improvement in the decision making process for a next similar decision, but the question arises whether consumers should perhaps be protected from making this very detrimental mistake in the first place. Allowing the consumer to learn in this situation is very costly, and might not be warranted from a social welfare point of view.

To summarise, consumers' biased behaviour is not necessarily detrimental, but it can be. Education and learning could overcome faulty decision making when appropriate feedback is provided, aided by spill-over effects. Education by sellers or information intermediaries, when costs of education are not prohibitively high,

[127] See for a discussion of how sellers might be abusing consumers' biased decision making below, section 4.3.2.

[128] Next to severe information overload, other factors causing biased decision making are not easily counteracted, such as the dread factor linked to decisions involving death and huge suffering. Even when people know that the dread factor influences their decisions, this might not cause them to change their feelings or decision strategy. Procrastination, linked to present bias, is another flawed choice strategy that seems to be employed over and over again even when people know it is detrimental.

could also correct the market failure; however, there has to be an opportunity to improve the decision based upon the mistake. When the consequences of the mistake are particularly detrimental, learning by making mistakes might not be an advisable policy strategy.

4.3.2. SELLERS TAKING ADVANTAGE OF CONSUMER BIASES

If consumer decision making is constrained by biases and heuristics, and these biases potentially lead consumers to make welfare decreasing decisions, a question remains whether sellers respond strategically to these biases. This could result in a further welfare decrease. In order be able to respond to them, sellers need to be aware of the biases and heuristics and they need to be able to take advantage of biased consumer decision making. Although marketing literature does suggest a general awareness of consumer biases in the market, this awareness can be disputed, especially when it comes to small and medium enterprises. The same goes for sellers' strategic ability to take advantage of biased decision making employed by consumers: even though empirical research suggests that sellers are able to abuse consumers' biased decision making, reputation and competition between sellers might be sufficiently effective to deter sellers' abuse of biases. Sellers could overcome consumer biases by education or lowering switching costs. Also, private party information intermediaries could help consumers in correcting their faulty decision making. Whether sellers are actually abusing consumer biases and heuristics needs to be clearly established in the process of deciding on and developing market interventions.

a. Sellers' awareness of biases and heuristics

In behavioural literature, it is often claimed that the private sector has known about human biases for a long time, adding that companies frequently take advantage of these biases to increase their profit (see for instance Ariely, 2009: 1–27).[129] To support the claim that sellers are highly informed of biases and heuristics that affect consumers, economic scholars often refer to marketing literature. To illustrate the discussions on consumer decision making, a model of consumer sophistication taken from marketing literature will be briefly discussed (Lee, Christensen and DeRosia, 2008). This model exemplifies how different biases

129 Hanson and Kysar (1999a: 726) claim that "manufacturers will behave as if they know the behavioral literature *and then some*" (italics in source), implying that the knowledge of sellers will go beyond that of behavioural scholars as they are driven by competition and profit.

and heuristics, such as risk perceptions, contextual circumstances and cognition are interpreted in marketing literature (see figure 5).[130]

In this model both motivation and ability are incorporated as primary factors for consumer care in buying decision processes. Elements of motivation are: the interest in the decision, perceptions of corresponding financial, social and physical risks and whether the buyer is a professional, avid hobbyist or not very involved in the transaction. The extent to which a consumer is aiming to employ and enjoys exerting cognitive skills in the decision process is also relevant to factor of motivation. The ability to exercise sufficient care in decision making comes down to personal traits such as knowledge, age, education, problem solving skills and cognitive abilities in general such as the capacity (hardware) and capability (software) to take sufficient care.

Figure 5. Model of Consumer Care

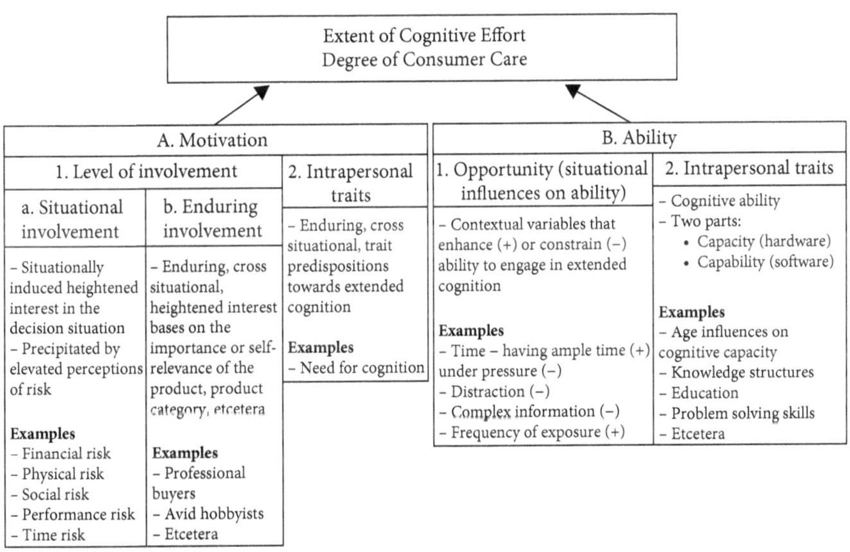

Source: Lee, Christensen and DeRosia (2008: 589).

Besides by personal traits, the ability to take care is influenced by contextual variables such as distraction, limited information, limited comparison opportunities, time pressure, frequency of exposure and complexity of information. Economic literature takes only a couple of these issues into account, such as the amount of information and the frequency of exposure. The behavioural literature does focus on the contextual variables and the cognitive ability to a

130 As Lee, Christensen and DeRosia (2008) describe, this model is set up to allow for detailed predictions regarding the circumstances in which consumers can be expected to experience source confusion, in relation to trademarks.

larger extent than economic literature does, even though not all of the elements mentioned in the model are included. A very interesting observation in the model is the need for cognition, which refers to a preference for thinking: consumers who enjoy thinking more than others get a positive (or less negative) impact from the decision making process itself (Lee et al., 2008: 593–4).[131] Behavioural literature often argues that conventional economic theory is too output-focused and that it neglects the decision making process; the disutility of this neglect is claimed to be habitually overlooked in economic assessments. Utility of the decision making process itself is however a new insight to even behavioural theory.[132]

Consumer protection regulation does not incorporate all of these aspects of the consumer decision making process, and whether full incorporation would be required is highly doubtful. This model however does illustrate how consumer decision making is perceived in marketing literature. As sellers can be assumed to base their marketing strategies on relevant information, marketing literature would be a useful source of such information. The suggestion that knowledge about consumer biases and heuristics can be acquired in the market however does not provide adequate justification for the enforcement of (intrusive) regulation onto sellers. It needs to be established whether sellers are in fact able to use this information to their advantage, and if so, whether this in fact results in a consumer welfare detriment that should be addressed by regulation.

b. Strategic responses to biases

Many scholars argue that sellers abuse biases of consumers in their own interest and even provide evidence to substantiate that claim.[133] Camerer et al. state that firms may exploit consumer errors and that better choices by consumers should increase total welfare (Camerer et al., 2003: 110). As argued by Hanson and Kysar, if consumers suffer from heuristics and biases, the search for gain will make sellers exploit these tendencies. They claim that manipulation of consumers by sellers is an "inevitable result of the competitive market" (Hanson and Kysar, 1999a: 726). Market participants, driven by market forces, will exploit the cognitive 'shortcomings' of potential clients in their own interest. A failure to do so will make companies fail in the market; abusing consumer biases is therefore the only viable survival strategy.[134] Della Vigna and Malmendier also argue that firms have

---

131 A comment with respect to cognition: in marketing, psychology, law and economics jargon is different. Cognition in marketing, meaning need for cognition, implies a preference for thinking and going over these decisions. Cognition in psychology refers generally to decision making processes in the mind.

132 It does relate to self-fulfilment or feelings of self-efficacy, which are mentioned in psychological literature, see for instance Gist (1987).

133 See above, chapter 3, section 3.3.1 for examples of situations in which sellers are argued to take advantage of consumers' biased decision making.

134 This position is echoed by many scholars, such as Korobkin (2006: 6), Loewenstein and Haisley (2008: 234), and White (2009).

incentives to accentuate consumer biases in order to profit from them, and they provide evidence of corresponding contract design in several business sectors such as credit card, gambling, health club, life insurance, mail order, mobile phone and vacation time-sharing industries (Della Vigna and Malmendier, 2004). Several studies show that firms take advantage of the non-rational expectations that consumers have of their own capabilities in for instance self-control or avoiding procrastination, such as the expected amount of times they will go to the gym. The profit-maximising strategy for firms is to magnify this bias, not to counteract it (Della Vigna, 2009: 363).[135] This strategy is not necessarily driven by malicious motives, it is the market mechanism; if competitors use this strategy to make money, other companies cannot afford to stay behind.

However, the potential abuse of consumer biases might not be as problematic as these examples suggest. Firstly, not all sellers might be able to take advantage of the biases and heuristics in consumer decision making, because they are biased themselves (Garvin, 2005). This especially refers to small to medium enterprises. Secondly, as has been explained above, sellers could respond to biases and for instance complex decision making by educating consumers, for example by offering simpler choices to attract consumers (Epstein, 2006). Sellers do respond to consumer biases, but the outcome is not necessarily detrimental to consumer welfare. Another example is related to switching costs. As rational apathy can be seen as an extra burden on switching costs, competitors could try to make switching even easier or less costly, so as to attract more consumers. They could provide information about how to switch, compensate switching costs or take over all administrative procedures that the switching entails. As has also been described above however, when consumer biases are difficult or costly to correct, sellers might be better off making use of these biases instead of correcting them. Thirdly, private industry can also be incentivised to help people make better choices when interests of consumers and sellers are aligned. This strategy to enhance social welfare takes advantage of the information possessed by sellers to help consumers (Loewenstein and Haisley, 2008: 216). Examples of industries where interests align between commercial parties and consumers are savings and adherence to drug treatments.

A careful assessment of welfare decreasing effects of biases should be part of behaviourally informed consumer policy making. Behavioural insights might cause consumers to suffer a decrease in their utility, possibly due to strategic behaviour by sellers. Evidence of sellers' abuse of consumer biases and heuristics can be found in some circumstances. However, sellers might not be able or not even be out to abuse consumers' decision making. Actual abuse by sellers should be empirically investigated in the relevant market setting, before behaviourally informed policy aiming to enhance decision making and social welfare is designed and implemented.

135 See Della Vigna (2009: 362–3) for an overview of such studies.

4.3.3. THE CAPABILITIES AND INTERESTS OF POLICY MAKERS

The next topic concerning welfare-enhancing policy is the capability of policy makers themselves. Scholars disagree on the extent to which policy makers are able to counteract biases in consumer decision making, and how their own personal interests influence their perception of consumers' best interest. This is an important issue in paternalistic government interventions. Paternalist interventions inherently imply the claim that the policy maker is better able to make this decision for the consumer in the interest of the consumer, than the consumer him- or herself. This is generally a disputed claim. Opponents of paternalistic intervention argue that policy makers might be biased themselves. The critics claim that behavioural insight increases policy makers' discretion as behavioural insight offers a wide range of justifications for government interventions. The possibility of manipulating consumers' decisions wilfully and deliberately is viewed with great apprehension by conventional economists and liberal policy makers alike.

a. Deciding for the consumer

Paternalism, deciding for someone else in their own (perceived) best interest, can serve two kinds of motive (Henderson, 2009: 4). The general justification offered in policy discussions is most often that consumers are in need of protection from themselves.[136] The first motive is then that policy makers genuinely believe that they are increasing social welfare by either helping individuals to increase their own or by forcing them to internalise the external effects of their actions. The second possible motive for paternalistic intervention however is that policy makers are trying to manipulate policy to impose decisions onto consumers, whether these decisions are in the best interest of consumers or not. Economists are very sceptical of the ability of policy makers to decide what is best for other people. They heavily criticise the notion of dismissing consumer sovereignty and thereby doing away with the authority consumers have over their own decisions and the freedom to decide as they see fit.[137] The costs of government decision making are argued by these critics to be much higher than the costs of private decision making (Glaeser, 2006). Consumers have a direct incentive to overcome personal errors, as they themselves are affected by these errors. When policy makers are deciding for other people, they might err in deciding what is best for the others. Error costs in deciding "what is best" might be higher when the government decides

---

136 As is for instance suggested by Sheldon (1974: 17).

137 The following quote from Issacharoff (1998: 1745): "... it would be indeed ironic if greater insight into the complexity of human decision making became the justification for taking the freedom to decide, even if imperfectly, from those very individuals." See also Van den Bergh (1990).

for others than when individuals make that choice for themselves. Furthermore, policy makers can suffer from biases as well as consumers do (see next section): why would they be any better in making welfare enhancing decisions than consumers?

There is a danger involved in allowing policy makers to intervene in consumer choices (Bernheim and Rangel, 2005: 3). Policy makers might be forcing their own preferred choices upon other people, regardless of whether that would be beneficial to social welfare. Certain decisions such as the choice regarding certain foods, preference of hygiene or safety standards, or even sexual orientation and religion could be interpreted as not revealing people's "true interests". The principle of revealed preferences protects consumers against government's inaccurate estimations of the desirability of decisions. If choices made by consumers are however no longer deemed to provide valuable information on what consumers want, policy makers could be able to justify far-reaching interventions into people's life choices. Caution is therefore required when policy makers are allowed to decide on behalf of consumers what is in the consumer's best interest.

b. Policy makers are biased too

Policy makers, just like any other individuals, are prone to suffer from biased decision making.[138] As mentioned above, policy makers might genuinely aim to make people better off and thereby increase social welfare, but the decisions they make in order to accomplish this benefit might be biased. There are several biases that are especially relevant to policy making.

Overoptimism causes people to overestimate their success rate. As this bias occurs predominantly in situations where people feel that they can influence the outcome of their actions, it can be argued to also apply to policy makers' decisions. Policy makers might be overoptimistic about the impact and the consequences of their own policy plans. When making a decision on behalf of citizens, the availability heuristic will cause lawmakers to respond to only some risks and problems, namely the ones that are salient to the public (Korobkin, 2006: 9–11). Self-serving biases, which cause people to interpret data in their favour, might trigger policy makers to (consciously or unconsciously) construe the available information advantageously, or to be inexplicably drawn towards their own preferred policy option. Most policy decisions are unlikely to be a clear cut case, because the consequences of policies are not always very clear. Policy evaluation is not an exact science (Van Boom et al., 2008: 41). As policy is affected by a myriad of viewpoints, facts can have uncertain consequences or consequences that are positive in some aspects, but negative in other. Consequently, selection bias might play a role in policy decisions as well. In addition, policy makers can fall short to

138 Mentioned by several scholars, such as Harrison (2008), Benjamin and Laibson (2003) and Zanitelli (2009: 13–5).

hindsight bias. Hindsight bias causes people to estimate the risk that a particular event will occur differently once the event actually has taken place. This might result in welfare decreasing policies, and the creation of too many provisions against some event that has just happened but is unlikely to materialise again anytime soon. Interested parties can even use this bias to influence policy making for their own benefit using "availability campaigns" (Kuran and Sunstein, 1999: 712).

As people tend to employ biases and heuristics, it is likely these biases will be found in policy makers too. As intelligence is no guarantee against biased decision making, even these presumably very capable and usually democratically elected government officials cannot be assumed to consistently make unbiased decisions. Behavioural insights therefore also provide a *warning* against government interventions in the choices of civilians (Benjamin and Laibson, 2003: 8–9). Glaeser argues that biased decision making is actually an argument against paternalistic interventions, as people have better incentives to correct their own biased mistakes than biased government decision makers do (Glaeser, 2006: 134). However, one could also argue that policy makers have more information and a better overview of that information. They might be better able to steer people's decisions towards better choices than people can themselves, especially when the choices are complex and they require the processing of loads of information (Loewenstein and Haisley, 2008: 214). Even though policy makers are also confronted with biases, their decision making might be less flawed than that of consumers. The argument that policy makers are likely to be affected by biases and heuristics in their policy decisions, as well as other human beings, remains however a worthy consideration.

c. *Discretion of policy makers*

The use of behavioural insight in the development of policy is claimed by critics to increase the discretion of policy makers. Behavioural economics is portrayed as supplying policy makers with a *Laundry List*: a list of biases and heuristics that have been empirically tested to apply in some circumstance and that policymakers can resort to whenever they are in need of a justification for their political endeavours (Rachlinski, 2000: 749). The problem with this sort of list is that it would not necessarily relate to a context in which those biases would actually occur (Korobkin, 2006: 12). Not only would this list be too extensive, the relative weight of these biases and heuristics could never be assessed in a general way either; a general way that would apply in each and every context, to each and every person, or to an identifiable group of people (Frijters, 2008). A list like this would merely provide a suggestion to be taken into account when devising policy. Behavioural insights on the list, it is argued, could have one effect in some situations and in other situations quite an opposite one. The assessment of which effect is relevant and stronger in which case can be difficult. The greater the number of such insights to be accounted for in policy, the more difficult the weighing of different arguments becomes. As this weighing of arguments is in the end up to policy makers, the inclusion of behavioural insights into policy decisions could increase the discretion of policy makers to a great degree. Policy makers, so it is argued by critics, will then always be able to find a behavioural notion to support their policy action.

Further concerns regarding government discretion are that the political processes might be hijacked by minority interest groups (Harrison, 2008: 62).[139] Critics claim that demands for regulation often come from rent-seeking producers; the regulation resulting from these demands might very well be detrimental to consumers (Field, 2008: 96). They also argue that once the first steps in the direction of paternalist policies are taken, the risks of outrageous constraints of consumer choice are lurking.[140]

d. Manipulating consumer decisions

The fear of government interventions into free will has caused behavioural literature to focus on the regulatory approach of soft paternalism.[141] Behavioural literature points out several cases in which governments have to provide a starting point, a default rule, a choice between opt-in or opt-out, et cetera. This starting point inevitably affects choices and preferences of affected individuals (Sunstein and Thaler, 2003: 1165). Policy intervention is therefore unavoidable, even if the intervention does not aim to steer consumer decision making in any direction. As soft paternalism keeps free will intact, consumers are free to decide in whichever way they want.

Soft paternalistic approaches, in which consumer decisions are nudged in a certain direction, are however also criticised. The main fear is that even though consumers are in theory still able to make their own choices, their choices will in fact be manipulated by the government's choice architectures to an unacceptable degree. Even when choice architectures were already in place, these architectures would not necessarily have been devised to deliberately push consumers' decision making in a certain direction. The manipulation of individuals justified by behavioural law and economics through soft paternalism is claimed by opponents of soft paternalism to be inconsistent with consent, will and dignity (White, 2010). They argue that consumers are not free to choose, as they are deliberately pushed towards certain decisions. Soft paternalism can be devised in such a way that the motives of policy makers do not even have to be made known; it is just a change of the default, who would mind that? A change in policy without

---

139 The risk of regulatory capture will be briefly discussed below, section 4.4.1e, and more extensively explored in chapter 7, section 7.2.5g.

140 These arguments are known as slippery slope arguments, see for instance Whitman and Rizzo (2007) and Zanitelli (2009: 17–8).

141 See above, chapter 3, section 3.3.2.

a requirement for the (actual) motivation behind this change to be known runs a high risk of being unacceptably manipulative, the opponents claim.

The concern of unacceptable (degrees of) manipulation of policy plans is argued to be especially relevant to those cases where policy makers are in some way discontented with the choices that people make and therefore nudge them in a different direction, irrespective of which decisions will be in the best interest of individuals. Policy makers, so the critics argue, have no way of knowing what is in the best interests of individuals, besides basing themselves on the choices of the individuals. Therefore, the autonomy of individuals should be respected. Perceived unacceptable manipulation of policy is regarded to be a specific problem of soft paternalism and this point provides a strong caution for the translation of behavioural insights into policy. Government interventions could be perceived as excessively or wrongly manipulating because they are not in the best interest of consumers but a result of politicians wrongly interfering with consumer decision making. Consumers might reject these behaviourally informed policies, mistrust the government or respond in other ways that have undesirable consequences. The risk of perceived manipulation when consumers' decisions are deliberately nudged in certain directions should be carefully acknowledged.

4.3.4. COSTS OF PATERNALISTIC GOVERNMENT INTERVENTIONS

Market interventions that aim to correct a market failure or biased decision making will cause society to incur several types of costs that are a burden to social welfare.[142] Administrative, monitoring and enforcement costs are all connected to government interventions and can potentially be very high. Regulation that is enacted and fully implemented might be hard to remove later on. Policy that aims to correct consumers' biased decision making might result in several other costs. As not all consumers might suffer equally from the same biases, interventions that aid vulnerable groups might thereby also damage sophisticated consumers. Companies affected by consumer regulations will have certain costs connected to compliance with these regulations. Furthermore, paternalistic regulations can have adverse effects. Whether the costs of government intervention outweigh the benefits should therefore be carefully assessed. Two specific kinds of cost connected to paternalistic government interventions will now be discussed in more detail: distributional effects and negative effects on consumer learning and dependency.

142 See above, chapter 2, section 2.2.3.b.

a. *Distributional effects*

Interventions in the market to protect or benefit some individuals can have distributional effects, which means that other people might suffer a loss due to these interventions. Government interventions might aid certain consumers more than they benefit other ones. Regulation to benefit the 'unsophisticated' consumer might not be of any benefit to sophisticated consumers, whereas they are contributing to the payment of intervention costs through taxes. Sometimes, interventions could even be detrimental to sophisticated consumers, as some of the products they prefer can no longer be acquired in the market due to consumer protection interventions. Risky financial products could here serve as a possible example. Distributional effects might still increase general social welfare, but deserve some attention nonetheless as some parties do lose out (Amir and Lobel, 2008: 2123). Sophisticated consumers have no need for such interventions, and the help to unsophisticated consumers could come at their cost. Camerer et al., aware of this fact, hence dubbed their type of soft paternalism 'asymmetric paternalism': benefits and costs of the interventions will not affect different groups to equal measures, and will therefore be allocated asymmetrically (Camerer et al., 2003).

Furthermore, when governments help consumers to overcome biases and to become more sophisticated regarding for instance saving, credit cards, and telephone subscriptions, the companies that offer these products will suffer losses (Amir and Lobel, 2008: 2123). On the one hand, companies affected by consumer regulations have to incur certain costs in order to comply with these regulations, for instance information disclosure policies. On the other hand, these companies may have relied upon specific market procedures and product types in response to consumer biases. They will suffer losses as a consequence of a change in consumer decision making. Even though total social welfare might increase due to the interventions, the losses suffered by companies should be taken into account as a consequence of government interventions.

These distributional effects are real and unavoidable when biases in consumer decision making are corrected. Paternalistic interventions will very likely result in sophisticated consumers and companies having to face costly consequences. All distributional effects, where some groups benefit but other groups are less well off, should be taken into consideration, not only the effects to the group of consumers this intervention aims to benefit.

b. *Decreased learning and increased dependency of consumers*

Government interventions to overcome consumer biases can also have adverse effects in the sense that consumers do no longer feel the need to act prudently and or to learn from their mistakes. Regulatory interventions might prevent individuals from learning from the consequences of their actions, therefore becoming totally dependent on government protection (Winick, 1992: 1756–9). Klick and

Mitchell claim that costs of government interventions to overcome consumer biases in the long run will outweigh short term benefits due to negative learning and motivational effects. Paternalistic interventions reduce an individual's incentive to act deliberately and carefully, resulting in consumer moral hazard. Interventions such as restricting choice options and muting feedback signals are likely to restrict learning opportunities. Also, as contractual freedom is required for the development of competence in decision making, the overall competence in this respect will decrease and the need for paternalistic oversight in other domains could be intensified (Klick and Mitchell, 2006). Consumer moral hazard can thus be an adverse effect of paternalistic interventions and increase the dependency of consumers on government instruments and interventions.[143]

Minimising consumer accountability for poor choices reduces incentives to choose well. Consumers might be lulled into a false sense of security since the government will protect them, even when they have failed to assess the consequences of their decisions sufficiently. Consumer vigilance is an important asset in the market place, as consumers are the best suited party to look out for their own interest (Hviid, 2009).[144] If consumers no longer feel responsible for the consequences of their own actions, this sentiment could lead to bad decision making on the part of consumers. The fact that consumers make poor choices is not by itself a justification for regulation (Silber, 1990: 73).

However, it is important to note that (softly) paternalistic policies do not completely preclude learning. Interventions to correct biases and heuristics can employ other strategies than merely the instruments of changing defaults or minimising options. Debiasing, which entails giving less but better information, can strengthen careful decision making and induce consumers to make informed choices in cases where they used to rely on defaults. In these cases people might actually learn from positive reinforcement, which could result in more informed decision making in other situations as well as the one in which the government has intervened (Loewenstein and Haisley, 2008: 214). Also, in cases where consumers do not deliberate their decisions, and are not likely to do so even when their decisions prove faulty, learning is unlikely to take place anyway. In these cases, decreased learning due to behaviourally informed interventions is less of a problem.

---

143 See above, sections 2.3.3b.

144 Hviid (2009) also points out that it is not always easy for consumers to distinguish which offers are 'too good to be true' or whether they are genuinely innovative improvements to the current standard. Consumer protection might help innovative sellers to deservedly gain market space, as consumers are less fearful of trying new and unknown products.

4.3.5. SUMMARY AND CONCLUSIONS

Biases and heuristics might very well influence consumer decision making in a way that is detrimental to consumer welfare. When aims are undertaken to correct consumers' biased decision making through (softly) paternalistic government interventions however, several issues arise that complicate the effective translation of behavioural insight into policy. These normative issues, which have been discussed above, will be summarised here. Following that, conclusions will be drawn from this discussion, resulting in an overview of normative cautions and considerations that should be taken into account when translating behavioural insights to policy.

a. Summary: normative cautions for behaviour consumer policy

Consumer decision making is likely to be affected by biases and heuristics that provide an opportunity for sellers to take advantage of consumers. However, even if several biases affect consumer decision making, policy interventions are not automatically warranted. Decision making which relies on heuristic shortcuts can be a quite efficient decision strategy for consumers to reach relatively good outcomes. However, when choices are complex, not made on a daily basis, holding consequences that are dreaded or that lie mainly in the (distant) future, consumers could easily be deceived by their own biases and heuristics. Self-commitment strategies might work, but are a crude mechanism. Allowing consumers to learn from their mistakes and to correct their own decision making strategies could be a very efficient way of preventing faulty decision making. Learning however is not always possible. Feedback, incentives to learn, spillover effects to other people, costs of educating consumers, being able to improve the decision making strategy are all important aspects of people's ability to benefit from learning. Some mistakes are just too costly to make, and government intervention might be justified to prevent such a decision from ever being made.

Even though information on consumer decision making is available to sellers, they might not be able to use this information to the detriment of consumers. Sellers might be biased themselves. Competition between sellers might cause sellers to educate consumers about their biases; it might however also force sellers to abuse consumer biases as they cannot stay behind in the market. Policy makers might not be better able than consumers themselves to decide what is in the best interest of consumers. Even though policy makers are biased too, they might have more and a better overview of information at their disposal, enabling them to make more sophisticated decisions on behalf of consumers. The incorporation of behavioural notions in policy will increase the possible justifications for new policy plans and is therefore likely to increase policy makers' discretion. The possibility of abusive manipulation of consumers' decisions by deliberately nudging them in certain directions against their best interest is another cause of concern. Admittedly, some policies involve choosing a starting point or default position, which necessarily includes a policy choice. However, increased discretion and perceived manipulation of consumers' decisions are an issue in behaviourally informed consumer policy that is worthy of serious consideration.

Finally, next to the costs that are related to government interventions in general, paternalistic interventions aiming to improve consumers' decision making can come with specific types of additional costs. Policies that aim to provide support for unsophisticated consumers might have detrimental effects for sophisticated consumers, and will also be costly to sellers. Whether the increase in welfare to one group merits the decrease in welfare to another is a policy decision; from a social welfare perspective however, such effects should always be taken into account. Government intervention can also increase consumer moral hazard as consumers become less vigilant when they no longer have the ability or incentive to learn from their mistakes. The intervention instrument of debiasing however might provide an example of soft paternalism which nudges people into (rational) deliberations. Consumer learning could therefore be increased by soft paternalism and stimulate consumers to make careful assessments in other situations.

b. Conclusions: normative cautions and considerations for behavioural consumer policy

Before implementing interventions that aim to correct consumers' biased decision making, several cautions and considerations that are connected with the translation of behavioural insight into (consumer) policy should be considered. The main normative considerations for the use of behavioural insight to improve consumer policy can be identified as follows:

- It should be assessed whether *perceived* consumer biases are detrimental for consumers *in reality*. Consumers might learn from mistakes, or they might be able to be educated by sellers and information intermediaries. Also, it should be established whether sellers in fact abuse consumer biases. When choices are complex, not made on a daily basis, holding consequences that are dreaded or that lie mainly in the (distant) future, the government is more likely to efficiently improve consumer decisions.
- Policy makers should be well aware of the difficulties in deciding what is in the best interests of other people, including the fact that they may be biased themselves. The reason that people decide as they do might very well be that they actually prefer this decision; consumers might also prefer to be able to decide for themselves, even erroneously.
- The increased discretion allowed to policy makers and risks of manipulating consumers' decisions against their best interests are special concerns of behavioural theory. Consumers perceiving 'benign' interventions as wrongly or exceedingly manipulating could have counter-productive effects.

- Paternalistic interventions can result in costs to sophisticated consumers and sellers, and risk increasing consumer dependency while deterring consumer learning. These adverse and distributional effects should be taken into account when deciding on the welfare-enhancing effects of interventions.

These cautions and considerations should be taken into account when behavioural insight is included in consumer policy design. The negative consequences of a behaviourally informed policy should where possible be counteracted. The increased discretion and risks of manipulation are especially relevant concerns that have to be addressed in policy making procedures. Some policy measures for devising behaviourally informed consumer policy, that do take the cautions and considerations mentioned here into account, will be discussed in the next section.

4.4. GUIDELINES FOR CAUTIOUS BEHAVIOURAL CONSUMER POLICY

The behavioural claim is that even when one acknowledges the increase in transaction costs, the complexity of the analysis, the risk of regulatory capture, the difficulty of pinpointing true preferences and the other concerns mentioned above, the use of the assumptions of rational man as a basis of policy prescriptions could still have more negative consequences than the incorporation of behavioural theory. Behavioural notions point out several issues that could result in a decrease in social welfare. These issues, which are linked to consumer decision making processes, are regularly overlooked by standard economic analysis. The concerns that have been specified in the previous sections should however be taken into account whenever behavioural insight is employed as a basis for policy. In the following section, some policy measures will be discussed to address the methodological and normative cautions that were reviewed previously. These policy measures will be used to generate (non-exhaustive) guidelines for the cautious development of behaviourally informed consumer policy.

4.4.1. ADDRESSING THE CAUTIONS AND CONSIDERATIONS

The cautions and considerations from both the methodological and the normative or policy perspective are valid concerns and they should therefore be addressed. This section will provide ways of accounting for some of these cautions and considerations.

a. *Scientifically sound basis for policy analysis*

First, the methodological concerns that have been raised with respect to the effects of behavioural insight on theory or policy will be discussed. A sound scientific basis should underlie any policy analysis and recommendation. When in a certain market consumers are argued to behave under the influence of biases and heuristics, this statement should be carefully assessed. Behavioural studies should also be conducted in contexts that are equal or similar to the market conditions in which the bias is argued to be effective and detrimental. Empirical studies should be undertaken to enhance the scientific basis. Data should be interpreted cautiously, refraining from undue generalisations. Statistical studies merely suggest certain observations; evidence about biased consumer decision making should not be inferred from one study. Literature or a collection of articles of which the common message is not heavily disputed, suggesting a common observation, is more trustworthy. Only when a sound scientific basis has been established and the claim that consumers are biased in a certain market can be credibly asserted, a market-based welfare analysis can be conducted.

b. *Economic welfare analysis is more than rational choice*

Economic theory provides highly valuable insights about markets, the behaviour of agents within that market, market failures and the costs and benefits of government interventions correcting those market failures. Economics has produced further insight on the basis of RCT than merely predictions of individual behaviour. For instance, market failures and social welfare considerations provide rationales for government intervention. Also, different costs and benefits to government interventions have been established. An example is the insight that consumer protection will in the end be borne by consumers themselves, and also that increasing costs to consumers do not necessarily decrease consumer welfare if consumers get higher quality in return. Economic theory has a long history of establishing a general framework for analysing the economic effects of laws and policies. The costs and effects of rules, law and regulations, the incentives that they create for market parties and desirable strategies for intervention in the market can be described using economic analysis. Economic analysis is therefore an extremely useful tool for the development of efficient and effective consumer policy. Traditional economic analysis should not be abandoned in favour of behavioural insights, even in those cases when behavioural notions are better able to explain and predict behaviour than rational choice. Rational choice is only one part of the entire set of economic insights. Economic insight can still be valid and relevant to policy issues even when consumer behaviour in certain situations is better explained and predicted using biases than RCT. In these cases RCT could be abandoned in the pursuit of accurate predictions of the behaviour of market parties in favour of behavioural insights. However, other relevant insights that have been pointed out by economic theory still hold, such as reputational concerns of commercial parties, costs and adverse effects of government interventions and the working of the market mechanism as a whole. The entire picture required for policy analysis includes more aspects than only individual behaviour; economic analysis therefore still has a role to play even when individual behaviour in certain cases is more accurately predicted by behavioural insights. Sound economic principles and a rigorous evaluation of the costs and benefits should provide the foundation of any proposed government intervention.

c. Market-based analysis of consumer behaviour

Studies should be conducted in the relevant markets to assess the discussed consumer behaviour, taking as much of the particulars of that market into account. In cases where consumer biases are argued to be detrimental to social welfare, these behavioural assessments should portray the following characteristics:[145]

- Behavioural assessments should be sound scientific and preferably empirical market-based studies of relevant consumer behaviour. This includes the contexts in which consumers take decisions. When analysing consumer behaviour, both conventional economics and behavioural insights should be explored for explanations of the observed behaviour. Both sets of insights should be evaluated according to their accuracy at explaining and predicting consumer behaviour in this particular context;
- When biases are shown to affect relevant consumer decision making, the assessment should shown whether or not these biases are abused by sellers to the detriment of consumers;
- The assessment should provide a full examination of consumer and social welfare effects of relevant consumer behaviour and strategic response of sellers. This assessment should explore the decrease in welfare suffered by consumers due to inhibitions in their decision making process, whether those inhibitions stem from information asymmetries or from heuristics and biases. Consumer learning, education by sellers and other market corrections to overcome consumer biases should be also be regarded as relevant material to be included in the assessment.

d. Designing behavioural interventions: efficient, context-specific and heuristic-savvy

An intervention that is designed to counteract the negative consequences of biased consumer decision making should correspond to three criteria: it should be *efficient*, so that the benefits of the intervention outweigh its costs but also that no other intervention is more effective at similar costs; it should be *context-*

145 As is discussed in Ogus (2005), OECD (2007) and Bar-Gill (2008: 801–2).

specific, meaning that it should address particular issues within consumer decision making and refrain from overly general solutions; and it should be *heuristic-savvy*, which implies that it should account for choice architectures and where possible employ biases.[146]

Efficient

For any government intervention, the requirement of efficiency implies that the intervention should (1) be effective in counteracting the negative consequences of the consumer bias, (2) provide more benefits than costs, and (3) be the most desirable option in comparison to other policy options, including the option of no intervention.[147] First, to be effective and actually remedy the problem, the devised intervention has to address the cause. For the development of intervention strategies information can be taken from both economic and behavioural literature. When behavioural notions are shown to apply to the issue at hand, the intervention should aim at correcting them or otherwise account for these biases. When the decrease in welfare is caused by information asymmetry however, the intervention should be based on economic insights because such a market failure can best be counteracted by typical information remedies. Secondly, an analysis of all costs and benefits of the devised intervention is should be made. Intervening in the decision making of other people can be costly, not only for the government, but also for the targeted individuals as they might have to forgo on certain options. The cost-benefit analysis should include possible distributional effects and other negative consequences of policy interventions, which have been described in this chapter. Preferably, and when applicable, intervention on behalf of biased consumers should not distort the decision making of well-informed consumers. Sellers' welfare should also be taken into account, especially when the policy intervention implies costly efforts on their behalf.[148] The accurate weighing of intervention consequences, including the different effects that they will have on different groups, can represent a difficult policy question (OECD, 2007). It is one however that needs to be provided with an answer. Thirdly, all available policy options to remedy the market failure or the behavioural problem should be considered, including the option of no intervention. Due to the costly nature of government interventions and the difficulties connected with deciding for other people, policies corresponding to soft paternalism have benefits over more intrusive policy suggestions. Especially when the consequences of interventions

[146] The term "heuristics-savvy" is borrowed from Korobkin (2006: 14).

[147] Many scholars point towards the continued necessity of conducting a(n) (economic) cost-benefit analysis of government interventions, also when these are based upon behavioural insights. See for instance: Ogus (2005), OECD (2007), Amir and Lobel (2008: 2122–3) and Field (2008: 94).

[148] For instance, placing information duties on sellers, even when the aim is to provide less and better information to debias consumers, will be a burden to sellers.

are unclear, as is often the case with 'newly devised' interventions such as behaviourally informed ones, less intrusive interventions are to be preferred over far-reaching interventions (Loewenstein and Haisley, 2008: 216).

Context-specific

If anything, the psychological literature suggests that biases and heuristics are highly context-specific. The question is then to what extent an overarching and general theory such as rational choice is actually required. Predictions that apply to specific contexts might be just as helpful, as policies usually target specific contexts as well. For instance, consumers might respond differently to the risks provided by faulty product design than they respond to the risk of a possible loss of income which is relevant in mortgage contracts. Specific policies can be developed to address the respective contract types. Insights from psychology can be used to develop policy for specific areas, taking the available information about the specificity of the cases into account (Brennan, 2008: 142). Empirical and experimental research should pinpoint the contexts in which the different types of decision making processes are used. The validity issues connected to experimental research however result in the fact that experimental observations may not provide a sufficient justification for policy changes that are more general in nature (Harrison, 2008: 60). Policy interventions based upon behavioural insights should therefore be applied within limited contexts; an intervention based upon behavioural notions might be efficient in some situations, but not in all.

Heuristic-savvy

Behavioural insights could be especially relevant to the design of intervention instruments. Mulholland claims that "the principal value of behavioural economics to consumer protection lies in its ability to help in the more efficient implementation of existing policy goals" (Mulholland, 2008: 68). The interventions should be *heuristic-savvy*: taking due account of the biases and heuristics at play in the relevant decision making process, and where possible even employing consumer heuristics to accomplish beneficial results (Korobkin, 2006: 14–6). The consumer behaviour that is addressed through policy instruments is affected by certain decision contexts or choice architectures. It should be assessed which biases and heuristics, as well as which choice architectures, underlie the biased decision (Amir and Lobel, 2008: 2122–3). A (creative) solution should be proposed and assessed accordingly.[149] This proposed solution will aim to correct or account for the biased decision making of the policy target group, for example

[149] As behavioural policy solutions are not yet common or wide-spread, some creativity is required in the design of behavioural interventions.

by switching the default rule or by debiasing or rebiasing the consumer.[150] The efficiency of several interventions should be duly assessed. Naturally, the proposed correction should be examined to see to what extent it actually aids consumers in their decision making abilities or causes an improvement in their resulting decisions. It would be valuable to distinguish the circumstances which 'trigger' rational thinking as opposed to intuitive thinking, or the dominance of one bias over the other (Amir and Lobel, 2008: 2122–3). Depending on the ease with which consumers can switch their decision making strategy, one instrument might be more efficient than others within the context of one specific policy question.

e. *Transparent and rigorous decision making procedures for policy*

The implementation of behavioural insights consumer policy increases the discretion policy makers have in designing policies, which gives rise to fears of possible manipulation of policy to further the ends of policy makers instead of consumers. Also, as policy makers are biased themselves, their decision making might be just as flawed as the consumers' decision making. Cost-benefit analysis, transparency, field testing and rigorous decision making procedures could have be used to overcome some of the difficulties connected to using behavioural insights in policy making.

Cost-benefit analysis and transparency

Sunstein however argues that a cost-benefit analysis is an excellent strategy for lawmakers to overcome cognitive biases in the development of policy (Sunstein, 1999). A sound cost-benefit analysis can create an *accurate overview of all foreseen consequences*, including the *chances* that these consequences will actually take place, the *cost-effectiveness* and the *efficiency* of policies: will they meet the goals they are supposed to? The cost aspect of policy options should include the wide variety of possible costs, such as administrative costs, monitoring costs, enforcement costs, but also other consequences that government intervention can have such as changing consumer demand, increasing prices, stimulating moral hazard, et cetera. An overview of all costs and benefits of the preferred policy option, set out against the consequences of other policy options, could result in more objective decision making which is less influenced by biases and heuristics and guards against policy makers abusing their discretion. Sound cost-benefit analysis can also aid policymakers in being more transparent about their considerations for new policy plans. *Transparency* is a vital part of valid policy making. The application of Rawls' publicity principle to government interventions results in

150 See above, chapter 3, section 3.3.3, also for a discussion of the benefits and consequences of these intervention strategies which is relevant for the selection of the most appropriate intervention strategy.

the publicity condition: the requirement that these interventions should stand up to public scrutiny (Rawls, 1993: 66–7). If a government cannot or will not defend a (nudging) strategy in public and refuses to disclose its true intentions for implementing this policy, the intervention should not be put into practice.

Field testing

The procedures for the development and implementation of behaviourally informed policy should furthermore include *field testing* of the proposed interventions to reduce uncertainties regarding the costs and benefits of policies. If possible, economic policy interventions and especially the behaviourally informed ones should be tested in small-scale field experiments to determine the actual effects of the policy intervention before they are applied to a large population (Greenstone, 2009: 118–9). Consumers who are affected by biases might therefore not respond in the way that had been envisaged by the policy intervention (OECD, 2007). Undue generalisation of behavioural observations can be corrected at this stage of the policy making process. Soft paternalism is not yet a common concept and therefore "unchartered territory", in need of careful testing before being implemented (Loewenstein and Haisley, 2008: 216). This solution can however not guarantee a successful implementation: some relevant behavioural effects, such as learning effects, might take years to effectuate. The possibility of such delayed effects should also be taken into account in the development of behavioural policy (Benjamin and Laibson, 2003: 28–32). The credibility of policy evaluations that are undertaken with the use of experiments should furthermore be enhanced by making the data and the evaluations transparent and publicly available, again increasing the transparency of the considerations that underlie government plans (Greenstone, 2009: 119).

Stakeholder participation

Slippery slopes and the distrust towards policy makers do not necessarily call for the rejection of all paternalistic interventions. These cautions are however relevant and support a rigorous set of preconditions that should be met before government officials are allowed to intervene in markets (Sylvan, 2008). Therefore, the procedures for decision making should allow different interest groups, stakeholders and experts to voice their opinions and review policy suggestions.[151] Organisational structures and review processes should be put in place to counteract excessive discretion on the part of the policy makers. Also, experts can be employed to increase the quality of the decision making of policy makers. Amir and Lobel argue that this type of cooperation between government, regulated

[151] See also Stiglitz (2009: 18) arguing that parties who are likely to be hurt by a failure of regulations should be well represented in the regulatory structures.

entities and other stakeholders in the development of new policy corresponds to the 'new governance approach'. This approach ensures public participation, transparency and sharing of best practices and information. It takes insights from behavioural theories that regard adversarialism as counterproductive and therefore aim to stimulate companies and individuals to share information by engaging in mutually beneficial problem solving (Amir and Lobel, 2008: 2127–37). Europe has since 1998 known the requirement of a Regulatory Impact Assessment (RIA) in cases where a regulatory proposal is expected to have an effect on business, charities and voluntary organisations (Ramsay, 2007: 59). The implementation of RIAs is aimed at stimulating rigorous and transparent policy making, which can also aid behaviourally informed policy proposals.

Policy making that involves many stakeholders, experts and other interested parties will admittedly require a complicated decision making process. The involvement of many people in this process will imply lengthy procedures with a higher cost of decision making. Also, there might be a risk of regulatory capture, where interest groups try to influence policy makers into decisions that are merely beneficial to the interest group itself; this might apply to both business and consumer organisations (Bates, 2002: 88–9).[152] Policy strategies that aim to promote of interests of consumers should require consumer participation, both at the level of policy decision making and the level of enforcement. However, consumer participation (at least in the EU) is limited and outweighed by the influence of business interest groups (Ramsay, 2007: 19–22). Policy makers should be aware of the respective agendas of the relevant interest groups; interest groups are however also valuable sources of information. Inviting different stakeholders with adverse interests to partake in policy development processes could limit the risk of capture (Cafaggi, 2008: 138).

Policy makers' discretion

Transparent procedures which involve all relevant stakeholders should prevent policy makers from making self-interested decisions that they claim to take on behalf of consumers, unless there are (actual) sound arguments to do so. Also, procedural transparency should limit the policy makers' discretion and the possibility of undue manipulation or biased decision making, and reduce the risk of regulatory capture (Rachlinski, 2003: 1214–9; Cafaggi, 2006: 57). Furthermore, rule-making should be separated from rule-monitoring to avoid possible conflicts of interest on the monitoring agent's part (Cafaggi, 2008: 138). Behavioural insights increase the palate of available justifications for welfare-enhancing consumer policy interventions, extending beyond situations that do call for

[152] See below, chapter 7, section 7.2.5, for a discussion about involving interest groups in regulatory decision making process. See also Dayagi-Epstein (2006) more specifically about difficulties concerned with representation of consumer interests through consumer organisations.

intervention on the basis of rational choice and standard economic insights. The risks of unsuccessful interventions should however be taken into account, as policy makers can err. The potential of undue government manipulation is very real, even though this danger is far from new and hardly limited to behaviourally informed interventions to consumer policy. Transparency in decision making procedures and procedural aims, the involvement of stakeholders, experts and other interested parties and the conducting of field experiments should increase the understanding of possible effects of policies before they are implemented and guard against manipulation. The implementation of these prescriptions for policy procedures is crucial. Issues such as which parties should be involved and at what stage of the process they should be, and how to ensure transparency, are all facets that greatly influence the effectiveness of policy procedures to prevent error and manipulation (Tiemeijer, 2009: 307–8). Since policy procedures are costly however and can offer no guarantees, the issues of error and manipulation remain delicate.

4.4.2. SUMMARY: GUIDELINES FOR CAUTIOUS BEHAVIOURAL CONSUMER POLICY

To address the cautions and considerations concerning the implementation of behavioural insights into consumer policy that have been the topic of this chapter, guidelines can be put forward to steer consumer policy into welfare enhancing directions. These guidelines call for:

- *A scientifically sound basis for policy analysis.* When a behavioural bias is argued to influence decision making to consumers' detriment, sound and preferably empirical studies should be undertaken to provide a reliable basis for policy. Also, the results of these studies should not be over-generalised.
- *Economic welfare analysis to be seen as more than rational choice.* Economic insight should be seen to encompass both rational choice and behavioural theory; when behavioural insights are shown to influence decision making, economic insights can still be the foundation for socially beneficial consumer policy.
- *Market-based analysis of consumer behaviour.* Consumer behaviour should be assessed in the markets that it applies to. The explanations and predictions for behaviour that are shown to be valid, whether they are behavioural or rational, should form the basis of the analysis. The possibility of sellers' abuse of consumer decision making should be carefully examined, as well as the detrimental effects of biased behaviour including market corrections and consumer learning.
- *Efficient, context-specific and heuristic-savvy behavioural interventions.* Like any policy intervention, behaviourally informed policy should be cost-effective, it should target a clearly established issue and it should be more efficient in its aim than other policy options including the option of

non-intervention. Because behavioural insights are context-dependent, behaviourally informed policy should address specific issues and refrain from providing general solutions. It should be aware of the choice architectures relevant to the decision making process of consumers, and where possible take advantage of biases and heuristics to steer decision making towards welfare-enhancing options.

- *Transparent and rigorous decision making procedures for policy.* Transparent and rigorous decision making procedures which are based upon a cost-benefit analysis and which allow stakeholders, experts and other interested parties to have a say in the development of policy should guard against government error, biased policy decision making and undue discretion in or manipulation of policy. These rigorous procedures however come at a cost, and offer no guarantees. However, the demand for profoundly researched policy measures of which the consequences can be established with relative certainty is rising, not only in government, but also in society. Mere rational choice predictions without further empirical insight might no longer be accepted as a justification for policies.

These guidelines should be a starting point for the design of behaviourally informed consumer policy interventions that aim at improving consumer and social welfare and that are founded on insights from both traditional economic analysis and behavioural theory.

4.5. CONCLUSIONS

To conclude, this section aims to answer the research question of to what extent the application of insights from behavioural economics to economic analysis can be depended upon to improve consumer policy from a social welfare perspective.

4.5.1. CAUTIONS AND CONSIDERATIONS FOR BEHAVIOURALLY INFORMED CONSUMER POLICY

The chapter has reviewed the concerns that are raised regarding the question whether and to what extent behavioural insights can be used to inform welfare-enhancing consumer policy, and has also considered several policy strategies that can be employed to address some of these cautions and considerations. In conclusion, it can be asserted that none of these cautions and considerations presented in this chapter justify a complete rejection welfare-enhancing behaviourally informed consumer policy. The concerns raised can however justify a rejection of behavioural policy interventions in certain cases. Policy interventions aimed at curing presumed consumer biases and heuristics are not justified when rational choice can provide a more accurate prediction of behaviour or when the hypothesised bias cannot be shown to be detrimental to consumers in specific markets. Neither should the behavioural intervention be implemented when it is too costly. Policies can also be ineffective in improving social welfare due to government error or when the policy is motivated by a desire to unduly manipulate rather than aid consumers in their decision making. Thus, the concerns that have been described in this chapter should be taken into account in behaviourally informed consumer policy.

The discussion that has been reviewed in this chapter has resulted in the following cautions, considerations and guidelines for the incorporation of behavioural insights in welfare-enhancing consumer policy interventions: first, from the methodological perspective, statistical studies providing psychological insights and social data should be interpreted cautiously; their results should not be over-generalised and they should be checked for soundness. Empirical studies are to be preferred over laboratory experiments. Furthermore, the studies should be context-specific, when applicable illuminating cases of conflicting insights regarding behaviour. Behavioural insights can improve the accuracy of predictions in some cases; this improvement should however be traded off against increased context-dependency, analytical complexity and costs.

Secondly, in response to normative concerns, it should be clearly established that the respective biased decision making is indeed detrimental to consumers and abused by sellers strategically. Market corrections such as consumer learning and education by sellers or information intermediaries should be considered. Traditional economic welfare analysis of markets, market failures, government interventions including the cost and benefits of regulation should not be abandoned. A behavioural bias that has been proven detrimental to social welfare does not automatically justify government intervention. The development of behaviourally informed policy should take notice of the difficulties of deciding what is in consumers' best interest while not relying upon the information provided by their decisions, as well as risks concerning increased discretion in and undue manipulation of consumer policy. Costs, adverse and distributional effects such as consumer dependency and losses to sophisticated consumers and sellers should also be taken into account.

Third, when behavioural policy is developed, implemented and enforced, the negative consequences of this policy should where possible be counteracted. Guidelines for cautious and welfare-enhancing consumer policy include a full market-based assessment of consumer behaviour based on both economic and behavioural insights. Interventions should be efficient and context-specific, accounting for and even taking advantage of consumer biases. Procedures concerning policy decision making should be transparent and rigorous: they should employ a cost-benefit analysis, take insights from stakeholders and experts, and guard against government error, undue discretion and manipulation of consumer policy.

4.5.2. ANSWERING SPECIFIC POLICY QUESTIONS: THE CASE OF CONSUMER STANDARD TERMS

As has been established in this chapter, the possible additions that behavioural insights can make to conventional economic theory should be assessed in specific situations and address specific policy questions. To further assess the extent to which behavioural insights can inform a welfare-enhancing consumer policy, a specific situation will be examined, namely the issue of standardised terms in consumer contracts.

This issue has been argued by behavioural scholars to be an example of a case in which behavioural insights provide better explanations and predictions of consumer behaviour than rational choice.[153] That claim will be assessed in the following chapter, chapter 5. It will be established that behavioural insights, corroborated with empirical data, can indeed be argued to improve policy recommendations on government interventions in consumer standard terms. Therefore, in chapter 6, common policies in European legal systems concerning standard terms in consumer contracts will be discussed, concluding with the claim that the European common core could be improved allowing for behavioural insight to inform consumer protection policy. Chapter 7 then examines several policy strategies that could be followed when aiming to improve current consumer policy concerning standardised terms. The aim of the assessment in chapter 7 is to discuss and provide a rough assessment of different strategies to improve consumer policy concerning standard contract terms, taking the lessons from the analysis in this research into account.

[153] See above, chapter 3, section 3.3.1.

CHAPTER 5

BEHAVIOURALLY ENHANCING POLICY RECOMMENDATIONS – STANDARD TERMS IN CONSUMER CONTRACTS

5.1. INTRODUCTION

In the previous chapters, the rationale for consumer protection from the perspective of mainstream economics has been explained and the insights of behavioural economics towards consumer protection have been introduced. Furthermore, the discussions regarding the methodological issues and normative concerns with the implementation of behavioural insights into policy have been analysed. It has been concluded from these chapters that behavioural insights can provide welcome additions to economic policy recommendations with the aim to enhance social welfare provided that several cautions are taken into account and that these policy recommendation apply only to certain contexts. Which contexts allow for an improvement of consumer policy and policy interventions on the basis of behavioural insights should be assessed by focusing on specific policy questions in specific cases. This chapter will therefore focus on the issue of the desirability of policy interventions in standardised terms in consumer contracts. The welfare-enhancing effects of policy interventions in standard terms in consumer contracts have been extensively discussed in economic literature. This chapter will provide a re-assessment of the discussion on the basis of new insights developed in behavioural literature. The aim of this chapter is to discuss whether the insights from behavioural economics and empirical or experimental research change the (mainstream) economic policy recommendations on standard terms in consumer contracts. Two research questions, which correspond to the overall research questions of this research, will be the focus of this chapter:

1. To what extent is government intervention in standard terms in consumer contracts justified from a social welfare perspective?
2. To what extent can the application of insights from behavioural economics and empirical research into economic analysis improve policy recommendations regarding standard terms in consumer contracts?

To provide an answer to these questions, the policy recommendations regarding standardised consumer contracts based on neoclassical economics, information economics, behavioural insights and empirical literature will be discussed.[154] Neoclassical economics will focus on the market failure of (insufficient) competition to provide the justification and the input for recommendations for interventions in standardised terms in consumer contracts. The neoclassical claim is that as long as competition is uninhibited, consumers are protected from being confronted with onerous terms. A minority group of informed consumers will discipline the market.

Next, the perspective of information economics will be presented, which identifies information asymmetry and adverse selection as the main causes for welfare deterioration. One-sided standard terms which favour sellers over consumers will result in a lower quality than is efficient from a social welfare perspective. Information economics' policy recommendations therefore focus on information duties, while acknowledging that information asymmetry might persist even when information remedies are enacted. Consumer vigilance is however considered to be the most efficient instrument in disciplining the market, as the focus is on improving the conditions for consumers to read standardised contract terms.

The behavioural insights to consumer standard terms focus on the ability of consumers to read and assess terms in consumer contracts. Behavioural notions suggest that this ability might be limited, which would aggravate the information asymmetry problem and make it very difficult for consumers to discipline the market. The reliance upon consumer vigilance to discipline the market to provide efficient standard terms, even if consumer vigilance is aided by information remedies, is therefore ill-advised from a behavioural perspective. Behavioural insights suggest a shift in policy focus, moving away from depending upon information remedies to enhance consumer vigilance.

Fourth, empirical research is examined to clarify the issues that have been brought forward by neoclassical economics, information economics and behavioural notions. Even though the empirical research projects are limited in number, some interesting suggestions follow from their results. Empirics for example suggest that consumers are unlikely to read terms and that information duties are unlikely to improve reading. This observation would undermine the informed minority theory. Terms are, consequently, shown to be one-sided, favouring the seller over the consumer. Furthermore, the data suggest that sellers do not attempt to draw consumers with attractive standard terms, which means that competition with respect to standard terms will be unlikely. Therefore, the instruments of regulation and judicial enforcement are equally unlikely to bar

[154] As has been mentioned in the introduction, section 1.2.3, this research distinguishes between the *neoclassical* or *traditional economic* approach, the *information economic* approach, and the *behavioural economic* approach, even though the boundaries of these approaches (mostly between the first two approaches) are not clearly drawn in literature. This distinction has been made to clearly separate the views in mainstream economics before information issues were deeply considered, the economic views that do consider the impact of information on consumer protection, and the economic views that consider insights from psychology and other social sciences.

onerous terms from contract or improve the quality of terms. In the discussion of the desirability of one-sided terms in consumer contracts, the argument that one-sided terms are in fact desirable from a social welfare perspective is refuted by this research. This chapter will draw two main conclusions. First, when the aim is to enhance the quality of standard terms in consumer contracts from a social welfare perspective, government interventions beyond providing information remedies can be justified, and the reliance on consumer vigilance to discipline the market into providing efficient standardised terms should be limited. Second, as behavioural notions and empirical research provide the foundation for the shift in policy focus away from the reliance on consumer vigilance and information remedies, behavioural notions and empirical research can result in an improvement to classic, mainstream economics' suggestions for policy recommendations.

5.2. NEOCLASSICAL ECONOMICS AND STANDARD TERMS

One issue within consumer protection that has been criticised since it was developed is the standardisation of terms in consumer contracts. With the industrialisation and standardisation of goods came also the standardisation of contracts. Contract law doctrines and policies, depending upon traditional insights towards freedom of contract and legality of contract terms, largely upheld the view that consumers have a duty to read the forms and are bound by them.[155] This sparked a wide-spread discussion about the legality of standardised contract terms. A standard contract may be defined as: "a contract entered into totally or partially according to pre-drawn terms and intended to be applied similarly in a large number of individual cases irrespective of individual differences" (Sheldon, 1974: 17). Usually, standard terms in consumer contracts are drafted by sellers. This offers no guarantee that the interests of consumers are represented in the standard terms. Standardised terms, also referred to as boilerplate or terms of adhesion, are criticised for their lack of actual assent. The users of standard terms were reproached for disallowing freedom of contract to the assenting party, usually the consumer. Neoclassical economics however largely argues in favour of the standardisation of terms. The use of standard terms reduces transaction costs. Neoclassical economics claims that competition between firms and

155 This chapter focuses on the economic, law and economics, and behavioural perspectives towards the issue of standard terms in consumer contracts, and provides empirical suggestions which support, or refute, these perspectives. Chapter 6 will review the legal perspective will be portrayed and featuring a more detailed discussion of actual contract law policies and doctrines concerning consumer standard terms, which are commonly shared among European legislative systems. The introduction that follows here does touch upon the legal context, but only for the purpose of setting the stage for the economic discussion. The legal perspective will follow in the next chapter.

reputation will ensure that efficient terms, meaning terms that maximise the benefit of seller and buyer combined, will be offered in the market. Neoclassical economics assumes that a small group of informed consumers will drive the market mechanism. Some critique towards the abilities of this marginal group of informed consumers to discipline the market is occasionally granted; however from the viewpoint of neoclassical economics, the standardisation of consumer contracts is a most welcome development in the market.

5.2.1. THE SETTING: FREEDOM OF CONTRACT VERSUS STANDARDISATION

Issues such as unequal bargaining power, the take-it-or-leave-it nature of standard terms, the practice of signing-without-reading and the fact that standardisation of contracts result in the application of similar terms to nearly all contracts concluded within business sectors have given rise to scepticism regarding the fairness of standard terms. Llewellyn, Kessler and Slawson were among the first to argue that standardisation of contracts between strong and weak parties can result in the strong party dictating the terms of the contract (Llewellyn, 1939; Kessler, 1943; Slawson, 1971). These scholars criticised standard term contracts on the basic premise that if no voluntary agreement had been reached, which as they argued is the case with standard terms, these contracts give rise to serious concerns.

Llewellyn made a distinction between clauses that serve the better functioning of the transaction as a whole and clauses that serve the sole interest of the drafting party. Arguing that it might not be so easy for judges to make that distinction, he adds it is important to realise that free contract presupposes free bargain. Where free bargaining is absent, he argues that the conditions and clauses that should be read in the contract should not be those which happen to be printed on the unread paper, but should be those which a sane man might reasonably expect to find on that paper (Llewellyn, 1939: 704). The freedom of contract principle, which should ensure that everyone can construe contracts in any way they please (why else would they enter into the contract?), no longer holds only positive connotations. The freedom of contract stands to become a "one-sided privilege" (Kessler, 1943: 640). As Kessler details, the freedom of contract principle is desirable not only for moral reasons; it also has a very pragmatic component. Contract law cannot provide for every contingency and arrangement that might be preferred by the contract parties. Parties therefore should be free to decide on the terms that govern their own contract. People themselves know most about their own preferences and are therefore in the best position to decide which contract terms would correspond best to their own preferences. Freedom of contract enables parties to make contracts as they see fit to enhance their own welfare in the best way possible. Standardisation of contracts then creates difficulties if it no longer corresponds to the wishes of the parties.

The standardisation of contract terms brings clear benefits to both contract parties, mostly by decreasing transaction costs like drafting and negotiation costs. However, if the weaker party to the contract is not able to change the content of the contract due to the 'take-it-or-leave-it' nature of the terms, and shopping for terms is not of much use either since all firms offer the same terms, consent of the weaker party to these contract terms can no longer be assumed. This leads to a de facto monopoly over contract terms by the industry, which is not necessarily welfare enhancing.[156] Slawson developed the idea that when standard terms govern a transaction between a consumer and a commercial party, these terms cannot be viewed as a legitimate contract, as they do not reflect the agreement of the consumer (Slawson, 1971).[157]

5.2.2. ECONOMIC DEFENCE OF STANDARD TERMS

These first critical notes on the terms in standardised consumer contracts focused on the fact that consumers cannot change the terms of the contract, and that they were bound by the contract even if they had never read the terms or actively assented to them. The issue of whether or not consumers were able to understand and assess standard contract terms was not yet considered very important. Indeed, it was argued that these instruments, even when the negative side-effects are taken into account, still promote the welfare of society as a whole. Neoclassical economics found that benefits resulting from a reduction in transaction costs will be awarded to both parties, not in the least to the consumer, as the seller would be argued to be constrained by competition from the setting abusive terms and prices.

According to neoclassical economic insight, the issues with standard terms that have been pointed out above do not pose serious challenges to contract terms being welfare enhancing. Through the use of standard terms transaction costs can be reduced, and consumers are shielded from onerous terms through sellers competing for business. Negotiating for terms is likely to be impossible, yet

156 Kessler (1943: 640): "Society, when granting freedom of contract, does not guarantee that all members of the community will be able to make use of it to the same extent. On the contrary, the law, by protection the unequal distribution of property, does nothing to prevent freedom of contract from becoming a one-sided privilege. Society, by proclaiming freedom of contract, guarantees that it will not interfere with the exercise of power by contract. ... Standard contracts in particular could thus become effective instruments in the hands of powerful industrial and commercial overlords enabling them to impose a new feudal order...".

157 One possible response to the issue of legitimacy of standard terms in consumer contracts is provided by Barnett (2002). He argues that the agreement to standard terms should be seen as a manifestation of an intention to be legally bound. Therefore, standard term contracts can be seen as perfectly legitimate, even though some judicial scrutiny might be required regarding overly one-sided terms.

neoclassical economics argues that it is also unnecessary in order for consumers to receive better terms. Instead of negotiating, consumers could shop for better terms, the neoclassical theory claims.[158]

a. Reduction in transaction costs

All scholars, from economists and from other relevant disciplines alike, agree that standard terms have resulted from cost considerations.[159] The use of standard terms has resulted in a considerable decrease in contracting costs. This refers not only to the costs of negotiations, but also to the costs of drafting the contract (Hatzis, 2008: 3). Furthermore, standard terms reduce costs associated with the principle-agent problem. This refers to the fact that sellers would not like their agent, the employee that actually concludes the deal, to decide on contract terms themselves at the expense of the seller (Posner, 2003: 115).

Saving on transaction costs should reduce prices, which also stands to benefit consumers greatly. Contract terms allocate risks between seller and consumer. Within a certain business sector, the most efficient risk allocation is likely to be similar in all contracts between sellers and consumers. Consequently, standardised contracts in a business sector are not necessarily a sign of abuse. Lastly, the duty to read is efficient, as it stimulates consumers to read the contract, to thereby make sure the transaction they are about to conclude is welfare enhancing.

b. Competition drives efficient contracts

Competition between companies with respect to their standard terms should ensure a 'fair' (welfare-enhancing or efficient) contract for all consumers. The issue of what constitutes an 'efficient contract' is worthy of a more detailed examination. According to the Coase theorem, transactions between parties that willingly agreed to the contract are thought to be necessarily welfare enhancing, since the negotiations ensure the presence of benefits for both parties.[160] Negotiations about the terms of the contract should allow both parties to make sure that the contract terms correspond to their preferences. Efficient contract clauses are clauses that allocate risks efficiently, which implies that risks should be allocated to the party that is better able to bear that risk, has the best ability to insure against that risk, or that is the most efficient in preventing the fulfilment of the risk.[161] An inefficient

158 See for overviews of the neoclassical position on standard terms in consumer contracts among others: Meyerson (1990) and Katz (1998).

159 One of the first scholars to draw attention to this feature was Llewellyn (1939: 701).

160 See above, chapter 2, section 2.2.1c; external effects could of course render the contract inefficient.

161 This is referred to as the 'cheapest cost avoider principle'. See for a discussion: Schäfer and Leyens (2009: 102–3).

contract clause would create higher costs for one party than the corresponding benefits to the other party (Ben-Shahar and Pottow, 2006: 217).

Economic theory argues that consumer contracts will be efficient in the market even when the majority of consumers does not read standard terms. The invisible hand of competitive market forces will be assumed to drive an information flow about better terms. As competing firms will need to attract as many consumers as they can, they cannot afford to lose even those few consumers that do inform themselves of the contents of the contract (Schwartz and Wilde, 1979). As profit-maximising sellers do not want to lose consumers, they will adapt their standard forms to correspond to the preferences of the majority of their customers, economic theory claims. Competition therefore drives sellers to draft terms that correspond to the preferences of consumers (Priest, 1981). This drive to efficient drafting of contract terms requires a "margin of informed, sophisticated, and aggressive consumers" who discipline the market by negotiations or by shopping for better terms (Schwartz and Wilde, 1979). The other consumers can free ride off the efforts of the informed few, unless the informed consumers are positively discriminated and given a preferential treatment (Trebilcock, 1993: 120). When sellers are able to sort out which consumers are informed and provide them (and only them) with better terms, these few informed consumers could be prevented from disciplining the market.

c. *Shopping for terms renders negotiating irrelevant*

As has been mentioned above, the question of whether or not consumers are able to negotiate for better terms is considered to be irrelevant in traditional economic theory. According to this view, consumers do not need to negotiate terms; they can simply shop around until they find the contract terms that best suit their preferences. If enough consumers shop for terms, economic theory assumes that businesses are likely to compete on terms. This marginal group of savvy consumers can discipline the market (Schwartz and Wilde, 1979: 647–50). Only a small group of readers and shoppers is required to discipline the market to the point that sellers hunting for the marginal consumer will adopt efficient terms (Schwartz and Wilde, 1983). The necessary volume of this group is also indicated in literature; the percentage of 30% is mentioned by Schwartz and Wilde, and confirmed by Goldman in a study (Schwartz and Wilde, 1979: 659–62; Goldman, 1992: 719). To enhance the ability of the savvy consumers to accomplish this task, their costs in becoming informed should be reduced as much as possible. Therefore, standard contracts should be made easily available, and written in simple, short, plain language. The ability of a marginal group of consumers to become informed and to discipline the market does depend on enough consumers being "term conscious", a term that refers to whether or not consumers are fully able to interpret the consequences of terms, as is mentioned by (Schwartz and Wilde, 1979: 650).[162]

d. *Standardisation does not equal abuse*

As standardisation lowers per unit costs of contracting, standardised contracts will be used both in competitive and monopoly markets. They are not necessarily a consequence of market power. Costs will be lower if terms are standardised. If terms are standard and the terms do not contain vague concepts or misrepresentations, the market is quite likely competitive (Schwartz and Wilde, 1979: 656). Standard terms allocate risks between consumers and businesses. A firm offers a bundle of rights in the contract, at a corresponding price.[163] For the allocation to be efficient, some risks should be dealt to the seller, some to the consumer. This depends on which party is better able to prevent the fulfilment of the risk, which party is best able to reduce the costs resulting from that fulfilment, or which party is best able to bear the risk or insure him or herself against the risk. The 'best' allocations of risks, corresponding to the preferences of consumers and business, are unlikely to vary between businesses. Standard forms used by different firms allocating these risks will therefore be comparable (Priest, 1981: 1300). In one sector, the allocation of risks and rights in a certain way would not differ from one company to another. Therefore uniformity in terms might be expected in highly competitive markets (Schwartz and Wilde, 1983: 1389–91). Standardisation is not a clear sign of unfairness of the standard terms; a situation of full information and allocation of risks that corresponds to consumer and business preferences and therefore is welfare enhancing could also result in similar standard terms throughout the business sector. If terms are alike in a business sector, this would promote competition over the other product attributes such as price, to the benefit of the consumer (Cooter and Ulen, 2003: 288–9).

e. *Duty to read stimulates reading*

The last aspect of standardised contracts that is often regarded with some suspicion is the fact that consumers are bound to a contract even if they have never read it; they are bound simply by entering into the contract. It is a legal principle that contract rules hold.[164] The consumer therefore has a duty to read the contract before entering into it. After assenting to the transaction itself, the assent also covers all the terms in the contract.[165] Economic discussions focus on

---

[162] This remark could be seen as a first hint at the behavioural discussion that follows in the next section.

[163] See more generally on this issue: Hatzis (2008: 4–5).

[164] In chapter 6, the common doctrines and policies regarding the legal evaluation of standard terms in consumer contracts will be discussed in more detail.

[165] This is described as "blanket assent", a term ascribed to Llewellyn (1960: 370–1).

the responsibilities of each contract party to assure that the contract is welfare enhancing and therefore recommend the duty to read. A 'duty to read' clause is said to support the responsibility of parties to a contract for their own decisions, thereby counteracting consumer moral hazard problems (Rakoff, 1983: 1187). Consumers themselves are in the best position to maximise their own welfare, economic theory reminds us. The doctrine promotes stability and reliance on contracts, even if the contract turns out to be less beneficial than was estimated by one of the parties before. 'Duty to read' as well as the general economic approach focuses on the ex ante perspective more than the situation ex post. Consumers' best defence is their own vigilance (Schwartz and Wilde, 1983: 1414–5). This would result not only in consumers avoiding onerous terms in their own benefit, but also in the aggregate push to businesses to adopt more benevolent terms, neoclassical economics argues.

5.2.3. CONCLUSION: DESIRABLE GOVERNMENT INTERVENTIONS BY NEOCLASSICAL ECONOMICS

From the perspective of neoclassical economics, the use of standard terms is largely efficient and beneficial for social welfare. As a consequence of the above reasoning, neoclassical economics sees a limited role for government intervention in standard terms in consumer contracts. Schwartz and Wilde argue that intervention by government is ill-advised when the market is competitive. The market will provide the optimal standard terms and the optimal amount of information when it is competitive. Government intervention is likely to increase costs, even when some decreases in search costs for comparison shoppers are achieved. Standard terms should be enforced as contracts, as they decrease transaction costs and are likely to be competitive (Schwartz and Wilde, 1979: 667–72). Issues like unequal bargaining power, the 'take-it-or-leave-it' nature of contracts, the 'duty to read' obligation placed on the accepting party and firms offering the same standard terms throughout the industry are not problematic from a neoclassical law and economics perspective.

When markets are not competitive, some government intervention could be justified.[166] Even in such cases the benefit of those interventions is criticised, however. Baird claims there is not much reason to worry about sellers abusing consumers through standard terms, as there is not much to be gained for them (Baird, 2006: 937). When sellers want to make profit, a focus on product quality, service and other product elements would yield a higher benefit than an attempt to create a profit through abusing consumers via standard terms. Neoclassical theory points out that sellers have limited time and effort to devote to the development

[166] See above, chapter 2, section 2.2.2 for a discussion of market failures and how they lead to a decrease in social welfare.

of profitable strategies, and that they will therefore focus on improving their product and service instead of abusing consumers via standard terms. Schwartz and Wilde do however suggest that government interventions could consist of a standardisation of how terms should be communicated, so that they can be more easily compared (Schwartz and Wilde, 1979: 677). As argued above, imperfect competition in a market could lead to one-sided terms being drafted by sellers. As to the policing of courts over standard terms, courts should identify a market failure before striking down with a standard term (Schwartz and Wilde, 1983: 1458). Therefore, in markets with imperfect competition, some judicial review over the terms could be exercised to make sure they are not overly one-sided, which would result in welfare losses instead of welfare gains.

Deciding which terms, whether they are bargained for or not, deserve to be reviewed in light of their one-sidedness, is a difficult task (Kornhauser, 1976: 1164). Neoclassical theory also remarks that judicial interventions could wipe those legal terms that are deemed unreasonably onerous from the contract and add certain other rules. Again, interventions in legitimate contracts should not be taken on lightly. As mentioned above, by drafting the contract, the seller allocates risks between him and his transaction partner. This allocation of risks is argued by neoclassical economics to be more efficiently conducted by businesses than by courts or other institutions, as businesses are under the influence of consumer opinion through competition and reputation (Rakoff, 1983: 1204). Neoclassical economics therefore stresses that intervention in contract terms should be exercised with caution and should only be enacted when deemed absolutely necessary to improve social welfare, and only in cases of imperfect competition.

5.3. INFORMATION ECONOMICS AND STANDARD TERM CONTRACTS

Where the neoclassical economic reasoning would argue in favour of the use of standard terms, information economics brought a different view on the benefits in transaction costs and the countervailing forces of competition against abuse. The issue of information asymmetry and the resulting problem of adverse selection in contract terms, which decreases the quality of the terms offered to consumers, is an essential insight brought forward by information economics. Due to rational apathy, consumers will sign contracts without reading them. This will lead to an adverse selection problem, resulting in low quality one-sided terms which favour sellers over consumers. This calls for an intervention in the market. As the lack of information underlies this particular market failure, the most obvious remedy would call for the provision of information. Another intervention that information economics might suggest to counteract this market failure is changing the default rules. To a limited extent an intervention in the content of contracts might also be justified, but only if all other interventions fail to reach an efficient market outcome. The interplay between government intervention and the competitive cures of competition and regulation must continuously be taken into account.

5.3.1. INFORMATION: A DIFFERENT FOCUS ON STANDARD TERMS AND MARKET FAILURES

On the basis of information economics, competition and market structure can no longer be regarded as the only potential source of decreasing welfare regarding consumer standard terms.[167] Providing efficient default rules can reduce transaction costs and thereby increase social welfare. Furthermore, the presence of information asymmetry in the context of standardised consumer contracts seems obvious. Consumers fail to read contracts, as it is rational for them not to do so. The resulting asymmetry of information will lead to adverse selection, also known as the lemons problem: sellers are able to draft one-sided terms in their contracts which favour the drafter. This information asymmetry is therefore now seen as the main market flaw leading to a decrease in social welfare.[168]

a. *Competition failure is not the main issue*

Information economics find the main cause of inefficient terms not in market structure or competition issues but in the information problem resulting from signing-without-reading, (De Geest, 2002: 222). Even when a monopoly would exist, the monopolist has an incentive to offer efficient quality levels and depress the quantity of production (Katz, 1998). A monopolist would make the largest profit by making the quality of his product as attractive as possible to the greatest possible number of consumers.[169] This quality of the product has many aspects, such as service quality, an easy-to-reach selling location and the quality of the

[167] On market failures related to information issues in consumer standard terms, see for instance: Schwartz and Wilde (1979: 659–62), Meyerson (1990), Eisenberg (1995: 240–8), Katz (1998), Hillman and Rachlinski (2002: 445–54), Schäfer and Ott (2004: 370–3), Wilhelmsson (2006) and Gillette (2009). For an overview of rationales for intervening into unfair terms in consumer contracts, see Ramsay (2007: 158–65). See also Van Wijck and Theeuwes (2000) for an overview of the welfare implications of consumer protection against unfair contracts and the different market failures addressed by interventions in the market. Furthermore, see Armstrong (2008: esp. 119–125) on the interaction between competition and consumer policy related to standard terms.

[168] Other market failures, such as an externality problem or imperfect competition due to a small number of suppliers, could of course also exist within the markets that employ consumer standard term contracts. These market failures are however not thought to be directly linked to the standardisation of contract terms, as they could occur within any contract and any market regardless of whether these market use standardised consumer contracts. These market failures will thus largely fall outside the scope of this analysis, which focuses on welfare problems due to standardisation of consumer contract terms.

[169] This statement only holds under certain assumptions such as homogeneous demand, which implies that all consumers desire a similar good. See above, chapter 2, section 2.2.2.

contractual terms. The instrument that monopolists use to increase their profit is not decreasing quality below efficient levels, but offering fewer products on the market than demand would require. Offering fewer products increases the price of goods, which enables monopolists to extract an extra profit. It is in the interest of monopolists to offer the quality that consumers demand in their product. By attracting as many consumers as possible through offering a desired quality in product, service and contract terms, monopolists can increase demand for the entire package, and thereby the price. Higher prices can boost profit levels even more.

The main reason for concern regarding standard terms in consumer contracts, which used to be argued to be sellers' economic power position vis-à-vis consumers, is nowadays quite commonly thought to be the lack of information on the part of consumers.[170] Besides curing the market failure of information asymmetry, social welfare could also be improved by reducing transaction costs.

b. Default rules reduce transaction costs

One of the discussions fuelled by the focus on information is the discussion about transaction costs, especially contracting costs and search costs. Contracting costs can be decreased by providing default rules for parties to use. Through the provision of default rules, contracting parties no longer have to draft contract terms themselves. Also, consumer search costs can be reduced by making sure default terms are easily available, intelligible, free from overly complicated terminology, et cetera. Lengthy negotiations can be avoided because parties can just refer to the default rules. Or, in cases where the default rules that have been suggested do not conform entirely to the parties' wishes, parties can contract around the default terms. The default rules can be a starting point for negotiations, thereby even reducing contracting costs even when they are not adhered to in the final contract. The minor issues being settled by default rules, parties can focus their negotiations on the issues that are really important to them. Default rules should thus be provided to contracting parties to reduce transaction costs. The reduction in transaction costs that is thus accomplished results in benefits to social welfare.

c. Information asymmetry: signing-without-reading and adverse selection

Information economics applied Akerlof's lemons problem to the perceived one-sidedness of standard terms in consumer contracts. This insight turned out to have great implications. As has been explained above, asymmetric information between the parties to a contract can not only lead to deterioration in the quality

170 See for instance Grundmann (2002: 275) and Van Boom and Kottenhagen (2006: 136) who all claim that this statement is essentially undisputed nowadays.

of the product itself, but also in the quality of the underlying contract terms.[171] Asymmetric information is clearly an issue in the subject of contract terms, as consumers fail to read these terms. Consumers will be subject to rational ignorance or rational apathy: it is not in their best interest to carefully read the terms as it is just too costly. As a result, sellers are able to draft one-sided contract terms which favour the seller. Price competition forces the (unobserved) quality of terms even further down, which will not be observed by consumers because they are not reading the terms. The resulting adverse selection is the most likely market failure which to occur in the context of standard terms in consumer contracts.

Consumer rational apathy: signing without reading

The asymmetry of information regarding standard terms in consumer contracts is a consequence of the limited benefit that consumers stand to gain when they inform themselves about the contents of the contract they are about to sign.[172] Reading standard terms is costly in time and effort, it is boring, and there is little to be gained by these costs. Standard terms are usually printed in small font sizes and the clauses are drafted in long sentences, which are difficult and taxing to read. The form will be long and full of 'legalese', while the consumer in a typical day-to-day consumer transaction is in a hurry. Consumers skim rather than carefully read these documents, if they give them any attention at all. Contracts must be precise, in order for them to be understood and explained by courts in the way that the sellers have meant them to be. Therefore, contracts are written in specific legal language that lay people will find hard to understand. For instance, important information might be buried in certain definitions that lawyers recognise as important but lay people may not. A consumer is confronted with different sets of contract terms, and does not have specific knowledge about any of these forms. Sellers on the other hand are the more sophisticated parties because they frequently engage in contracts governed by the same standard terms. Consumers may not even know what kind of information they should be looking for because they lack background knowledge. This again increases the difficulty of getting the relevant information out of the contract. Precise contracts do contain the information that is relevant for a consumer, but those relevant items might be buried in the long and complicated form and difficult to extract for the lay consumer.

Apart from the high costs of reading the standard terms, the consumer stands little to gain from this taxing activity. The terms of a contract cannot (easily) be changed, as the agent with whom the consumer is currently negotiating is unlikely

171 See chapter 2, section 2.2.2e.

172 See for a comprehensive discussion on consumer rational apathy regarding standard terms: Sovern (2006: 1671–72). See also Meyerson (1990: 596–600) and Hillman and Rachlinski (2002: 435–37).

to have a mandate for changing the terms of the contract. Even when standard terms are read, the tremendous amount of information prevents the consumer from thoroughly analysing all terms, let alone comparing all terms in different contracts. Shopping for better terms would imply incurring even more reading costs, since different sets of standard terms would need to be compared. Also, as terms are likely to be standardised throughout an industry, it is unlikely that a competitor's contract will contain significantly better and less one-sided terms. In addition, the terms in the contracts will specify contingencies with small and remote risks, so the benefit of changing these term will be (seen as) relatively low. Furthermore, the reputation of the firm itself and the law or legal institutions will be seen as providing a safeguard against overly onerous terms anyway. In other words, consumers are suffering from *rational apathy* (also referred to as rational ignorance): they rationally choose not to incur the costs of reading standard terms as the costs outweigh the gains of doing so. This however leads to information asymmetry, resulting in adverse selection with respect to standard terms.

Adverse selection: one-sided standard terms

'Signing-without-reading' leads to a typical case of information asymmetry (De Geest, 2002).[173] Standard terms in consumer contracts will be known by the professional party, but are unlikely to be known by the consumer. Contract standard terms deal with many issues, such as the allocation of the risks for certain contingencies, complaint procedures, warranty terms, et cetera. If buyers would be informed of which terms they would prefer in the contract, sellers would be forced to draft (more) efficient contract clauses corresponding to the wishes of the consumer. But this is not the case as consumer do not know which risks they would like to take upon themselves, which contingencies they would like to see settled and which risks they would prefer the sellers to take on at a given price, which is all predetermined in contract terms. Buyers are rationally ignorant. As a consequence, the market mechanism suffers from an adverse selection problem, due to information asymmetry. Consumers are unaware of the content of the contract. They are (at least to some extent) aware of certain other salient product features, such as price, colour, warranty period, convenience and so on. Some contract terms might be taken into account: terms that allocate high risk contingencies or are in other ways important to consumers. The majority of terms will however go unnoticed, as if the terms were invisible (Rakoff, 1983: 1251).

As consumers do take product aspects such as price into account, but cannot fully assess the quality of certain other product aspects such as contract terms, consumers will opt for lower prices while making a gross estimation of the contract

[173] The adverse selection problem in standard terms has been described by several scholars. See for instance: Goldberg (1974), Rakoff (1983), Korobkin (1998; 2003), Ben-Shahar (2006), Becher (2008) and Schäfer and Leyens (2009).

quality. It is not beneficial for consumers to check for inefficient clauses when these clauses only come into effect in relatively unlikely events, even if he suspects he is being exploited. Because firms deal with many consumers however, the profits that they obtain from such exploitation could be significant (Armstrong, 2008: 120–1). A demand for lower prices drives down the unobserved quality of contract terms. Offering high quality terms, which give privileges to consumers over sellers, is more costly to sellers. As the high quality terms go unnoticed, offering high quality terms is not a business strategy that attracts consumers. Sellers have no incentive to attempt to lure consumers by offering a better deal in the hidden terms. Because of competition and the market mechanism, the quality of terms in consumer contracts is driven down. Schäfer and Leyens refer to this situation as a "flea market", in which consumers are offered low prices, but can only conclude transactions in which they get allocated only a minimum of rights vis-à-vis the seller (Schäfer and Leyens, 2009: 107). Both consumers and sellers are trapped in the flea market: even if they are aware of this situation and would prefer to see it changed, they are unlikely to be able to establish a higher quality of terms in consumer contracts. Information asymmetry creates an adverse selection problem respect to standard terms in consumer contracts.

To illustrate, a standard term could for example specify that in case of damage resulting from the delivery of a household appliance to the house of a customer, the store should be notified in writing within three days.[174] The majority of consumers, when actually considering this term, could prefer to have this term extended to seven days, even if that would imply incurring a small cost for the extension of the time span. However, since this term will not be read nor be salient to consumers, the seller is able to draft a term with a short time span for notification. Prolonging this time span could result in more notifications of damage made to the seller, and therefore would likely be more costly to the seller. Providing a short time span for notification is less costly to the seller, enabling the seller to charge a lower price for the good. Competition between sellers for the favour of the consumer only affects those product attributes that are noticed by the consumer, but contract terms can be seen as product attributes too. As the price is a likely to be noticed by the consumer, competition between sellers induces them to set the price at a competitive level. A standard term regarding notification duties in case of damages caused by the delivery service will simply be provided low-cost and low quality, as the consumer will not be aware of this term anyway. As the consumer will not be more likely to buy this product or service when the notification duty is set more to her benefit, and sellers do incur costs from being more lenient in their terms, there is no gain for the seller in drafting the notification duty term more favourably to the consumer. This implies that the

174 Example taken from the Media Markt standard terms (term 8.15; www.mediamarkt.nl, consulted January 5, 2006; this particular standard term is currently no longer part of the Media Markt standard terms, consulted November 6, 2009).

notification term will be one-sided and low quality in the sense that it favours the seller and not the consumer. This constitutes an adverse selection problem.

Other standard terms in consumer contracts that could be interpreted to be of low quality are for instance disclaimers of implied warranties, limitations of certain damage types, or terms that specify the choice of law or choice of forum and caps on damages. A term allocating the right to collect and disseminate a consumer's personal information to a seller can also be seen as a low quality term, as well as restrictions on the manner in which a consumer may bring future legal grievances against a seller or producer. Other low quality terms could specify a long notification period in order to cancel contracts or specify a rather cumbersome procedure that has to be followed in order to cancel a contract, for instance sending a registered letter three months before the automatic renewal date of the contract.[175]

Market failure and welfare loss

One-sided terms, even though they are low in quality, do not necessarily decrease welfare. Consumers could have a preference for low quality terms, since products can then be offered at low cost. A price deduction could be passed on to consumers. In negotiations, contract terms could be stipulated in which the consumer agrees to take on certain risks for a price premium (Van den Bergh, 1998: 135). However, there is no guarantee that one-sided terms will coincide with the preferences of the consumer. As consumers are more likely to be risk averse than firms are, the fact that a consumer is taking on risks instead of a firm is likely to be inefficient. Whether one-sided standard terms will generally be welfare enhancing should be severely doubted (Gazal-Ayal, 1999; Korobkin, 2003). Which level of quality in contract terms is efficient depends on the preferences of consumers. These might however be hard to establish, precisely because the typical consumer is unaware of contract terms. Interventions in the market to correct for the market failure of adverse selection should accommodate for this ambiguity.[176] On the whole however, the market failure of information asymmetry indicates that society would gain from improvements in the level of quality in standard terms in consumer contracts. As adverse selection depresses quality in the market, the market is likely to produce sub-optimal levels of quality in standard terms in consumer contracts. In theory, a total market failure of information asymmetry would result in a collapse of the market. This is however not to be expected in the market for standard terms (Schäfer and Leyens, 2009: 108). Consumers will not

175 As will be discussed below in section 5.5.3a, some of these examples of low quality standard terms have been studied in empirical research and are in these studies shown to be drafted in consumer contracts regularly. It is important to note however, as is discussed in section 5.5.4a, low quality terms are not necessarily a sign of abuse.

176 The issue of the efficiency of one-sided, low quality terms will be discussed below, section 5.5.4.

refrain from entering into contracts. Transactions will continue to be concluded, however they will be governed by terms that favour the seller over the consumer.

One-sided terms are cheap to provide for the drafter, but are not necessarily welfare enhancing. Businesses have an incentive to draft terms according to their interest, or might even be forced to draft one-sided terms by competitive forces even if they would see potential benefits to mutually beneficial terms (Rakoff, 1983: 1204). Adverse selection resulting from information asymmetry thus leads to a decrease in social welfare and therefore constitutes a market failure. This market failure is to be found in the loss associated with a certain level of quality in standard terms not being offered in the market, even though consumers would have bargained and paid for this higher level of quality in terms if transaction costs and information asymmetries would not have prevented them from doing so. Even though the quantity of profit that is gained by the seller from this exploitation of standard terms in consumer contracts will not be tremendous, it can still be considerable (Armstrong, 2008: 121).

It is frequently argued that intervention in standard terms on behalf of consumers is uncalled for, as consumers willingly accept the allegedly undesirable terms in the contract (Field, 2008: 99). However, when consumers and sellers know they are trapped in a flea market, such a contract might indeed be entered into willingly, yet at the same time be welfare decreasing and justify government intervention. The mere fact that consumers and sellers are aware that low levels of quality in standard terms will be offered does not imply that government should not intervene on behalf of consumers. Neither consumers nor sellers are able to accomplish a higher quality of terms in the market due to the market failure of adverse selection, which as has been explained above is very likely to be present. The fact that consumers and sellers are aware of this market failure does not necessarily mean that they are in a position to bring about a higher level of quality in standard consumer terms.

5.3.2. MARKET CORRECTIONS OF INFORMATION ASYMMETRY IN STANDARD TERMS

It has now been established that an important market failure (adverse selection) is likely to occur with regard to standard terms in consumer contracts. Before however government interventions in consumer standard contracts can be justified from a social welfare perspective, several issues should be taken into account. One issue is the existence of market corrections that might counteract the market failure of information asymmetry, such as reputation and unravelling of information. Also, it could be argued that informed minority will discipline the market. However, as the discussion below will illustrate, market corrections are unlikely to sufficiently improve the quality of standard terms in consumer contracts.

a. Reputation and consumer learning

The reputation of firms is an important instrument in disciplining markets and market parties and to counteract detrimental effects of market failures. It might also induce sellers to draft higher quality terms in standardised consumer contracts. Accordingly, some scholars in the law and economics literature campaign for a return to a market-based approach to consumer contracts even when consumers are uninformed of the content of standard terms (Gilo and Porat, 2009). They argue that when markets are sufficiently competitive, standard terms in consumer contracts can be assumed to be efficient and fair as a result of reputation and competition. Courts do not have to be concerned with assessing the 'fairness' of standard terms. They claim that reputation and competition will either lead to efficient and fair contracts, or at protect consumers from detrimental terms being enforced against them.[177]

The effectiveness of reputation as a mechanism to induce less one-sided terms should however be questioned, especially in consumer markets. The effectiveness of repeated purchases, learning effects and the reputation of sellers to stimulate high quality terms in consumer contracts is assessed critically (Bar-Gill, 2008: 755–6; Harel and Procaccia, 2009; Schäfer and Leyens, 2009: 109–10). Consumers are likely to enter into contracts less frequently than sellers, and not to have a great amount of information at their disposal about the reputation of the sellers that are operating in the market.[178] Even when consumers frequently enter into the same contracts, they might not assess the standard terms even once. Only a small number of consumers will actually be confronted with the specific contingencies that are dealt with in typical standard term clauses. To the extent that reputation can be argued to be effective, it will only be effective in contract terms which allocate high risk contingencies and terms that consumers actually assess in their decision making process. These terms are unlikely to be many.

Interpersonal learning among consumers with respect to standard terms is not likely to be sufficiently effective either. Standardised products can usually be argued to reach efficient quality due to information sharing, because standardised products can be tested and used by everyone (Epstein, 2006). This argument however does not necessarily apply to standard terms, because they might not be scrutinised by a sufficiently large group of consumers, as has been explained above. Although consumers might seek expert advice in cases that involve big and important decisions, they will be unlikely to do so when deciding whether or not to accept the standard terms. It is too costly, considering the (relatively low)

---

177 See also: Johnston (2006) and Bebchuk and Posner (2006). This argument will be further explored below, section 5.5.4.

178 See Macaulay (1963) on the relational theory of contracts, which points to the observation in sociology that business conflicts are hardly ever resolved in court, as the relationship between businesses requires that partners search for a non-legal out-of-court solution. Whether reputation and business relationships have the same effect in consumer contracts is doubtful.

benefit that could be obtained through the use of the information intermediary in this case. Learning effects therefore are unlikely to develop sufficiently in the market.

The reputation of sellers is more dependent on the product itself than on the contingencies that are provided for in the standard terms. If the quality of the terms is not well known to consumers and information does not flow from one consumer to the other, reputation might be affected by the quality of the standard terms only to a very limited degree. It might be more beneficial for the firm to exploit the ignorant consumers or offer different terms to the savvy consumers (Rakoff, 1983: 1225; Schwartz and Wilde, 1983: 1450). Sellers can waive a specific term if a consumer complains (Ibrahim, 2005). This saves reputation, but does not allow all consumers to benefit from a less one-sided contract.[179] Only the consumers that complain obtain these benefits. This is problematic as not all consumers would take the trouble of complaining if they expect the firm to invoke the one-sided term against them. Also, consumer standard terms often allocate remote risks. Consumers might not learn of businesses invoking these terms against their customers, and these terms then have little or no effect on the reputation of the firm. Lastly, businesses might also be managed by short-run players who are not concerned with reputation. The reputation mechanism, even though it does guide behaviour to some extent, will not be sufficient to overcome the market failure of information asymmetry.

b. Unravelling, signalling and screening

When sellers offer terms that are more benevolent towards consumers than those that are offered by their competitors, sellers have an incentive to make this information known to consumers. The information will thus become unravelled. However, it is doubtful whether the possibility to unravel information regarding the quality of standard terms will be effective and thus used by sellers. The information that is provided will still need to be assessed according to the specific situation and preferences of the respective consumer. As consumers suffer from rational apathy, they might choose not to take the information into account (Meyerson, 1990: 600–3). As consumers consciously choose not to include the information in their decision making process, they are unlikely to screen businesses for information about standard terms. If consumers do not assess this information, sellers have no incentive of providing information about high-quality terms, nor an incentive to offer these higher quality terms.

Standard terms can be regarded as having many characteristics of a credence good: even when the good is bought, or the standard terms accepted, the quality of these terms is very difficult, bordering on impossible, for individuals consumers

179 See Trebilcock and Dewees (1981: 106–13) for a discussion on sellers discriminating between informed and non-informed consumers.

to ascertain (Meyerson, 1990: 598). When information about quality is too costly or too difficult for consumers to interpret, sellers could also provide some sort of signal of quality. However, whether this device can be expected to sufficiently counteract the market failure of information asymmetry with respect to standard terms in consumer contracts is questionable, as a reliable signal of quality cannot be maintained (Schäfer and Leyens, 2009: 108–9).[180]

Reputation, learning effects, unravelling of information, screening for high-quality terms and signalling of terms are therefore unlikely to be sufficiently effective in stimulating the market to provide higher quality standard terms and overcome the welfare loss described above. This negative assessment might not be valid for all standard terms; for the majority of terms however, the terms that are subordinate, that are not considered to be of high importance to consumers or that involve unlikely contingencies, the effectiveness of market corrections can be argued to be limited.

c. *The abilities of the marginally informed group to discipline the market*

As has been argued above, in neoclassical economics the claim is presented that a small group of informed consumers is able to discipline the market into providing the terms that consumers have a preference for.[181] Several scholars however doubt the disciplining power of this marginal group of consumers. They claim that protection from inefficient contract terms through an informed minority group will not be effective with respect to the majority of standard terms. It is argued that competition with respect to price cannot be understood in the same way as competition with respect to standard terms, because in the latter consumer preferences are more likely to be heterogeneous, consumer costs with respect to these terms might differ, and evaluation of the terms is more costly (Schwartz and Wilde, 1983). The aggressive consumer, searching for a bargain, is a minor player in the market and unlikely to have a lot of influence (Goldberg, 1974: 485). Searching for, reading, understanding and comparing standard terms is too costly; a competitive market for standard terms requires more consumers than there will be to drive the market for efficient terms (Meyerson, 1990: 601; Harel and Procaccia, 2009: 24–26).

A second possibility is shopping for terms, and thereby disciplining the market, which grants a positive external effect to other consumers. From the perspective of one consumer, it would be best if all the other consumers undertake the costs of reading, shopping for and negotiating beneficial contract terms, so that she can obtain her preferred terms 'for free'. Consumer reading

---

180 As will be discussed in chapter 7, signals for quality of standard term forms have been developed in for instance Israel and Mexico, where sellers can obtain a sign of approval from a specific tribunal or other institution to establish that the terms offered in the seller's contract meet the applicable legal standards. See below, section 7.2.4.

181 See above, section 5.2.2b.

and shopping for terms are likely to be underproduced in the same way as public goods. When one consumer reads and fully assesses the implications of that contract, she can obtain benefits from the knowledge she gained by reading and assessing. Knowledge and information are public goods; by informing other people of this knowledge, consumers could use it to their benefit as well and social welfare would be increased. These consumers would not have to undergo the costs of reading and assessing themselves, and could thus free ride on the efforts of the reading consumer. The benefit gained by free riding consumers will however not serve reading consumers (fully). The reading consumer will not take these extra benefits into account when deciding whether or not to read and assess the contract. Society at large would gain from a few consumers reading the contract and sharing their knowledge, but that the consumer herself will gain from reading and assessing the contract is unlikely. As consumers cannot reap the full benefits of reading and shopping for contract terms, they are unlikely to engage in this behaviour to the extent that is optimal from a social welfare point of view (Hillman and Rachlinski, 2002: 447).

5.3.3. GOVERNMENT INTERVENTIONS CORRECTING ADVERSE SELECTION IN STANDARD TERMS

As it has now been established that the market failure of adverse selection is likely to occur in connection to standard terms, government interventions aimed at counteracting the adverse selection in standard terms can be contemplated. Regulatory interventions can consist of procedural or substantive rules: procedural rules would in this case mainly aim at the improvement of information, while substantive rules would relate to the content of the contract and could for example prescribe defaults or ban certain terms. Information duties correspond better to party autonomy and are therefore to be preferred over substantive interventions. As has been stated above in the introductory chapter, this research focuses on regulatory efforts to increase the quality of contract terms, as the expected quality of one-sided terms can be argued to be too low from a social welfare perspective. However, enforcement issues relating to the improvement of the quality of standard terms will be briefly examined, as well as the comparative benefits of public and private enforcement.

a. *Procedural and substantive interventions in information economics*

The most obvious interventions to counteract information asymmetry problems, constituting a lack of information on the side of the consumer, are information based remedies. Only when the information asymmetry cannot be sufficiently corrected through information measures, other means should be considered, such as interventions in the content of the contract. Stimulating the provision of information could be the most effective and direct way to overcome the asymmetry in information and thereby possibly correct the market failure. Furthermore, information remedies are less intrusive than substantive interventions, as the first do not limit the range of terms that are available to consumers and sellers. Interventions in the provision of information only target procedural aspects of the transaction; they do not affect the content of the contract. Party autonomy and freedom of contract are left intact. In information economics, procedural interventions are therefore to be preferred over substantive interventions.

When dealing with information asymmetry, the lack of information is the core of the problem; procedural interventions therefore focus on information rather than the content of the contract. Only when information remedies and the market forces of competition cannot sufficiently counteract the market failures which are detrimental to consumers, there is a clear justification for the intervention of public authorities (Howells, 2005). Examples of these more far-reaching interventions could be a fairness standard, bans on certain terms, shifting the risk in existing risk sharing arrangements and altering default rules. Information asymmetry is however not the only market failure that should be addressed in the context of standard terms in consumer contracts. Undesirable practices such as fraud, duress, and misrepresentation might also occur. These issues should be regulated and dealt with by (criminal) courts, since such practices are abusive and lead to welfare decreasing transactions (Van den Bergh, 2003: 1).

b. *Regulation and enforcement*

The interventions that are undertaken in consumer protection, including standard terms in consumer contracts, are often a combination of regulation and enforcement. Through regulation, standards can be set that can be evaluated on a case-by-case basis in court. Procedural requirements can be laid out, the observance of which can be assessed by the judiciary. The timing of the intervention distinguishes regulation from enforcement. An intervention can either target an undesirable act before it is committed (ex ante control), or it can be addressed to a harm that already has occurred (ex post monitoring) (Van den Bergh, 2007: 200–1). Ex ante control is more likely to be based upon regulation, whereas ex post monitoring often implies enforcement. That being said, ex ante and ex post interventions cannot always be clearly distinguished, and a clear line between interventions that are purely regulatory and court inventions is often difficult to draw. Interplay exists between enforcement and regulation concerning the correction of market failures, and also with respect to information asymmetry in standard term contracts. A "fairness test" might be set in regulation, of which the details need to be filled in through court intervention ex post. Also, court interventions in one case would set a precedent for future cases, thereby having an ex ante effect. The effectiveness and efficiency of consumer protection thus rely on both regulation and enforcement.[182]

c. *Public and private enforcement*

The enforcement of consumer protection law, including regulation of standard terms, is confronted with many challenges. Private enforcement over consumer standard terms is unlikely to take occur to a sufficient degree to discipline the market. Baird claims that most buyers will not go to court, and that sellers are aware of this fact (Baird, 2006: 937). Consumers suffer from rational apathy because the expected benefits from going to court do not outweigh the costs of doing so. As individual losses are small and seeking court intervention is costly in time and effort, let alone in financial cost, consumers stand to gain little from prosecuting, or will even lose out. The total social loss due to consumer law infringements might warrant an intervention that cannot be expected from consumers themselves as they are merely confronted with their own (relatively) small loss. Also, consumers are likely to lack the required knowledge; which terms are considered to be onerous, and whether violations of consumer protection law have actually occurred for instance. The information asymmetry which is present in consumer contracts prohibits effective private enforcement.

Public enforcement might be more efficient in getting onerous terms stricken from contracts. Public agents possess more information about laws, regulations and possible infringements of the law. Furthermore, public agents are able to take the entire loss to social welfare into account and thus make a more informed cost-benefit analysis of whether or not enforcement would be beneficial to social welfare (Van den Bergh, 2007). Public agents however do not always have the required standing in court to seek the enforcement of consumer protection laws. The collective action problem which is present in private enforcement can also be overcome by group enforcement, but that is not always available and can give rise to other problems such as interest representation and financial constraints. Even though this short overview of enforcement issues brings up many interesting research questions, this research will focus upon regulatory efforts to enhance the quality of terms in consumer contracts.[183]

182 Other interventions in the quality of terms can of course also be conceived, such as giving guidance to companies with regard to trade practices, negotiating standard terms with trade associations et cetera. This part of the research focuses on typical interventions suggested by information economics in the context of standard terms in consumer contracts. In chapters 6 and 7, consumer policy and policy proposals directed towards standard terms in consumer contracts will be more thoroughly assessed.

183 See for a coherent overview of the difficulties with private enforcement and how collective enforcement might improve social welfare, Trebilcock (2003), Van Boom and Loos (2007) and Van den Bergh and Visscher (2008) for a focus on consumer protection; Keske (2010) for a more elaborate discussion of this issue in the context of competition policy.

d. *A focus on regulatory interventions aiming at efficient contract quality*

As has been mentioned in the introduction, this thesis will focus on regulatory interventions aimed at increasing the quality of terms in consumer contracts. Enforcement issues and undesirable practices such as fraud and misrepresentation fall outside the scope of this research. This research focuses mainly on regulation which addresses the adverse selection problem in consumer contracts. There are several reasons for limiting the focus of this research. First, limiting the scope will enable an in-depth discussion of regulatory issues connected to standard terms in consumer contracts. It will allow for a discussion of and suggestions for improvements to regulation and ex ante policies aiming to provide a higher quality of standard terms in consumer contracts. Secondly, as will be argued in chapter 7, most policy recommendations that aim to improve the quality of standard terms entail more and further reaching regulation than is implemented nowadays. This thesis focuses on the regulatory interventions that typically occur in European legal systems, and discusses if and how improvements to this kind of regulation could provide a higher quality of standard terms.[184] Thirdly, considering the interplay between regulation and enforcement, it would be important to address the costs and benefits of regulation and possible improvements to regulation and policy. Before going deeper into issues of how enforcement of certain regulations can be improved, the desirability of those regulations itself should be assessed.[185] The interventions that will be described in the following sections are regulatory interventions that can justified from the perspective of information economics aiming to improve the quality of contractual terms and to counteract adverse selection in consumer standard forms.

5.3.4. POSSIBLE REGULATORY INTERVENTIONS 1: SETTING DEFAULT RULES

Through the use of default rules, society can save on transaction costs. Contracting parties can resort to the default terms set by the government instead of drafting contract terms themselves. This not only saves on drafting costs, but also on negotiation and research costs into the consequences of terms. It is therefore important to set default rules as efficiently as possible.

[184] See chapters 6 and 7.

[185] As a fourth reason, it could be mentioned that the general instrument of administrative regulation is likely to be more effective than a case-by-case treatment of claims through courts, as is for instance claimed by Leff (1970a: 356–7). As the effectiveness of regulation and the effectiveness of enforcement will not be juxta-posed in this research, this claim will not be further developed here.

a. *Efficient default rules*

What would constitute as an efficient default rule is discussed most notably by Ayres and Gertner (Ayres and Gertner, 1989; 1999). First, default rules should be set in such a way that they would be preferred by the majority of contracting parties. The result is that the majority of parties can contract according to the default terms without (much) further negotiation, thus reducing transaction costs for the largest group of people. These default rules are called *majoritarian default rules*: default rules that are favoured by the majority.[186] Secondly however, it might be the case that not majoritarian default rules are most efficient, but *minoritarian default rules*. This situation arises when it is not costly for the majority to contract to their preferred terms, contrary to the default terms, but comprehensive costs are faced by the minority when they would like to opt for their preferred terms. In these situations, social welfare is most improved when the minoritarian rule is set as the default, even though nominally more parties have to diverge from the default term. Third, the default rule could be set to the disadvantage of the party that possesses important private information, stimulating them to reveal that private information. This kind of default is called a *penalty default rule*. The disclosure of private information enables the contracting counterpart to perform more efficiently than they would have if they had been left uninformed.

An example of a penalty default rule can be provided by low reimbursement rates for postage parcels that get lost. The transporter does not know what is transported in the parcel. The contents of the parcel could be very valuable, or not be valuable at all. Efficiency considerations would prescribe the transporter to take more care in handling valuable parcels than invaluable ones. Information concerning the contents of the parcel is private; the sender knows the value of the parcel, but the transporter will only know if he or she is informed of the contents. If the sender knows that this parcel contains particularly valuable items, she could inform the transporter, who could respond by taking adequate care. Most likely, this added care would entail an extra cost. This however is efficient. If the transporter were to reimburse the full costs of each parcel that could be lost or damaged, he would take more care than if he would only have to reimburse up to the damage cap. Extra care entails extra costs, which would then also be passed on to those consumers who send invaluable parcels. The sending of valuable packages, which is more costly, would be cross-subsidised by the sending of the cheaper parcels, to the detriment of these latter senders. By setting the damage

186 Note that the majoritarian default rule does not have to be most efficient for the majority to be favoured by the majority and to be the most efficient default rule to set. Parties could be mistaken as to what would be the most efficient rule for them to stipulate in their contract. If the default rule is set to the rule that would be in fact more efficient, but is not favoured by the majority of parties, parties would contract away from the default anyway (at least in theory). This would yet again increase transaction costs. Therefore the majoritarian default rule should be the one that is *preferred* by the majority, not necessarily the one that is most efficient for the majority of contracting parties.

cap relatively low, consumers (who hold private information about the value of their parcel) have an incentive to reveal a high value of the contents and pay for the additional care, giving an incentive to the transporter to exert this extra care.[187] The efficiency of penalty default rules is therefore based on the disclosure of private information.

It is likely that consumer contracts require different default rules than business-to-business sales. Furthermore, default rules are likely to be sticky, whether they are efficient or inefficient (Ben-Shahar and Pottow, 2006). Diverging from default rules might be too costly to match the benefit of having a rule that fits the preferences of contracting parties better. Default rules are therefore likely to be followed, instead of being diverged from.[188] It is therefore even more important to set efficient default terms. Lastly, default rules matter only in some situations. When transaction costs are low and information is distributed symmetrically, parties are more likely to negotiate than to resort to default rules (Korobkin, 1998: 623). The characteristics of this situation however do not apply to the typical consumer standard term transaction, making default rules in consumer contracts very relevant.

b. Mandatory or default

Even though consumers are unlikely to negotiate for better terms, contract rules should be default rules instead of mandatory rules.[189] Mandatory rules are likely to be inefficient for several reasons (De Geest, 2002: 224). One is that legislators and courts choose the rules; these parties might not have the most relevant information about cost structures and preferences of affected parties at hand. The sellers do have this information, as they have first hand knowledge of which costs are related to which kind of term, and are in much closer contact with consumers. Again, competition will force sellers to take consumer interest into account. Sellers are the *cheapest information provider* when it comes to standard terms (Van den Bergh, 1997). Mandating the power to make contract terms to a party outside the actual contract (government of judge) implies that this outside party has more or better information, and is better able to set the optimal quality level for all contracts this term applies to than the parties to the contract themselves; these are very demanding conditions, unlikely to be often fulfilled (Kornhauser, 1976: 1182).

Also, which terms are efficient can be different in the various business sectors, depending on cost structures and consumer preferences. As consumer preferences are likely to be heterogeneous, some clauses might be efficient in one

187 But see Posner (2006) arguing that in actual contract law, no penalty defaults can be found.
188 See also below, section 5.4.
189 See for a general discussion of the differences between mandatory and default rules and cases in which they are applied, Van Bijnen (2007: 59–67).

business sector but inefficient in the other. Consumers and sellers that prefer rules other than default rules should be allowed to contract contrary to the default. Default terms can reduce transaction costs in situations where the default term is the preferred contract term and no longer needs to be stipulated in the contract. In other situations, parties are able to contract around the default terms.

5.3.5. POSSIBLE REGULATORY INTERVENTIONS 2: INFORMATION DUTIES

A central theme within information economics is that in order for consumers to discipline the market, they should read terms and negotiate or shop for better terms. Consumers are best protected by their own vigilance. To overcome the market failure of information asymmetry, information should be provided for consumers. This information will enable consumers to discipline the market on their own accord. To stimulate consumers to actually read standard terms, a *duty to read* for consumers combined with information requirements rendering the assessment of contracts less costly for consumers, can be argued for. The effectiveness of disclosure duties is however highly questioned. Due to rational apathy and the fact that information is a public good, the adverse selection problem might persist even with information duties to aid consumers.

a. Duty to read

The *duty to read* stems from traditional views such as adherence to terms of the contract and upholding the freedom to contract. Giving consumers an incentive to think carefully about the costs and benefits of the contract terms they are about to assent to, can result with relative certainty in a welfare enhancing transaction.[190] The duty to read consists of holding consumers responsible for the consequences of (not) reading the contract. It does not impose a sanction such as a fine on consumers when they fail to read contract terms, but it entails that contract terms will be legally binding to consumers even if they did not read the contract terms before entering into the contract. The duty to read therefore does not involve a punishment for not reading the terms, but implies that consumers will be held to the contract even if they choose not to read it beforehand. This should stimulate consumers to read contracts, or allow them to take the rational decision not to read the contract while being held to the contractual terms nonetheless.

[190] See above, section 5.2.2e.

The duty to read is however heavily criticised.[191] Eisenberg for instance states that "the duty to read", which implies that consumers consciously choose not to read contracts, is not linked to human reality at all (Eisenberg, 1985: 311). Ben-Shahar contends that the opportunity to read is a 'myth'. In effect, the option to read does not exist, due to the difficulties consumers encounter when trying to read the terms (Ben-Shahar, 2009). Standard terms are unlikely to be read by consumers, and the duty to read is argued by these authors to be an ill-advised instrument for solving the information asymmetry problem.[192]

b. Disclosure duties

Combined with the duty to read, consumers' transaction costs for becoming informed of the content of the terms should be decreased. Accordingly, there should be a requirement for sellers to make sure that contract terms are timely and easily available before the deal is made, known as the *availability requirement*. Furthermore, information policies should stimulate sellers to draft and disclose terms that are relatively easy to understand; this is referred to as the *transparency* of terms. Transparency can also be referred to as *readability* and *intelligibility*. All these notions are connected to the ease with which terms can be interpreted and understood, and often relate to issues such as font size, long sentences, the use of '*legalese*', et cetera. These interventions decrease the amount of time, financial cost and effort that consumers need to invest to understand the content of the contract. Consumers are given a true opportunity to read and assess the standardised contract terms. This opportunity, combined with consumer responsibility for the choice not to read, should optimally incentivise consumers to take care when entering into contracts. Signing-without-reading is still allowed and could (and will) therefore still occur. However, information economics claims, uninformed conclusion of contracts is in such a case a choice of the consumer, as she has had the opportunity to read the contract. Through the use of disclosure duties, such as availability and transparency, consumer reading should be increased, as it reduces consumer search costs, making consumer reading more beneficial to consumers.[193]

---

191 Some examples of this critique will be discussed here, as they have been provided in the economic literature. The duty to read will be more thoroughly assessed from a legal perspective in chapter 6, sections 6.2.1 and 6.3.2.

192 Chapter 7 will discuss several strategies for enhancing standard term policy, including solving the signing-without-reading problem and the option of doing away with the entire system of standardised terms in consumer contracts. See below, chapter 7, sections 7.2.1 and 7.2.2.

193 Hillman suggests requiring that e-business terms are online available, which however may backfire as this would make suspect terms more likely to be enforced; see Hillman (2006b).

c. *The effectiveness and efficiency of disclosure duties*

Whether or not disclosure duties can induce consumers to become informed and use that information to discipline the market is highly debated. Insights from modelling and game theory suggest that it is very unlikely that all consumers read, and that markets are disciplined by consumer reading (Priest, 1981). Katz argues that a duty-to-read cannot solve the signing-without reading problem. He shows that as long as costs of reading are positive, no consumer would read standard terms, and sellers would write low priced harsh terms as a consequence (Katz, 1990).

In addition, Gazal-Ayal shows that unless all consumers read the contract before signing, inefficient terms are very likely to occur (Gazal-Ayal, 1999). Consumers only read contracts (theoretically) if they have a low reservation price, which is the price that they are willing to pay for the product in relation to the actual price of the product. When a consumer values a certain good just above the price that she will have to pay to obtain this good, the consumer is said to have a low reservation price. A low reservation price could render the entire value of the contract to be lower than the price they are willing to pay, if the contract contains onerous terms. Therefore only consumers with a low reservation price could be expected to read and assess contracts, not all consumers could be expected to do so.

Information is only useful if consumers can act upon it. Consumers might be aware that even if they would acquire certain information, it would not make them shop or negotiate for better terms anyway. Obtaining the information is then of little use. If consumers believe that they have no alternative but to accept the standard terms that are put before them, they will not be inclined to read standard terms (Howells, 2005: 358). Furthermore, when consumers expect the quality of standardised contract terms to be low, and expect that sellers will be favoured over consumers throughout the business sector, consumers will not expect to gain anything by reading standard terms. According to their expectations, they would not find better terms in the contracts of competing firms, and will therefore choose not to read the terms at all. These consumers then start a self-fulfilling prophecy, as their expectation of one-sided contracts could in fact cause contract terms to be written one-sidedly due to the before mentioned adverse selection mechanism.[194]

194 In theory, consumers could be more easily made to read contract terms in cases of internet contracts, as terms can be made immediately available to consumers, and they do not feel the pressure of a sales agent or a waiting line behind to hurry the closing of the sale. See Hillman (2006b) and Mann and Siebeneicher (2008) on the specific problems related to e-standard terms and a discussion of mandatory website disclosure of e-standard terms. Mann suggests that internet retail contracting is in reality not much different from face-to-face contracting, at least not concerning the quality of the contract terms.

Grether, Schwartz and Wilde agree that consumers are unlikely to make optimal choices, even if they are enabled to read standard terms. This is partly due to the fact that information is a public good and therefore will be underprovided.[195] Consumers as rational information seekers balance costs and gains of searching for and processing information. Furthermore, special skills might be required to fully assess contract terms, skills which consumers might not have (Grether, Schwartz and Wilde, 1985: 277).

d. Information overload caused by disclosure duties

Disclosure duties sparked a discussion about overly burdening consumers with information. Eisenberg contends that too much information may lead to consumers refusing to take in any information at all (Eisenberg, 1985). Eisenberg argues this behaviour is not at all unreasonable: as consumers know that they will not understand the information anyway, taking in and assessing all this information will be costly and extremely frustrating, yet unlikely to yield great benefits to consumers. Grether, Schwartz and Wilde however argue against the view that disclosure requirements lead to an information overload and will therefore be ineffective (Grether et al., 1985). They argue that too much information will not cause consumer choice dysfunctions, as consumers will *satisfice* rather than optimise. As has been discussed above, satisficing entails looking for product characteristics that are satisfying, rather than optimal. The choice set is reduced by choosing some product characteristics, and screening products to see whether they correspond to acceptable levels of quality regarding those characteristics. Satisficing enables consumers to deal with large choice sets. Consumers know how to handle large amounts of information, and will simply ignore irrelevant information. Information overload which might make it more difficult to find the product attributes that the consumer is looking for should not be a "big concern". Therefore, only disclosure duties that increase search costs might be problematic, but disclosure duties would be still welfare enhancing on average. The concern that the vast amounts of information cause consumers to be unhappy can also be discarded, as this view is "implausible and unsupported by data" (Grether et al., 1985: 286).[196]

---

195 See also Hillman and Rachlinski (2002: 447) for a more elaborated discussion of this argument; mentioned above, section 5.3.2c.

196 See however below, section 5.4.1a, for a description of how information overload might cause a decrease in consumer welfare after all.

5.3.6. POSSIBLE REGULATORY INTERVENTIONS 3: MANDATORY SUBSTANTIVE INTERVENTIONS

Government interventions targeting information asymmetry should not stop at information duties. Some situations might call for mandatory substantive interventions. These interventions are more far-reaching than information duties, as an intervention in the substance of contracts does not correspond to the ideal of party autonomy.[197] The substantive interventions that can be used on standard terms in consumer contracts are a combination of ex ante and ex post interventions: within regulation a standard for onerous terms can be given, and lists of (presumably) onerous terms can be provided. When sellers do not comply with these regulatory measures, they can be enforced through the legal system.[198]

a. *Barring onerous terms*

As has been argued above, information remedies are the preferred option when aiming to overcome the market failure of information asymmetry. Therefore, mandatory interventions in the content of the contract should only be resorted to in cases where information duties and competition are unlikely to have a sufficient effect in counteracting the adverse selection problem. In line with this reasoning, Hatzis argues that substantive fairness of terms, the fairness of the content of terms, should not be investigated by courts. Instead, courts should focus on procedural fairness and bar unfair commercial practices that do not allow the consumer to become sufficiently informed about contract terms, et cetera (Hatzis, 2008: 48). Substantive fairness tests stimulate consumers into not-reading, as they can comfortably expect terms not to contain onerous terms (Gillette, 2004: 716–7). De Geest argues that if it can be shown that certain clauses will never be agreed to by consumers, these clauses should be banned (De Geest, 2002: 225). Restricting contractual freedom amounts to welfare losses for the consumer who would read and shop for or negotiate other terms. On the other hand, allowing contractual freedom leads to decreases in social welfare through adverse selection. In this delicate trade-off, restricting choice can be justified in cases of terms that are quite unlikely to be ever bargained for. An example would be clauses that exempt liability for intentional losses, basically creating in incentive for fraud on behalf of the drafter.

Terms that are unlikely to be agreed upon in negotiations for could be banned by 'blacklisting' them. A black list of standard terms is a regulatory list of standard terms that stipulates these terms as being onerous. These terms should be stricken from the contract, and cannot be enforced against the non-drafting party. In some cases, a grey list is a better option. When a term is mentioned

197 See above, section 5.3.4b.

198 See above, section 5.3.3.

on a grey list, this term is invalid unless the seller can prove these terms to be based upon true consent. When clauses are suspicious, greylisting them could ensure that these terms are deemed to be void unless plausible evidence of true consent can be presented. Likely, the burden of proof would be on the seller to establish the following circumstances: that the term that deviates from the default terms (also) increases costs for the seller instead of for (only) the consumer, that the terms were clearly and individually negotiated and understood, that they were stated in plain and intelligible language, and/or that there were very clear warnings in the contract so that the consumer must have been aware of these terms before signing the contract (De Geest, 2002: 226–7).[199] When terms are the product of negotiations, Hatzis argues that black and grey lists should not be applied as the consumer clearly assented to the terms (Hatzis, 2008: 54). Also, if the market is competitive, the price/quality ratio of the contract should be taken into account when assessing terms. The reasonableness of the contract should be evaluated concerning the contract as a whole, not just in relation to the mere term in question.

b. *Barring low-quality but permissible terms: using availability as proxy*

Not all consequences of the market failure of information asymmetry can be targeted through enforcement. Courts can only strike onerous terms from consumer contracts. This implies that the quality of terms can be improved to permissible levels, which could still be lower than the actual preferences of consumers. When a contract term is driven out of the market due to the high quality, the consumer cannot go to court and demand this higher level term to be supplied again if a lower level quality is also deemed permissible by courts.[200] As courts only ban the most onerous terms, the level of quality in terms is slightly elevated, but not much. The "flea market" therefore will probably still exist, be it offering slightly better quality than before, but still unable to offer high quality terms to consumers should they prefer them.

To overcome this gap between acceptable and preferred terms, consumers may resort to challenging the procedural requirements of availability and disclosure to be able to get out of a low quality term contract. Cserne claims that the availability requirement is more and more criticised as being a proxy (Cserne, 2009). This requirement is a procedural necessity that is not linked to the substance of the contract terms. However, it is only invoked when a party feels disadvantaged by the substance of one or more particular terms in the contract. By focusing on a procedural test when the complaining party is unsatisfied with

199 Behavioural insights criticise this view, referring to risk perceptions of consumers; see below, section 5.4.1d.

200 This reasoning is analogous to Kornhauser (1976: 1180), who argues that court intervention is insufficient because products that have been driven out of the market due to their high quality cannot be reinstated by courts.

the content of the contract terms, the availability test fails to address the need for more substantive control over contract terms. It enables courts to intervene when the content of a term is considered to be undesirable by the costumer, but only in cases where a procedural requirement has not been met.

This implies that court intervention is not fully effective at improving the quality of terms to the level preferred by consumers. When the availability and disclosure requirements are fulfilled, only onerous terms can be barred from contracts, but not terms that are barely permissible, and inefficient due to their low quality.

5.3.7. REGULATION AND ITS EFFECT ON COMPETITION

Above, it has been argued that both competition and regulation can protect consumers from abuse by onerous terms.[201] Regulation however also comes with costs, and might have a negative impact on the effectiveness of competition to counteract the market failure. Heterogeneous consumer preferences can limit the benefits of regulation, and cause detriment to consumers with a preference for low priced low quality standard terms. As consumers feel more protected, their propensity to be vigilant and to take care in transactions may be reduced. The interplay between competition and regulation should therefore be carefully assessed.

a. *The costs of regulation*

Regulation, correcting a market failure, comes with costs. These costs consist not only of the administrative costs of implementing the regulation itself, but also of the adverse effects that the regulation might have, for instance in hindering competition and error costs. Also, there is a paradox in using costly information measures as a solution to problems that started with the cost of becoming informed being too high. Insight into the issue of transaction costs has taught that information costs are both a part of markets and of regulatory interventions. The relative costs of the problem and the solution must be understood clearly (Hadfield et al., 1998: 145).

Furthermore, as consumer preferences are heterogeneous, regulatory intervention could benefit some groups of consumers, while harming the interests of others. Consumers who have a preference for low-quality low price terms could find that their preferences can no longer being fulfilled, as regulation has banned the terms that they prefer. Whether a ban on a low-quality term is welfare enhancing depends on the number of consumers who prefer one-sided terms. The fact that some consumers might be harmed in their interest when the

201 See also above, section 5.3.3.

quality of terms is improved, even when this intervention increases social welfare as a whole, should not be overlooked.

b. *The cures of competition and reputation*

In theory, competition between sellers should make terms less one-sided, as beneficial terms should attract consumers. If consumers can easily observe and evaluate product attributes at the time of the sale, if search costs are not significant, and if most consumers are capable of making reasonably good decisions concerning the product attribute in question, competition on its own can protect consumers very well (Armstrong, 2008: 100).

The one-sided drafting of standard terms is discouraged by various legal institutions, such as unconscionability, fairness tests, the *contra proferentem* rule et cetera (Kessler, 1943).[202] Consumers will be protected from onerous terms by the company's need to uphold its reputation, and by the protection of legal institutions. Therefore, standard terms in consumer contracts are unlikely to be onerous (Schäfer and Ott, 2004: 370–3). These competitive cures however can arise only with respect to the terms that the consumers are consciously aware of, not with respect to the ones that information asymmetry relates to. Also, savvy business strategies can mute the effect of competition and the influence of the marginal informed consumer group by giving favours to the smart and complaining consumers. Furthermore, disagreement over terms that are connected to remote risks might not influence reputation. Moreover, short term players are not deterred from onerous practices or terms by the prospect of a bad reputation.

Goldberg argues that the characteristics of contracts correspond more to private regulation on the part of the drafter and that standardised terms cannot be seen as a voluntary agreement. Equilibrium terms could come forward from this market, but harsh and low priced terms could also drive out the good and higher priced ones (Goldberg, 1974: 483–6). Of course, both consumers and producers have an incentive to cure this situation. Market solutions like brand names and advertising could ameliorate the effects of the market failure, but are unlikely to sufficiently counteract it. Gazal-Ayal analyses how consumers could use readily available information such as price and reputation to estimate the quality of products and thereby of standard terms. Both a high reputation and higher prices could signal a higher quality of the terms. Yet Gazal-Ayal also shows that neither reputation nor price can be sufficient indicators for quality (Gazal-Ayal, 1999: 26–39). Both items can be perceived as signals of quality, and have some effect in that sense, but neither can create full knowledge on the quality of

[202] See chapter 6 for a discussion of the common core of the European legal approach towards standard terms in consumer contract.

contract terms. Government intervention is therefore warranted to counteract the adverse selection of standard terms.

c. *The interplay between competition and regulation*

When an industry is more regulated, suppliers have less freedom in setting their own terms. Theoretically at least, this hinders competition, and decreases welfare for consumers with heterogeneous preferences. There is a concern that regulation will induce even less reading by consumers. Moral hazard of consumers (or rational apathy, rational ignorance) is reinforced by paternalistic consumer protection (Hatzis, 2008: 11). Standard contract terms can in most cases be safely ignored by consumers (Baird, 2006: 936). Law protects consumers anyway and might thereby actually stimulate consumer moral hazard. Why would consumers bother reading or comparing terms if they know that the onerous terms will be stricken from the contract anyway?

However, the extent to which competition is in fact hindered by regulation in the context of standard terms is hard to ascertain. The more terms are affected by adverse selection, and the further these terms are removed from the scope of consumer information, the less positive the effect of competition is. When there is no competition with respect to standard terms, sellers cannot distinguish themselves from the competition by offering better terms. Therefore, all sellers will try to offer terms at as low a cost as possible, and all terms will be offered in the same quality: one-sided, harsh terms with a low price. In this scenario, regulation that aims to improving the quality of terms can thereby only improve the market if it can successfully distinguish the terms that have disappeared due to adverse selection. The quality of terms is too low from a social welfare perspective, and should therefore be corrected. Very intrusive forms of regulation could even prescribe terms in consumer contracts. In this situation, consumers still have only one type of standard term to expect, but now these terms will be of higher quality than they would have been in absence of the regulation. As has been argued above, due to adverse selection the efficient level of quality in standard terms is likely to be higher than the quality of terms that is provided by the market. When there is no competition with respect to a large portion of standard terms due to information asymmetry, regulation on these terms could not possibly hinder competition much.

Whether a form of contract provided by regulation should be preferred over the option of non-interference, which means leaving it up to the market, could however also be questioned. It can be doubted whether the regulator retains sufficient information about which standard terms would be efficient. Different policy proposals which aim at improving the quality of terms, including the option of prescribing terms, will be assessed below.[203] Suffice it to point out for now that a trade-off does exist with respect to competition and regulation.

The interaction between competition and regulation is delicately balanced. In general, regulation should be regarded as the second-best option, as it interferes with the market mechanism. Before regulation is enforced in order to correct the market failure, it should be established that the effects of competition fail to have sufficiently ameliorating effects.[204] With respect to standard terms, it should ideally be established which terms are effected by adverse selection, and which terms are subject to sufficient competition between sellers.[205] Heterogeneous preferences complicate the question of whether certain terms are actually subject to sufficient competition. In the case of standard terms, due to information asymmetry, a substantial part of the contract might not benefit from the competitive cure of the market mechanism. The costs and benefits of both regulatory interventions and the mechanism of competition, and the interplay between them, should be carefully assessed.

5.3.8. CONCLUSION: DESIRABILITY OF GOVERNMENT INTERVENTION BY INFORMATION INSIGHTS

Scholars agree that the asymmetry of information and the resulting adverse selection problem is the main cause of concern for consumer welfare with respect to standard terms. Competition issues and market structure are unlikely to be the cause of welfare decreases related to one-sided terms. Based upon the insight of information economics, asymmetric information and transaction costs provide the main rationale for government intervention. Consumer rational apathy and adverse selection are likely to result in consumer contract terms that are overly one-sided, favouring the seller over the consumer. The quality of terms can be said to be too low, and this problem is unlikely to be corrected through market instruments such as the sellers' reputation, consumer learning, information unravelling, quality signals and the competitive cures of a marginal group of informed consumers. Therefore, interventions in the market are justified. Procedural interventions are usually to be preferred over substantive interventions. Interventions will often consist of a combination of regulation and enforcement. This research focuses regulatory efforts to improve the quality of terms in consumer contracts.

Intervention comes in different shapes and sizes. The provision of efficient default rules will allow contracting parties to save on transaction costs. Drafting

203 The analysis of different policy proposals aiming to improve standard terms consumer policy is the subject of chapter 7.

204 As has been argued above; see above, chapter 2, section 2.3.2.

205 See below for a discussion of empirical results regarding the one-sidedness of terms, section 5.5.3.

efficient default rules would partially remedy the signing-without-reading problem. The insertion of better rules in cases where a contingency has not been specified will improve the quality of the contract. Disclosure duties such as availability and transparency for sellers, combined with a duty to read obligation for consumers, create an incentive and an opportunity for consumers to read the terms and discipline the market.

Whether this requirement actually enables consumers to discipline market is however questionable. The use of a substantive test, combined with black and grey lists, should result in the most onerous terms to be stricken from contracts. As low quality terms that are also undesirable but just above the threshold of being deemed onerous slip through the judiciary test, the procedural requirements of availability and transparency will come into play. Court intervention can therefore only establish a limited improvement to the quality of standard terms. Competition and regulation are both instrumental in improving social welfare, but competition can also be hindered by regulation. Whether or not (specific) standard terms are affected by adverse selection, or whether they are drafted to attract consumers by their content and thus are subject to competition, should be carefully assessed. Due to heterogeneous preferences, some consumers might actually desire low-quality low priced terms. Intervening by banning these one-sided terms might stand to benefit society as a whole, but the fact that some consumers are harmed in their interests should not be neglected. Distinguishing which terms are subject to competition, and which terms are affected by adverse selection and therefore stand to be improved through regulation, is a challenging task for the policy maker. Whether or not the intervention can be regarded as efficient depends on a careful evaluation of the effects of both competition and regulation with respect to standard terms in consumer contracts, in light of information asymmetry and adverse selection, and heterogeneous preferences.

Information economics has thus resulted in a focus on information. It has identified a 'different' market failure, the one of information asymmetry, and relies largely on information remedies as a cure. Whereas information economics does mention that information remedies can fail to overcome the adverse selection problems caused by information asymmetry, the first focus of information economics remains the provision of information to the market to increase social welfare.

The focus on information has also shifted the focal point of distinguishing decreases in social welfare related to consumer contracts. Instead of largely focusing on competition and market structure, the decision making process of the consumer has been brought to the forefront. The assumptions that are normally included in the assessment of the decision making processes of consumers also became topics of more frequent discussion. This development relates to a new current in economic literature to focus on standard terms in consumers' contracts, a current that occupies itself mainly with decision making processes: behavioural law and economics.

5.4. BEHAVIOURAL NOTIONS ON CONSUMER BEHAVIOUR AND STANDARD TERMS

This section will review the additions from the perspective of behavioural law and economics to the issue of quality of standard terms and the role of consumers in disciplining the market. It will be concluded that the insights of behavioural law and economics largely correspond to the concerns raised in the information economics debate regarding one-sided standard terms in consumer contract. Behavioural insight however also exacerbates the previous story, as it sheds even more doubt on the effectiveness of information remedies. Taking the biases and heuristics of behavioural economics into account, effective readership and consumers disciplining the market become even less probable. It is extremely unlikely that a sufficient percentage of consumers that actually read standard terms will be present in the market. Consumers will suffer from information overload and social pressures, and will therefore not have a high propensity to read the terms. Also, consumers might feel more compelled to abide by standard terms once they have signed the contract than is suggested on the basis of economic insights, even if the terms do not correspond to their preferences. Furthermore, to the extent that consumers do read standard terms, their interpretation might be flawed: the evaluation of terms by consumers might be overoptimistic, to their own detriment. Regarding policy recommendations, behavioural analysis of standard terms in consumer contracts calls the effectiveness of information duties and consumer vigilance to improve the quality of consumer standard terms into question.

5.4.1. CONSUMER BIASES AND HEURISTICS RELATED TO STANDARD TERMS

Behavioural law and economics has zoomed in on the decision making process of consumers and takes insights from other social sciences such as psychology and, to a smaller extent, sociology. Social sciences identify several biases and heuristics that could be applicable to standard term contracts. When these biases influence consumer readership or assessment of standard terms, this could have implications for the ability of consumers to act in a disciplinary capacity in the market. The problem of one-sided standard terms might be more severe than economic theory would predict or understand. The reliance upon information remedies to overcome the market failure of information asymmetry should be reconsidered. Even when consumers read terms, their assessment of the risks described in the contract terms might give cause for concern. Biases and heuristics at play in the context of standard terms in consumer contracts can be divided into four categories: information overload and propensity to read, perceptions of self-commitment, risk perceptions and emotional status or social pressures.[206]

a. *Information overload and propensity to read*

The first category of consumer bias that is claimed to be applicable to the issue of standard terms in consumer contracts, information overload and propensity to read standard terms, relates to the claim that consumers do not read standard terms. Behavioural biases and heuristics regarding information overload and propensity to read corroborate this claim. One of the implications from behavioural economics is that an accurate distinction between informed and vulnerable consumers is more complicated than had been previously thought.[207] In some situations all consumers could be considered to be vulnerable, because they are unable to consistently make rational and informed decisions even when they are aided by information disclosure. Consumer standard terms might constitute one of these cases, meaning that (nearly) all consumers should be considered vulnerable.

An opportunity to read standard terms cannot be compared to the opportunity to inspect goods (Ben-Shahar, 2009: 12–20). Consumers do not possess the necessary capabilities to read and understand standard terms; they cannot assess unlimited amounts of information since they are not computers.[208] Assessing the content of a contract to find out whether this contract is worth the asking price is very difficult, and likely to be too demanding for a consumer. For the consumer to be able to attach a fair price to the terms that she encounters in a contract, she should have a very deep understanding of the market and its cost structures, and roughly know what competitors are offering. Consumers are not able to perform this task (Ben-Shahar, 2009: 17).

To deal with vast amounts of information in the assessment of standard terms, consumers are argued to use satisficing rather than optimal decision making.[209] However, balancing the different aspects of a decision is difficult. Also, consumers focus on a few salient items, ignoring the other terms of the boilerplate (Korobkin, 2003). Competition in standard terms is likely to take place with respect to these salient product attributes. The other, non-salient, terms are ignored by the consumer, excluded from the decision making process, and therefore likely to be provided one-sidedly, favouring the seller over the consumer as much as

[206] Division loosely based on Becher (2007); for further overviews of behavioural biases related to standard terms in consumer contracts, see for instance: Stark and Choplin (2009), White (2009) and Ben-Shahar (2009).

[207] See above, chapter 3, section 3.3.2b.

[208] As empirically established by Miller (1956), consumers can take up to seven aspects into deliberation.

[209] See above, chapter 3, section 3.2.2a.

possible.[210] Linked to salience is another bias, namely attention focus. As has been discussed above, specific information items that have been disclosed might attract much more attention from consumers than would be called for considering their preferences. Consumers can feel paralysed by the vast amounts of information that are to be assessed in standard terms of consumer contracts; they could therefore refrain from assessing these terms altogether. Behavioural insights indicate that consumers can be very much confused by an overload of information, which does not increase their state of well-being (Jacoby, 1984; Malhotra, 1984). Confusion also decreases propensity to read; decision paralysis and inertia, which cause people to refrain from taking any action at all, are even more likely to occur when actions are considered to be unpleasant (Brennan, 2005).

Biases related to information therefore prevent consumers from fully assessing, or even reading, standard terms in consumer contracts. If some salient terms are assessed and taken into account in the decision making process of consumers, these terms are likely to be few. Evaluating the consequences of the terms mentioned in the contract is likely to be too burdensome for consumers, as they do not possess the relevant information and necessary capabilities to make this assessment.

b. Emotional status and social pressures

Certain social norms are in place, prescribing consumers not to read contracts. Actually reading contracts is seen as socially inappropriate, and consumers are expected not to read them. Social psychology research indicates that people tend to conform to expectations and tend to trust others, even strangers.[211] Contract terms might be presented at the end of the meeting, when there is little time left. A long line of other customers might be waiting. Sellers might flip through the contract and point out certain relevant passages, but not allow enough time to adequately read the document before ending at the page where the contract can be signed. If the consumer does insist on reading the contract, agents might be

[210] Klick (2005: 565) reports that another view to standard terms is just as likely as the one proposed by Korobkin. Klick suggests that standard terms offer a mechanism for firms to price-discriminate, giving benefits to consumers who want to negotiate. It is therefore "analogous to clipping coupons to get a better deal on a product". As anyone can get the better deal, consumers make a rational decision not to. Between these two theories, Klick recommends to experimentally test which theory is consistent with observations from reality; explanations relying on biases and heuristics should not just be taken for granted. As will be mentioned below, empirical research does not support the thesis that sellers discriminate between consumers who do not and who do read standard terms, but the data is limited.

[211] See for instance: Snyder and Swann (1978). Weber, Malhotra and Murnighan (2005) point out that such trust however also provides certain benefits. Even though immediate trust might seem irrational, research indicates that it does make people better off. Trust apparently makes people happier, and it leads to people being trusted by others more than if they would not have a trusting nature themselves.

fidgeting, sending bored blank looks, et cetera. Social pressures could counteract a possible desire to investigate the details of the contract (Eisenberg, 1995: 243).

Businesses may make the consumer feel uncomfortable when she is reading the standard terms. The salesman himself, or other customers, might be in a hurry and stand waiting impatiently for the consumer to finish. Reading standard terms might seem confrontational and give the impression that the consumer does not trust the business or its agent. Distrusting people also makes the consumers themselves feel uncomfortable, like calling the counterparty a liar. Business agents might try to develop a relationship with the consumer when negotiating, so that the consumer does not want to seem difficult. They might downplay the importance of the standard terms, by handing over the contract while adding: "Lawyers make me give you this", and a quick wink. This would make people feel they should not be difficult. Social pressures and the emotional status of individuals thus furthermore decrease the propensity to read standard terms.

c. *Perceptions of self-commitment*

When consumers are already committed to the contract through attraction to the product itself, a test drive, going through the entire sales process, negotiations or maybe an application fee, they may not be prone to let standard terms impede the transaction. The *sunk cost effect* causes consumers to be more inclined to continue with the sale after they have invested time and effort in it. This is the result of a desire not to have wasted time and effort, to justify previous choices and to maintain their self-esteem with regard to previous actions (Thaler, 1980; Becher, 2007: 10). The fact that standard terms are usually presented at the end of the transaction process only intensifies the effect of the sunk cost bias. A corresponding effect is *cognitive dissonance*: consumers at this stage of the transaction already feel morally committed to go through with the contract. When consumers read terms, if they read standard terms at all, they might discount the disclosed information even if this information would ordinarily have persuaded the consumer not to sign (Whitford, 1973: 426). The information does not concur with previously held thoughts, and is therefore discarded.

Empirical research suggests that people interpret standard terms more favourably than these terms really are. Solan et al. describe how false consensus bias might lead people to believe that their interpretation of terms is the one that is shared by other people, when actually it is not.[212] This might cause consumers to be mistaken in the rights and obligations that a contract assigns to them (Solan, Rosenblatt and Osherson, 2008). Combined with self-serving bias, this might lead consumers to interpret contracts in their favour and be more confident about their interpretation. When it is pointed out to them that this term should be interpreted differently, they are likely to feel bound by the contract terms and not

[212] In this overview of studies, even judges are shown to be subject to the false consensus bias.

to challenge these in court (Becher and Unger-Aviram, 2009). Furthermore, as has been mentioned by Becher and Zarsky, consumers are more likely to read a contract ex post, after the contract has been concluded. When a dispute between parties has arisen, reading the contract terms can be highly beneficial from an informational perspective. Especially when a dispute has arisen, consumers wish to know where they stand (Becher and Zarsky, 2008: 312–4). At this point however, consumers will also feel more committed to the terms, as they have already agreed to the contract.

Interpretation of contract terms might further enhance the problem of self-commitment. The *confirmatory bias* suggests that people are looking for information that confirms what they expect, not information that contradicts it (Wason, 1960). With self-serving bias and false consensus bias linked to confirmatory bias, it is unlikely that consumers will find information in the standard terms that contradicts the positive terms that they expect to find and in that they will fact interpret the terms to state. Consumers could thus be biased against finding information that will make them pull out of the buy.

Lastly, but not unimportantly, people like to stick to what they have. The *status quo bias* causes people to stick to default terms to a larger extent than can be expected from rational behaviour.[213] Consumers are therefore also more likely to stick to standard terms. Omission-commission bias, a subcategory of status-quo bias, makes consumers hesitate before changing terms of a contract, because they fear an undesirable consequence of their active decision more than an undesirable consequence of them remaining passive. Consumers can also infer from the fact that a certain terms has been drafted in a standard term, that this is likely to be the best option. Perceptions of self-commitment thus decrease the propensity of taking action against standard terms even if these terms do not correspond to consumer preferences. Before the contract is concluded, the consumer might feel committed as she already decided to buy the product. Reading standard terms after the transaction is concluded is more likely than reading terms before agreeing to the contract; at this point however, perceptions of self-commitment will be enhanced, decreasing the propensity of consumers to challenge undesirable standard terms.

d. Risk perceptions and uncertainty

Risk perceptions influence the way in which consumers interpret the consequences of standard terms. For the few salient terms that are included in the decision making process of consumers, this raises concerns regarding the abilities of consumers to decide which risk divisions would be in their best interest. People want to believe what is in their favour, so they will interpret ambiguous boilerplate in a way that is favourable to them. Consumers are prone to neglect

213 See for the discussion of default terms above, section 5.3.4.

low probability risk, excluding remote risks and the standard terms related to those risks from the assessment of the contract (Eisenberg, 1995: 240–2). This is known as *low probability neglect*. Individuals have an inclination to eliminate uncertainties and simplify decisions. Some risks are overestimated though, when consumers have had close experience with the contingency this risk relates to, or when it has been frequently publicised (Becher, 2007: 25). Furthermore, people underestimate the chances of bad risks coming to fulfilment and overestimate the possible good consequences of contracts (*self-serving bias* and *overoptimism*). This might cause them to take less care in for instance assessing contracts.[214] Overoptimism also causes consumers to overestimate their own ability to comply with procedural requirements necessary in for instance claiming a rebate, or cancelling a contract before the notification period. Even when consumers notice that claiming rebates or cancelling contracts is rather cumbersome, they overoptimistically will think that they will be able to benefit from the rebate, or will not forget to send a registered letter to cancel the contract in time. As is for instance claimed by Edwards (2007), consumers regularly forget to comply with the necessary procedural requirements. They therefore underestimate the true costs of procedural requirements.

The dread factor, related to very negative occurrences such as death and pain, causes certain terms to be excluded from the decision making process, even though rationally these terms should be contemplated. Terms that would exclude liability for severe consequences of product malfunctions such as disability or even death could therefore not even be accounted for in the decision, simply because people do not want to think about those consequences from even being possible. Furthermore, when people think that the consequences of their decision are unlikely to involve a high risk or serious consequences, consumers tend to be more passive as well and invest less effort into the decision. As standard terms frequently refer to unpleasant events that might occur in the future, often with low risk, these terms and risks are likely to be under-evaluated in the decision making process, or excluded from this process completely. Risk perceptions are very important with respect to standard terms, as standard terms can be argued to allocate risks between the seller and the consumer. The division of risks should therefore be reflected in the end-price of the contract. If consumers misinterpret these risks, the expected value of the contract including the expected losses from risks that fall upon themselves might be much less than consumers understand beforehand.

Hypothesised behavioural biases can also contradict each other. Self-servingly, a consumer might expect that onerous terms will not be enforced or even be enforceable against her. Overoptimism will thus cause consumers not to feel bound to the contract. The effect of cognitive dissonance however might

214 See however also Posner (2004) for a discussion on how levels of care might be higher instead of lower, even when people suffer from overoptimism, under certain conditions.

have quite the other outcome. Cognitive dissonance can be described as the psychological state in which an actor feels uneasy because apparently he has done something which was not in his best interest. In other words, a person feels bad for making a mistake. To retrospectively justify his actions, this person might commit to his decision even more. Signing a contract containing onerous terms might counter-intuitively compel even more people to feel bound by the contract (Eigen, 2009: 7–8).[215]

Uncertainty and/or asymmetric information concerning use-patterns enable sellers to exploit consumer biases (Bar-Gill, 2007). Where price calculations are difficult, such as can be the case in credit card contracts, consumers might err in making realistic assessments of future gains and costs of the contract. Consumers do not know how often people in their situation will be confronted with late payment fees. The seller has more information about user averages, and is thus better able to make an estimate of how much a consumer on average will have to pay in late fees. Information on average use patterns could decrease the information asymmetry between seller and consumer, and re-bias the consumer by providing her with an anchor to correct for her self-serving assessment.

e. *Conclusion: behavioural additions to insights in consumer behaviour*

Regarding consumer behaviour, behavioural notions do provide additional insights that should be taken into account in the analysis of the welfare effects of consumer behaviour regarding the issue of intervening in standardised consumer contracts.

Due to bounded rationality, information overload, emotional status and social pressures, consumers are even less likely to read standard terms than has been hypothesised by information economics. The perception of self-commitment sheds doubt upon the propensity of consumers to take action against onerous terms or terms that do not correspond to their preferences. Feeling committed to buy a product might further decrease the propensity of consumers to regard the standard terms, or to feel the need to deal with undesirable terms should they be encountered. As consumers are more likely to read standard terms ex post, after concluding the contract, they will feel bound by these contract terms by the time they are able to assess them. Risk perceptions affect those few standard terms that are taken into account in the decision making process. Even when terms are considered by consumers, risk perceptions might undermine consumers' ability to decide which risk division would be in their best interest.

Biased risk perceptions caused by self-serving bias and overoptimism, combined with the low probability neglect and dread factor, cause consumers

[215] Upon empirical testing, Eigen (2009) finds that that people are inclined to feeling bound to adhere to a contract they have signed, even though the contract terms are undesirable. See below, section 5.5.3c.

to misinterpret the expected value of the contract. Even though the behavioural economic analysis of risk perceptions might be most decisive in setting apart 'standard' economic theory from behavioural economic analysis, with respect to standard terms in consumer contracts in general these biases are less influential. This is because most standard terms are unlikely to be read, fully assessed or challenged by consumers. Therefore, the interpretation of risk does not really enter into the analysis of consumer standardised terms in general. In some contexts however, such as consumer financial products, these biases might have some influence on the assessment of specific standard terms.[216] Consumer behaviour with respect to reading and assessing standard terms in consumer contracts can thus be argued to be affected by behavioural biases and heuristics, which could justify behavioural interventions in policy.

5.4.2. BEHAVIOURAL IMPLICATIONS FOR STANDARD TERM POLICY

Behavioural analysis of standard terms in consumer contracts suggests a lesser focus on information duties. Consumer vigilance should only be expected to improve the quality of standard terms in consumer contracts to a very limited extent, if at all. The question of which interventions should be recommended for policy that aims to correct consumers' biased decision making also deserves some discussion.

a. *The effectiveness of information remedies*

In general, the application of behavioural insights such as information overload, emotional status and social pressures concerning standard terms in consumer contracts corresponds to the insights of information economics. Consumers fail to read and assess standard terms sufficiently, which results in low quality terms being offered in the market. Admittedly, this view is not new to information economics. Information overload was already theorised in information economics to be a possible cause of suboptimal decision making. The salience or rather the non-salience of standard terms, which is seen as a behavioural addition to explanations of consumer behaviour, does in fact not differ much from the insights that had already been gained by economic theory concerning rational apathy. Information economics also allows for the possibility that information asymmetry cannot be sufficiently counteracted through information remedies, at which point substantive interventions might be warranted. The preferred solution

[216] Risk perceptions relating to particular standard terms will not be assessed in the following section on the suggestions of empirical research, as this research takes a more general perspective on standard terms. See also below, chapter 8, section 8.2.2.

within information economics is reliance upon information remedies, also in the context of standard terms in consumer contracts. Information remedies are argued to correct adverse selection and increase social welfare by increasing the quality of standard terms. Since these information remedies however are dependent on consumers' informed decision making, their effectiveness can be doubted as a result of behavioural biases and heuristics.

Behavioural theory brings the argument of low quality terms that result from consumers not fully reading and assessing terms to a further level. The biases with regard to information overload and social pressure result in even more doubts about the effectiveness of information remedies. While information economics relies upon information remedies to correct information asymmetry, it can be concluded from behavioural notions that information might not be a sufficient remedy for information asymmetry in the case of standard terms. As has been discussed previously, the instrument of information disclosure should be carefully re-assessed in the light of behavioural notions.[217] Behavioural insights suggest that even if adequate information is available in the market, this no longer necessarily means that welfare enhancing government intervention is redundant in the context of consumer protection. Consumers are overwhelmed as it is; their psychological capacities might render the extra information provided through information remedies ineffective. This implication of behavioural insights to policy can be clearly argued to be relevant to the context of standard terms in consumer contracts. This change of focus and different view on information remedies can be seen as one of the major implications of behavioural insights applied to standard terms, and consumer protection in general.

b. *Reliance upon consumer vigilance*

Behavioural notions suggest that consumer vigilance should not generally be depended upon to discipline the market for standard terms. The findings on consumer behaviour regarding reading, assessment and commitment to terms after having decided to acquire the good further increase doubts about the capability of consumers to discipline the market and to effectuate efficient standard terms to be drafted by sellers. Consumer biases and heuristics might impede consumers in this challenging task. As consumers are more likely to read terms ex post, and feel committed to the contract, consumers' propensity to actively negotiate a higher quality in standard terms is reduced. These insights regarding propensity to read also provide more arguments against the theory of the informed minority of consumers who are able to discipline the market. In addition, these insights provide further arguments to doubt the effectiveness of private enforcement of regulation that aims to ban onerous terms, in excess to the

217 See above, chapter 3, section 3.3.2c.

concerns already mentioned above.[218] Again, the concerns raised in (information) economics are aggravated by behavioural insights.

Behavioural literature has furthermore distinguished certain terms that are likely to be disregarded and therefore non-salient, such as low probability risks and dreaded risks. Moreover, defaults that were already seen to be sticky from a transaction cost perspective are now shown to be even 'stickier' due to behavioural biases. In general, behavioural insights suggest that the effectiveness of consumer vigilance to cure the market failure of information asymmetry, which results in adverse selection, should be doubted.

c. *Behavioural intervention strategies to correct biased decision making*

This section aims to provide some arguments relating to the question of which intervention strategy should be recommended for the task of improving consumer decision making with regard to standardised contract terms.[219] In light of the fact that behavioural insight suggests that consumers will fail to negotiate over standard terms in consumer contracts and that effective strategies that should enable people to truly read, assess and shop for terms are hardly (or even im-) possible, a change in policy focus might be justified. Policy measures should go beyond the aim of enabling consumers to read (Becher and Unger-Aviram, 2009: 22).[220] Furthermore, recommendations for policy should relate to the issue which interventions would allow the market to operate best in an environment where consumer reading and negotiations of terms are not or only to a very limited extent possible (Baird, 2006: 935). As has been explained above, behavioural intervention strategies can aim at debiasing consumers, changing the default of the decisions or rebiasing consumers by employing the effects of one bias to overcome the detrimental effects of another one. The question remains which intervention strategy that accounts for behavioural insight should be recommended to address the issue of standard terms in consumer contracts.[221]

In general, debiasing is to be preferred over the other intervention strategies as it allows consumers to make an informed decision. This intervention strategy could entail the implementation of an instrument in which less and better information is disclosed, perhaps by disclosing some standard terms separately

---

218 See above, section 5.3.3c.

219 In accordance to the cautions, considerations and guidelines that have been developed in chapter 4, it must first be established whether behavioural interventions are justified. Only then should intervention strategies based upon behavioural insights be contemplated.

220 Becher and Unger-Aviram (2009: 22) instruct: "Policymakers, devote less attention to improving plain language!".

221 The question of how the issue of standard terms in consumer contracts should be addressed in a way that accounts for behavioural insights is only limitedly discussed in current behavioural economic literature. Bar-Gill (2009), mentioned above, suggests to inform consumers of average use patterns; and Becher (2009) suggests a "fair contracts approving" mechanism to overcome the one-sidedness in consumer contract terms. These and other policy suggestions aiming to improve standard terms in consumer contracts will be discussed in chapters 7.

from the contract, or information on the package of the product or on a label that is provided where the good is displayed, in large text size and simple wordings. There are however not a great number of terms that can actually be included in the decision making process as a result of debiasing, and these terms, even though they are disclosed, might still not be assessed by consumers. Another way of (limitedly) debiasing consumers and making their decision more informed is providing sellers with a reliable signal of the higher quality of their terms. When a credible signal of quality can be established through a certificate or some other kind of seal of approval, or some rating or labelling scheme for the quality of the contract standard form, this intervention might to some extent be able to increase the quality of standard terms.

The intervention strategy of changing the default however also seems promising. When policy instruments directly change the standardised consumer terms into terms of higher quality, consumer decision making processes do not need to be altered. The standard terms could be upgraded to a higher level of quality by a combination of legal standards and some sort of authority monitoring of terms. The quality of terms could also be raised by inviting consumer interest groups to have a say in which terms should be included in standard forms. Also, certain higher quality terms could be mandatorily included in consumer standard forms; even entire contracts could be prescribed to sellers and consumers.[222] The intervention of rebiasing does not seem very applicable to the case of standardised consumer contracts.

5.4.3. CONCLUSION: BEHAVIOURAL ADDITIONS TO STANDARD TERM POLICY RECOMMENDATIONS

In behavioural literature, several insights to consumer behaviour regarding standardised contract terms are discussed that do not correspond to conventional economic theory. Due to information overload and emotional pressure, consumers are not likely to read and assess standard terms. Even though this view has also been presented by information economics, behavioural notions aggravate this concern. As consumers feel committed to contracts that they have signed, they are not inclined to file suit even when terms are of low quality and they would have preferred or even expected better terms. When terms are considered, they might not be assessed in ways that are described by RCT. Consumers have different risk perceptions than can be theorised on the basis of economic theory; they have

222 Barr, Mullainathan and Shafir (2009: 37–54) suggest several ways in which behaviourally informed regulation could improve the consumer financial market, including the provision of a opt-out standard mortgage offer that would make us of 'sticky defaults' and enable consumers to better be able to compare different mortgage offers. Similarly, they argue that an opt-out payment plan for credit cards should be introduced that automatically requires consumers to make necessary payments within relatively short periods of time.

difficulties in deciding which terms and risk allocations would be in their own favour.

On the basis of behavioural literature, several implications to consumer policy regarding standard terms should be considered. First and foremost, the effectiveness of information duties can be criticised. To increase the quality of terms, interventions beyond information remedies should be developed. Behavioural notions address and undermine the informed minority theory. Consumer vigilance is a doubtful instrument to discipline the market for efficient standard terms. Intervention strategies to address the notions developed in behavioural literature can either aim at debiasing consumers with regard to standard terms, or at changing the default by improving the quality of standard terms directly.

As has been mentioned several times, when behavioural insights and economic theory seem to (partially) contradict each other, empirical testing should be conducted to determine the validity of both (sets of) hypotheses. In the next section, the results from empirical studies on consumer reading, shopping and negotiating and the content of standard terms will therefore be discussed. Other issues that will be addressed in this section are empirical studies on the effectiveness of information remedies and disclosure duties, as well as the presence and desirability of one-sided terms in consumer contracts. The main issue that empirical research should shed light on is the question of whether consumer vigilance, combined with the provision of certain information to aid consumers in their endeavours, can be expected to sufficiently discipline the market into drafting efficient standard terms.

5.5. CONSUMERS' ABILITY TO DISCIPLINE THE MARKET: EMPIRICAL RESULTS

Until a few years ago, the academic and policy discussions regarding standard terms in consumer contracts were informed mostly by theory, and lacked an empirical base. Since then, empirical research has been undertaken to answer the question of whether the adverse selection problem actually occurs with respect to consumer standardised contracts. This research centres on questions such as whether consumers read, shop and negotiate for terms, and whether or not standard terms in consumer contracts can be found to be one-sided. Also the influence of competition on standard terms has been assessed, as well as the extent to which consumers feel compelled to abide by the contract they have signed.

The results of these studies are shown to largely correspond to the insights from both information and behavioural economics. The empirical studies, even though they are few in number, indicate that the majority of consumers does not read standard terms; this does depend on the type of contract. The typical remedies that information economics suggests, such as availability of the contract, the provision of easy to read and understandable terms et cetera, do not seem to greatly enhance consumer reading. The supposed effectiveness of information remedies can therefore not be supported. The aspects of shopping and negotiating for contract terms have not been much examined yet, but the research that has been done does not suggest convincingly that consumers actually shop and/or negotiate for terms in a consistent manner. Lastly, standard terms in consumer contracts do appear to be one-sided, and to favour the seller over the consumer. Competition between firms, championed by economic theory, does not seem to be able to sufficiently counteract this problem. Availability of terms before the conclusion of the contract is cannot be shown to have a positive effect on contract term quality either. The informed minority theory that has been brought forward by neoclassical economics cannot be confirmed through empirical studies. The claim that consumer vigilance will be able to discipline the market in the context of standard terms in consumer contracts, a claim which is supported by both neoclassical and information economics, cannot be maintained on the basis of empirical findings.

A further question is whether, even if standard terms in consumer contracts are found to be one-sided, this calls for government intervention. One-sided terms do not necessarily signal abuse. Sellers could use the one-sidedness of terms to distinguish between consumers prone to moral hazard, or screen for consumers who would benefit from a more beneficial treatment. They are prevented from abusing their discretion through competition and reputation. Such views can however be challenged. Sellers' incentives might not correspond to the interests of society at large. It is therefore doubtful that the distinction of which consumer is to benefit from better terms and who should be confronted with one-sided terms, should be left solely up to companies.

5.5.1. CONSUMER READING AND UNDERSTANDING OF STANDARDISED CONTRACT TERMS

As mentioned before, a lot of studies mention that consumers are unlikely to read standard terms: it would not be rational, they suffer from biases, et cetera. Even though a considerable number of authors suggest that consumers do not read standard terms, evidence to this effect is hardly ever provided.[223] A limited number of surveys and empirical studies on whether or not consumers reported that they had read standard terms have been undertaken (Hillman, 2006a; Becher

[223] To mention just a few of the instances where the claim that consumers do not read standard terms is made without referring to any significant empirical evidence: Whitford (1973: 426), Kornhauser (1976: 1163), Trebilcock and Dewees (1981: 104), Rakoff (1983: 1177), Gillette (2004: 680) and Becher (2008: 724, also stating that numerous commentators have mentioned this). De Geest (2002: 221) claims "(e)veryday life experience teaches us that typically less than 1% of all consumers read standard term clauses before buying the item".

and Unger-Aviram, 2009; Stark and Choplin, 2009). Even less studies of actual reading behaviour have been conducted (Bakos, Marotta-Wurgler and Trossen, 2009; Stark and Choplin, 2009). The results of all these studies point in the same direction: very few consumers read standard terms. In some contexts however, consumers report they would read the standard terms, which allows for a further examination of the factors that could influence consumer reading behaviour. Also, the effectiveness of disclosure duties is discussed in the light of empirical findings.

a. *Do consumers read standard terms?*

The informed minority theory that is championed mainly in neoclassical economics but also referred to in information economics requires a minority of about 30% of consumers to read standard terms in order for this reading minority to be able to discipline the market. In empirical studies, research has been done to establish whether this required percentage is met. Based upon a survey of reported reading behaviour of e-standard forms, Hillman concludes that people generally do not read e-standard forms beyond price and description (Hillman, 2006a). The Internet might provide benefits for comparing sellers and contracts and thus render reading contracts potentially more worthwhile.[224] However, consumers do not seem to take advantage of this new development. Hillman reports that most consumers do not read all terms in e-standard contracts. Only 4% of the participants reported they would read e-standard terms under any circumstance. 44% reported they would not read. The other consumers would read only under specific circumstances. Generally, less than the before mentioned required 30% of consumers reads standard terms, whether these terms are online or in paper version. However, when the vendor is unknown, or when the value of the contract is high, more than a third of consumers report that they would read the standard terms.

Bakos, Marotta-Wurgler and Trossen test actual reading behaviour in internet contracting. They find that only 0,2% of consumers access the standard term form on the website. The average time spent reading the standard terms was about 48 seconds. Therefore, Bakos et al. assess the reported percentage of reading consumers to be a "substantial overestimate of the number of effectively informed consumers" (Bakos et al., 2009: esp. 26). In their study that reveals actual reading of standard term contracts in an experimental setting, Stark and

224 See Hillman and Rachlinski (2002) and Hillman (2006a; 2006b) for a discussion on how online boilerplate is different from paper versions. Both the survey of Hillman (2006a) and the survey of Becher and Unger-Aviram (2009) report not much difference between online or paper versions of standard term contracts. This research will not treat the two versions differently either. Compare Hillman and Rachlinski (2002: 474–86) who conclude that even though online contracting lessens the need for legal intervention as it will be easier to compare contracts and thereby should enable consumers to protect themselves from abuse, consumers might not be able to take advantage of these benefits due to cognitive difficulties.

Choplin find that 95,6% of participants fail to read the contract before signing it (Stark and Choplin, 2009).[225] In a survey asking respondents about their contracting behaviour, they again find that a sizeable number of consumers signed the contract without reading (all) the terms. This does depend on the type of contract. In their survey on reported reading behaviour, they find the following (Stark and Choplin, 2009: 691–6): terms on downloading software are hardly ever read in full (only by 5% of consumers) but mortgage contracts on the other hand are reportedly read fully by 73% of consumers. Car rental contracts are reportedly read by 72% of consumers, and a mere 57% of participants in the study claim to have read the contract to purchase their home in full. The study undertaken by Becher and Unger-Aviram confirms the results of the other studies by concluding that consumers in many cases do not read standard terms (Becher and Unger-Aviram, 2009). Again however, whether or not consumers read standard terms is reported to depend upon the context. Signing up for a bank account will make most people sign without reading the terms (92%), a car rental induces a little more reading but still not much (81% do not read). Standard terms at the laundry service are read even more often than at the car rental (75% do not read). The only situation in this study that apparently gives an incentive to read standard terms is signing up a child for a nursery school (24% not reading the contract terms).

From these empirical results, it can be concluded that the common view that consumers do not read standard terms can empirically be confirmed in some contexts. However, some other contexts or contract characteristics might give an incentive to read to number of consumers that is sufficiently large to possibly enable them to discipline the market. Therefore, the reasons that consumers gave for reading or choosing not to read the contract deserve some further consideration.

b. *Reasons given for failure to read*

In the study on actual reading behaviour, Stark and Choplin tried to find out what were the reasons for participants for choosing not to read the contract (Stark and Choplin, 2009: 684–6). Following that study, the most important issue for not reading terms according to consumers, is trust. When consumers trust their counterparty, and they trust the institutions to make sure that any onerous contract terms will not be enforced against them, they do not read standard terms. Other issues that contributed to a failure to read were the length of the form

225 See Stark and Choplin (2009: 678–80) for details on the materials and procedures of the study. It consisted of asking students to sign a standard form of 3 pages for participating in an experiment. The form contained rather onerous terms, such as the requirement to give electric shocks to fellow students even if they screamed or cried for help. Students themselves could be forced to do push-ups, and would not be allowed to leave if they wanted to. Even though the terms themselves indicated that signing the form would not be in the best interest of participants, less than 5% of the participants read the terms, and only 3% refused to sign the form.

(even though the form in question was only 3 pages), the fact that the form was perceived as boring, and that participants were lazy and impatient and wanted to get on. Some items were, perhaps surprisingly, not rated as very important factors in the decision not to read, such as difficulties in understanding the form, font size, long sentences, inability to negotiate, and the preservation of the image of good and trustworthy counterpart. Participants moreover believed that if their counterpart would have insisted that they read the standard form, they would have been more inclined to do so. Additionally, they did not think the standard terms would contain anything important for them to know, or anything other than forms they claimed to have read in the past.

Trust in the company is confirmed as an important factor in reading behaviour by Bakos et al. (Bakos et al., 2009). They find that online standard terms are more likely to be accessed when the company is small, or when 'suspicious' products such as freeware (free software) are being offered. Furthermore, consumers who are older and consumers who have a higher income are more likely to access online standard forms. Search and reading costs might be lower for these groups, as they are likely to have more time (older consumers) and are confronted with less difficulties when reading standard terms (higher income consumers have on average enjoyed higher levels of education). The value of the contract is also an important positive factor to the probability of consumers reading the contract. Hillman finds that the main reason that consumers fail to read is that they are in a hurry. Less important, but still a significant factor in the decision not to read are certain underlying beliefs, such as the belief that nothing will go wrong, that the terms will be fair, and that competitors' terms will be comparable (Hillman, 2006a: 297–8). A higher value of the contract and unfamiliarity with the vendor further increase the likelihood of reading.

Becher and Unger-Aviram report that legal language, font size and print density cannot be shown to have a large impact on the failure to read (Becher and Unger-Aviram, 2009). According to this report, the value of the contract is the most important factor in deciding whether of not to read standard terms, followed by the length of contract and the possibility to change contract terms. The importance of contract value is illustrated by the high number of consumers that report reading terms of a nursery school (only 24% report not reading the standard terms). This contract holds a higher value, as any potential damage is likely to affect (among others) a loved one who the consumer feels responsible for. The possibility to change or improve contract terms is a factor in the decision (not) to read. Consumers are more likely to read contracts when they are able to change contract terms, even when consumers in the end decide to opt for the default rule. The mere possibility of choosing one's contract makes one more inclined to read the default (Becher and Unger-Aviram, 2009: 21). Similarity among contracts is not a key factor.

Most of these aspects hold in ex ante and ex post settings on whether consumers opt to read their contracts. However, in the ex post setting, the factors that influence consumers' intent to read contract terms are slightly different (Becher and Unger-Aviram, 2009: 19–20). The most influential factors are shown to be the cost of transaction, opportunity to learn new things, and opportunity to change or improve contract terms. However, the empirical results indicate that contract length, contract density, and font size are not considered important by consumers in their decision to read the standard terms. Generally though, consumers are much more likely to read standard terms ex post, when a conflict has arisen, than ex ante before signing the contract.

c. *Discussion of the empirical results on consumer reading*

The empirical studies reporting on whether or not consumers read standard terms reveal that not many consumers read. Bakos et al. conclude from their and other empirical tests that the informed minority theory, which is persistent in economic theory and claims that a minority of informed consumers can discipline the market, cannot be maintained (Bakos et al., 2009: 28–33).

Reasons that are reported by consumers for reading or failing to read largely correspond between studies, but not in all cases. The value of the contract is found to be important in all studies. When the value of the contract is high, consumers are more likely to read the contract. This can be explained by the fact that when the value of a contract is high, one-sided terms can be expected to result in higher losses. Whether or not the consumer knows her counterparty, and finds that she can trust him or her is indicated to have significant impact. These factors can be related to the reputation argument, and the fact that consumers rely upon legal institutions to provide protection from onerous terms. The length of the form and time constraints are also considered important factors in the decision not to read the form, but the inability to understand terms is not. Consumers might be (overoptimistically) assuming that they would be able to understand the terms. The possibility to negotiate the terms to the contract might be another factor, as consumer report that not being able to change the terms is a factor in them deciding not to read.

Not all factors are found to be important in the different studies. Although Hillman, Stark and Choplin report that similarity between contracts is a mildly important reason for not reading terms, Becher and Unger-Aviram do not report this factor to be significant. Also, the ability to negotiate terms is not considered an important factor in the study by Hillman, but Becher and Unger-Aviram report that the possibility of choosing and negotiating contract terms increases the likelihood of consumer reading, even when consumers decide to opt for the default rules.

Becher and Zarsky note that reading standard terms is more likely ex post when a legal dispute arises (Becher and Zarsky, 2008: 312–4). When a dispute between parties has arisen, reading the contract terms can be highly beneficial from an informational perspective. Especially when a dispute has arisen, consumers wish to know where they stand.[226] Even if the contract terms are likely to be binding, becoming familiar with rights and obligations can be a starting point in seeking to alter the contract ex post. Sellers might be willing to change the contract terms in individual contracts when confronted with a complaining consumer. Assertive consumers who take the effort to verbalise their complaint are more likely to have a negative impact on sellers' reputation than silent consumers. Sellers have an incentive to appeal to these assertive consumers, and they know exactly who these consumers are: the ones that come up to the store and complain. This also implies that consumers that do not complain are unlikely to be able to receive better terms. This observation increases concern on discrimination between complainers and silent consumers (Becher and Unger-Aviram, 2009: 22).

Furthermore, empirical research suggests that not all consumers will benefit equally from information disclosure. Consumers who are well-educated stand to benefit to a larger extent from information disclosure than consumers from socio-economically challenged backgrounds.[227] These empirical studies make the concern regarding discrimination between silent and complaining consumers more important from an equity perspective (Whitford, 1973: 470; Stark and Choplin, 2009: 696–7). As has been mentioned above, Bakos et al. (2009) also find that higher income consumers are more likely to access online standard terms, confirming the equity-based suspicions. It can be concluded however that most contracts will only be read by a small minority of consumers. High value contracts might inspire higher percentages of readers, but they are not often concluded whereas consumers enter into numerous small value contracts on a daily basis. More empirical research is needed to determine the sectors of industry or the contract types in which consumer reading is more likely.

d The effectiveness of disclosure duties on improved reading and understanding

Empirical data also sheds doubt on the effectiveness of disclosure duties in stimulating consumers to read standard terms. The typical disclosure duties regarding increasing the opportunity to read for consumers, namely improving transparency, readability and intelligibility, are not considered important factors on the decision to read. Font size, legalese and long sentences are not put forward by consumers as being of great consequence in their decision to read the contract. The length of the form is considered to be a significant factor. Restricting the length of a standard form however is not a typical requirement under disclosure duties.

226 As Baird (2006: 938) already mentioned, legal terms only matter when something goes wrong.

227 See for instance McNeil et al. (1979), who show how information disclosure in the second-hand car market promotes the interest of well-educated consumers more than lower-class consumers, as the first are better able to understand, utilise and benefit from the provided information.

Related to disclosure duties and more specifically to the requirement of availability, Bakos et al. claim that the accessibility of contract terms does not have any positive influence on readership. They claim that consumers do not read online standard forms, "regardless of how accessible they are" (Bakos et al., 2009: 4–5). Mann and Siebeneicher find that only 6% of internet retailers have enforceable contracts on their websites. The other contracts would not survive court scrutiny as they do not correspond to the legal requirement of that respective legal system (Mann and Siebeneicher, 2008). The enforcement of disclosure duties therefore lacks in effectiveness. In addition, empirical studies suggest that consumers do not seem to gain better understanding from credit contracts that corresponded to relevant information duties than from contracts that do not conform to information requirements in relevant regulation (O'Shea, 2005). In a related point, some employees who were under the impression that their contracts stipulated that they, employees, could only be let off *for cause*, have been shown to have had in fact signed a contract in which they could be fired at will (Sunstein, 2001). Tenants will also believe terms of the contract to be more favourable than they actually are (Müller, 1970). The contractual terms were available to the employees and consumers; they were just not interpreted correctly. The empirical studies thus suggests that disclosure duties are ineffective in increasing consumer reading and to some extent even the apprehension of the contract, and that disclosure duties are insufficiently enforced to induce compliance within the market.

e. Limitation of studying reported behaviour vis-à-vis actual behaviour

The difference between reported behaviour and actual behaviour is clearly relevant. Stark and Choplin, Becher and Unger-Aviram, and Hillman do surveys in which consumers themselves report on their contracting behaviour, as has been discussed above.[228] An observation should be raised with respect to the difference between studying reported behaviour and actual behaviour. Surveys on reported consumer behaviour provide information about what people claim they do or will do, but they do not measure actual behaviour. Reported behaviour, even though it is a valid research method, should be evaluated correspondingly (Becher and Unger-Aviram, 2009: 23).

Surveys that depend on reports of behaviour instead of testing actual behaviour can be influenced by perceptions of behaviour, of what is seen as appropriate behaviour by society, and consumer biases and heuristics such as overoptimism. Interestingly, even though social norms prevent people from actually reading a contract, as has been explained above, the behaviour that is theoretically seen as appropriate in this case is reading the contract. All consumers know they 'should read contracts before signing them'. Therefore, the percentages of consumers

[228] See above, section a.

that report reading in these surveys are likely to be higher than actual reading behaviour would warrant. Indeed, the study by Stark and Choplin testing actual reading behaviour reports lower percentages of reading than the before mentioned surveys, even than their own survey on reported behaviour.[229] Both studies that did research on actual reading behaviour, Stark and Choplin (2009) and Bakos et al. (2009), find much higher percentages of non-reading than the studies on reported behaviour. Stark and Choplin themselves call the relatively high reading percentage reported by consumers in mortgage contract terms (73% in mortgage contracts) in their survey highly unlikely, and a result of the self-reporting nature of the survey.[230] The public attention to predatory loans might make consumers to be more optimistic about their actual behaviour. Also, when participants had read some of the terms, when they have signed all pages of the contract, or when they had been giving a summary by the sales person, they might have perceived themselves as having fully acquainted with the contract even though not all terms have actually been read (Stark and Choplin, 2009: 695–6).

Furthermore, the fact that standard terms are reported to have been read, or that an online standard terms form has been accessed, does not necessarily imply that that all the terms in the contract have been fully assessed and comprehended. As has been mentioned by Bakos et al. (2009), and also Stark and Choplin (2009), the reported percentages of reading consumers might result in an overestimation of effective and full assessment of the contract. Regarding the (average) time spent on assessing the contract, both articles conclude that the limited amount of time allocated to the contract could not possibly have resulted in full and comprehensive readership.

5.5.2. CONSUMERS SHOPPING FOR AND NEGOTIATING CONTRACT TERMS

Next to consumer reading, it would be interesting to see whether consumers shop for and negotiate terms. Even though this issue is hardly researched in empirical literature, some evidence to support the position of consumers shopping for and negotiating standard terms can be found. Unfortunately, these arguments are not very convincing.

229 The authors themselves also highlight this aspect; see for instance Stark and Choplin (2009: 684), Becher and Unger-Aviram (2009: 23).

230 Stark and Choplin (2009: 695) timed a research assistant, having a history in financial sales, when he read through all of the terms of a typical mortgage contract; it took him over 3 hours. Stark and Choplin concluded it would be unlikely that consumers, who typically do not have a financial background, would take considerably less than 3 hours. Therefore, they assess it to be unlikely 73% of the participants really read all of the mortgage terms.

a. *Evidence of consumer renegotiations*

Johnston reports that faced with repayment schedules in cases of consumer debt and return sales policies, consumers renegotiate the price and terms of the contract. He cites the examples of hospital bills, consumer credit cards, mortgage contracts, rent-to-own contracts, and retail sales return policies (Johnston, 2006).[231] This claim is largely based on informal sources such as newspaper articles and anecdotal evidence, combined with the observation that the involved institutions have dedicated personnel for negotiating repayment schedules. One survey on negotiating the price of a medical bill is also mentioned, finding evidence that 10–17% of consumers have tried to reduce their hospital bills, in which 45–48% of those consumers were successful (Harris Interactive, 2002).

When companies allow consumers to renegotiate their debt, these companies are able to screen the consumers and decide which consumers they want to offer more favourable terms. Even when consumers do not bargain before engaging into the contract, the standard terms of the contract invite consumers to (re)-negotiate and start a conversation about the terms of the contract with the provider (Johnston, 2006: 864–77). Repayment will be offered to consumers that are valuable to retain as customers, in light of future sales. Strict return policies provide retail shops with the option of (not) enforcing the strict policies. When retail shops expect abuse on the side of the consumer, such as buying a dress to wear for one night, and then returning it, the retail agent can resort to the strict policy.[232] Bona fide consumers will not be faced with this strict enforcement, which again allows the company to screen consumers. This opportunity to screen depends on the ability to identify abusers.[233] Standard terms in a consumer contract facilitate bargaining and are a crucial instrument in maintaining cooperative relationships. The standard terms set the base line situation, and provide a starting point for parties to start conversing and build relationships. Therefore Johnston concludes that negotiation of standard terms is possible and is frequently entered into, and that one-sided terms are efficient since they enable companies to screen and distinguish between consumers.

---

231 As the first four examples concern repayment schedules in cases of debt, they can be considered comparable situations. This leaves only two situations in which consumers are claimed to renegotiate terms: repayment schedules in cases of consumer debt and return sales policies.

232 As has been mentioned above, the economic term for abuse on the side of consumers is *consumer moral hazard*; see sections 2.3.3b and 4.3.4b.

233 Johnston (2006: 875–6) reports the existence of a database that screens for abusive consumers in return sales, which is able to indicate 0,1% of all consumers as return abusers.

b. *Discussion of the reported results on consumer negotiations*

Whereas Johnston claims that this "overwhelming evidence" of consumers renegotiating terms is only "the tip of the iceberg", and maintains that anything can be renegotiated (Johnston, 2006: 876), this study unfortunately fails to convincingly show that consumers actually do negotiate their standard terms. Besides the fact that the study is based on mostly anecdotal evidence, the evidence that is presented is related only to a limited number of contract terms, which is insufficient to justify the general conclusion that consumers (re)negotiate standard terms.

Negotiating or sticking to the default

In his article, Johnston focuses on situations of renegotiation of contract terms, which is negotiating the terms ex post, after the contract has been concluded, instead of negotiating the terms ex ante. A first issue to be discussed is whether consumers will negotiate terms of the contract at all, or whether they are likely to stick to the default terms as they have been provided. There are hardly any empirical studies that have tried to shed some light on the percentage of contracts that consumers have bargained over with respect to standard terms, or surveys that ask consumers on whether they are prone to negotiate standard terms. A few studies have looked into the stickiness of default rules, arguing that default standard terms in consumer contracts tend to persist in consumer contracts even when it would have been easy to change. It is unlikely that these terms reflect the preferences of contract parties. Johnson et al. describe the following situation that concerns default insurance terms for car owners (Johnson et al., 1993). New Jersey and Pennsylvania are neighbouring states in the US. When both states introduce the option of a limited right to sue, entitling automobile drivers to attain lower insurance rates, different default rules where chosen in the legal regime of the respective states. New Jersey drivers needed to acquire the full right to sue, and the default rule was a limited right, whereas in Pennsylvania, the full right to sue was the default, which could then be forfeited in favour of the limited alternative. Transaction costs of switching to the alternative endowment were minimal: only a signature was needed. Whereas only about 20 percent of New Jersey motorists opted to acquire the full right to sue, approximately 75 percent of Pennsylvania drivers chose to retain this right. As these are neighbouring states in the same country, it is unlikely that these choices represent the existence of very different preferences in the respective motorist communities. Transaction costs neither seem to be prohibitively high.

This default allocation of rights exemplifies how defaults can indeed be sticky, and that people are not prone to negotiate the terms of the contract ex ante. In line with the reasoning by Johnston, the timing of negotiating about contract terms could more likely be ex post through *re*negotiations.

Renegotiating over price or standard terms in general

Johnston claims that people frequently renegotiate the price of their contracts or standard terms such as payback schedules. The question is whether these negotiations, if they are indeed found to occur frequently, can sufficiently counteract the market failure of adverse selection in all standard terms, and not just a few salient ones. Negotiations over price could imply the negotiation over other terms in the contract as well, as standard terms might be adjusted to account for a lower price. An assessment of the allocation of risks to either the seller or the consumer can attach a certain value to all contract terms. This value is reflected in the end-price of the contract. By renegotiating terms in the contract the contract price could be correspondingly adjusted. A standard term that could be related to this issue is the payment window. Price negotiations and negotiations over payback schedules are thought to be quite common. Negotiations on less salient standard terms are however highly doubtful, and experimental or empirical insights on this issue would be very welcome to the discussion.

Tendency to adhere to contracts

Another issue that could shed doubt upon the tendencies of consumers to renegotiate standard terms is the obligation that people feel to uphold their promises. In empirical tests, Eigen found that people generally feel duty-bound to adhere to the contracts that they had consented to. He finds that people continue performance under a contract largely due to moral obligations such as keeping one's word. This effect was stronger than a legal threat. People feel more compelled to abide by contract terms when they have been given an option between two terms, than when they were presented with a take-it-or-leave-it offer. Being able to scroll through a contract also increases the propensity to adhere to contract terms (Eigen, 2009: 41–2). Eigen furthermore finds empirical suggestions that people from lower socio-economic backgrounds are more likely to feel bound to contracts than people who are more educated, more skilled and earn higher salaries (Eigen, 2008). In a related point, Müller finds that tenants who were faced with undesirable terms were under the impression that these terms would be enforceable, decreasing their inclination to renegotiate or even to go to court. This finding corresponds to the claim that people feel committed to terms, even if the terms deviate from their expectations ex ante (Müller, 1970). Therefore, it can be argued on the basis of empirical research that consumers feel a tendency to adhere to contracts instead of renegotiating them.

Ability to screen consumers

The extent to which companies and other institutions are able to screen consumers on the basis of standard terms can also be doubted. In case of payment windows and repayment schedules, there are some indications that companies screen the consumers that can pay their bill straight away from the ones that need to be offered a repayment schedule.[234] Also, the repayment terms could be set to the needs and characteristics of that particular consumer. Consumer screening with respect to the ability to pay their bills is one instance where screening is likely to take place. With respect to return sales policies, this ability to screen is debatable. In case of any doubt about consumer abuse, sellers might be prevented from enforcing the strict return policy by reputational concerns. Furthermore, the database that is reported to be used as a selection instrument only designated 0,1% of consumers to be likely to be return abusers (Johnston, 2006: 875–6). This percentage might be correct, in the sense that there really are not many return abusers out there; it could also indicate that this screening device is not very effective. Unfortunately, it is difficult to estimate the effectiveness of the screening device, and no arguments are presented to confirm its accuracy. Johnston's insights about renegotiation do correspond with the previously discussed evidence that consumers are more likely to read standard terms after a conflict, in this case the inability to pay the bill, has arisen.[235] However, more research should be conducted both on consumer negotiations of standard terms, and on the question of whether or not consumer shop for better standard terms.

5.5.3. PRESENCE OF ONE-SIDED STANDARDISED TERMS IN CONSUMER CONTRACTS

Lastly, the reported one-sidedness of terms in standardised consumer contracts has been examined to assess the claim that the standard terms in consumer contracts are being affected by adverse selection. A suggestion of one-sidedness can be taken from these studies. Neither competition nor availability of terms can be shown to enhance the quality of standard terms in consumer contracts. Furthermore, regulation and court enforcement can be argued to be insufficiently effective in barring undesirable terms from contracts.

a. *Evidence of the one-sidedness of terms*

Marotta-Wurgler is one of the few scholars who have done impressive empirical research into the contents of standard terms. Upon examination of the use of dispute resolution clauses, Marotta-Wurgler assumes that choosing a forum with a less consumer-friendly status over one with stronger consumer protection could be interpreted as a one-sided term. She does not find evidence that forum

234 Payment windows therefore have characteristics of a penalty default rule, stimulating the revelation of private information, as described by Schwartz and Wilde (1979).

235 See above, section 5.5.1.

selection clauses are employed by sellers to the detriment of consumers (Marotta-Wurgler, 2007a). In another more general study of the contents of standard terms, she does find however that the vast majority of the examined contracts are more favourable to the seller, the drafting party, than the default rules that would govern the contract in absence of the standard term agreement (Marotta-Wurgler, 2007b).

Mann and Siebeneicher perform a study in which they survey the contracts of 500 large internet retailers (Mann and Siebeneicher, 2008). They report finding less one-sided contract terms than might be expected on the basis of theory. Still, examples like a disclaimer of implied warranties, or limitation of certain damage types were found in 49% of the contracts; choice of law, choice of forum and caps on damages were found in respectively 40%, 32% and 22% of the contracts (Mann and Siebeneicher, 2008: 999).[236] Another suggestion of one-sided standard terms has been found by Hillman and Baraka. Upon surveying over 100 software publishers, they find that most of publishers in their survey would offer certain warranties on their website, which were subsequently disclaimed in their standard forms (Hillman and Baraka, 2009).

b. *The effectiveness of competition and availability on quality of terms*

In a study on software licence agreements between businesses and consumers, Marotta-Wurgler finds that market structure and corresponding intensity of competition in a market is not correlated to the quality of standard terms offered to consumers (Marotta-Wurgler, 2008). The empirical data suggest that the quality of standard terms in consumer contracts is not decreased when competition decreases. The same study finds no evidence of salient terms within the set of standard terms that are influenced by competitive efforts. Priest, examining the warranties of 62 household appliances and corresponding market structure data, did not find that more restrictive terms were being offered by firms with a larger market share (Priest, 1981). Both empirical studies therefore report not being able to find evidence that sellers compete with each other on the basis of making their standard terms more attractive to consumers.[237] Market pressure as a disciplining tool can therefore be considered problematic (Hillman, 2006a: 298–9).

In another study on software licence agreements, Marotta-Wurgler compares terms in contracts that were available before the sale to terms that were not

[236] Mann and Siebeneicher (2008: 1000) brand these terms and corresponding contracting interfaces "surprisingly benign".

[237] Wright (2007) turns the argument around: he claims that as terms do not seem to decrease in quality when the market structure is more competitive referring to both Priest (1981) and Marotta-Wurgler (2008), the claim of adverse selection of non-salient standard terms cannot be proven. However, the influence of competition is only part of the story. Together with the empirical results on reading behaviour and the one-sidedness of terms, the absence of a competitive cure with respect to standard terms seems to support the view that the market is not disciplined by consumers, through competition or otherwise.

available until after the sale. Terms that are provided only after the sale were not worse in quality than the terms that were available before-hand; they were in fact slightly better (Marotta-Wurgler, 2009). This would suggest that availability to read does not improve the quality of standard terms in consumer contracts (Becher and Unger-Aviram, 2009: 18–9).

c. *The effectiveness of regulation and court enforcement on deterrence of onerous terms*

When discussing the content of standard terms, it would also be interesting to see whether firms adjust their terms when regulation and courts rule specific terms to be onerous. Unfortunately, very limited research has been undertaken to provide clarity on this issue. One study that is worth mentioning has been conducted by the Dutch Consumer Authority together with Belgian and Luxembourgian partner institutions. This research study focused on standard contract terms of large chain stores in the Benelux market for consumer electronics. It found that in several of these contracts standard terms were drafted that did not conform to legal requirements (Consumentenautoriteit, 2010). Out of the 18 chains with in total over 3800 stores, 10 chains were shown to use illegitimate standard terms. The terms in question would for instance grant consumers a lower warranty period than is legally obligated, would require consumers to pay for shipment, repair and research costs under all circumstance, or would set unreasonable procedural requirements for returning damaged goods. These terms were thus not only one-sided, they would not even pass court scrutiny.

Furthermore, several statements about the issue can be found in literature. Sullivan for instance mentions a "puzzling persistence of unenforceable contract terms", referring to this as a "common phenomenon" that justifies scrutiny even when empirical evidence is lacking (Sullivan, 2009: 2). With regard to disclosure duties however, as has been mentioned above, Mann and Siebeneicher find that enforcement of disclosure duties is lacks effectiveness (Mann and Siebeneicher, 2008: 998). As this study indicates that sellers in their behaviour largely do not conform to the disclosure duties that have been stipulated by regulation and by courts, it should be doubted that they would adjust the content of their terms to regulation and court rulings.

From their finding that consumers turn to the terms of their contract only when a legal dispute arises, Becher and Unger-Aviram infer that consumers expect the contract terms to be binding and to be held up in court (Becher and Unger-Aviram, 2009: 15). This would render them hesitant to face the costs of a court trial. Eigen in addition finds that consumers are likely to abide by contract terms, instead of challenging them, even if these contract terms do not correspond to their preferences. He furthermore finds that the moral obligation of having to go through with the contract you signed induces people to comply with the contract, more than being confronted with possible legal consequences (Eigen,

2009: 41–3). Also, Stolle and Slain find that exculpatory clauses deter people from pursuing their legal rights. This sheds even further doubt on the effectiveness of enforcement when it comes to deterring sellers from their onerous behaviour and from drafting onerous contract terms (Stolle and Slain, 1997).

d. *Discussion of the empirical results on presence of one-sided terms*

Regarding the one-sidedness of terms, studies by Marotta-Wurgler indicate that the vast majority of standard terms in consumer contracts is one-sided and favours the seller over the consumer (Marotta-Wurgler, 2007b). Mann and Siebeneicher report finding less one-sided contract terms than would be expected on the basis of theory, but their results still indicate a considerable amount of one-sided terms in the contracts investigated (Mann and Siebeneicher, 2008). The results regarding the effect of competition in deterring one-sided terms in consumer contracts are more conclusive. The researchers in both studies, Marotta-Wurgler (2008) and Priest (1981), agree that no evidence can be found for the claim that sellers compete with each other on the basis of their standard terms, which would result in terms that are more attractive to consumers. Note that this result both applies to the possibility that consumers would prefer high quality high price terms, and the possibility that they would prefer low quality low priced terms.

In addition, empirical research indicates that sellers do not fully conform to disclosure duties even though these duties are set by regulation and enforced by courts. This would indicate ineffectiveness of enforcement and insufficient deterrence properties of onerous disclosure duties. This, combined with the study of the Benelux market for consumer electronics, raises doubt on the extent that sellers do conform to regulations and court rules regarding the onerous content of terms. Therefore, the effectiveness of courts and regulation in barring onerous conduct and onerous terms from sellers can be debated. Mann and Siebeneicher (2008) find that a remarkably low percentage of investigated sellers conform to disclosure duties. The studies by Becher and Unger-Aviram (2009) and Stolle and Slain (1997) indicate that consumers expect contract terms to be held up in court. Even though merely indicative, this raises some hesitation with respect to the effectiveness of regulation and courts to deter onerous practices and terms from consumer transactions. One-sided terms can therefore be argued to be present in contract terms. This has been suggested by theory on adverse selection and has been confirmed by empirical findings. Furthermore, empirical results on the ineffectiveness of competition and enforcement of regulation in deterring one-sided terms justify the conclusion that terms in consumer contracts are one-sided and favour the seller over the consumer.

5.5.4. DESIRABILITY OF ONE-SIDED STANDARDISED TERMS IN CONSUMER CONTRACTS

The existence of one-sided, low quality and low priced, terms in consumer contracts is likely, a claim which is based upon theory and the empirical results discussed above. This claim has sparked a discussion on the (un)desirability of one-sided standard terms in consumers' contracts. Some authors argue that one sided terms might be preferred by consumers. Others points out that these one-sided terms are harmless, or that they have a function in controlling consumer moral hazard. They claim that one-sided terms allow sellers to distinguish abusive consumers from reliable ones, but that sellers themselves are prohibited from abuse of their discretion through competition and regulation. These observations warn against government interventions out of welfare considerations, even when is has to be acknowledged that standard terms in consumer contracts are one-sided and favour sellers over consumers.

a. One-sided terms as a sign of abuse

The one-sidedness of terms is commonly understood to suggest information failures and thus welfare decreases, even when the market itself is competitive (Hadfield et al., 1998: 146). However, it is important to point out once again that one-sided contract terms are not necessarily inefficient. Consumers might be quite willing to trade off better contract terms for lower prices, thereby increasing their opportunities to buy products and services (Van den Bergh, 1998: 135). Also in the case of penalty default rules, which are designed to encourage parties with private information to reveal that information, a harsh term might be quite reasonable and efficient. Consumers are more prone to risk aversion than sellers and are therefore more likely to prefer higher quality terms. Due to the adverse selection problem which is aggravated by behavioural biases and supported by empirical results, terms are likely to be offered in a lower quality than preferred by consumers. The problem of a "flea market" is likely to occur with respect to standard terms. The quality is provided on a lower level than preferred by consumers, and the market is not able to provide a higher quality in terms (Schäfer and Leyens, 2009: 107). It should be mentioned that when low-quality low-priced terms are being drafted, sellers invoke them against consumers, and consumers are bound to the contract, this has been argued to not constitute wilful abuse of consumers by sellers. Both sellers and consumers are 'caught' in the flea market: consumers know standard terms are generally of low quality, but accept them since they have no other option. Sellers offer low-quality terms as the market mechanism forces them to do so. It is not in the interest of sellers to offer a better quality of terms, nor in the interest of consumers to read and assess them, let alone to try to accomplish better terms. It is also important to realise that not all consumers would prefer more protection and privileges for a higher price. Not all terms should be offered in a high quality to correspond to consumer wishes. Distinguishing which terms should be offered in higher quality, and which terms should be offered in low quality, remains a difficult issue.

b. Consumer moral hazard and sellers' ability to invoke one-sided terms

Bebchuk and Posner acknowledge that standard terms in consumer contracts are one-sided in the sense that they favour the sellers (Bebchuk and Posner, 2006). They assert however that this is efficient due to the fact that it deters the consumer from behaving opportunistically. Not only sellers can display abusive behaviour; consumers can also abuse sellers. This is referred to as *consumer moral hazard.* Bebchuk and Posner claim that sellers are less inclined to behave opportunistically than consumers in a competitive consumer market as sellers are constrained by reputational considerations. For example, hotels will never ask their clients to pay for an extra night if they check-out a mere ten minutes late (e.g. 11.10 am instead of 11.00 am), even though that is a term of the contract. A term which is unlikely to be invoked due to reputation constraints does enable the hotel to use its discretion and only use this term against opportunistic consumers.

Baird argues that one-sided terms will not cause great detriment to consumer welfare, as sellers are unlikely to invoke them (Baird, 2006: 938–9). The reason for this is that one-sided terms are unlikely to be upheld in court. Thus, even when one-sided terms are drafted into consumer contracts, they are unlikely to be invoked and thus will not have great detrimental effects to consumer welfare.

c. Consumer (re)negotiations and screening

Another motivation for the suggestion that one-sided terms in standardised consumer contracts are relatively harmless relates to consumer (re)negotiations and screening. Some standard terms are designed to be 'forgiven', meaning they will be invoked in very few situations (Johnston, 2006: 877–84). The argument goes that when an unforeseen contingency is fulfilled and this results in dissatisfaction with certain contract terms, these terms will not be enforced against the consumer, provided that she is of good faith. An exception will be made in the benefit of the consumer because that is in the best interest of all contracting parties. However, not all consumers are worth the effort to keep them as customers. Ex-post consumer screening is enabled by one-sided consumer standardised terms. Johnston refers mainly to the examples of repayment schedules to support this claim (Johnston, 2006).[238]

As consumers are unlikely to read standard terms, renegotiation ex post is likely to be the only occurring instance of negotiating standard terms. This corresponds to the findings of Becher and Zarsky, who were the first to empirically

---

[238] See above, section 5.5.2a.

show the importance of the ex post function of standard terms (Becher and Zarsky, 2008). Consumers are far more likely to read standard terms ex post, after a conflict has arisen, than before concluding the transaction. The consumer thus only knows about the standard terms when a problem occurs that is dealt with in standard terms. These terms might not correspond to the preferences of the consumer, which she only finds out upon reading the terms ex post. Therefore, the consumer approaches the seller to complain about that term, e.g. renegotiate the term. This enables sellers to screen individual situations, and offer the terms that would be most beneficial for both seller and consumer. Before the contingency arises, this screening is not possible. As consumers renegotiate their terms ex post, the presence of one-sided terms in consumer contracts should according to these authors not be seen as alarming or detrimental to social welfare.

d. *Discussion of the desirability of one-sided standard terms*

The literature which focuses on providing information about standard terms and behavioural theory with respect to standard terms implicitly assumes that these terms govern the contract. In reality, these terms might not actually be enforced by the drafting parties on a regular basis. The analysis of standard terms could take this factor into account, and distinguish between the cases in which standard terms are usually upheld and the cases in which these terms will usually be waived. This would be an interesting issue to take up in further empirical research. There are quite some concerns that arise from the sellers' discretion in deciding when one-sided terms should be upheld. Sellers can be argued to be prevented from invoking one-sided terms against consumers as they know it will not stand up in court; on the other hand consumers are shown to feel committed to the contract after signing it, so they might also feel bound to one-sided terms. This provides an incentive to sellers to invoke the terms.[239] Therefore, it might not be in the best interests of consumers or in the interest of social welfare to allow companies to decide between the invocation of standard terms and the provision of a better treatment than the standard terms would warrant (Radin, 2006: 1233; Linzer, 2008: 205–6). Bebchuk and Posner do grant that when the influence of reputation is less relevant one-sided terms can be invoked inefficiently, and that social welfare would then benefit from a more generous treatment of the consumer (Bebchuk and Posner, 2006). Typically, consumer sales are not characterised by long term relationships. Also, social norms might be at play here to protect consumers from abuse of sellers. Whether consumer moral hazard provides a sufficient justification for the presence of one-sided terms in consumer contracts should therefore be questioned.

The question of whether the possibility of renegotiating contract terms is a sufficiently effective tool to overcome detrimental consequences of one-sided

[239] See above, section 5.5.2b.

terms to social welfare also deserves some discussion. Renegotiation can occur in cases of divergence between ex ante and ex post preferences of contract parties. With regard to consumer debt, the offer of a repayment schedule will most likely enable the company to recoup a larger amount of the debt than consumer bankruptcy would. A negative consequence for sellers of offering these repayment schedules is that they distort the ex ante incentives that other consumers have for putting effort into paying their debt on time. Depending upon renegotiation to sort *bona fide* consumers from *mala fide* consumers could thus have adverse effects regarding consumer moral hazard.

Also, not all consumers will renegotiate the terms of the contract. If the seller simply waives the standard term in the one contract after the consumer's complaint instead of changing the term in the standard form, the complaint by the marginal consumer does not protect the infra-marginal consumer from unfair terms in the contract.[240] This implies that only complaining consumers stand to benefit from screening practices. A related equity concern can occur with regard to consumer characteristics that are shown to have an effect on the outcome of negotiations (Hadfield et al., 1998: 138). Examples of characteristics that according to economic theory should not have an effect on the outcome of negotiations, but that have in fact been shown to be relevant, are sunk costs and the race or gender of consumers (Ayres, 1991).

In addition, it is not clear whether companies actually do distinguish between customers. Repayment schedules could be offered to nearly all customers in debt, in order to increase the likelihood of repayment; repayment schedules are then not necessarily instruments to screen between consumers and to decide which consumers the company wants to retain. Complaints about return sales policies are linked to consumer moral hazard. It is doubtful that companies can accurately distinguish between consumers who behave opportunistically and those who do not. A strict or lenient return policy could be part of general company policy, and therefore not be a screening instrument at all. Whether these screening methods therefore imply that sellers are able to distinguish between situations in which social welfare might benefit from invoking the one-sided terms and situations in which social welfare requires sellers to be more lenient is unclear. Moreover, it remains to be seen whether sellers have incentives that correspond to social welfare considerations, and whether they will always act in the benefit of social welfare. Even if companies do use standard terms as screening instruments, screening by

[240] The marginal consumer is the consumer for whom the expected benefits of making a complaint outweigh the costs by a very small amount; it is therefore in his interest to complain, but only barely. For the infra-marginal consumer, the expected benefits of complaining do not outweigh the costs, therefore this consumer will not complain. Whether the complaint made by the first consumer aids the second type, as Johnston (2006) claims, depends on whether the terms of the contract are changed for all consumers or whether the complaint only affects the individual contract of the complaining consumer. A similar argument has been made above with regards to the effectiveness of reputation as a means of inducing less one-sided terms. See: Ibrahim (2005), and above, section 5.3.2.

companies in this way is not likely to be socially optimal. Renegotiation might not benefit all complaining consumers. In the absence of perfect competition, screening companies could distinguish between them and for example offer more lenient terms only to the most valuable consumers. Not all of the cases in which it would be efficient to offer more lenient terms need necessarily be given this discretion. The evidence and arguments given for consumer bargaining over standard terms are insufficient to justify one-sided contract terms in consumer contracts without further scrutiny. One-sided terms are likely to occur in standard terms, and their presence seems to be detrimental to social welfare rather than beneficial.

5.5.5. LIMITATIONS OF THE EMPIRICAL STUDIES

On the whole, unfortunately, empirical research regarding standard terms in consumer contracts is lacking. The discussion would benefit from more input, and it would not be warranted to arrive at far-reaching conclusions merely on the basis of the available evidence. However, the insights gained by the available empirical results described above are very relevant to the discussion of the purported adverse selection in consumer standard terms and the ability of consumers to discipline the market. The suggestions provided by empirical research, even though they are based on a limited number of studies, should not be overlooked. The fact that the empirical results all seem to be pointing in the same direction should shed some doubt on traditional economic insights relating to the (limited) need for consumer protection in standard terms of consumer contracts. As will be described in the following chapter, these economic insights have been very influential in the design of consumer policy regarding standard terms. A re-assessment of these policies seems warranted, even on the basis of these few empirical studies. Another limitation of the empirical studies described here is that they have predominantly been conducted in the United States. As this dissertation mainly focuses upon European policy regarding standard terms in consumer contracts (see the next chapter), it should be borne in mind that these empirical results could be influenced by factors that are more likely to be present in the United States than in Europe. Before the implementation of far-reaching new policy can be contemplated, empirical studies should be conducted within European contexts to understand how one-sided terms are effected by competition, reputation, enforcement and consumer reading in the different European states. Research that has been undertaken in the United States can inform European research in aim, structure and methodology.

A further remark to the empirical studies concerns the accuracy of their method. As in some contexts such as mortgages and child day care contracts quite high percentages of consumer reading are reported, it might be concluded on the basis of these studies that intervention on behalf of consumers is ill-advised in these contexts. With respect to this observation however, the differences between reported reading behaviour and actual reading behaviour should once again be brought to mind. The studies on actual reading behaviour suggest that the percentages found in studies of reported behaviour might be overestimations. Furthermore, merely scanning the contracts or even reading it fully does not automatically constitute an effective assessment of the contract. Especially in the case of financial consumer products such as mortgages, where assessment of financial risks is vital, consumers reading contracts might not therefore necessarily be able to discipline the market.[241] Again, more context-specific empirical research is needed to examine the efficiency of contract terms, also in contexts where terms can be expected to be read. Therefore, before adapting policies to correspond to behavioural and empirical insights, further empirical studies are required. These studies should be context-specific and study the exact questions that are relevant for the developed policies.

A possible example might be this: since standard terms have been shown to be one-sided in the study by Marotta-Wurgler (2008), and even overly one-sided in the Benelux consumer electronics market, can standard terms in other sectors of industry and in other countries also be shown to suffer from one-sidedness? This question would especially be relevant in contexts where consumers do report that they read the standard terms, such as in the context of mortgages. The fact that terms are one-sided in online contracts might suggest that terms are one-sided in other sectors of industry as well, if consumers in these sectors are faced with similar difficulties in disciplining the market for efficient standard terms. This suggestion however by itself is insufficient as a ground for (far-reaching) policy interventions. Also, empirical confirmation of Marotta-Wurgler's findings regarding the effect of competition and availability of terms on the quality of standardised terms in software license agreements is required (Marotta-Wurgler 2008 and 2009). Another example of a relevant empirical study could research the extent to which sellers invoke one-sided terms against consumers. Again, these studies should refer to the contexts that they are conducted in, and are relevant only for that industry sector or type of contract. As can be noticed from a review of the empirical studies regarding standard terms in consumer contracts, all of these studies are recent. The large majority of the empirical research in this area has been conducted within the past few years. As the results from this research can have far-reaching implications, especially for policy, more empirical work in this area is to be expected and indeed very welcome.

Discussions about a change in policy strategy on the basis of available empirical research, even though the quantity of empirical results is still insufficient, can be very helpful. These discussions can raise awareness for empirical insights in policy discussions, and put empirical research in the area of consumer protection on the policy agenda, including more specific research into standardised terms

[241] See below, chapter 8, section 8.2.2.

in consumer contracts. Discussions in this field should include the awareness that more specific empirical research is necessary to justify far-reaching policy interventions. Behavioural insights can identify the hypotheses that should be tested empirically and the factors which might be relevant in the given contexts.

5.5.6. CONCLUSION: SUGGESTIONS FROM EMPIRICAL RESEARCH

The empirical studies confirm that there are clear signs of information asymmetry and adverse selection present with respect to standard terms in consumer contracts. Even though these empirical studies are few in number, all data points in the same direction and arrives at the conclusion that the claim that consumers are able to discipline the market regarding standard terms, either through reading, an informed minority group, competition and/or reputation is highly doubtful. One-sided terms are likely to occur in markets, which in turn is quite likely to have a detrimental effect on both consumer and social welfare. The examined empirical studies and overviews suggest that consumers fail to read standard terms in the majority of the contracts that they enter into, and that information duties cannot bring consumers to read contracts either. Only in cases of an unfamiliar vendor and a high value of the contract, consumers report to read the contract. The typical issues that are addressed by disclosure duties, such as availability of the contractual terms and their complexity, do however not seem to enhance readership. Furthermore, the availability of contractual terms before the conclusion of the contract is shown not to enhance the quality of terms. Data from reported consumer reading behaviour points to much higher percentages of consumer reading than studies which research actual readership. Therefore, the effectiveness of information remedies to correct information asymmetry and adverse selection in consumer standard terms cannot be supported in light of the empirical findings.

Consumers cannot be shown to shop for, nor negotiate over standard contract terms. Standard terms in consumer contracts are likely to be provided one-sidedly and favour the seller over the consumer, whether or not that corresponds to the preferences of the consumer. The alleged cure of competition cannot be concluded to have any positive effects on increasing the quality of standard terms; the provision of contractual terms before the contract is concluded cannot be shown to have any positive effects either. Positive effects can neither be expected from private enforcement by consumers; this is again corroborated by empirical insight. These claims are furthermore supported by the finding that people believe that terms will hold up in court, and that they feel bound to the contract. The likelihood of consumers going to court over standard terms and therefore the effectiveness of private enforcement in deterring onerous practices and terms is small. Distributional effects are also a concern, as people from higher socio-economic backgrounds are shown to read standard terms to a larger extent, and to feel less bound to one-sided terms. The question whether the one-sidedness of contract terms actually implies a social welfare loss is also subject to discussion. Some scholars point out that one-sided terms are unlikely to be enforced, and that they serve a function in providing a starting point for renegotiations. Others argue that sellers are unlikely to invoke one-sided terms or to be able to enforce one-sided terms when they are taken to court. One-sided terms will not be enforced if that is not in the best interest of drafting party, who is prevented from enforcing the terms by competition and reputation. This claim would be especially relevant in cases of investments in long term relationships. These scholars conclude that one-sided terms should therefore not be considered a problem to society. However, the one-sidedness of standard terms should still be regarded as highly likely to be detrimental to social welfare, because consumers are more risk-averse than companies. Moreover, neither consumer moral hazard nor screening can sufficiently justify the drafting of one-sided terms in consumer contracts. It is remains doubtful whether the incentives that sellers have to adjust terms in the favour of consumers correspond to the interests of society at large.

The empirical data is as yet insufficient to form a sound basis for policy interventions, especially in Europe. However, whereas only suggestions should be inferred from these studies, the studies that have already been undertaken can inform new research in methodology and structure and can provide new research questions which are specifically oriented at the relevant policy issues. More studies should be targeted at different sectors of industry and different types of contracts to gain empirical insight on the one-sidedness of terms within that industry, the sector-specific effects of competition, the complaining behaviour of consumers and the extent to which consumers are faced with the invocation of one-sided terms against them. Such research would provide valuable further insight about the market for consumer standard terms. Also, even though consumers report that they will read contracts of high value and the contracts which are drafted by sellers that they do not trust, it should not be automatically concluded that consumers are sufficiently protected by their own vigilance in these cases. Further assessment of these contracts, especially in the light of biases regarding risk assessment, seems warranted. On the whole, empirical findings cannot support either the effectiveness of information duties to correct inefficiently low quality terms, or the capability of consumer vigilance and action to discipline the market for efficient standard terms in consumer contracts. Both these remedies are argued for in neoclassical and information economics. A shift towards other interventions in the aim to increase the quality of standard terms in consumer contracts, interventions which take behavioural and empirical insights into account, seems warranted.

5.6. CONCLUSIONS

To conclude this chapter, a summary will be provided of the policy recommendations that result from the insights from neoclassical economics, information economics, behavioural notions and empirical research. Using these recommendations, assessments will be made of both the desirability of government interventions in standardised consumer contracts and the extent to which behavioural insights and empirical data can improve mainstream economics policy recommendations to benefit social welfare.

5.6.1. SUMMARY OF THE DIFFERENT POLICY RECOMMENDATIONS

A short overview will be provided of the main policy recommendations that follow from the different perspectives discussed in this chapter. Next, the research questions that have been posed at the beginning of this chapter will be provided with an answer.

a. The informed minority theory and the vigilant consumer

This chapter started with a discussion of the policy recommendations on standardised consumer contracts from a neoclassical economics point of view, which focuses on the market failure of competition. The standardisation of contract terms raises suspicion as the consent to terms was maintained to be insufficient, but neoclassical economics expects that competition will cure this market failure. An informed minority is argued to be able to discipline the market by stimulating competition between sellers. Sellers are then forced to attract as many consumers as they can, otherwise they will fail in the market. They cannot afford to offer consumers anything less than efficient terms. The market mechanism thus provides the ultimate protection to consumers. As long as there is competition, neoclassical economics claims that government interventions are unnecessary, as there is no problem in the market.

b. Information remedies to stimulate consumer vigilance

The insights from information economics have been presented next, which identify information asymmetry as the main cause of welfare deterioration. Consumers are insufficiently informed about the content of standard terms in consumer contracts. They will opt for desired salient aspects such as a low price, but will likely only make a superficial assessment of the quality of terms. As offering higher quality is more expensive and yet will remain unobserved by consumers, the market mechanism drives the quality of standard terms down in the absence of sufficient market corrections, constituting an adverse selection problem. Policy recommendations focus on information duties, the duty to read and striking onerous terms from contracts. Consumer vigilance is depended upon to discipline the market, as information economics focuses on improving the conditions for consumers to read the terms. Information remedies are therefore the preferred policy solution to overcome the market failure of information asymmetry. Information economics does acknowledge the fact that it might not always be possible to sufficiently counteract information asymmetry in some cases, in that in such cases mandatory substantive interventions might be justified. The preferred policy focus however is based upon information remedies.

c. *Information remedies and consumer vigilance undermined*

The behavioural insights into consumer standard terms focus on the ability of consumers to read and assess terms in consumer contracts, exacerbate the information asymmetry problem and suggest that it might be very difficult for consumers to discipline the market. The informed minority theory and the reliance on consumer vigilance to discipline the market do not correspond to the findings of consumer biases resulting in information overload, low propensity to read and consumers feeling committed to terms even when they do not consider these terms acceptable. These insights shed doubt on the relevance of information remedies as preferred policy solutions to overcome the problem of undesirably low quality terms.

d. *Empirical clarity*

Empirical research has provided some clarity in the issues challenged by neoclassical, information and behavioural economics. Even though the number of experiments, and therefore the corresponding data, is still insufficient to justify any definite conclusions, the results do suggest that consumers are unlikely to read terms, that information duties are unlikely to improve reading, and that consumers cannot be shown to negotiate for terms. Terms are likely to be one-sided, of low quality and to favour the seller over the consumer. Furthermore, the data suggest that sellers do not attempt to catch the fancy of consumers with attractive standard terms. Therefore, no competition with respect to standard terms is likely to occur, and regulation and court enforcement are unlikely to bar onerous terms from contracts or to improve the quality of terms. The empirical data therefore confirm the basic insights of both information economics and behavioural theory. An adverse selection problem occurs with respect to standard terms. However, in a finding which supports behavioural notions, information remedies are shown to have limited effect in inducing consumers to read. Consumer vigilance cannot be shown to be sufficiently effective to stimulate competition and enforce regulation against sellers, and a policy strategy which depends on consumer vigilance can therefore not be supported.

e. The presence and desirability of one-sided terms in consumer contract

A further topic of discussion is whether the presence of low quality standard terms in consumer contracts is in fact detrimental to social welfare. It is acknowledged in this research that not all one-sided terms are inefficient, as consumers might have a preference for low priced low quality terms. Adverse selection however suggests that terms will be offered in a lower quality than would be desirable considering consumer preferences. One-sided terms are claimed to have a function in the sense that they protect sellers against consumer moral hazard and enable sellers to screen consumer preferences, which in turn enables them to offer a better contract to certain consumers. In short, some authors claim that one-sided terms will not be invoked against consumers when that is not in the interest of social welfare, as that would then neither be in the interest of sellers. This claim lacks empirical support however. Also, the interests of sellers might not correspond to the interests of society. The presence of low quality terms can thus not be sufficiently justified. Social welfare could be improved by government interventions which aim to increase the quality of standard terms in consumer contracts.

5.6.2. CONCLUSIONS: BEHAVIOURALLY ENHANCING POLICY – CONSUMER STANDARD TERMS

As has been mentioned in the introduction, two research questions have been the focus of discussion in this chapter:

1. To what extent is government intervention in the quality of standard terms desirable from a social welfare perspective?
2. To what extent can insights from behavioural notions and empirical research improve the policy recommendations from mainstream economics within the context of improving the quality of standard terms from a social welfare perspective?

To conclude this chapter on policy recommendations regarding the quality of standard terms in consumer contracts, an answer to these questions will be provided.

a. Desirability of government interventions in standard terms

Due to information asymmetry and adverse selection, the quality of standard terms that is provided in the market is likely to be too low from the perspective of social welfare. This implies that consumers prefer a higher level of quality in standard terms than the level of quality that is provided by sellers, even if consumers would have to face extra costs from a higher level of quality. Market corrections are not sufficiently able to overcome this welfare loss. However, consumers are unlikely to be able to discipline the market into providing efficient standard terms, not even when they are aided in this endeavour by information remedies. Biases and heuristics impair consumer decision making and consumer vigilance. Sellers will therefore not be induced to draft efficient terms in consumer contracts by competition or by litigation. The claim that low quality terms will not be invoked against consumers when this is not efficient from a social welfare perspective, cannot be supported. Social welfare therefore stands to be improved by government intervention that aims to improve the level of quality of standard terms. Consumer policy cannot rely on consumer vigilance to discipline the market; even when information duties are provided to stimulate this vigilance, consumer vigilance is likely to be insufficiently effective. This conclusion justifies government interventions that reach beyond the provision of information in order to improve of the quality of standard terms in consumer contracts.

b. Can behavioural insights and empirical data improve policy recommendations?

Regarding the issue of standard terms in consumer contracts, neoclassical economics recommends reliance on the market mechanism, provided that imperfect competition problems are dealt with by competition policy. According to neoclassical economics, an informed minority of consumers will discipline the market. Information economics points to the market failure of information asymmetry and recommends information duties in order to improve consumer vigilance. Behavioural insights aggravate concerns about the information asymmetry problem by highlighting the fact that information remedies are less likely to sufficiently counteract information asymmetry than is theorised by information economics. Empirical data suggests that information asymmetry and adverse selection are indeed more severe, that competition will not have any substantial effects, and that information duties are also unlikely to be very effective. The empirical data support the insights from information economics to some extent, and confirm the doubts raised by behavioural economics relating to the limited effectiveness of information remedies and the effectiveness of consumer vigilance to discipline the market. More extensive empirical research in specific market contexts is warranted to assess the claim that consumer vigilance and information duties are insufficiently effective. This research should distinguish between different sectors of industry, as the influences of competition, sellers' reputation and reading behaviour of consumers is likely to be dependent on industry-specific characteristics.

Therefore, it can be concluded that behavioural insights and experimental data do provide reasons for a change in consumer protection policy regarding standard terms in order to improve social welfare. As the effectiveness of information duties is undermined by consumer biases and heuristics, consumers are even less likely to be able to discipline the market than information economics have theorised. If governments wish to improve the quality of standard terms, policy suggestions that look beyond the provision of information and the reliance upon consumer vigilance should be considered. These recommendations are not the same as information economics or neoclassical economics recommendations. The empirical results do indicate that such improved recommendations could enhance social welfare. It is therefore concluded in this research that behavioural insights and empirical data can indeed improve policy recommendations related to unfair terms in consumer contracts from a social welfare perspective.

This change in policy recommendation consists of a shift in policy focus away from consumer vigilance aided by information remedies. Information duties are insufficiently able to induce consumers to read and discipline the market, and therefore insufficiently able to improve the quality of terms to a more socially desirable level. This suggestion is based upon theory from information economics, behavioural insights and empirical data.

c. *To continue: standard term policy and policy suggestions*

In the following chapter, the discussion turns to actual consumer policy related to standard terms in contracts by reviewing the common core of European consumer policy related to standardised contract terms. This overview focuses on European legal systems, while providing some insights on legal rules and policies prevalent in the US. This chapter will conclude that current policy aims and strategies, like information economics, rely to a large extent on information provision and consumer vigilance to enhance the quality of standard terms in consumer contracts. As behavioural insight has shed doubt upon this strategy and this doubt has been supported by empirical research, chapter 7 discusses several possible policy strategies that aim to improve regulation concerning standardised consumer contract terms, such as solving the signing-without-reading problem, doing away with standard contract terms in the consumer market, or establishing some sort of administrative control over standardised contract terms. That chapter aims to provide a starting point for the discussion of how the behavioural insights and empirical results can be implemented into policy.

CHAPTER 6

CONSUMER POLICY AND THE QUALITY OF STANDARD TERMS – REVIEW OF THE COMMON CORE

6.1. INTRODUCTION

The previous chapter explored the issue of the desirability of interventions in consumer standard contract terms from several perspectives. It has been established that behavioural insights and empirical data can improve policy recommendations regarding the issue of consumer standardised terms that stem from both neoclassical and information economics. This chapter will discuss the legal discussion and literature as well as actual consumer policies related to the issue of standard terms in consumer contracts. It will provide a review of the European common core in legal approach to consumer standard terms and assess its correspondence to the insights developed in traditional economics, information economics, and behavioural insights. The review will focus on the common policies, doctrines and rules that are used in unfair terms regimes in European legal systems but will occasionally refer to legal systems in the United States. The aim of this chapter is to establish to what extent common policies in Europe correspond to the policy prescriptions that follow from the assessment in the previous chapter. It will therefore first determine the extent to which this common core relies upon the effectiveness of provision of information and consumer vigilance in generating a sufficiently high quality of consumers' standardised terms. Next, the chapter will establish the effectiveness of the common approach in unfair terms itself in improving the quality of contract terms. This chapter will establish that the current common core of European consumer policy related to standardised contract terms largely corresponds to the insights of information economics. Information remedies currently form the main intervention strategy in standard terms, which depend strongly on consumer vigilance to provide improvement to the quality of terms. This chapter will question the effectiveness of the common approach in unfair terms regimes in this respect. The next chapter, chapter 7, will discuss several policy strategies that could be resorted to when aiming to improve current consumer policies regarding standard terms.

As has been stated above, this chapter will review and analyse a European '*ius commune*' or '*common core*' of the legal approach on standard terms in consumer contracts. This method, which extracts a common core in legal approaches instead of addressing the specificities of several legal systems in detail, is common in comparative law and economics.[242] A prime source for common legal principles in European contract law is the Draft Common Frame of Reference (DCFR). The DCFR is a project within the European Union which draws upon the EC Consumer Acquis and on best practices found in Member States' legal orders to develop clear definitions of legal terms, fundamental principles and coherent model rules of contract law.[243] Although these European policies differ in many ways, they commonly share their main instruments of consumer policy. Examples from different Member States will throughout the review serve as illustrations to this point. This chapter will first provide a description of the common legal approach, followed by an assessment to establish the extent to which this common legal approach corresponds to the insights developed in chapter 5 of this research.

The scope of this research does not allow for an extensive comparative overview of legal systems and the way in which they target onerous terms in consumer contracts or try to improve the quality of consumer contracts in general. General and comparative overviews with respect to the regulation of unfair terms in consumer contracts and consumer protection regulation in general have been provided extensively elsewhere.[244] This research will focus on the common

242 See for instance: Bussani and Mattei (1997: 340).

243 For an introduction to the DCFR, see Schulte-Nölke (2007) and Clive (2008). The project has been heavily debated. See for instance: Smits (2008a), Smits (2008b), Rutgers (2008), Jansen (2008), Beale (2008a), Mak (2008), Hesselink (2009) and Eidenmüller (2009).

244 See for a general comparative overview of regulations and policies regarding unfair terms in consumer contracts in the European Union, see European Commission (2000), EC Consumer Law Compendium (2008). Bates (2002) compares unfair terms regimes in the US, UK, Germany, Sweden and Israel. Maxeiner (2003) provides an overview and comparison between US, EU and German law regarding unfair terms in consumer contracts, Micklitz (2008) compares the legal rationales for controlling unfair terms in Germany, France and the UK, and Alpa (2008) compares the Italian and UK legal system. See also Collins (2004: 792–94), Ben-Shahar (2009: 7–20) for a general description of private law regulation of standard form contracts, where Ben-Shahar also introduces the US approach. For earlier discussions of the topic of standard terms in consumer contract from a legal perspective in Europe, see for instance: Lando (1966) and Bourgoignie (1983). Weatherill (2005: 113–34) gives an introduction to EC Consumer Law and Policy regarding the regulation of the substance of consumer contracts. De Boeck and Van Hoecke (2008) also provide a very general overview of European unfair terms regimes, referring to several national systems such as France, Germany, the UK, Belgium, the Netherlands and Spain. For national perspectives, see for instance Howells and Weatherill (2005: 261–94), Ramsay (2007: 157–213) discussing the UK perspective, Sheldon (1974) and Bernitz (1973) focusing Swedish law, Wilhelmsson (1993) on the Nordic model in general and Pavillon (2006) reviewing the Dutch unfair terms regime, including commenting upon the difficulties encountered when implementing the EC Directive into national law. On the European Directive on Unfair Terms in Consumer Contracts (93/13/EEC), see: Bernitz (2000), De Geest (2002), Weatherill (2005: 115–28), Van Boom and Kottenhagen (2006), Collins (2008), EC Consumer Law Compendium (2008). For an in-depth comparison between the DCFR and the Proposal Consumer Rights Directive (as will be introduced below, see note 267), see De Booys, Hesselink and Mak (2009).

legal approach related to standard terms in consumer contracts in Europe. The resulting insights and conclusions from this research could provide a starting point for the analysis of individual legal systems in Europe and elsewhere.

After commenting upon basic legal concepts and principles of consumer law in these systems, this chapter will discuss common instruments of intervention in consumer contracts. To do justice to the differences between legal regimes, the third part of this section examines to what extent various unfair terms regimes can differ in scope. The fourth part of the chapter provides a review of enforcement practices.

First however, the common legal approach to standard terms in consumer contracts is assessed. Recently, the ability of consumers to discipline the market has been questioned and policy discussions have called for more substantive control in this field. It might be possible and necessary even to improve unfair terms policy in order to generate a higher quality in standardised consumer contract terms.

6.2. POLICIES REGARDING UNFAIR TERMS IN CONSUMER CONTRACT

This section will provide an overview of the common legal approach to standard terms in consumer contracts, exploring the common core of legal principles, policies, rules, doctrines and practices regarding consumer standardised terms, within European legal systems. The analysis will occasionally refer to the US legal system for further illustration. Standard term policies are often referred to as *unfair terms* policies. Other denominators for standard terms are *boilerplate*, *pre-formulated* or *adhesive terms*. Freedom of contract and laissez-faire are principle concepts within general contract law and more specifically in standard term policies. With respect to standard terms, consumers have a duty to read the terms. Their acceptance of the price and main subject matter covers the contract terms like a blanket, and causes consumers to be bound to the contract even if they did not read the terms. These legal consequences do call for some protection of consumers against onerous terms. Procedural intervention tools related to unfair terms in consumer contracts include information duties and remedies. The availability requirement, transparency, readability and intelligibility should allow and stimulate consumers to read and understand the terms of the contract. Substantive intervention in the terms of consumer contracts usually consist of a substantive test, such as unconscionability, fairness or reasonability, and can be supported by the addition of black and grey lists of unfair terms The enforcement measures within unfair terms regimes focus on the elimination of unfair terms in consumer contracts. To enhance the efficacy of enforcement measures, consumer interest groups in EC Member States have now been awarded the right to apply for an injunction against unfair terms in court. Also, regulatory agencies with some power of enforcement have been established; these agencies can issue fines and injunctions.

6.2.1. BASIC LEGAL CONCEPTS AND PRINCIPLES IN UNFAIR TERM REGIMES

This section will start with an exploration of the concepts and principles that form the basis of standard terms policy. When contract laws and policies were first applied to contracts, they were designed with an 'arms length transaction' in mind. This refers to a situation where seller and buyer meet face-to-face, discuss the details of the buy, inspect the good and agree on the transfer. As the unfair term regimes are derived from general contract law, consumer contract law has inherited some of the basic principles of general contract law such as freedom of contract and individual responsibility. Within the realm of standard terms these principles apply as well, be it that they are balanced by objectives such as protection of consumers against onerous terms in consumer contracts. Policies and rules that have been enacted to provide protection to consumers from onerous standard terms are justified by the (weaker) position that consumers occupy vis-à-vis sellers. One major issue within consumer law in general and more specifically in unfair terms regimes is the question to what extent a consumer can and should be held responsible for her own actions. This question is complicated by the clear dichotomy between the informed and capable consumer on one end of the spectrum, and the incapable and weak consumer on the other.

a. *Freedom of contract and laissez-faire*

Freedom of contract, consumer choice and active consumerism are main concepts within consumer law of European and United States' legal systems.[245] The principles share the common claim that parties to a contract themselves are best able to decide what contracts they wish to engage in, and that they should therefore have the freedom to set the terms to a contract as they see fit. European consumer law has a strong focus on consumer choice, which allows the consumer to profit from the increases in quality, diversity and decreasing prices that have been the result of enhanced competition within the EU (Weatherill, 2005: 34–7). Competition law and consumer protection might thus be understood to have the same goal: to improve the position of the consumer by campaigning for consumer sovereignty (Waller, 2005: 631; Wilhelmsson, 2006: 72). The active consumer is

[245] The foundation of governing methods on the autonomy of individuals and individual private power is a general characteristic of European Contract Law. See Grundmann, Kerber and Weatherill (2001: 7). See also Wilhelmsson (1993: 445–6) for a discussion of the importance of principles of freedom, autonomy and responsibility in the Finnish unfair terms regime.

however a necessary factor in this process: the active consumer needs to discipline the market and to generate welfare enhancing transactions to fuel the positive effects from increased competition. This vision on the consumer is portrayed for instance in the EC Consumer Policy strategy 2007–2013, which states that 'confident, informed and empowered consumers are the motor of economic change as their choices drive innovation and efficiency' (European Commission, 2007).[246]

The *laissez-faire* approach that is common in contract law is extended to policy related to standard form contracts (Kornhauser, 1976: 1154). Government intervention which affects autonomy and personal choice is criticised for interfering with basic notions such as freedom of contract and individual freedom or autonomy (Weatherill, 2005: 114). Following these basic notions, parties are free to decide which transactions they would like to enter into and on which terms contracts will be concluded. Principles of autonomy and personal choice similarly oppose after the fact intervention in contract terms by courts, as such intervention would undermine the certainty of contract and the autonomy of parties to decide for themselves which terms should govern their contract. The fact that courts can bar a term ex post, a term which parties have agreed on ex ante, would give an incentive to parties to agree to an unfavourable term in exchange for a certain benefit in exchange, only to challenge the unfavourable term at a later point. The view here described thus claims that because standard terms decrease transaction costs and are therefore favourable to both producers and consumers, these terms should be held up in court unless they are obviously abusive (Hillman and Rachlinski, 2002: 455).

b. Individual responsibility, duty to read and blanket assent

The notion of freedom of contract might be said to have two dimensions: the freedom to set the contract as one wishes, and the freedom to make mistakes while doing so. *Caveat emptor*, an assertion of individual responsibility, was and is the guiding principle in contract law and enforcement in European legal systems (Van Boom et al., 2008: 25). The basic rule therefore is that parties will be held to the contract, even if the contract turns out to be less favourable in hindsight. This principle has greatly influenced contract laws and policies, including those related to standard terms (Leff, 1970b: 143). In the context of standard terms in consumer contracts, the fundamental idea is still that parties assent to the terms of the contract and that contracts are binding.[247]

The basic principle of freedom of contract therefore includes a duty on contract parties to carefully consider their transactions. This duty refers to

[246] See Beale (2008b: S83) who criticises the DCFR for this view of "competent consumers".

[247] See also Träger (2008: 59–60) for a historical survey of freedom of contract and individual responsibility in unfair terms regimes.

standard terms as well as to terms that were explicitly agreed on in the contract procedures. Both consumers and sellers have a *duty to read*, which does not imply that they are obliged to read contract terms, or that will get a fine when they do not read contract terms, but it does mean that the contract terms will govern the contract even when parties choose to not read the terms.[248] The consumer concludes the contract under a presumption of assent, or *blanket assent* (Hillman and Rachlinski, 2002: 455).[249] By accepting the price, the good, and other aspects of the transaction, the consumer automatically accepts all the terms of the contract. The assent to the transaction covers all contract terms like a blanket. When consumers have had a meaningful opportunity to read the terms before entering into the contract, they are presumed to assent to the terms of the contract without actually reading them, and are therefore bound to the contract.

c. Dichotomy: consumer responsibility and inability

There is an important dichotomy within consumer protection law between two different views of the consumer: the confident and informed consumer on the one hand, who can discipline markets by active pursuit of the best deals in quality and price, and on the other hand the weak consumer who is unable to discipline the market as she is confronted with too many hurdles to complete this task. Maxeiner refers to these both views as the *contract model* and the *consumer model*: the contract model protects the freedom of contract, and the consumer model protects consumers (Maxeiner, 2003: 160). The first view could only call for interventions that aid the consumer in his task, his pursuit, if any interventions could be required at all. Interventions of this sort could include information requirements, which allow the consumer is to make an informed decision. Consumer law according to the contract model should support consumers in making their own informed decisions, and leave the autonomy of the consumer intact. The second view, the consumer model, is more closely linked to paternalism and could justify more substantial interventions to protect consumers. This protection could shield consumers not only from sellers' abusive behaviour, but even from their own flawed decision making.[250]

The dichotomy between the contract model and the consumer is very visible in unfair terms regimes. To the extent that consumers are presumed to be able to discipline the market, information remedies are provided to help consumers make informed choices. In such cases, the consumers now have the main responsibility for striking the deal that is in their best interest, as consumers have been given

---

248 As has been discussed above, chapter 5, section 5.3.5a. See also Bernitz (1973: 21).

249 The theory of *blanket assent* is attributed to Llewellyn (1960: 370–1).

250 Reasons for intervention in consumer contracts are discussed by several authors. See for instance: Ramsay (1984: 15–35), Haupt (2003), Van den Bergh (2003), Levitin (2007), Rischkowsky and Döring (2008). See Van Boom, Tuil and Dijkshoorn (2008) for an interesting collection of discussions on autonomy, paternalism and the role of private law.

the means to protect themselves from bad deals: the necessary information. Consumers will not be protected from their own flawed decision making as long as the required information is available, whether they choose to use that information or not. When consumers choose not to read standard terms, even though the contract form is available and the terms are properly disclosed and transparent, they will be bound by the contents of the contract. Excessive protection of consumers may lead to adverse effects, and could for example stimulate consumers to enter into all kinds of transactions without any careful consideration. Consumers, not sellers, are the best party to look out for consumer interests. Therefore, they are given an incentive to pursue their goals actively and thoroughly (Barnett, 2002).[251] This line of argument clearly rests on the contract model.

On the other end of the spectrum lies the view that consumers are just not able to sufficiently perform the task of disciplining the market. The bargaining position of consumers is not equal to that of sellers because (individual) consumers lack size and resources. The capabilities and effort that the task of disciplining the market would entail are so huge that consumers cannot be expected to successfully complete this task. In this view, the consumer model, consumers are regarded to be "somewhat naïve and (in) need to be protected against a tendency to be easily impressed and to act hastily and thoughtlessly" (Hartlief, 2004: 254). This view tends to regard consumer law as a set of rules that should protect 'weak' consumers from 'abusive' producers and sellers, and that should allow contractual agreements between the two parties to be more equal. Therefore, consumers should not (always) be held responsible for their choices in situations where sellers abuse their relative position towards consumers. Consumers cannot be expected to read standard terms in consumer contracts. It is too strenuous to even attempt to understand these terms, let alone to compare them to other contracts or to negotiate better terms. It makes no sense for consumers to read standard terms; they can therefore not be expected to be able to discipline the market. The consumer model claims that consumers have not really assented to onerous terms in consumer contracts and therefore cannot be held responsible for accepting them. The enforcement of standard contract terms against the weaker party would according to this line of argument actually deny that party the freedom of contract, because the weaker party is then subjected to terms that he never asked for nor agreed to (Rakoff, 1983: 1237).[252]

The legal approach to standard terms in consumer contracts, and in consumer policy in general, should be understood in the light of this dichotomy. Finding the right balance between consumer responsibility (aided by information) and

251 Kornhauser (1976) discusses this view extensively and argues that even though at that time (1976) this view was the main basis for standard term policy, the policy basis for intervention in contract terms was already changing.

252 See Linzer (2008) for a discussion of both views, where Linzer argues for the second approach.

consumer inability is difficult. The main question is the limit of the responsibility of the consumer.[253] European unfair terms regimes generally strike a compromise between both views. Consumers are generally protected against onerous terms: terms that are considered to be so disadvantageous that consumers would never rationally and knowingly assent to them. The fact that such terms are included in the contract suggests that sellers are taking advantage of consumers' inequality. In many cases however, consumers are still expected to take action against onerous terms in contracts. Beyond the level of the onerous, terms which consumers might find undesirable but which are not strictly considered to be onerous by legal standards are a different category all-together. With respect to undesirable terms, consumers themselves are supposed to stimulate the market in providing the terms that they prefer. They can either negotiate for better terms or file suit against sellers who included undesirable but not strictly onerous terms in the contract, and argue that in this particular case the undesirable term should not govern the contract.[254]

d. *Legal rationales for policy intervention in consumer standard contracts*

Two main rationales for intervention in consumer (standard) contract terms can be identified in the common core of legal approaches towards standard terms: *abuse by sellers* and *transaction costs and information asymmetries* (EC Consumer Law Compendium, 2008: Part 2 C.I). In consumer transactions, the two parties

---

253 This subject is related to another issue, namely which type of consumer should be the benchmark in regulations and court proceedings. EC policy takes the stance that the average consumer is to be the benchmark, which means that people are responsible for their own weaknesses if such weaknesses are beyond average (EC Directive 2005/29 recital 18). This benchmark has often been criticised, for instance by Incardona and Poncibò (2007). They argue that the benchmark of the average consumer should be replaced by the benchmark of the weak consumer. This issue is linked to the question whether consumer law has a special stance within contract law, or whether the legal system should maintain 'Sonderprivatrecht', a singular legal regime that applies to all contracts. The latter option might call for protection of the weak instead of merely the average consumer in order to provide adequate protection to consumers who do inhibit a different position in reality than commercial parties do, even if the law does not wish to grant them an exception. For example, both Germany and the United States did not have special consumer protection provisions within general contract law and employed the benchmark of the weak consumer. The Netherlands, and also EC legislation, do provide for specific consumer protection legislation and apply the benchmark of the average consumer. Also, ECJ rulings that enforce the benchmark of the average consumer would augment the importance of this particular view of the consumer in national legal systems, even when this view was not a part of that legal system before. The issue will not be extensively explored in this research, but merits further investigation.

254 EC consumer policy is dominated by the view of the competent consumer who is capable to look after her own interests as long as she has been properly informed or has had a fair opportunity to acquire that information (Wilhelmsson (2006: 52). The right to information is a fundamental right of consumers, already recognised in the first EC Resolution on consumer protection, as is mentioned by Van den Bergh (2003: 25). However, EC consumer policy does recognise that there are situations in which the consumer is not able to discipline the market, and should be protected from sellers' abuse.

to the contract have important differences in characteristics, which could allow of the parties to take advantage of the other. Sellers are generally the larger party, they have a better financial position, they engage themselves regularly in these contracts and they possess over a number of resources competences.[255] One rationale for intervention in consumer contracts is therefore provided by the protection of consumers' abuse by sellers. Consumer contract law aims to balance the position of the two parties to the contract by the introduction of interventions to protect the weaker party.[256] In the European common core, the *inequality* between contract parties thus provides a legal rationale for the protection consumers with regard to (standard) contract terms. The identification of inequality however is just a starting point for consumer protection law. The specific aspects of that inequality, the factors generating it and its consequences are vital for the determination of the appropriate legal response (Howells and Weatherill, 2005: 261).

Inequality between sellers and consumers does not provide the only rationale for monitoring or otherwise intervening in pre-formulated consumer contract terms. Another important rationale is provided by transaction costs and information asymmetries. The seller, who has drafted the contract terms, is usually better informed about the content of standardised terms than the consumer. For the consumer it is often too expensive to obtain the information required for negotiating the conditions of the transaction. High transaction costs of the assessment of the contract and information asymmetries should be counteracted by consumer protection policy.[257] This second rationale has the underlying claim

255 Consumer protection law can be restricted to apply only to natural persons, which depends on the legal system or on the specific laws, acts and directives that apply to the issue at hand. See below for a brief discussion concerning the definition of consumer.

256 The ECJ states in the *Oceano Gruppo* case that the EC Unfair Terms Directive is based upon the weakness of the consumer vis-à-vis the seller or the supplier, with respect to both his level of knowledge and his bargaining position (ECJ, 27 June 2000, in joined cases C-240/98 to C-244/98, *Océano Grupo Editorial SA v Roció Murciano Quintero)*. This would correspond more to abuse theory than to transaction cost considerations. There might however also be a different theory behind EC policy. Schillig (2008) for example argues that the adverse selection motivation is behind the Unfair terms regime. Hesselink (2007: 856) discusses a company lawyer of Siemens, who in one of the regulatory workshops of the European Commission DG SANCO argued that the necessity of protecting large companies from consumers should not be overlooked. Although Hesselink seems to regard this comment is rather comical, it might also indicate that EC policy makers are open to economic insights which argue that companies can suffer from consumer moral hazard and should possibly be protected against the consumer.

257 It is furthermore argued that the legal systems in the EU have different views on which rationale is more important with respect to protecting consumers. See for a discussion of these differences in scope below, section 6.2.3. For example, in legal systems where the consideration of transaction costs was a main reason for policy interventions, the standard terms regime would typically include business-to-business contracts, but not individually negotiated terms. Examples of legal systems that base their unfair terms regime on transaction cost considerations would be German, Dutch and Portuguese law. On the other hand, legal systems that adhere to the abuse theory will typically only protect the consumer in the standard terms regime, and apply the regime only in business-to-consumer contracts. In such systems the

that when the consumer is adequately informed, she is able to prevent abuse by sellers. All legal systems can be argued to recognise both rationales, abuse by sellers on one hand and transaction costs and information asymmetries on the other, as valid reasons to intervene in consumer contract terms, and to have used these rationales in the construction or intervention measures. The most common interventions in European legal systems will be reviewed in the following part of this section.

6.2.2. INTERVENTIONS IN TERMS OF CONSUMER CONTRACTS

Even though freedom of contract is the leading principle in contract law, and consumers are assumed to have assented to the contract terms, some protection against onerous terms is commonly deemed necessary. Therefore several legal doctrines and rules aim to improve the position of the consumer in order to counteract abuse by sellers or transaction costs and information asymmetries. Policies with regard to standard terms in consumer contracts relate to two main issues: one is the principle of transparency and the other is control over the content of the contract. The first type of policy will aim at balancing out the information asymmetry that is typical of a consumer contract, and the second will aim to eliminate onerous clauses (Ferrante, 2005: 116). Interventions can also be divided along different lines, into three groups: ex post intervention by courts, ex ante regulation by legislators and competition enhancement (Becher, 2009: 749). As has been mentioned above, these interventions cannot be clearly divided; for instance, the effectiveness of many regulatory interventions depends on the effectiveness of court interventions.[258] It has already been pointed out that this research focuses on regulatory interventions. This research however acknowledges the interaction between these regulatory interventions and enforcement issues, and will briefly discuss enforcement issues from a legal perspective in this chapter.[259]

Regulatory interventions in consumer contracts can relate to the *substantive part* of the agreement and therefore aim to influence the content of the transaction, or they can relate to the *processes and procedures* that have led up to the contract and the communication and interaction between parties (De Hoon, 2007: 6–9).[260] The main legal and regulatory interventions of standard terms in consumer contracts include procedural rules that aim to stimulate consumer reading and meaningful assent to contract terms, and substantive rules which bar onerous

scope of the regime would however be extended to individually negotiated terms. Examples of legal systems which base their unfair terms regime on abuse theory would be French, Belgian and Luxembourgian law.

258 See above, chapter 5, section 5.3.3b.

259 See above, chapter 5, section 5.3.3d.

260 See above, chapter 2, section 2.3.3c.

terms from consumer contracts.[261] Furthermore, default rules are employed to decrease transaction costs. This results in the following list of common instruments to address pre-formulated terms in consumer contracts:

a. Procedural rules, consisting in information rules and remedies;
b. General substantive rules for striking onerous terms, to be assessed by courts;
c. Banning the use of specific contract terms through the use of black and grey lists;
d. Default rules.

a. Procedural rules and interventions: information duties[262]

Nearly all legal systems use information remedies to address the issue of unfair terms in consumer markets.[263] The main consumer policy instrument to counteract information asymmetry is *information disclosure* (Hadfield et al., 1998: 143; European Commission, 2005: 10).[264] This also follows from the *Cassis de Dijon* case, in which the court gives preference to information remedies.[265] Interferences with the content of the contract are generally only deemed admissible if information requirements provide insufficient protection. As Howells states, the provision of information is undoubtedly "one of the key tools available to enhance consumer protection... Information and warnings are the traditional tools of consumer protection" (Howells, 2005: 352–3). The obligation on sellers to disclose information to consumers is "(t)he most widely used means of consumer law of the European Union" (Haupt, 2003: 1139). The imposition of pre-contractual information duties on sellers has been a particularly popular tool in consumer protection policy (Whitford, 1973: 400; Wilhelmsson and Twigg-Flesner, 2006: 452). Information disclosure by sellers can therefore be seen as the preferred

261 Howells and Weatherill (2005: 263–4) argue that doctrines such as undue influence, misrepresentation, duress and fraud are not aimed at targeting standard terms in consumer contracts. They claim that unfair terms merely create issues of inadequate information and limited choice for consumers, and that these other doctrines target different issues, such as deceit and taking advantage of unfortunate circumstances on behalf of the counterparty. Therefore, these authors argue that the doctrines of misrepresentation, undue influence, duress and fraud should be not discussed within the scope of standard terms. For a more recent comparison on a number of regulatory interventions, see Beale and Schulte-Nölke (2007). See for a discussion of these instruments: Johnston (2006: 860–4). Some comments about the use of regulatory approaches in various legal systems will be provided in the footnotes below.

262 Information duties have been introduced in the chapter 5, section 5.3.5.

263 See Armbrüster (2008) for a comprehensive discussion of the role of information and information rules in standard contract terms from a European perspective.

264 Gozzo (2005: 18) contends that party autonomy and information requirements have been set as rationales for consumer protection policy by the European Commission to avoid cultural problems between Member States' legal systems. He claims that these relatively abstract notions as underlying goals of consumer protection policies have become a strategic instrument for the pursuit of harmonisation of European contract law. Harmonisation is beyond the scope of this research; see below, note 282.

265 ECJ, 20 February 1979, in case C-120/78, *REWE-Zentral AG* v. *Bundesmonopolverwaltung für Branntwein*. See Micklitz (2008) for further discussion of this case.

policy solution to counteract information asymmetry, including information asymmetry related to standard contract terms. EC consumer law in particular is strongly committed to the information paradigm and the belief that through information consumers can discipline the market (Wilhelmsson, 2006: 71).

The policy instrument of information disclosure consists of several procedural rules. One of these procedural rules, which is part of nearly all European and United States' legal systems with regard to consumer unfair term regimes, is the *availability requirement*. This requirement stipulates that the contract terms have to be (easily) available to the consumer should she wish to read them. Following another procedural rule, the contract should be *transparent*, which basically means that reading and comprehending the form should not be too difficult.[266] The contract therefore should be written in *plain language*, the *font size* should not be too small and the terms should be *intelligible*. Excess amounts of '*legalese*' and long sentences decrease transparency. Contract terms that are particularly questionable from the perspective of the consumer can call for *evident disclosure of specific terms*. To further enhance the opportunity for consumers to become acquainted with the terms of the contract, *cooling off periods* can be set to allow the consumer an extended period in which she can reflect on her decision to enter into the contract and reverse it if need be.

The *contra proferentem* rule, which stipulates how unclear contract terms should be explained, can also be understood as an information rule. The *contra proferentem* or *ambiguity rule* is a rule of contractual interpretation which stipulates that an ambiguous term will be construed to the disadvantage of the party who has drafted the term in question. As sellers are usually the drafters of terms, this rule will often benefit and protect consumers. Contra proferentem also provides an incentive for sellers to draft intelligible terms, because ambiguous or unclear terms will be explained in favour of the consumer. Sellers can only invoke clear and comprehensible standard terms against consumers.[267] Another kind of intervention which aims to improve consumer information is the provision of information about consumer rights. Government agencies can provide information to consumers, information that educates them their rights, or subsidise organisations to provide comparative pricing and term information.

[266] On the requirement of transparency and the consequences of a lack of transparency in the EC Member States, see EC Consumer Law Compendium (Part 2 C.V).

[267] Stated to be interpreted in the way "most favourable" to the consumer in art. 5 of the EC Directive on Unfair Terms in Consumer Contracts (93/13/EEC), from here on referred to as EC Unfair Terms Directive. The same formulation is used in art. 36 of the Proposal for a Directive of the European Parliament and of the Council on Consumer Rights, as published by the European Commission (2008) (from here on: Proposal Consumer Rights Directive). This directive is at the moment still a proposal, and does not yet apply legally to consumer contracts in EC Member States (January 2010). See also Proposal Consumer Rights Directive, art. 31. For a discussion of the *contra proferentem* rule, see for instance Bernitz (1973: 29–31) and Cserne (2009).

The procedural rules that govern standard terms in consumer contracts aim to improve the position of the consumer vis-à-vis the seller through the provision of information. By enhancing the opportunity for the consumer to read the contract, assent to the contract terms can be more easily established even if the consumer chose not to read the terms. The procedural rules thus complement the duty to read and blanket assent principles. Information duties allow the consumer to become informed and therefore allow her to make an informed decision. Consumers can opt for the contract terms that they prefer, either by negotiating or by shopping for terms. Information duties aim to establish a fair content of the contract by encouraging informed decision making (Wilhelmsson and Twigg-Flesner, 2006: 449–50). The information disclosure rules can even be seen as normative, because they encourage consumers to base their decisions on the information that is provided more carefully (Whitford, 1973: 438). Now that consumers have had the opportunity to read contract terms, the consequences of the duty to read can be legitimately imposed on them even if consumers did not read the terms.

b. Substantive tests

The take-it-or-leave-it nature of standard term contracts and the difficulties to read the terms are regarded important issues in the legal discussion of unfair or standard terms in consumer contracts. The take-it-or-leave-it nature of standard term contracts refers to the fact that the content of these terms is set by sellers, who might be bound by reputational concerns only. Legal literature has also expressed great concern that sellers will draft contracts that are primarily in the interest of sellers and do not concern the interest of consumer.[268] Therefore, in addition to the procedural rules that aim at increased provision of information, European legal systems have implemented a substantive test on which contract terms are evaluated: the *fairness test*.[269] Similar doctrines and rules are referred

268 Maxeiner (2003: 114) quotes a legal counsellor to a US Fortune 500 company, saying that: "(t) he purpose of form contracts is primarily to protect to needs of our [internal] clients, not to protect the interests of our customers."

269 The fairness test in the EC Unfair Terms Directive, Art. 3, reads that if a contract term shall be regarded as unfair if, "contrary to the requirements of good faith, it causes a significant imbalance in the parties' rights and obligations arising under the contract, to the detriment of the consumer". According to Art. 4(1), the unfairness of a contractual term "shall be assessed by (1) by taking the nature of the goods or services for which the contract was concluded into account, and (2) by referring, at the time of conclusion of the contract, to all the circumstances attending the conclusion of the contract and (3) in relation to all the other terms of the contract or of another contract upon which it is dependent." Additionally, the annex to the EC Unfair Terms Directive has a certain indicative effect in the assessment of the fairness of a clause. About the legal consequences of unfairness in the EC member states, see EC Consumer Law Compendium (Part 2 C.IV). In the Proposal Consumer Rights Directive, this definition has not changed, nor the fact that the circumstances of the contract have to be taken into account (in art. 32).

to as *reasonability*, *fairness* and *unconscionability*.[270] These doctrines differ among legal systems with respect to details in implementation, but share very similar basic principles and aims.[271] Substantive tests allow courts to strike onerous terms from consumer contracts. The 'unfairness' can both refer to substantive terms or procedural terms (Willett, 2007: 1–3). Substantive unfairness regards the division of rights and obligations provided for by the contract terms. Procedural terms regard what happens in the process leading to the conclusion of the contract, which would be negatively affected by a lack of transparency or a lack of choice. These could lead to an unacceptable compromise on the ability of the consumer to protect his interests at the procedural or pre-contractual stage. When a contract term is so onerous that consumers would not reasonably expect it to be included in the contract, when the terms is incompatible with the conscience of the courts or if the term can be deemed unfair in the sense that it benefits the seller greatly to the expense of the consumer, the term can be stricken from the contract.

c. *Black and grey lists: barring onerous terms ex ante*

The substantive tests described above provide standards and thresholds to evaluate the contents of contractual terms in consumer contracts. The assessment of these standards can further be aided by the provision of black and grey lists.[272] Black and grey lists illustrate and clarify the proper implementation of the substantive test, which increases legal certainty and decreases the workload of courts. In most to all legal systems, blacklisted contract terms should always be considered onerous, which renders them immediately null and void. Grey lists can also be employed and refer to terms that are merely presumed to be onerous. The consequences of striking a term from the contract can differ among legal systems. Sometimes, the term is replaced with a similar default rule stipulated in contract law. In other cases the entire contract can be seen as void.[273] The burden

---

270 See also above, Chapter 5, section 5.3.6, where substantive tests for standard terms have been introduced. Most Commonwealth countries employ a general concept of unconscionability; the English courts however did not up until the EC Unfair Terms Directive. The English Unfair Contract Terms Act 1977 did contain a reasonableness test, but this Act only applies to exclusion and limitation of liability clauses and to indemnity clauses in consumer contracts. See Ramsay (2007: 168–191) for a discussion. Collins (2004: 794) mentions that the fairness test in the European Directive on Unfair Terms is interpreted differently in the various Member States.

271 See Hillman and Rachlinski (2002: 456–8) for a discussion on how the fairness concept in European civil law relates to the unconscionability concept in the United States.

272 The EC Unfair Terms Directive only contains a grey list; other systems like the Dutch regulations of standard terms contain both a black and a grey list. For a comparative overview of EC Member States, see EC Consumer Law Compendium (Part 2 C.IV.3). The Proposal for a Consumer Rights Directive opts for both a black and a grey list (Annex II and III). The US legal system does not incorporate any black or grey lists; Bates (2002: 94–5) suggests implementing a policy instrument that would enumerate general categories that would be presumed not to pass the substantive test into the US legal system.

273 See Maugeri (2008) for a discussion. See also below, section 6.2.3a.

of proof for the claim that these standard contract terms are not onerous would be placed with the drafter and user of the terms.

Terms that are black- and greylisted can serve as an illustration of the standard that is applied by substantive tests. Examples of terms that are blacklisted can for instance be found in the Proposal Consumer Rights Directive, in Annex II.[274] The Proposal Consumer Rights Directive states that "… (c)ontract terms, which have the object or effect of the following, shall be unfair in all circumstances:

(a) excluding or limiting the liability of the trader for death or personal injury caused to the consumer through an act or omission of that trader; …[275]

(c) excluding or hindering the consumer's right to take legal action or exercise any other legal remedy, particularly by requiring the consumer to take disputes exclusively to arbitration not covered by legal provisions; …[276]

(e) giving the trader the right to determine whether the goods or services supplied are in conformity with the contract or giving the trader the exclusive right to interpret any term of the contract; …"[277]

In Annex III, some examples of terms that are presumed to be unfair can be found: "(c)ontract terms, which have the object or effect of the following, are presumed to be unfair: …

(b) allowing the trader to retain a payment by the consumer where the latter fails to conclude or perform the contract, without giving the consumer the right to be compensated of the same amount if the trader fails to conclude or perform the contract; …[278]

(d) allowing the trader to terminate the contract at will where the same right is not granted to the consumer; …[279]

(h) obliging the consumer to fulfil all his obligations where the trader has failed to fulfil all his obligations; …"[280]

All these terms are examples of terms that allow more privileges to sellers than to consumers. The example of Annex III term b) is an obvious unbalanced privilege, which enables the seller to retain consumer payment without having to provide any form of compensation. Some terms, such as Annex II term e), might even give adverse incentives to sellers. When this term applies to the contract,

---

274 The suggested terms on the black and grey lists in the Proposal Consumer Rights Directive have been derived from Member States' regulation. This renders these lists interesting examples of blacklisted and greylisted terms. The original EC Unfair Terms Directive only provides a grey list, which was the result of a compromise between Member States. See Wilhelmsson (2006: 57–8) for further discussion of that topic. The terms that are mentioned here are comparable to the terms that are greylisted in the Annex of the EC Unfair Terms Directive, which is the directive that currently applies since the Consumer Rights Directive, at this point, merely has proposal status.

275 Comparable to term (a) in the Annex of the EC Unfair Terms Directive.

276 Comparable to term (b) in the Annex of the EC Unfair Terms Directive.

277 Comparable to term (m) in the Annex of the EC Unfair Terms Directive.

278 Comparable to term (d) in the Annex of the EC Unfair Terms Directive.

279 Comparable to term (f) in the Annex of the EC Unfair Terms Directive.

280 Comparable to term (o) in the Annex of the EC Unfair Terms Directive.

sellers have an incentive to state that they determine every good to conform to the contract, even if the good cannot reasonably and objectively be argued to conform to the contract specifications.

Furthermore, it can easily be argued that these terms are all quite undesirable from the perspective of consumers. It could of course also be argued that consumers knowingly take a risk with respect to these terms and accrue a benefit in the form of lower prices in return; the undesirability of these terms is therefore not undisputed. However, because the possible consequences of these risks are considerable and these terms might even give adverse incentives to sellers, consumers are assumed not to have knowingly assented to these terms.

d. Default rules

Besides the procedural and substantive rules, consumer contract law also provides for default rules to fill gaps in incomplete contracts. The freedom of contract provides that parties are free to set the rules as they please; when they do not decide on specific rules to govern their transaction, the default rules in consumer contract law can be referred to in order to settle disputes should they arise. Also, when an unfair term is stricken from the contract, default rules can be used to fill the created gap.

6.2.3. SCOPE OF UNFAIR TERM REGIMES

The scope of the unfair terms regime differs among legal systems of European Member States.[281] This scope can be restricted to business-to-consumer contracts, but it can also be extended to include business-to-business contracts. Another issue is the exclusion of price and main subject matter from the substantive test. A third way in which the scope of the unfair terms regime can differ among legal systems is whether it excludes negotiated terms from the assessment. The EC Unfair Terms Directive has a narrow approach and limits its scope to business-to-consumer contracts and excludes price, main subject matter and negotiated terms from review. EC consumer law is governed by the principle of *minimum harmonisation* and thus establishes the lower threshold level of consumer protection that has to be provided by Member States. The currently proposed Consumer Rights Directive however will change this situation. The Proposal Consumer Rights Directive aims to apply *full harmonisation* in European Consumer Protection law, at least with respect to the issues that are dealt with in the Consumer Rights

[281] See also Beale (2008a), who argues that it is hard to find a real common core in European contract law as contract law regimes differ in EC Member States. He cites the example of mistake and disclosure duties.

Directive, which includes issues of standard terms in consumer contracts.[282] This will imply that EC Member States can no longer diverge from the legal approach prescribed in the Proposal Consumer Rights Directive.

As long as this directive has not been adopted, Member States can opt for a broader scope of application of the unfair terms regime; in fact, many Member States have done just that. This broader scope can consist of the applicability of the unfair terms regime to business-to-business and consumer-to-consumer contracts (instead of only business-to-consumer), the inclusion of price or main subject matter in the unfair terms regime, and the subjection of negotiated terms to the same regulations as standard terms.

a. Business-to-consumer, business-to-business, and consumer-to-consumer[283]

"Consumer law" or consumer protection law refers to all laws and regulations that affect consumption and consumer markets. The concept of consumer which is adhered to in legislation and regulation often depends on the area of application.[284] In some contexts a different concept of consumer might be applied than in other legislative areas. A typical definition might be: "a consumer is a

282 See Proposal Consumer Rights Directive, pages 3, 6–7. See also above, note 267. This research will not explore the issue of whether harmonisation of European Consumer Protection law is desirable; this very interesting discussion falls outside the scope of this research. See for contributions to this discussion: Collins (2004), Hondius (2004), Gozzo (2005), Weatherill (2005: 61–83), Loos (2007), Cherednychenko (2007), Poncibò (2007) and Mak (2009; 2010). See for a discussion of harmonisation in the area of unfair contract terms, Amato (2008). Harmonisation of European Private Law is difficult to defend from an economic perspective, mainly due to the differences in consumer preferences and market structures throughout the European Union, which makes different model forms efficient in various parts of Europe; see Van den Bergh (2002a; 2002b).

283 See for a comparative overview with respect to wider notions of consumer and types of contracts, EC Consumer Law Compendium (Part 2 C.III.1.a, b and c; Part 3 A.III).

284 This research will merely portray the differences in scope between Member States with regard to parties that are included in the regime as a part of the introduction to unfair terms policy in Europe. It will not address the topic of the desirability of different scopes, business-to-consumer, business-to-business, or consumer-to-consumer, or the topic of harmonisation of these scopes in much detail. See for a discussion of this issue for instance Howells and Weatherill (2005: 262), who claim that commercial parties should also be protected by the unfair terms regime. Similar problems as the ones addressed by the unfair terms regimes protection consumers might occur in relationships between large and small trading parties. Aquaro (2003) argues that the scope of consumers should be extended from private to also legal persons, which is also discussed by Luth and Cseres (2009: 262–5). See Roppo (2009) for the claim that European legislation is focuses more and more on asymmetric contracts, referring to contractual relationships that suffer from inequality between parties, whether those parties are natural or legal persons. Roppo argues that this focus is desirable from efficiency and fairness perspectives. See furthermore Heiderhoff and Kenny (2007: 5) who argue that small businesses, entrepreneurs or professionals cannot be defined as consumers following European case law.

natural person who acquires the goods or services in question outside the scope of his or her professional expertise" (Terryn, 2008: 57).[285]

Professional expertise refers to both experience and knowledge about the transaction at hand. Small to medium enterprises generally do not enjoy the same protection as consumers, even though they might sometimes have a similar position vis-à-vis larger contract parties, for example when a medical practitioner buys a computer for his office. When the product or service is acquired for both a private and a commercial use, the buyer usually cannot enjoy the protection that is awarded to the consumer. Consumer protection regimes can be extended to cover such cases, even if the level of protection can be somewhat diminished (Hondius and Rijken, 2006: 85).[286] In some cases, when the unfair terms regime is wide in scope and governs both business-to-consumer and business-to-business contracts, even consumer-to-consumer contracts are governed by the unfair terms regime.[287]

b. Price and main subject matter[288]

Within European consumer law, most legal systems more specifically exclude *essential terms* from the scope of the general and the fairness test in the unfair terms regime, such as price and main subject matter and certain substantive tests.[289] These product aspects should then either be considered by the consumer herself, or they might fall under other contractual doctrines such as misrepresentation, fraud and duress. The doctrine of *iustum pretium*, which holds that a just price must be paid and that unjust price should be prevented, is not commonly held in European legal systems. This means that parties should for themselves decide how much they want to pay for a certain good. It might for example be argues that insufficient competition could result in prices that are too high; and as this practice is usually dealt with by competition law, the *iustum pretium* doctrine is usually not applied within consumer contract law. With respect to the fairness test however, some legal systems do incorporate price and main subject matter into the assessment.[290] Price and main subject matter are however excluded from review by the fairness test in the Proposal Consumer Rights Directive; when this proposal and resulting limitation in scope will be enacted, the extended

---

285 For a discussion on the concept of *consumer*, see Terryn (2008: 56–60).

286 See for instance the case *Gruber* (ECJ, 20 January 2005, in C-464/01, *Johann Gruber v Bay Wa AG*).

287 This is for instance the case in the Nordic countries.

288 See for a comparative overview with respect to assessing price and main subject matter, EC Consumer Law Compendium (Part 2 C.IV.1 and 2).

289 Insurance contracts are, at least in European legal systems, usually not governed by the general approach to unfair terms in consumer contracts, as all terms in these contracts relate to price and can be considered to be essential terms. See for a discussion, Van Boom and Kottenhagen (2006).

290 This is the case in Austria, Denmark, Greece, Latvia, Luxembourg, Romania, Slovenia, Spain and Sweden.

scope that is currently applied in some legal systems at this moment could be compromised.[291]

c. *Individually negotiated terms*[292]

Also individually negotiated terms are frequently excluded from the review of fairness tests. When consumers have negotiated one or more contract terms with the sellers, the respective unfair terms regime may no longer apply to those terms. Individually negotiated terms are not standard terms and can be seen to cater to the specific wishes of the consumer that negotiated for these terms. A negotiated term might hold up in court even if this term would have been deemed unfair if it had been a standard term. In these cases, consumers can be argued to have knowingly assented to certain terms through negotiations; therefore, the fairness test is no longer applied. Here, the risk that sellers abuse information asymmetries suffered by consumers is not considered to be a concern, as consumers are clearly aware of terms they negotiated for. Even though some Member States include individually negotiated terms into the scope of their substantive tests, the unfair terms regime in the Proposal Consumer Rights Directive does not apply to negotiated terms. The burden of proof however remains on the seller to support his claim that the term was individually negotiated. Again, the Proposal Consumer Rights Directive could limit the scope of the fairness test in all Member States to exclude negotiated terms from review.[293]

In the DCFR, the definition of a term that is *not* individually negotiated is given as follows: "a term supplied by one party is not individually negotiated if the other party has not been able to influence its content, in particular because it has

291 See Proposal Consumer Rights Directive, art. 32 sub 3. The Green Paper on the Review of the Consumer Acquis, published by the European Commission (2006: section 4.6, at page 19), did suggest to extend the scope of the fairness test mentioned in the EC Unfair Terms Directive regarding consumer standard terms to also cover price and main subject matter. This policy option will be discussed below, see chapter 7, section 7.2.3.

292 DCFR II. – 1:110; see EC Consumer Law Compendium (Part 2 C.III.3.b) for a comparative overview of which EC Member States include individually negotiated terms in the scope of the unfair terms regime: Belgium, Czech Republic, Denmark, Finland, France, Latvia, Luxembourg, Malta, Slovenia, Sweden. Germany has excluded individually negotiated terms from review, but has defined that notion very narrowly, in the sense that the consumer has to fully understand the substance of the contract and be aware of its legal consequences.

293 See Proposal Consumer Rights Directive, art. 30 sub 1. The DCFR does not take a stand on the issue of in- or excluding individually negotiated terms from the scope of the unfair terms regime. In II.-9:403, "which has not been individually negotiated" has been put between square brackets. In the introduction to the DCFR, it is stated (under 72, page 46 of the online version) that "the question is a delicate one and better left to a political decision". The Green Paper on the Review of the Consumer Acquis did suggest extending the scope of application of the EC Unfair Terms Directive to also cover individually negotiated consumer contract terms (section 4.4.1, at page 18). This policy option will be discussed below, chapter 7, section 7.2.3.

been drafted in advance, whether or not as part of standard terms." Additionally, the DCFR contains the following restrictive conditions:

- If one party supplies a selection of terms to the other party, a term will not be regarded as individually negotiated merely because the other party chooses that term from that selection.
- If it is disputed whether a term supplied by one party as part of standard terms has since been individually negotiated, that party bears the burden of proof that the term has been negotiated.
- In a contract between a business and a consumer, the business bears the burden of proving that a term supplied by the business has been individually negotiated.
- In contracts between a business and a consumer, terms drafted by a third person are considered to have been supplied by the business, unless the consumer introduced them to the contract.

As a consequence of these conditions, it is questioned whether the practical consequences of thus extending the fairness test would have been very great due to the limited amount of terms that can be determined as being individually negotiated under the definition of the DCFR.

6.2.4. ENFORCEMENT OF UNFAIR TERMS REGIMES

As has been mentioned previously, the effectiveness of regulatory provisions with regard to unfair terms in consumer contracts depends to a large extent on (court) enforcement. Although this research focuses on regulatory efforts to enhance the quality of consumer standardised terms, some remarks about the enforcement of unfair terms regimes will be presented. The unfair terms regimes are mainly enforced by private enforcement, but recently public enforcement has been more and more effective in barring onerous terms from consumer contracts. The consequences of the identification of certain terms as unfair may differ among legal systems. In EU legal systems, consumer organisations can also challenge terms on behalf of consumers.

a. Elimination of unfair terms

The enforcement efforts with respect to standard terms in consumer contracts within the EU focus on the elimination of unfair terms (European Commission, 2000: 20–9). The consequences of the fact that a certain term has been deemed unfair can however differ.[294] In some systems, terms that are deemed unfair are regarded as never having been written and therefore have no legal consequences even when they are part of contracts. In other systems the term is part of the

[294] EC Consumer Law Compendium (Part 2 C.III.4).

contract until the party that is supposed to be protected by these rules, usually the consumer, calls for the nullity of the term. However, even when an onerous contract term is deemed to be invalid and should not have any legal consequences, sellers might still be able to (illegally) invoke these terms against consumers. When a consumer confronted with unfair contract terms fails to take the necessary initiative against them, sellers can invoke these terms against consumers even when they would not have held up in court. Therefore, the deemed nullity of terms will not be of any assistance to consumers unless they are aware of the unfairness of terms and corresponding legal rights, and take action against them.[295]

The fact that consumers can be confronted with unfair terms and might not (be able to) act against them is one of the reasons that in recent years enforcement agencies such as consumer authorities have been set up in nearly all EC member states. The enforcement agencies are usually able to issue fines or injunctions when they detect the use of unfair terms.[296] The public body of the Consumer Ombudsman is also active in some EC member states, most notably in the Nordic countries.[297] In these countries, the Consumer Ombudsman reviews standard forms from industry, following a complaint or by own initiative. Upon finding an undesirable term, the Ombudsman would usually seek compliance by the company primarily through negotiations. In the odd case that this approach is not successful, a complaint may be filed at the Market Court.[298]

---

295 See for a further discussion of enforcement difficulties connected to European unfair terms regimes, below, section 6.3.2d. Both the US and the UK opt for this model. However, the ECJ has stipulated that judges are obliged to assess whether terms can be considered onerous, even if a consumer who brings a claim against a seller does not challenge this and other terms as being onerous (ECJ, 4 June 2009, in case C-243/08, *Pannon GSM Zrt. v. Erzsébet Sustikné Győfi*). How this ruling will influence national law adjudication will become clear in the coming years.

296 See for an introduction to the Dutch Consumer Authority: Ammerlaan and Janssen (2007). The Dutch Consumer Authority has been operating only since 2006; see art 2.2, 2.5, 2.7, 2.9 and appendix B of the Wet Handhaving Consumentenbescherming. For the Dutch Consumer Authorities' approach to consumer standardised terms, see consuwijzer.nl/Consumententhema_s/Algemene_voorwaarden. As has been mentioned above, chapter 5, section 5.5.3c, the Dutch Consumer Authority together with Belgian and Luxembourgian partner institutions has conducted a study on the legality of standard terms in the Benelux consumer electronics market. In the UK, the Office of Fair Trading (OFT) can be viewed as both a regulatory and enforcement institution. It uses abstract review and assesses terms outside the contexts of their use in individual cases. See Ramsay (2007: 194–204) for a discussion of the role of the OFT in policing unfair terms in consumer contracts.

297 In Sweden, unfair terms in consumer contracts are reviewed and controlled by the Consumer Ombudsman and the Market Court. See Sheldon (1974: 37–59) for an discussion of the achievements of the Swedish Consumer Ombudsman and Market Court in the first two years of their focus on standardised terms, and Bates (2002: 67–79) and Viitanen (2007) for more recent overviews of the Swedish resp. the Nordic approach to consumer protection.

298 In Israel, a Standard Terms Tribunal has been specifically set up to deal with unfair terms issues. This Tribunal can also give pre-approval to standard forms. See Deutch (1990), Bates (2002: 79–90) and Becher (2009) for discussions of the Israeli unfair terms regime. See below for a discussion of this policy alternative, chapter 7, section 7.2.4.

b. *Standing before the court*

In most legal systems and for a long time, only courts have had the official power to prohibit the use of unfair contractual terms. The regulations concerning standard terms in consumer contracts largely rely on private enforcement, which means that private parties need to challenge these terms in courts (Howells and Weatherill, 2005: 292). However, as has been argued in the previous section, consumers are unlikely to file suit against unfair standard terms. In light of the concern that consumers might not take legal action against unfair terms and in order to enhance the deterrent value of the enforcement mechanism, the right apply for an injunction against unfair terms in court has been granted to consumer organisations. In addition to consumers that have been confronted with unfair terms themselves and consumer organisations, the right to seek injunctions against unfair terms can be extended to other associations, such as trade and professional associations and public authorities.[299] This usually includes institutions such as the Consumer Authority and the Consumer Ombudsman which were referred to in the previous section. As has been stipulated within EC Directive, all EC member states provide for collective court procedures, which usually allow some representative party, such as a consumer organisation, to challenge unfair terms on behalf of consumers (EC Consumer Law Compendium, 2008: 252).

c. *Consistent enforcement in EU: the CLAB*

An interesting instrument within the context of enforcement against unfair terms in consumer contracts is the European Database on Case Law about Unfair Contractual Terms (*CLAB*, which stands for "clauses abusives"). This project, which is initiated and financially supported by the European Commission, aims to create a comprehensive database on consumer contract terms that have been deemed onerous within EC Member States' court proceedings. The CLAB would have a potential beneficial impact not only in harmonious and consistent enforcement of unfair terms throughout EU legal systems, but might also allow courts to save valuable time and effort (European Commission, 2000). Furthermore, it could be a valuable research tool for academics and practitioners. This database is however criticised for not being very user-friendly, and its

[299] In Sweden however, individual consumers have no standing in the Market Court, which is reserved for appointed consumer representative organisations and the Consumer Ombudsman. In Israel the Attorney General is also authorised to stand up in court on behalf of consumers, as well as consumer groups. See Bates (2002: 69–70, 73, 84) for a discussion; see for a further discussion of control via public agencies and private organisations below, chapter 7, section 7.2.5. See also Van den Bergh (2008) for a discussion of the enforcement of consumer law through consumer associations. Furthermore, see Proposal Consumer Rights Directive, Art 41, for an example of expanding the rights to take legal actions in the enforcement of consumer law.

existence was very well-known (Micklitz and Radeideh, 2005: 344; Van Boom and Kottenhagen, 2006: 139–40). The CLAB database also does not seem to be very well maintained.[300] The effectiveness of this instrument in the generation of a more consistent enforcement of unfair terms throughout EU legal systems should therefore be questioned.

6.2.5. SUMMARY

European unfair terms regimes generally compromise between the competent and the incapable consumer, or the contract model and the consumer model. The principles of freedom of contract and *laissez-fare* in general contract policies are also applied to consumer standard contracts. Consumers are generally held responsible for agreeing to contractual terms they do not desire. A duty to read is enforced against them, which implies that standardised contract terms will govern the contract even when consumers did not specifically agree to these terms, as long as consumers have agreed to the transaction at large. However, consumers are protected against onerous terms.

Consumers are not supposed to (be able to) protect themselves from onerous terms, or rather, when onerous terms are drafted into consumer standard forms abuse by sellers it is assumed that consumers would not knowingly assent to these terms and assent is therefore deemed not to have taken place. The consumer model applies; assent to onerous terms in standardised consumer contracts will therefore not be held against consumers. Regulation such as substantive tests, black and grey lists and the extension of enforcement rights to other parties such as consumer associations, protect consumers from unfair terms. They do not have to discipline the market on their own; other parties such as consumer authorities, associations and regulatory agencies are able to bar onerous terms from consumer contracts. Onerous terms are stricken from the contract and cannot be held against the consumer, even if she assented to the standard form. However, the necessary initiative to act against unfair terms will largely remain with the consumer. When a consumer is confronted with unfair terms in consumer contracts, and she does not act against them, sellers are able to invoke unfair terms against consumers even when this term would not have held up in court.

Substantive tests and black and grey lists can only affect the quality level of terms up to the level of unfairness. A term that is undesirable from the view of a consumer, but meets the substantive requirements, will hold up in court and will be binding to the consumer. The contract model applies above the level of

[300] At least not up until 2000, see European Commission (2000: 28–9); see also Micklitz and Radeideh (2005) for an extensive introduction to the CLAB and even statistical analyses of the entries, on the basis of which they discuss the strengths and weaknesses of the database and present a critical review of the effectiveness of the project.

unfairness: when consumers have assented to contractual terms, these terms will be held against them. Consumers themselves are supposed to be capable of stimulating the market into providing the terms that they prefer. When contract terms are not deemed to be unfair according to the substantive measures, sellers' abuse of consumers' lack of knowledge is more difficult to establish. Consumers themselves are in these cases responsible for obtaining the contractual terms that they desire into the contract. Procedural rules, which often relate to information duties, help consumers in this endeavour. Procedural rules reduce the transaction costs that consumers face in the assessment of contractual terms. Following these rules, contract terms have to be made easily available, transparent and intelligible. When terms are drafted ambiguously, they will be construed to the disadvantage of the drafting party, usually the seller. When terms are likely to be considered undesirable by consumers, specific disclosure of these terms might be required. Also, cooling off periods might be mandatory, which grant the consumer a longer period of time to become acquainted with the terms of the contract. Furthermore, government institutions provide consumer education to make consumers aware of their rights in issues of standard terms in consumer contracts. Also, default rules are provided in contract law to lower transaction costs for both sellers and consumers.

Substantive rules protect consumers from onerous contract terms. Procedural controls such as information duties help consumers to accomplish the task of disciplining the market with regard to certain terms, terms that meet certain substantive requirements. It remains the responsibility of the consumer to bring about terms that are higher in quality than just-above-onerous should they prefer this higher quality, and to take care of their own interest in negotiations. This is how the balance between substantive and procedural requirements in unfair terms regimes has generally been struck until now. The answer to the dichotomy of the competent consumer vis-à-vis the incapable consumer is provided by securing a threshold level of quality, namely unfairness, below which consumers are not considered capable to discipline the market, but above which consumers are held responsible for bringing about the quality of contract terms they wish to obtain. That being said, many cases involving onerous terms still depend on consumer initiative to start enforcement procedures.

Furthermore, the scope of application of different European unfair terms regimes differs. Some unfair terms regimes apply to business-to-business and consumer-to-consumer contracts in addition to business-to-consumer contracts. Furthermore, price, main subject matter and negotiated terms can but are not necessarily excluded from the application. The elimination of unfair terms mainly depends on private enforcement procedures, in which the consumer has to initiate the necessary actions, sometimes assisted by consumer organisations. Besides private, also public institutions have recently become more active in barring onerous terms from consumer contracts.

6.3. ASSESSMENT OF UNFAIR TERMS CONSUMER POLICY

The description of the common core of European unfair terms regimes regarding consumer contracts that has been presented in the previous section will serve as a basis for an assessment of unfair terms consumer policy. This sections aims to establish which insights correspond most to the common core of unfair terms regimes. It will be established that the common approach corresponds mainly to the insights developed in information economics, even though the legal rationale of sellers' abuse is not so easily reconciled with economic theory.

Furthermore, it will assessed whether the policy recommendations that have been provided in chapter 5 have been already implemented in the legal approach on unfair consumer terms, or whether consumer policy could still be improved by these recommendations. It will be shown that the recommendations from chapter 5, which suggest looking beyond information provisions and consumer vigilance in the aim to enhance the quality of consumer standardised terms, do correspond to some policy measures in the common core of consumer policy on standard contract terms. However, this policy still depends to a large extent on information provisions and consumer vigilance. In fact, several difficulties that have been brought forward in the legal debate concerning unfair terms regimes also question the effectiveness of information disclosure and the dependence on consumer vigilance. In the legal debate, these difficulties have resulted in a call for more substantive interventions. The balance that is struck between procedural and substantive control has recently been more and more criticised. Policy makers argue for a shift to more substantive control in unfair terms and present several policy proposals to enhance consumer standard terms regimes through increased substantive control.

6.3.1. UNFAIR TERMS REGIMES: CORRESPONDENCE TO INFORMATION ECONOMICS

This section aims to assess the common core of European unfair terms regimes. When the insights developed in the previous chapter are taken into account, it can firstly be argued that European unfair terms regimes correspond mainly to the notions of information economics. The view that sellers abuse consumers is less easily reconciled with this perspective. Also in the legal debate, some concerns have been raised with respect to the common approach of standard terms in consumer contracts. These concerns can be argued to correspond to behavioural criticism. Based upon these concerns, a call for more substantive interventions is brought forward in policy discussions. Whether this call can be justified based upon the policy recommendations developed in the previous chapter will be considered in the next chapter, which will assess several proposals for amending standard term consumer policies.

a. *Correspondence with notions of information economics*

In the context of policy interventions on standard terms in consumer contracts, the main rationale for protecting consumers is nowadays provided by insights from information economics. In fact, both the procedural and substantive interventions can be argued to correspond to information economic insights. The line of argument is roughly as follows: information asymmetry and the corresponding adverse selection problem decrease the quality of standard terms, which justifies government intervention (Eidenmüller, 2009: 127).

In earlier decades, the main argument for the regulation of terms in consumer contracts focused on the abuse of monopoly power, which would correspond to neoclassical economic insights. However, competition policy is now seen to deal with these issues in a sufficient way (Schäfer and Ott, 2004: 371). The information failures that occur even when the market itself is competitive provide the key motivation for government interventions and consumer policy in unfair contract terms (Hadfield et al., 1998: 146–7).[301] Schillig therefore argues that the legal paradigm of intervention in unfair terms has shifted from an "inequality of bargaining power" motivation to a rationale of "adverse selection" (Schillig, 2008).[302] The fact that sellers are able to abuse consumers is largely caused by the fact that consumers are not aware of the content of the contracts. This allows sellers to draft low quality standard terms in the contract, which can be detrimental to consumers even when prices are adjusted accordingly. The policy tools, principles and doctrines which relate to unfair terms in consumer directives seem to be mainly directed at making the consumer more informed (Willett, 2005: 10). The transparency principle, which requires expression in plain and intelligible language, combined with the duty to read, should enable and incentivise consumers to become informed. Information duties, even though they are mandatory, are aimed at increasing party autonomy (Grundmann, 2002: 280). A strong link between the information paradigm in EC consumer law and RCT can be established (Micklitz, 2008: 21).

Both the view of the rational and competent consumer as well as the view of the incapable and vulnerable consumer can be justified from the perspective of information economics. As a starting point, information asymmetries should be targeted by information remedies. However, the framework of information economics also supports the concept of rational apathy. Information economics

301 See also for a more general discussion on the on the role of information in private law: Van Boom, Giesen and Verheij (2008: 24–7).

302 Schillig (2008) also argues that EC Unfair Terms Directive corresponds more to the notions from information economics than to imperfect competition, because it takes its suggestions from ECJ case law.

therefore understands that in some cases consumer choice and private enforcement cannot effectively overcome market failures. Rational apathy, which refers to a wilful assent to unknown terms, would be most detrimental when it concerns onerous terms. Terms that meet the fairness test are arguably less detrimental to consumers even when they have been assented to without prior reading or assessment, and might not justify costly interventions. Cases of consumer assent to onerous terms as a result of rational apathy require a kind of government intervention which goes beyond merely providing information in order to avert considerable consumer detriment. The substantive interventions in the common core of unfair terms regimes, regarding substantive tests, black and grey lists, can therefore also be justified on the basis of information economics.

A very different discussion however is whether this particular standard is set at an optimal level from an economic perspective. As consumer preferences can differ, any mandatory standard will have distributional effects. Some consumers might prefer a lower quality than the substantive test prescribes, especially when they are sufficiently compensated by for instance a price reduction (Collins, 2004: 793). The assertion that substantive requirements can be justified from the perspective of information economics does not yet imply that the specific standard that has been achieved in unfair terms regimes in Europe is efficient from an economic perspective. This assessment would require an extensive study, primarily of the relevant case law, which is outside the scope of this research. However, it can be asserted that in principle, when terms can be argued to be undesirable to a large majority of consumers, economic considerations could justify banning these specific terms. The examples that have been provided in the black and grey lists suggest that this requirement has been met in unfair terms regimes in Europe.[303]

b. Sellers' abuse according to legal and economic insights

Abuse theory, the rationale for consumer protection that is provided by sellers' abuse of consumers through unfair terms, does however not fully correspond to information economics. The adverse selection that results from information asymmetries is not strictly regarded as wilful abuse of consumers by sellers in information economics. Information economics considers both seller and consumer to be 'trapped' in a flea market. Consumers are not able to generate a higher quality of terms, but sellers are neither able to do so as the market mechanism forces them to draft low-quality terms.

The consumer law model and corresponding abuse theory tend to view consumer law as a set of rules that should protect 'weak' consumers from 'abusive' producers and sellers. As consumers suffer from constraints in size and resources, their bargaining position is not equal to that of sellers. This weakness argument

[303] See above, section 6.2.2c.

however provides no information about the causes of quality deterioration on consumer markets (Van den Bergh, 2003: 19–20). Adverse selection could account for this observation. Based upon information economics, it could be argued that deterioration in quality is not so much caused by the 'weak' position of the consumer, but rather by the fact that the consumer is less informed than his counterpart. Consumer protection law however is still (partly) concerned with abuse of consumers by sellers. Therefore, not all aspects in consumer policy relating to unfair terms correspond to information economics.[304]

6.3.2. CRITIQUE FROM THE LEGAL DEBATE: ENHANCING STANDARD TERM QUALITY

The legal debate has also brought forward several points of critique against the current legal approach on unfair terms in consumer contracts. The criticism relates for example to the presumed assent to unread standard terms and the effectiveness of disclosure duties in securing informed assent or enhancing the quality of standard terms. Also, as the availability requirement is used as a proxy to bar undesirable terms from the contract, consumers are argued to be in need of a higher level of quality of terms. Furthermore, the legal debate has pointed out several issues with the enforcement of unfair terms regulation.

a. *Presumed assent and signing-without-reading*

As has been discussed above, several aspects of standard terms contracts have been criticised within the legal debate, which questions for instance the idea of blanket assent to standard terms in light of fairness considerations.[305] It is argued that consumers are unable to assess standard terms sufficiently. These contracts are take-it-or-leave-it; furthermore, similar terms apply to nearly all contracts conducted within the same business sector, which renders shopping for terms rather useless. Consumers thus sign contracts without reading them, and are then presumed to have assented to the terms. However the criticism points out that when consumers do not assent to terms, the contract can no longer be viewed to represent the wishes of both parties to the contract. The presumption to read, the critique claims, is not based on realistic views of consumer reading. It merely shifts the burden of information acquisition to the party that accepts standard terms, in this case the consumer (Ben-Shahar, 2009: 3, 7). Speidel argues that the

[304] Furthermore, other aims for consumer protection such as aims that serve more general social concerns, possibly rooted in equality and the protection of human dignity, cannot be excluded. Howells and Weatherill (2005: 33) argue that some rights are to be protected that transcend the rhetoric of economic efficiency.

[305] See above, chapter 5, section 5.2.1; these concerns have been raised most notably by Llewellyn (1939), Kessler (1943) and Slawson (1971).

element of assent should be eliminated from judicial review of unconscionability. When a consumer argues that a term is unconscionable, the burden of proof on whether or not the term should be held up in court should be laid with the seller (Speidel, 1970: 359–74). The assumption that consumers have assented to terms when they agree to the contract does not correspond to the reality of consumer decision making.

b. *The effectiveness of disclosure duties*

Another point of criticism relates to the effectiveness of disclosure duties with respect to standard terms.[306] It is argued that disclosure duties cannot effectively enable consumers to make 'rational', well-balanced decisions of what would be in their own interest in the context of standard terms (Wilhelmsson, 2006: 54–6). The party that is supposed to be protected by information remedies should be able to process the information easily and take a meaningful decision on the basis of this information (Grundmann, 2002: 282). However, making well-informed decisions is too costly in time and effort because standard terms are too complicated and it is very hard for consumers to accurately assess the consequences of assenting to the risk distributions proposed in standard terms. Consumers are therefore not willing or able to assess the information. Even though the information is considered to be disclosed, it does not reach consumers, or it is not included in their decision making process. Information remedies such as the availability requirement, transparency, readability and intelligibility are therefore argued to be insufficient to protect consumers from undesirable terms.

c. *Using availability as a proxy for substantive tests*

As has been mentioned above, when terms are not deemed onerous because they meet the substantive requirements, they will apply to the contract and be held against consumers even when consumers consider these terms to be undesirable. A specific element of regulating standard terms in consumer contracts, the availability requirement, can in these cases be used to bar undesirable terms from the contract. The availability requirement is argued to be a proxy that consumers use to bar the standard terms that they consider to be undesirable, but that do pass the fairness test (Cserne, 2008). Even though this procedure can therefore possibly offer additional protection, the protection of consumers from undesirable terms can still be deemed insufficient. As Cserne argues, the availability requirement is a procedural necessity that is not conceptually linked to the substance of the

[306] The argument that consumers will not benefit from information disclosure to the extent attenuated by consumer policy is not recent in legal literature, see for instance: Whitford (1973: 404). See Howells (2005) for a general discussion of the limitations of disclosure duties in consumer protection.

contract terms. However, it is only invoked when a party does feel disadvantaged by the substance of one or more particular terms in the contract. It could be argued from this practice that consumers apparently do feel a need for a higher quality of standard contract terms. The availability requirement does enable courts to intervene on behalf of the consumers when the substance of a term is considered undesirable by the consumer, but only in the case that a procedural requirement has (coincidentally) not been met. The availability test thus employs a procedural defect to overcome a substantial issue: the fact that the complaining party is dissatisfied with the content of the contract terms. The availability test therefore fails to properly address an apparent need for the improvement of the quality of terms in standardised consumer contracts.

d. Enforcement difficulties

Lastly, unfair terms regimes are criticised with respect to the enforcement of unfair terms regulation. In most cases, consumers have to call for nullity of unfair terms. However, there are a number of reasons why consumers are unlikely to take individual legal action against onerous contract terms; consumers will for example only sue if things go wrong. Even in that situation, as the potential gains from suing on the grounds of an unfair term are most often low, consumers might rationally decide not to incur the costs of trial. Consumers are unlikely to be aware of their rights in court, and are generally not used to court procedures. A trial can emotionally be a very vexing and unpleasant experience for the consumer, more so than for firms, organisations and institutions that frequently involve themselves in litigation. Consequently, consumers often fail to take action against unfair standard terms, and unfair terms are likely to persist in standard contracts. Bates therefore argues that systems that are dependent on liability and consumer redress action are doomed to fail (Bates, 2002).

Consumer organisations might provide assistance for consumers in trial, including information and legal assistance. Information about contract rights and trial procedures could furthermore be obtained from institutions such as the European Consumer Centres.[307] As has been argued above, the right to stand up in court and apply for an injunction against unfair terms has been granted to consumer organisations to increase the deterrent value of unfair terms regulation.[308] It is however suggested in the legal debate that granting this right to consumer and trade organisations has not had overwhelming or satisfying results.[309] The effectiveness of the extension of access to court therefore remains to

307 See for more information: www.ecc-net.info.

308 See above, section 6.2.4d; see also Van den Bergh (2008) and Schillig (2008: 342) who argue that in order to improve the effectiveness of enforcement, allowing by third parties acting in the public interest to initiate review and court procedures could have great beneficial effects.

309 For instance, Hondius and Rijken (2006: 83) describe how in the Netherlands, during the 14 years counting from 1993, consumer organisations have asked for injunctive relief against

be seen (Howells and Weatherill, 2005: 294). The same holds for the effectiveness of barring onerous terms through public enforcement by consumer authorities.[310] The effectiveness of the actions of the Consumer Ombudsman in the Nordic Countries against unfair terms in consumer contracts is more positively viewed by commentators.[311] As the public enforcement of unfair terms regimes through consumer authorities is a relatively new policy development, at least in some European legal systems, the success rate of these institutions with regard to barring onerous consumer standard terms might yet improve.

Several other procedural problems might complicate the enforcement of unfair terms in consumer contracts (European Commission, 2000: 22–3). First, procedures can be very time-consuming.[312] The potentially offending terms will continue to be used until courts take the decision to strike the terms. Secondly, when the court hands down the verdict of unfairness and passes an injunction against the use of the term, this injunction is only held up against the party that has been taken to court.[313] Other sellers who use this term have to be sued as well before they can be served with an injunction. Thirdly, the decision of the court applies only to the wording of the terms, not to the effect that the term produces. Sellers can therefore replace the unfair term with one of a different wording but with a similar unfair effect. This term then needs to be challenged in court again before an injunction can be served against it. Fourthly, when sellers ignore the

---

unfair terms in a mere three court proceedings. All three cases were however decided in their favour. Micklitz (2008: 31) mentions that in Germany the number of collective actions brought by consumer organisations to enforce the fairness of standard consumer contract terms has diminished considerably.

310 As has been mentioned above, chapter 5, section 5.5.3c, the Dutch Consumer Authority together with Belgian and Luxembourgian partner institutions has conducted a study on the legality of standard contract terms in the consumer electronics market. In the accompanying press release, it is stated that the companies involved have been approached and that they have adjusted the standard terms; see consuwijzer.nl/Consumentennieuws/Nieuwsarchief/2010/April_2010/Consumentenautoriteit_informatie_over_garantie_klopt_vaak_niet (in Dutch). The list of sanctions that have been administered by the Dutch Consumer Authority however makes no mention of sanctions for onerous terms in consumer contracts (sanctions to be found at: consumentenautoriteit.nl/Besluiten_en_oordelen/Sanctiebesluiten). Also, while unfair terms in general, not only warranties, were a focal area of the Dutch Consumer Authority in 2007 and 2008, this is no longer the case in 2009 (for the Dutch Consumer Authorities' approach to consumer standardised terms, see consuwijzer.nl/Consumententhema_s/Algemene_voorwaarden; the current focal areas to be found at: consumentenautoriteit.nl/Aandachtsgebieden).

311 See above, section 6.2.4, especially note 297. See also Viitanen (2007: 100).

312 Even though this research focuses on regulatory interventions in unfair terms regimes, the critique with regard to enforcement procedures is worthy of review as these issues further undermine the effectiveness of regulatory interventions. The policy proposals that will be discussed in the next chapter will however not focus on the improvement of enforcement procedures. See for a discussion of private enforcement of consumer law for instance: Van den Bergh and Visscher (2008).

313 In some regimes, such as the English unfair terms regime, the injunction only applies to the contract challenged in court. Other consumers dealing with the same seller would have to challenge the term again before they can have it declared void in their contracts. See Bates (2002) for a critical discussion.

injunction and continue using the unfair term, such infringement is usually served with a fine. In order to achieve the penalty of infringement however, the plaintiff must take the infringing party to court again, and convincingly argue that the plaintiff has repeatedly violated to the court decision.

Collins argues that many sellers will continue to draft and use onerous terms: the worst thing that can happen to them is an injunction against the use of that specific standard contract term. Even when a court has deemed a term to be onerous, few consumers will be aware of the onerousness itself, or of the fact that this term is still used in the contract. When the term is challenged again, a next court might decide otherwise (Collins, 2004: 793). The question is therefore whether having a substantive test that is mainly enforced through private enforcement can ensure the barring of unfair contract terms from consumer standardised contracts. These difficulties concerning the enforcement of unfair terms regimes suggest that enforcement of regulatory interventions is insufficient to guarantee fair consumer contract terms.

e. *Support of legal critique by behavioural insights and empirics*

As has been argued above, the common core of unfair terms regimes corresponds to insights of information economics; behavioural insights have as of yet been largely unable to influence consumer protection policy related to unfair terms.[314] The issues that have been raised in the legal debate concerning unfair terms regimes however do largely correspond to the points of critique that were raised in the behavioural debate and the issues that were addressed in empirical literature. The behavioural debate and empirical research therefore seem to support the legal critique, because they too criticise the effectiveness of disclosure duties.[315] Behavioural and empirical insights also point out that the reality of consumer decision making does not correspond to presumed assent. It is unlikely that consumers will want to become informed about standard terms. Even though information duties lower transaction costs for consumers who would want to get informed about the content of contracts, consumers are highly unlikely to be able or willing to read and assess standard terms, let alone to negotiate for better terms. Another point of legal critique is that consumers are unlikely to take legal action against onerous standard terms. Behavioural insights concur that consumers are unlikely to sue in cases of overly one-sided terms, but would explain this hesitation with a reference to rational apathy and bounded rationality,

---

314 As Micklitz (2008: 21) mentions, the information paradigm in EC consumer policy corresponds to rational decision making, which does not concur in all circumstances to insights from behavioural economics.

315 Of course, as has been mentioned above in chapter 5, section 5.5.5, empirical research into these issues is lacking in number and should be evaluated accordingly. However, the empirical research that has been conducted supports the legal critique presented here, and should not be overlooked.

and add that consumers will feel committed to the terms of the contract.[316] The claim that the availability requirement is used as a proxy to bar undesirable terms from the contract implies that consumers are in need of higher quality term. Indeed, adverse selection in standard terms can be justified on the basis of empirical insights, and of course also on the basis of information economics. Both with regard to consumer reading and the enforcement of their rights, the legal debate criticises the abilities of consumers to generate sufficient quality in standard terms or to effectively enforce unfair terms regimes. This corresponds to the policy recommendations developed in the previous chapter. The concerns that have resulted from behavioural discussions have also been topics of concern in the legal debate. Therefore, the recommendations that were developed in the previous chapter could be used to amend unfair terms policies to least partly address the legal concerns.

6.3.3. AMENDING POLICY: EXPRESSED NEED FOR MORE SUBSTANTIVE CONTROL

Recent discussions among scholars and policy makers in European private law and consumer policy show a desire for more substantive control with respect to terms in consumer contracts. Improved insight into consumer decision making processes has made the bargain lose its appeal as an unyielding expression of individual will. Information duties do not seem effective in enabling consumers to include what is considered relevant, or even vital information, into the decision making process. The discussions resulting from the behavioural law and economics debate can have contributed to the desire for more substantive interventions. The difficulties of addressing biases through the provision of pre-contractual information or through cooling off periods are argued to justify mandatory regulation of terms (Ramsay, 2007: 164).

A diminished faith in contractual bargaining and competitive markets has led to a call for more control over consumer contracts, instead of leaving the issue up to the market (Ely, 2009). The willingness among legislators to intervene to a larger extent into the content of the contract is evolving, and is no longer merely focused on the process of contract formation (Weatherill, 2005: 113–5). The current focus on procedural control, it is argued, should make way for a more substantive control with regard to unfair terms in consumer contracts (Howell, 2007). The current ability of regulators and courts to intervene in consumer contracts is thought to be insufficient, which implies that the perspective that consumers need to be protected from themselves has gained importance. The call is for more far-reaching interventions on behalf of consumers, which no longer depend on consumers to choose the best contracts for themselves. Discussions

316 See above, chapter 5, section 5.4.1.

about lotteries, price festivals, and warranties that are different from legal warranties are examples of this sentiment in policy. The main sector of industry in which more government intervention on behalf of consumers is called for is, due to the credit crisis, the financial industry. Public outrage about onerous terms in consumer financial contracts, such as credit cards and mortgages, has fuelled this desire for more far-reaching substantive interventions in consumer contract terms.[317] An example of this expressed need for more substantive influence in the terms of consumer contracts is among others provided by the Green Paper on the Review of the Consumer Acquis. The Green Paper suggests expanding the scope of the fairness test to include price, the main subject matter and negotiated terms within all EC legal systems.[318] These issues signal a wish to increase government control over the terms in consumer contracts, whether these terms are standard terms or related to key aspects of the contract.[319] In the DCFR, the autonomy of contract parties is also decreased (Eidenmüller, 2009: 116–17).

This expressed desire for increased substantive control could be argued to correspond to the recommendations from chapter 5. Information disclosure is a procedural intervention; a lesser dependence on information disclosure could imply that more substantive interventions should be considered. The doubts related to consumer vigilance would also argue for a more substantive protection on behalf of consumers. However, whether this call for more substantive interventions can be argued to be justified depends upon the actual proposed policy amendments. It would therefore be very interesting to review some of the policy proposals that have been suggested in order to amend current policy. In the next chapter, some policy proposals that aim to enhance unfair terms regimes will be discussed in light of insights taken from both economic and behavioural literature. Some of the policy proposals that will be discussed might be quite effective in enhancing the quality of standard terms in consumer contracts.

6.4. CONCLUSIONS: CONSUMER POLICY AND THE QUALITY OF CONTRACT TERMS

The aim of this chapter has been twofold: first to review the extent to which the common core in legal approach to consumer standard terms depends on the provision of information and consumer vigilance to generate a higher quality

---

317 The occurrence of the credit crisis can also be viewed to justify the claim that standard term regimes need to change, specifically with regard to mortgage contracts, but also more generally. See for instance Smith (2009) claiming just that.

318 See above, note 291 and 293.

319 See below, chapter 7, section 7.2.3, for a discussion of this policy option. In the Proposal Consumer Rights Directive, the proposals from the Green Paper that refer to an extension of the scope of the fairness test to include price, main subject matter and negotiated terms have been dropped (see art. 32 sub 3). However, the expressed desire to expand substantive control still stands.

of consumers' standardised terms. Second, and correspondingly, this chapter aimed to determine to what extent the common approach in unfair terms is able to enhance the quality of contract terms. The review of the common core of European unfair terms regimes has established that information remedies form the main intervention in standard terms, and that consumer unfair terms policy greatly depends on consumer vigilance. The insights developed in the previous chapter suggest that this dependence on information duties and consumer vigilance are ineffective in improving the quality of consumer standard terms. This statement can be corroborated by critique presented in the legal debate.

6.4.1. POLICY DEPENDENCE ON INFORMATION DUTIES AND CONSUMER VIGILANCE

This chapter has reviewed and assessed common policies, doctrines and rules that are used in unfair terms regimes in European, and to a minor extent US, legal systems. The previous chapter has developed policy recommendations that argue against the effectiveness of depending on information disclosure and consumer vigilance to enhance the quality of consumer standard terms. The review of the European common core in unfair terms regimes suggested however that the current common approach to consumer contract terms greatly depends on information disclosure and consumer vigilance.

Policies in unfair terms regimes correspond largely to the insights of information economics. The basic principles of freedom of contract and the *laissez-faire approach* include the freedom to make mistakes. Consumers are therefore required to be vigilant. The duty to read and blanket assent also call for consumer vigilance: when the consumer assents to a transaction under undesirable terms, these terms will be hold against her as long as they meet with substantive requirements. This chapter has discussed the dichotomy between competent consumers, corresponding to the contract model, and unable consumers, related to the consumer model. To the extent that they are based on the contract model, unfair terms regimes depend up information disclosure and consumer vigilance. A key factor in the discussion is the fact that the policy intervention of choice in the common approach is information disclosure. Information disclosure requires consumers to be vigilant, as the informed consumer, or the consumer that has had the opportunity to become informed, is assumed to be able to protect her own interests.

In addition to information duties, consumers are protected by substantive requirements for standard terms. However, the extent to which policy employs substantive requirements as opposed to information duties is arguably small. Substantive requirements set a threshold level of quality for standard terms. This fairness level can be argued to be rather minimal. Examples can be taken from the grey and black lists that have been discussed above.[320] These lists feature terms that are of quite low-quality. However, the blacklisted and greylisted terms serve to clarify and illustrate the implementation of substantive tests, which suggests that only very low-quality terms can be barred from the contract by the application of substantive tests.[321] It can thus be argued that the standard of unfairness, the threshold level below which consumers will not be hurt by their rational apathy, is rather low. Correspondingly, the extent to which the quality of terms in consumer contract depends on information disclosure and consumer vigilance is quite high.

Enforcement also depends on consumer vigilance. Consumers need to be active when they are confronted with unfair terms. They need to know which terms are unfair, that these terms are used against them, they need to be aware of their legal rights, and they need to take action against these terms. The rational apathy concerns that might be at play here suggest that the enforcement of unfair terms policy should not be overly dependent on individual consumers. Recently private as well as public organisations have been empowered to act on behalf of consumers. However, individual consumer action is still regarded to be a main instigator of the enforcement of unfair terms policies. The current European unfair terms regimes can therefore be argued to still be strongly dependent on information disclosure and consumer vigilance.

Another relevant topic is the scope of the unfair terms regime and how this scope is connected to consumer vigilance and the recommendations from in the previous chapter. When price, main subject matter and individually negotiated terms are excluded from substantive tests, generating a sufficient quality in these product aspects then depends on consumer vigilance. However, the insights that have been developed in the previous chapter apply to cases of consumer *standard* contract terms. The assessment that has been conducted in the previous chapter might not yield the same results for the contract terms of price, main subject matter or negotiated terms, as these product aspects are not standard and are usually known to consumers. A caution against the dependence on information duties and consumer vigilance with regard to standard contract terms should not be overly generalised.[322] The detrimental effects of the dependence on consumer vigilance with regard to standard terms might not result from the same reliance in the context of price, main subject matter and negotiated terms.

[320] See above, section 6.2.2c.

[321] This question requires further assessment, which should refer to examples in case law where the application of substantive tests has led to the barring of standard terms from consumer contracts. The scope of this research does not allow for such a case law study. The examples of blacklisted and greylisted terms do however suggest that the standard of fairness that underlies these substantive tests is not very high.

[322] See below, chapter 7, section 7.2.3, for a discussion of the desirability of extending the scope of the unfair terms regimes or the fairness test to include price, main subject matter and negotiated terms.

6.4.2. EFFECTIVENESS OF COMMON UNFAIR TERMS POLICIES IN ENHANCING QUALITY OF TERMS

Current European unfair terms regimes can be argued to largely correspond to the insights developed in information economics, and consequently be strongly dependent on information disclosure and consumer vigilance to a large extent. With the insights developed in the previous chapter, this dependence on information duties and consumer vigilance can be argued to be insufficiently effective in the policy aim to enhance the quality of terms in consumer contracts. Concerns relating to unfair terms regimes that were presented in the legal debate corroborate these doubts.

There are two main reasons to doubt that common unfair terms policies are effective in enhancing the quality of standardised consumer terms. First, information disclosure is the main policy intervention that is implemented in these policies. This policy requires consumers themselves to stimulate the market and to thereby generate the quality of terms that they desire. By choosing or negotiating the contract terms as they see fit, the informed consumer can look out for her own interests. This type of policy aids consumers in their endeavour by providing procedural requirements to overcome information asymmetries. However, as has been argued in the previous chapter, information disclosure and dependence on consumer vigilance are likely to be ineffective strategies in the aim for augmentation of the quality of terms.

Secondly, even though unfair terms regimes provide a minimum, threshold level of quality for terms in consumer contracts, below which a term is considered onerous and will be barred from the contract, this threshold level of quality might not be effective in truly enhancing quality. The level of quality that is aimed for by substantive tests is unlikely to be very high. Enforcement difficulties furthermore cause unfair terms that would not pass the substantive test to be maintained in consumer contracts and invoked against consumers. Presumed assent and difficulties with information disclosure and enforcement all provide grounds for the claim that current policies could be improved with respect to their effectiveness in generating a sufficient quality in standardised terms.

The assessment in the previous chapter determined that standard terms in consumer contracts are likely to be of low quality due to adverse selection problems. Behavioural insight suggests that policies that are dependent on information disclosure and consumer vigilance are insufficiently able to overcome this market failure. The review of the common core of European unfair terms policies has established that the current approach is likely to be similarly inefficient in enhancing the quality of standardised consumer contract terms. The legal debate has expressed the same concern. Some policy proposals that aim to augment consumer policy regarding standard terms will be assessed in the next chapter. These proposals aim at solving the signing-without-reading problem, which would constitute real assent to terms; at removing standard terms from consumer contracts altogether; at expanding the scope of the fairness test and at construing some form of administrative control over standardised consumer terms.

CHAPTER 7

PROPOSALS TO ENHANCE CONSUMER POLICY OF STANDARDISED CONTRACT TERMS

7.1. INTRODUCTION

The review of the common approach in unfair terms policies in the previous chapter suggests that current unfair terms regimes in Europe depend too strongly upon information disclosure and consumer vigilance, which is argued to be ineffective in overcoming the adverse selection problem that affects consumer standardised contract terms. It is thus highly likely that standard terms in consumer contracts are of a low quality, giving more privileges to sellers than to consumers. This quality standard is likely to be lower than is efficient from a social welfare point of view. Unfair terms regimes and the quality of consumer terms in standard contracts thus stand to be improved. However desirable, there is not one simple solution to the problems presented by unfair terms in standard contracts (Bates, 2002: 90). The aim of this chapter will be to roughly identify possible solutions for low quality standard terms. The chapter will distinguish five approaches: solving the signing-without-reading problem, doing away with standard terms altogether, extending the scope of the fairness test, administrative approval and drafting contracts through negotiations between sellers and consumers. This chapter will argue that some of these approaches are better able to effectively and efficiently enhance unfair terms regimes than other ones, notably by generating an increase in quality of consumer standardised contract terms.

The aim of this chapter is therefore not to come up with definite, fully assessed and directly implementable proposals for policy. The scope of analysis in this research does not allow for an in-depth assessment of the different strategies, let alone the more specific policy proposals that fit within promising approaches. However, as the analysis conducted in the previous chapters indicates that the major concern with standard terms in consumers contracts is that they are of a too low quality from a social welfare perspective, some solutions that target this very problem are worthy of a (short) discussion. It should however be stressed that the claim that standard terms in consumer contracts attain a quality level that is too low from a social welfare perspective is at this point, and will remain in this dissertation, an assumption. As has been argued above, there are several reasons why the level of quality in standard terms can be argued to be too low to be found in information economic theory, behavioural insights and empirics.[323] The consequences of adverse selection would point in that direction and the informed minority theory cannot be supported by behavioural insights or empirical data. In addition, no beneficial effects from competition can be found to increase the quality of standard terms, and anecdotal evidence supports the view that consumers find standard terms to be of a too low quality. Of course, before steps to regulate more are undertaken, a more thorough assessment is required to establish that the quality of standard contract terms is indeed too low from a social welfare perspective.[324] Pending such an assessment, this chapter will roughly identify the type of solutions that would likely have beneficial effects if more extensive research will indeed make clear that the quality of standard terms is lacking within certain market sectors or even some consumer contracts.

Similarly, while the improvement of the quality of terms will be the main focus of the assessment, the fact that in some cases consumers might prefer a lower quality and lower price should not be overlooked. A policy instrument that can accommodate diverse consumer preferences will be assessed more positively. Furthermore, as has been argued above, the level of quality that is generated by substantive tests might be rather low.[325] This chapter will therefore discuss to what extent these policy proposals can incentivise quality of term increases, not only up to the level of the substantive tests but even beyond that level.

First, proposals will be assessed that aim at solving the signing-without-reading problem, which would constitute real assent to standard terms. Behavioural insights however suggest looking beyond solving the signing-without-reading problem, when possible to debias consumers and to nudge them into more informed decision making. Rating and labelling could provide valuable information tools for the assessment of the quality of terms by consumers. Second, this chapter will evaluate the proposals that involve removing standard terms from consumer contracts altogether, and to replace the standard form contract either by a general doctrine of reasonable expectations or by forced negotiations. Neither proposal is assessed benevolently in this research. The third type of proposal relates to an extension of the scope of the fairness test to enhance the scope of unfair terms regimes and to offer more protection to consumers. It will be argued however that these proposals are not very promising in enhancing the quality of contract terms, whether they regard standard terms or price, main subject matter and negotiated terms. Fourth, the possibility of

---

323 See above, chapter 5, most notably section 5.5.4a.

324 It would seem that the main concern in this regard is that the voice of the consumer is lacking. As there is no competition regarding standard terms, it not clear 'what consumers want', and what level of quality should be attained in consumer standard terms. To gain more perspective on this issue, consumer preferences can however be researched, for instance through consumer surveys, asking consumers about their wishes regarding contractual terms, or involving consumer interest groups.

325 See above, chapter 6, section 6.4.1.

construing administrative control over standardised consumer terms will be discussed. It will be concluded that this suggestion could be quite promising in the aim to enhance the quality of consumer standard terms, at least up to the benchmark level of fairness set in substantive legal interventions. The last type of policy suggestions provides an alternative in model forms of consumer contracts, which should either be provided by an authority or by negotiations between business and consumer representatives. This suggestion could attain an accurate representation of consumer and seller preferences for contract terms. This policy option will also be assessed to be very promising.

7.2. REVIEWING PROPOSALS TO AMEND UNFAIR TERMS POLICIES

In policy discussions, several options are presented which aim to improve unfair terms regimes. Some of these policy proposals will be assessed here.

7.2.1. PROPOSALS ON INFORMATION DISCLOSURE

In the development of policy amendments to enhance the quality of consumer contract terms, many suggestions fall back on the preferred policy instrument of information remedies. As signing-without-reading is interpreted to be the main cause of undesirable terms in consumer contracts, it is argued that consumers should be stimulated to read and truly assess contract terms. However, a focus upon information provision to try and stimulate consumer reading is inconsistent with the insights from behavioural theory. Consumers might also be nudged into more informed decision making by the provision of information through for instance rating standard forms and labelling the most sought-after standard terms. This would correspond to the provision of 'less and better' information that is frequently supported in behavioural literature. However, the extent to which ranking of contracts and labelling specific terms can be used to generally increase the quality of standard terms in consumer contracts remains unclear.

a. *Solving signing-without-reading*

The fact that consumers fail to read standard terms is in some policy discussions understood as the main cause of the persistence of unfair terms in consumer contracts. Consumers are held responsible for their assent to (dubious) terms. Therefore, many policy proposals that have been suggested to enhance unfair terms regimes aim at enhancing opportunities to read. Efforts are undertaken to increase consumer reading, such as enhancing intelligibility, drafting shorter forms of standard terms, using short sentences and a standardised way of presenting the information, et cetera. When consumers really read contract terms or have had a true opportunity to read but choose not to read standard terms, assent to contract terms can be more easily established. Hillman notes that a requirement to click on an "I agree"-button at the end of each term could be the most effective way to increase reading (Hillman, 2006a: 298). The format and layout of forms can be standardised in business sectors so that forms are more easily compared (Wilhelmsson, 2006: 55–6).

A transparency requirement can also be understood as including a duty to structure terms properly, which should enable consumers to better understand and assess these terms (Grundmann, Kerber and Weatherill, 2001: 27). Wendlandt argues that the structuring of the terms, which is very important for increasing transparency and being able to compare terms, should not be left to the vendor, but should be stipulated in the information requirements (Wendlandt, 2005: 85–6). Simply abiding by the law is easier and cheaper for sellers than choosing which structure to adhere to; the sellers' conformation to legal requirements would also benefit the consumer. Furthermore, a standard layout of contracts terms would enhance the comparability of terms. Key information should be required from sellers by regulators, as well as a serious offer from sellers to consumers to provide more information when that would be demanded by the consumer.

The question of which party should make a decision on which information to offer to consumers is also a topic of much debate. Van den Bergh argues that the seller, as cheapest information producer, would be the more efficient party to provide this information and therefore also the most efficient party to decide which information would be beneficial (Van den Bergh, 1997: 85). A better mix of less information should improve consumers' ability to use the information to their advantage. Another issue is whether regulators are sufficiently informed of the issues that are used by consumers as a basis for their decisions. Lists of information duties drafted by regulators could contain irrelevant information, which is costly for sellers to provide but does not benefit the consumer. If that is the case, the consumer is made to pay for information he or she does not need. Other solutions could involve asking consumers to validate specific contract terms by signing them, letting consumers re-write (onerous) terms, or having courts scrutinise individual cases to assess whether consumers meant to assent to the standard terms (Smith, 2009: 71–5). All these solutions aim in some way at solving the signing-without reading problem, and aim to stimulate consumers to actually read and assess, or at least consciously assent, to standard terms, which should create a more secure basis for presumed assent.

b. *Behavioural critique: look beyond signing-without-reading*

Policy proposals that aim to enhance consumer reading and try to create true assent to contract terms in this way, cannot be justified on the basis of the policy recommendations that have been developed in chapter 5. Correspondingly, Ben-

Shahar argues that contract law and policy both in the United States and in Europe fail to address to problem of unfair contract terms properly. Even though the problem that consumers do not read contracts is widely recognised, contract policies still depend on the provision of an opportunity to read as the means to overcome the disadvantaged position of consumers (Ben-Shahar, 2009: 10–1).

As behavioural research shows, supported by empirical studies, extensive informed decision making with respect to standard terms is unlikely to be attainable. The effectiveness of information disclosure is very limited in the case of standard terms. When effective at all, it can only relate to a small number of standard terms. Furthermore, as has been argued several times above, consumers have no incentive of extensively exploring the majority of standard terms. Consumers feel they have nothing to gain by properly taking standard terms into account. The reasons for this lack of assessment do not lie in the means of disclosure. The disclosure of information about these terms will not affect the decision making process. Results from empirical research suggest that making the disclosure of terms more transparent will not cause consumers to take the terms into account and unfair terms will therefore remain to be drafted into contracts. In addition, information disclosure does not account for other insights of behavioural literature, such as emotional pressure, risk perceptions and uncertainty.

Behavioural insights and empirical data suggest that less focus should be placed upon information duties that aim to solve the signing-without-reading problem. Policy proposals that aim to solve the problem of signing-without reading do not improve the standard terms consumers see themselves confronted with (Ben-Shahar, 2009: 5). The proposals that aim to solve signing-without-reading would increase transaction costs, but do not ensure a proper assessment of terms and inclusion of these terms in decision making processes. An adverse effect of these policy proposals can also be pointed out: they will possibly allow sellers to escape liability for dubious terms, as the 'validation' by the consumers will legitimise the standard terms. The requirement of specific assent to certain terms might induce consumers to *notice* the terms, but cannot guarantee that the terms will be properly *assessed* (Korobkin, 2003: 1246).

Behavioural insights suggest that the intervention strategies of debiasing consumers with respect to standard terms by providing less and better information are unlikely to be very effective. Standard terms will probably not be properly assessed by consumers even when it is made 'easier' for them to assess and comprehend the contents of the contract. Behavioural insights and empirical data suggest that such reading will simply not happen, as it is too costly, not beneficial enough, and consumers are overoptimistic with regard to the contingencies that are dealt with in the contract. Consumers will probably still validate and accept the terms. These proposals however are unlikely to enhance the extent to which consumers read or comprehend the content of the contract. As a result, the quality of standardised contract terms is not increased. Consumers will continue to sign without reading, and sellers will continue to draft low-quality low priced terms; the flea market persists.

c. *Rating and labelling*

Other policy interventions that aim at debiasing consumers, even to a very limited extent, might be more successful. The tool of information provision might therefore be used to improve the quality of standard terms after all. Becher and Unger-Aviram discuss policy proposals that aim to provide meaningful information to consumers about the quality of the contract, namely by *rating* contracts and by *labelling* the most sought-after terms (Becher and Unger-Aviram, 2009: 22–7).

Rating

The policy instrument of rating would collect data related to some product aspects, in this case standard terms, and score the contract on those items. It would then come to an overall rating of this form in relation to other forms. Ratings aggregate some aspects of the contract terms, but not all. Therefore, the terms that have been included in the rating process will necessarily become more salient and important in decision making processes than other terms. If these terms correspond to the aspects that the majority of consumers considers (highly) relevant, rating could be an effective way of providing information and trying to get consumers to take the quality of standard terms in account in the purchase of products or services. As has been discussed before, a higher quality does not necessarily mean that this term would correspond better to consumer preferences, as consumers might prefer a lower quality. It is unclear how a ranking would accommodate a preference for a lower quality.

The implementation details of the rating instrument and the connected ranking of contracts on the basis of this rating are very important. Questions such as who decides which terms will be assessed in the ranking, how this is decided and which institutes carry out the ranking will greatly affect the effectiveness of the instrument. The ranking needs to provide a trustworthy signal of quality; however, most ranking efforts are highly disputed, especially with regard to the issues that are included in the assessment and the measurement criteria. To allow the ranking to both correspond to consumer preferences and to include information from industry about cost structures and so forth, both these interest groups could be involved in the development of the ranking instrument.

Labelling

The policy instrument of labelling would entail the explicit disclosure of certain standard contract terms that are considered relevant to consumers on for instance a label that will be displayed with products. Specific and explicit disclosure of relevant standard terms, especially the negative aspects, could persuade the consumer to take the most onerous contract terms into account (Ben-Shahar, 2009: 25–6). Consumers would however still need to understand the impact of those terms themselves. This is a point of difference between the instruments of rating and labelling, because rankings attach scores to the respective terms. Labels only provide information, which consumers need to assess themselves. As behavioural insights have shown, consumers tend to make errors in the assessment of consequences, and especially in the assessment of risks. Of course, sellers do have an incentive to improve the quality of the specific items that are disclosed on the label. Consumer associations could also aid consumers by providing information about the significance of the standard terms on the label.

With respect to the quality of terms and a possible preference for a lower quality, the label could be preferred over the ranking instrument, as it provides more detailed information, which allows consumers to base their choice on the actual level of quality of the product. However, the instrument of ranking can include a higher number of terms in the assessment, while the label would only refer to a limited number of terms in order to maintain the informative value of the label.

d. Reviewing the policy tools of rating and labelling

Instruments like rating and labelling could have a beneficial impact on the quality of terms, even if this impact might be limited. Depending on the benchmarks that are used in rating efforts, sellers might even be incentivised to set the quality of terms well above the level of fairness that is effectuated by substantive interventions. Rating and labelling are essentially forms of debiasing consumers: by providing the sellers with a signal which they can use to provide information about the quality of their terms, consumers' decision making can become more informed. Consumers can take the quality signal into account and make a more argument-based decision about the quality of terms. Rating and labelling can decrease search costs by a significant level (with respect to the terms under assessment) and use consumer preferences for simple and easily comparable results to improve consumer choice.

An important limitation of both instruments is that they only include a selection of standard terms, even though rating is likely to have a more expanded scope than labelling. In both interventions however, several and maybe even the majority of terms are excluded from consideration. The instruments of rating and labelling will not affect the quality of these terms.

Furthermore, the implementation of these instruments will demand considerable (financial) costs and effort. (Mandatory) labelling requires some consumer authority to decide which terms should be specifically disclosed, and to incur the costs of monitoring the intervention. Sellers have to incur the costs of providing the labels. Rating of contracts could also be done by consumer authorities, but setting up the ranking system would again demand considerable investments. The implementation of these policy instruments could also give rise to other difficulties. Within one industry, terms are likely to differ only slightly. Ranking one competitor over another would then be difficult. All labels would be likely to provide the same information. Consequently, consumers might feel that they do not have much to gain by comparing ratings or labels of standard terms across companies.

It also remains to be seen how the information that is provided in ratings and on labels will affect consumer decision making. Consumers might still consider this information too costly or too confusing to include in their assessment. When consumers are overoptimistic with regard to the contingencies that are dealt with in standard terms, they might be even less inclined to take rating information into account. The question is in the end whether a rating of standard terms would incentivise sellers to draft a higher quality of consumer terms. The rating creates a signal of quality; consumers would need to respond to this signal in order for it to be effective. On the other hand, companies are very sensitive towards reputation, and presumably would like to score well on the rating of their contract terms or display positive information on the label. Furthermore, online instruments such as blogs, Facebook, et cetera could be used to increase the dissemination of information (Becher and Zarsky, 2008). Therefore, the rating and labelling of contract terms might be able to enhance the quality of the terms that are included in the evaluation of these policy instruments. Outside that scope however, rating and labelling will not have any significant impact.

If consumers cannot distinguish between different contracts because all contracts in a business sector are similar in quality, the effectiveness of these instruments in generating a higher quality of terms might be limited. Furthermore, the consequences of a certain score in ranking, or the consequences of accepting the terms that are disclosed in a label, might still be difficult for consumers to comprehend. Therefore, it is not clear to what extent rating and labelling can really increase the quality of the included terms. The effectiveness of these policy amendments would need to be tested before they can be implemented on a wide scale. Since these instruments are quite costly, the extent to which these policy proposals are efficient also remains to be seen.

7.2.2. REMOVING STANDARD TERMS FROM CONSUMER CONTRACTS

Because the issues related to stimulating consumers to read and truly assent to standard terms are so difficult to solve, some authors argue that standard terms should no longer be part of consumer contracts, or only to a very limited extent. Consumer contracts could be governed by a reasonable expectations doctrine. Also, contract parties could be forced to negotiate nearly all terms of the contracts, which allows for only a very limited number of standard terms. These proposals can however be argued to be very costly, and the extent to which the quality of terms is increased might be questioned.

a. *Reasonable expectations*

Consumers, it is argued, cannot be expected to wilfully assent to standardised consumer terms. Therefore, the consumer contract should not be regarded as a bargain between two or more parties to the contract, but as a one-sided rule-making effort on the behalf of the seller in which the interests of the consumer are not represented. Llewellyn argues that the conditions and clauses that should be read into consumer contracts should not be those which happen to be printed on the unread paper, but should be those which a sane man might reasonably expect to find on that paper (Llewellyn, 1939: 704). Slawson also argues that a standard form is not a contract, and that the buyers' reasonable expectations should govern the contract (Slawson, 1971: 541).[326] According to him, this policy intervention will enable courts to freely strike any term from the contract that they do not wish to uphold. Industry can no longer be certain that their terms will govern the contract. When sellers do wish to draft dubious terms into a contract, they will have to be very clearly present these terms to consumers to prevent them from being stricken (Slawson, 1974: 15–9).

b. *Forced negotiations*

Another option that entails removing standard terms from consumer contracts is to only allow for negotiated terms to govern the contract, or to severely limit the extent to which pre-drafted terms can be applied to consumer contracts. Behavioural insights suggest that policy should focus on the quality of information, not the quantity. Relevant characteristics of products and production process should be communicated effectively. In order to protect the consumer from an excess of information, Rischkowsky and Döring argue that the excessive use of 'small print' in purchase contracts should be governmentally prohibited (Rischkowsky and Döring, 2008: 306). This policy proposal is in fact another attempt at solving the signing-without-reading problem and trying to obtain true assent to the contract, only this attempt includes (largely) doing away with the standard terms.

An example of such a proposal is provided by Ibrahim. Ibrahim's suggestion still depends on both the enhancement of information provision and consumer

326 There is a difference between the tests of reasonable expectations or the substantive tests of unconscionability, fairness or reasonability, as is for instance discussed by Smith (2009: 56–60). These substantive tests will be assessed from the perspective of the judges. *Reasonable expectations* are to be evaluated from the perspective of the consumer. This doctrine however has been confined to insurance law in the US.

responsibility, but limits the extent to which the consumer is responsible for his assent to standardised terms (Ibrahim, 2005: 24–7). Ibrahim proposes that the possibility of including pre-drafted terms in consumer contracts should be severely limited. He argues that pre-drafted terms should fit on one page, that they should be limited to the most essential terms, that they should be presented in normal or large font sizes, should be easy to read and must not contain any legalese. Store managers should stimulate people to read by posting signs in stores and encouraging consumers. Reading would be an easier task, and consumers would therefore have a realistically meaningful opportunity to consent to standard terms and can consequently shop for terms. The tort principle of comparative responsibility should according to Ibrahim inform the applicability of the pre-drafted terms in the contract. Because a proper meeting of the minds is absent with regard to standard terms, the relative responsibility of sellers and consumers for ensuring beneficial contracts should be taken into account. Objective criteria related to the drafting of the form, its presentation and the act of acceptation should determine which party is more at fault when true assent has not been obtained. The consumer still has a duty to read, but the extent of this duty is proportional to the behaviour of the seller with regard to the presentation of the form and the way in which it is written. Ibrahim argues that this type of policy will induce sellers to draft forms with a less and simpler boilerplate, which would really enable consumers to read and shop for terms, and where possible negotiate about the terms. Non-salient terms are transformed into salient terms. Ibrahim's proposal is not very clear on which terms or which standard would govern the contract beyond the limited pre-drafted terms. It could be assumed that contract law would provide default rules for this purpose, and perhaps even some reasonability standard. Furthermore, assumedly, when sellers or consumers want to include more terms in the contract, they have to negotiate about these additional terms.

Comparative responsibility obliges sellers to decide which terms they deem to be important. When terms are low-quality, because they assign fewer privileges than the default rules, these terms have to be either on the disclosure form or be subject to negotiations; otherwise they cannot be invoked against consumers. Sellers therefore have to choose which low-quality terms they want to stick with, and which terms they will drop. Consumers then have a real opportunity to become informed about low-quality terms. The low-quality terms that do apply to the contract cannot be many, because only a limited number can be pre-drafted, and the other ones are subject to negotiations before they can be included in the contract.

c. *Reviewing the policy proposals of removing standard terms from consumer contracts*

Both options that imply removing standard terms from consumer contracts altogether or to a very large extent can be however criticised. Prohibition of standard terms would not be a good intervention to correct the market (De Geest, 2002: 224). Transaction costs would increase as all transactions, even buying an apple at a local fruit seller, would need to be negotiated. If no negotiations would take place, default contract rules specified in the law would in fact become mandatory contract rules, as they are always apply to (non-negotiated) contracts. These rules are unlikely to be efficient. One set of general default rules provided in contract law is unlikely to be efficient or desirable for all contracts and all business sectors, or to cover all the contingencies that should be dealt with in the contract.[327] Standards do not provide as much clarity as specific rules do, as standards need to be interpreted in the specific circumstances of the case. Therefore, these proposals are likely to create uncertainty in both parties, seller and consumer, about the rules which govern the contract. Furthermore, as Becher and Zarsky note, standard terms have an important function in providing information about what parties are entitled to under the contract (Becher and Zarsky, 2008). This information function would disappear when only reasonable expectations or negotiated terms can govern a contract.

Default rules in contract law are ill-equipped to cover all contingencies in all business sectors; it is therefore likely that sellers would prefer to deviate from the default rules. The terms that sellers would like to introduce could be better equipped to deal with the specific cost structures and contingencies in that business sector than the default rules. These introduced terms might even be more socially beneficial in these specific business sectors than the default rules, when they correspond better to the combined preferences of sellers and consumers in that business sector. As has been argued above, even when these terms have a low level of quality and favour sellers over consumers, consumer might prefer these terms under certain circumstances.[328] Consumers might not wish to face the high costs connected to certain privileges in standard contract terms, or maybe they do not mind bearing certain risks themselves. However, when standard terms are prohibited, or only a very limited number of terms can be pre-drafted, these terms are subject to negotiations. Requiring contract parties to negotiate nearly all terms of the contract would increase transaction costs to such an extent that economic transaction would come to a halt. Korobkin argues that any proposal that requires parties to negotiate most to all terms to the contracts cannot considered to be a viable alternative by any court or commentator (Korobkin, 2003: 1245). Furthermore, a limited number of pre-drafted terms being drafted

[327] See above, chapter 5, section 5.3.4b.
[328] See above, chapter 5, section 5.5.4a.

in the contract still calls upon consumers to actually assess the terms they are assenting to, and continues to depend on consumers disciplining the market, be it to a more limited extent. The extent to which consumers are willing to assess the standard terms that disclosed to them needs to be evaluated, even when these terms are only limited in number.

Kornhauser argues that the quality of standard terms will neither be improved by substitution with reasonable expectations, as it is hard to determine what reasonable expectations from buyers are. Consumers might not have any expectations about a great percentage of all possible terms, especially when they relate to contingencies that do not easily spring to mind. Furthermore, sellers and consumers will undoubtedly have different opinions of what is to be considered a reasonable expectation. Perceptions of what is to be considered reasonable can be influenced by biases and heuristics. These biases will most often lead both parties, both sellers and consumers, to interpret reasonability in their own self-interest, and therefore have an overoptimistic assessment of the implications of reasonable expectations covering the contractual conditions. Alternatively, consumers could base their expectations on faulty industry performance, which would not yield a desirable outcome either (Kornhauser, 1976). A reasonable expectation might in fact refer to a low quality in standard terms, when this is interpreted by courts to be reasonable and common in the business sector. This would even further decrease incentives for consumers to challenge contracts or sellers behaviour in court.

Both these policy tools, substitution by reasonable expectations or forced negotiations, do not seem very beneficial in increasing quality in consumer contract terms. Transaction costs are likely to increase considerably, and which terms govern the contract will become highly uncertain. Standard terms do come with benefits. Policy should take advantage of the benefits of standardised terms while correcting for the problems caused by adverse selection; these proposals do not seem to be able to do just that.

7.2.3. EXTENDING THE SCOPE OF THE FAIRNESS TEST AND UNFAIR TERMS REGIME

Not all policy proposals that aim to enhance the quality of terms in consumer contracts focus on standard terms. As has been mentioned above, the Green Paper on the Review of the Consumer Acquis suggests expanding the scope of the fairness test and the application of the EC Unfair Terms Directive to include price, main subject matter and negotiated terms, thereby expanding protection to consumers.[329] Even though this extension of scope is not mentioned in the Proposal Consumer Rights Directive, the original proposal can be seen as an expression of the desire to enhance substantive control over consumer contract terms.[330] The original proposal for the EC Unfair Terms Directive also included an expanded scope of the fairness test.[331] Such an expansion would correspond to the policy recommendations in chapter 5, where it was argued that the quality of *standard* consumer contract terms should depend less on consumer vigilance. Extending the scope of the fairness test would reduce the dependence on consumer vigilance to counteract unfair terms policy *in general*. Therefore, the proposal to extend the scope of the fairness test and the unfair terms regime will be examined here in the light of economic theory and behavioural notions.[332] It will be made clear that the policy recommendations with regard to consumer standard terms that were discussed in chapter 5 should not be over-generalised with respect to salient product aspects such as price, main subject matter and negotiated terms.

a. Expanding the scope of the fairness test: some economic remarks

It should be first pointed out that extending the fairness test to terms that the consumer incorporates in her decision making process, such as price and main subject matter, cannot be justified from the perspective of information economics. Effective competition policy would be much more effective and efficient in enhancing the quality of these very salient product aspects. The market failure of information asymmetry does not apply to these terms; they are known to consumers. Competition policy relates to the market failure that is the cause of sellers getting away with offering inferior quality at too high prices, which is insufficient competition. As consumers have an outside option of not entering into the contract at all, they are not forced to pay the high price and accept the low quality. Remedies in competition law should ensure a combination of fair prices and desirable quality.

The exclusion of negotiated terms from the discipline of unfair terms seems to offer less protection to active consumers than to inactive consumers. When consumers start negotiations, they will thereby forego on the protection from the relevant regulation. However, because active consumers know what they bargain for, they will not agree to welfare decreasing terms, save in cases of misrepresentation, fraud et cetera. Active consumers could very well be sufficiently protected in these cases as terms that are the result of fraud and

---

329 As published by the European Commission (2006: 18–9). See chapter 6, section 6.2.3, notes 291 and 293. See section 6.2.3 generally for a discussion of the differences in scope within the European common core of unfair terms regimes.

330 As published by the European Commission (2008).

331 See Maxeiner (2003: 160–4) and Wilhelmsson (2006: 57–8).

332 Expanding the scope of the fairness test to cover price and main subject matter has been previously explored in Luth and Cseres (2009: 266–72). See also Schillig (2008) for a critical discussion.

misrepresentation are already covered by other legal doctrines (Schillig, 2008: 346; Schäfer and Leyens, 2009: 113). Consumers therefore only suffer a decrease in welfare when they are denied the possibility to negotiate for the terms that they prefer. Consumers might still err in negotiations for certain contract terms and mistakenly agree to a term that decreases their welfare. This issue should be balanced with the costs of intervention in negotiated terms.[333] Consumer error might not be a sufficient rationale for mandatory legislation. The costs and benefits of this policy option require further exploration, which will be presented in the following paragraphs.

b. Enhancing the quality of price and main subject matter

The first question is whether the extension of the fairness test to include price and main subject matter is an effective, or even appropriate, method to increase the quality of contract terms, in this case the quality of price and main subject matter. To the extent that insufficient information is the main cause of high price and low quality of the subject matter, the low quality or unduly high price is likely to be caused by misrepresentation. This is an information failure that should be counteracted, but a rule which specifically targets misrepresentation would then be a better option than the general instrument of a fairness test. The same holds for undue influence, fraud, and other such malicious practices that might be the cause of unduly high prices. Protecting consumers from these undesirable practices directly would be much more effective than protecting them from the result of the practices, which could but does not necessarily consist of a too high price or a too low quality.

Low quality of the main subject matter could also be the result of adverse selection problems. However, this type of adverse selection might be counteracted by providing information about the quality of the good. The quality of the good might be not clear to consumers, but it is a salient product aspect. Salient product aspects are more likely to be corrected through market solutions and consumer learning than product aspects that are not salient, such as standard terms. Furthermore, a low product quality can be directly counteracted by setting quality standards for those products, provided that these standards are effectively enforced. Market solutions, consumers learning and specific standards are likely to be more effective in enhancing the quality of the product than the very general intervention of expanding the scope of the fairness test. Sellers can use some sort of signal to provide information about the quality of their product. The abuse of these quality signals, misleading information and unjust use of a quality signal, should be counteracted by enforcement. Again, enforcing rules that target the cause of the low quality and high price directly are likely to be much more effective than the general rule of extending the scope of the fairness test.

[333] See below, section 7.2.3d.

c. *Enhancing the quality of negotiated terms*

The effectiveness of extending the scope of unfair terms regimes to cover negotiated terms should also be assessed with respect to the effectiveness in enhancing the quality of contract terms, in this case negotiated terms. With regard to policy interventions into negotiated consumer contract terms, two different arguments can be raised: on the one hand, the fact that negotiations have occurred would indicate that a welfare enhancing deal has been concluded, at least with respect to the salient and negotiated terms. Consumers have negotiated about the terms, and therefore they must be aware of these terms. They would not have agreed to the terms unless they wanted the terms that they negotiated to govern the contract. The quality of negotiated terms can therefore be argued to be sufficient; as consumers have knowingly agreed to these terms, they must be beneficial to both parties. On the other hand however, negotiating terms with consumers might increase opportunities for sellers to exploit consumers and take advantage of their own more beneficial position, knowledge or capabilities. If sellers are aware of certain biases that consumer employ in their decision making behaviour, sellers might be able to use that knowledge against consumers and coerce them into making choices which are not in their best interest (Howells and Weatherill, 2005: 262).

There might be cases in which consumers negotiate terms on their own initiative that the seller knows is not in the best interest of consumers, but the consumer does not. In these cases, welfare enhancing decision making on the part of the consumer might be impeded by biases and heuristics. Behavioural insight and a desire to protect consumers from their own detrimental decision making could therefore have been at the basis of this policy proposal. However, the issue of negotiated terms is a very particular one.

First, similar to the question of whether consumers read standard terms, there is much doubt related to the question of whether consumers engage in negotiations of contract terms.[334] Unfortunately, empirical data on this specific issue are lacking. However, consumers are unlikely to invest a great effort in the terms of their contract. If they do even not read the terms, they are not very likely to bargain about them. Secondly, since the definition of 'a negotiated term' is quite narrow, as is for instance the case in the DCRF, it is improbable that many terms will fall under the definition of 'a negotiated term'.[335] Basically, unless a consumer asks for a specific term to be included in the contract, terms are not considered to be individually negotiated. Thirdly, in theory it is possible that a consumer would make a decision that is not in her long term interest, because she

[334] See above, chapter 5, section 5.5.2.

[335] See above, chapter 6, section 6.2.3c: recall that in the DCFR terms will be considered as "individually negotiated" only when a consumer introduced them to the contract; an option out of a selection of standard terms is not regarded to be an individually negotiated term.

is under the influence of biases and heuristics such as overoptimism, present bias and self-serving bias. The question however remains whether the seller induced this decision, or whether the consumer decided to negotiate this particular contract term on her own initiative. It is therefore still unclear whether the consumer should be protected from the seller, even if she does take a decision which is not in her interest. Fourthly, even when consumers negotiate a term that is not in their best interest, the unfair terms regime might not be able to offer any protection. The information requirements are not an issue, as the consumer brought up the negotiated term herself. As has been mentioned above, a term must be clearly unfair and quite onerous to be barred from the contract on the basis of the fairness test.[336] Substantive requirements will only bar the most onerous terms from consumer contracts. Negotiated terms are therefore unlikely to fail the fairness test. The term would have to favour the interest of the seller at the expense of the consumer, without reciprocal obligations in favour of the consumer. If the term is so blatantly undesirable that it cannot pass the fairness test, it is unlikely that consumers will ever bring it up on their own initiative. Arguably, sellers should not even be held responsible in these cases. The question can be raised what exactly can be accomplished by expanding the scope of the fairness test beyond the policy interventions controlling for misrepresentation, undue influence, fraud, and other such malicious practices. Whether cognitive errors in decision making justify the application of the standard of the fairness test to negotiated terms in court, remains an open question until further evidence of cognitive errors in negotiations over contract terms is provided. Also, the costs of the policy intervention should be considered, as well as possible adverse effects such as a decrease of the range of available options and consumer moral hazard. These will be explored in the next section.

Concluding, it is not certain that there really is a reason to be concerned about negotiated terms as long as abuse such as misrepresentation, undue influence and fraud is well-controlled by respective regulation. It is not clear whether sellers take advantage of consumers through negotiated terms. Neither has it been confirmed that extending the scope of the fairness test can remedy the problem should it actually exist. Even when there is a concern that consumers negotiate for terms that are not in their best interest, it is not clear that an extension of the scope of the fairness test will be of any benefit to these consumers. The benefits of this policy option can therefore be questioned; furthermore, costs can be pointed out that further undermine the efficiency of this policy proposal.

[336] See above, chapter 6, section 6.4.1.

d. *Costs and adverse effects*

Besides doubts about the effectiveness of extending the scope of the unfair terms regime to enhance the quality of contract terms, several adverse effects of this policy option can be pointed out.

Firstly, extending the scope of the discipline of unfair contract terms to include price, main subject matter and individually negotiated terms could result in consumer moral hazard.[337] The consequences of a transaction should be evaluated by both the seller and the consumer before the contract is concluded. Carelessness on the part of consumers can be induced when consumers are allowed to invoke the fairness test against any contract term, which is an example of consumer moral hazard. Carelessness in the conclusion of contracts and avoidable consumer error would not stimulate welfare enhancing transactions. Extending the scope of the fairness test to include negotiated tests would severely erode party autonomy (Eidenmüller, 2009: 129).

Secondly, extending unfair terms regulation to include individually negotiated terms in addition to standard terms could lead to a decrease in the range of available options for negotiations. Instead of protecting the consumer, an extension of the fairness test to include negotiated terms could bar certain welfare enhancing terms from the contract entirely. Even a welfare enhancing term might fail a fairness test, if that term allocates more risk to the consumer and therefore seems be to the detriment of the consumer vis-à-vis the seller. The seller could expect moral hazard on the part of the consumer and be unwilling to draft the term in the contract, even if so requested by the consumer. This infringes the freedom of choice, reduces the availability of options and delays the conclusion of transactions. The mechanism of reputation might prevent professional parties from engaging in moral hazard, but consumers will not be so affected (Bebchuk and Posner, 2006). As sellers can expect this kind of moral hazard on the part of consumers, they would not be willing to offer contracts to consumers that exclude certain privileges in exchange for a price premium, even when this corresponds to consumer preferences. They would only possibly be willing to do so after a lengthy negotiation process which included several assurances in the contract. These lengthy negotiations and assurances would further increase the costs of the contract.

Thirdly, the application of a general test such as the fairness test to include price, main subject matter and negotiated terms will cause society to face added costs. The application of this test is not always easy; the costs of court procedures will therefore have to be incurred even when the expansion of the scope is arguably ineffective in its aims. If this test can be invoked by consumers after the conclusion of contracts, sellers will face uncertainties with regard to the contracts they have concluded. They will have to account for the increased

337 See above, chapter 4, section 4.3.4d.

risks of being sued by increasing their prices. Extending the fairness test is a very general instrument that will have implications for all consumer contracts, not just for contracts that involve a problematic estimation of the price and gain for the consumer. The problems with 'unfair' price and subject matter and 'unfairly' negotiated terms might also be more likely in some business sectors than in others. These issues might be better addressed by special regulation which targets these specific contracts, instead of regulation which is applicable to all contracts.

e. *Conclusion: assessment of extending the scope of unfair terms regimes*

After the assessment of the policy proposal of extending the scope of the fairness test and the unfair terms regime to include price, main subject matter and individually negotiated terms, it can be concluded that this policy intervention would be inefficient, as the costs are likely to outweigh the benefits. The ability of these policy interventions to add any benefit to consumers beyond the benefit provided by rules concerning misrepresentation, undue influence and fraud should be doubted. It is unlikely that the quality of price, main subject matter and negotiated terms will increase much as a result of this very general policy intervention. Other more specific policy interventions can be more effective. Furthermore, this policy intervention would result in several costs and adverse effects, such as demanding court procedures and moral hazard. Consumer moral hazard, uncertainty, extensive negotiations and extra drafts lead to an increase in transaction costs without corresponding benefits to social welfare. As has been argued above, consumers might very well be willing to pay for the consumer protection that they desire.[338] If interventions are however unlikely to be effective, the costs of the interventions are likely to outweigh the benefits, which does not justify making consumers pay for their 'enhanced' protection. Policy recommendations with regard to interventions in standardised consumer contract terms should not be unduly generalised. The policy recommendations developed in chapter 5 cautioned against overly depending on consumer vigilance in cases of *standard* contract terms that are not salient to consumers. As price main subject matter and negotiated terms can be regarded as *salient* product items, these recommendations might not hold. Indeed, from the assessment conducted above, it can be argued that dependence on consumer vigilance can be justified in consumer protection measures regarding price, main subject matter and negotiated terms.

338 See above, chapter 2, section 2.3.3b.

f. *A behavioural policy proposal for enhancing quality of price and main subject matter*

As has been argued above, price and main subject matter are likely to be salient product items, which will be taken into account by consumers in their assessment of the contract. However, there are contracts in which sellers might be able to exploit consumer biases related to the value of the contract, for instance due to difficulties with price calculations. Examples of these contracts are credit card services, telephone and fitness club subscriptions.[339] In contracts where the gain out of the contract depends on the use that consumers make of the product or service, consumers might be vulnerable to biased decision making. Consumer might opt for an expensive fitness club contract, because they are overly optimistic about how many times they will actually go to the gym. They might therefore overestimate the value of the contract; after a few months, consumers find out they benefit much less from the subscription than they had previously thought. This problem could be even more likely to occur in contracts where the calculation of the expected benefit from the contract is complex, such as contracts for financial products.

A behaviourally informed solution to this problem has been suggested by Bar-Gill (Bar-Gill, 2007).[340] He suggests providing consumers with information about *average use patterns* of people who use these services. Neither sellers nor consumers have information about the specific price and gains of the contract for each individual consumer before the contract is concluded. However, the seller has information about average use patterns of the consumers that the seller already has a contract with. Providing information about average use patterns to new customers would decrease the information asymmetry between consumers and sellers. Average use patterns could even be made publicly available by issuing mandatory information obligations to sellers. Also, when the consumer has been using the good or service for some time, the seller acquires information about the *individual and specific use pattern* of that consumer. That information could also be disclosed to consumers, upon which they are enabled to re-assess the contract on the basis of their own use pattern. Market parties could even be of assistance by providing means to combine the assessment of individual use patterns and available contracts. For instance, a website could be provided where consumers can upload their credit card usage information, upon which the website calculates which credit card company consumers could best contract with.[341]

The information about average and specific use patterns could debias consumers, at least to some extent. The provision of less and better information

339 See above, chapter 3, section 3.3.1.

340 This example has been mentioned several times before in this research; see chapter 3, section 3.2.2e mainly. For reasons of completeness and clarity, this section will however discuss this policy option again.

341 See above, chapter 3, section 3.3.2e, note 94.

could nudge consumers into more deliberated decisions. Also, the provided information can serve as an anchor for consumer decision making and rebias consumers to allow for more welfare enhancing decisions. However, framing problems, overconfidence and other biases can also cause unrealistic assessments of benefits and costs of the contract. This proposal could still enhance consumer policy related to contracts with a problematic price and main subject matter due to complex decision making and biased value calculations. In these specific contracts, the specific policy proposal described here could enhance the combined quality of price and main subject matter.

7.2.4. ADMINISTRATIVE CONTROL OVER STANDARD TERMS

Another policy instrument that has been proposed frequently in the context of standard terms in consumer contracts is the possibility of pre-approval of standard terms forms by a public authority or a private interest groups. This is a type of administrative control over the content of standard terms. Administrative control can enhance the default option in consumer decision making: the consumer changes nothing in her decision making process, but bases her decision on a more welfare enhancing default, and is thereby nudged into a decision of higher quality.

a. Pre-approving content of standard terms

The policy option of administrative control implies that either public authorities or private interest groups would be approached to give their consent to the standard contract form that sellers would like to use. Through pre-approval, these consumer representatives would be involved in the drafting process of standard consumer contracts. They could make sure that standard terms will be drafted in higher quality, which could counteract the market failure of adverse selection. The pre-approval functions as a soundness check for the entire contract; the main difference with rating and labelling therefore is that an approved contract is sure to comply with all legal requirements related to all terms of the contract. The consumer does not need to interpret any label or ranking instrument herself, but can merely check for approval.

Several authors discuss the option of administrative control over the content of standard term contracts.[342] Becher discusses the certification of standard term

[342] Mainly by Becher (2009) and Gillette (2005). Becher discusses the proposal itself in more detail, while Gillette focuses on the circumstances under which this system would best be implemented. Furthermore, Kaplow and Shavell (2002: 217) mention the possibility of substantive control over standard terms by administrative organisations. The Israeli system,

contract forms by an approval agency to make sure these terms meet both the procedural and substantive requirements (Becher, 2009). Gillette also suggests a system of prior administrative approval of standard term contracts, and like Becher bases his suggestion on the Israeli system (Gillette, 2005). The Israeli legal system comprises a Standard Term Tribunal that can give pre-approval to standard terms.[343] Companies can ask for this approval on a voluntary basis. Pre-approval of a standard form contract by the Tribunal guarantees that the contract does not contain any "unduly disadvantages" or onerous terms (Becher, 2009: 757). A company that obtains approval for their standard terms would be allowed to show a seal of approval on their contract and other forms of communication, such as a website. Both sellers and consumers would be certain that standard terms drafted in the contract meet (at least) the legal requirements related to standard form consumer contracts.

Slightly adjusted policy proposals of administrative control could also be imagined. Pre-approval could be asked for parts of the contract as well as the contract in its entirety. Becher suggest that partly approved contracts can do more justice to the efficiency of terms which depend on the type of the consumer. Distinguishing between consumer types and offering them different terms would result in more efficient contracts. These terms should still be able to bear the pre-approved quality signal. Another option would be to offer a grading scheme for the approval of contracts (Becher, 2009: 759–67).

b. *Reviewing the policy proposal of administrative control over consumer standard terms*

The first question in the review of the policy proposal of administrative control is which benchmark would be used to assess the quality of standard terms. As has been argued above, the quality standard provided by substantive requirements in unfair terms regimes is unlikely to be very high.[344] However, as many unfair terms are argued to still be a part of consumer contracts irrespective of the legal substantive requirements, pre-approving standard terms could be a valuable way of enhancing the quality of standard terms at least up to the level prescribed by legal substantive tests. By applying this benchmark to standard terms in consumer contracts, quality of standard terms could be ascertained at least up to the level of the substantive requirements.[345] Arguably, it could be possible to enhance the quality of standard terms even beyond that level, for instance, by inviting consumer

which uses a form of administrative control, is discussed in more detail by Deutch (1990). See also Lando (1966: 138–43) and Bates (2002: 79–90).

343 The OFT in the UK and the Consumer Ombudsman in the Nordic Countries can also be asked for advice on standard terms, and the institutions can also give their pre-approval. In Mexico, a similar service is provided by Profeco, the Federal Attorney's Office of the Consumer. See above, chapter 6, section 6.2.4, and corresponding notes.

344 See above, chapter 6, section 6.1.4.

345 See above, chapter 6, section 6.3.2d.

representatives to review the standard terms. It could however be difficult to require companies to change their standard terms to account for more rights and privileges to consumers than is required by law. Furthermore, consumers might have a preference for lower quality terms if prices are adjusted correspondingly, and this might depend on the business sector at hand. The benchmark should therefore be set in a way that corresponds to consumer preferences, and that is a very difficult task. The less ambitious task of ascertaining quality up to the level of substantive requirements seems more desirable.

Secondly, the question remains whether consumer organisations and regulatory institutions are aware of consumer preferences of desirable standard terms and corresponding costs. As these parties are not sellers themselves, they have less information about the consequences of shifting risks from the consumer to the seller, especially with regard to the corresponding costs (Gillette, 2005: 987). Even though it could be assumed that regulators have the right motives to do what is best for consumers, Brooker and Cullum assert that they make "wild assumptions about how consumers behave and ... what kind of regulation is needed" (Brooker and Cullum, 2008: 6). Interests of buyers are unlikely to be homogeneous, which further complicates the assessment. Especially consumer organisations are argued to lobby for higher quality, perhaps at the expense of the consumer, because they are overprotective of consumers' interests (Dayagi-Epstein, 2006: 230).[346] Furthermore, regulatory institutions and consumer organisations are likely to underestimate the consequences of consumer moral hazard.[347] Regulatory agencies are argued to frequently issue regulation that favours consumers over sellers (Gillette, 2005: 1006).

Thirdly, the incentives for sellers to participate in the model form scheme should be examined.[348] If sellers could either reduce the risk of liability, or gain a competitive advantage that cannot be obtained otherwise, they would have an incentive to ask for pre-approval of their standardised contracts (Gillette, 2005: 990–1). Avoiding doubts about the legal validity of their contracts might even be a sufficient reason for parties to ask for pre-approval (Collins, 2004: 799). This approval might function as a signal of quality for sellers which they can use to enhance their reputation; also, the risk of being publicly accused and convicted of having imposed unfair terms upon consumers might provide a sufficient incentive (Sheldon, 1974: 21). As companies draft the standard terms themselves, these terms can cater to the needs of business sectors, which is a positive aspect of the proposal. The incentive to gain approval might however be decreased if the demanded level of quality is too high and therefore too costly for sellers. The attractiveness of pre-approved standard terms could be further enhanced by

346 Deutch (1990: 191) explains how consumer organisations have been involved in the review processes at the Israeli Standard Term Tribunal.

347 See for instance Hartlief (2004: 254) for this view on consumers.

348 See also below, section 7.5.

allowing the pre-approval for standard terms to be cheap and easily obtainable. An increase of the deterrent effect of enforcement against one-sided and onerous terms and enforcement efforts generally will stimulate sellers to ask for pre-approval. Consumers could be considered to have a 'relaxed' duty to read if they wish to oppose standard terms that have not been pre-approved (Becher, 2009: 770–86). Another option to enhance the attractiveness of pre-approved standard terms is holding non-approved forms as presumptively unenforceable against the consumer (Bates, 2002: 104–5).

It is relevant to note that both Becher and Gillette comment upon the limited success of the Israeli system, which could be caused by free riding problems (Gillette, 2005: 984–9; Becher, 2009: 758). Sellers who have gained approval for their standard contract terms are likely to make this accomplishment public. Usually, standard forms that sellers use are easily acquired, either by downloading them from a website or on simple request. Other commercial parties could take over these pre-approved contracts without having to face the costs of obtaining the approval. When the quality sign of approval however has more impact on consumer decision making than the terms themselves, free riding would be less of an issue. Trade organisations that hand in contract terms for pre-approval could also overcome free riding problems (Davis, 2006).

Fourth, and perhaps most importantly, the incentives that this policy proposal causes to consumers should be examined. An arguable downside of pre-approval of standard terms could be the fact that it provides incentives for consumers to refrain from reading the contract. However, as has been suggested by empirical data, the incentive for consumers to read terms is already so low that is it unlikely that is could be much further decreased.[349] Therefore, the adverse effect of decreasing consumer reading is likely to be very small.

Another issue connected to consumer incentives is whether consumers will base their buying decisions on for the presence (or absence) of a sign of approval on standard terms. The arguments that have been discussed in the context of rating and labelling apply here as well.[350] Even though contract terms themselves are unlikely to be a salient product attribute, the overall quality of the terms might be. Consumers, it is argued, could be incentivised to shop around for pre-approved contracts and to recognise pre-approval as a quality signal (Becher, 2009: 759–63, 86–7). Consumer organisations can also help create awareness about pre-approved contracts. Whether consumers will actually be affected by pre-approval remains to be seen, and should be empirically tested. However, out of reputation considerations, firms might wish to seek pre-approval even when consumers cannot be shown to actively search for pre-approved contracts. To enhance the credibility of the quality signal, sellers who claim to use pre-approved

349 See above, chapter 5, section 5.5.

350 See above, section 7.2.1.

terms without actually adhering to these terms should be penalised, possibly by public institutions.

As yet, it is not clear whether pre-approved standard terms provide an effective signal of quality that enables sellers to attract more consumers. This policy proposal should therefore be carefully assessed and empirically tested.

c. *Reviewing the slightly adjusted policy proposals of administrative control*

The slightly adjusted policy proposals of partial approval and a grading scheme can also be assessed. Pre-approval can be asked concerning parts of the contract as well as concerning the contract in its entirety. Approving contracts partly, and not in their entirety, would allow sellers to distinguish between consumer types and offer these consumer types different contracts while still being able to use the quality signal of pre-approval. Sophisticated consumers who consciously and upon deliberation would wish to opt for a lower quality of contract terms could through partial pre-approval have an opportunity to choose for those lower quality terms. Whether this adjusted proposal is more beneficial to consumers however depends on the extent to which consumers scrutinise the parts that have not been pre-approved. If sellers hide onerous terms in the part of contract terms that are not approved, sellers could abuse the system of pre-approval. Therefore, the governing body should be allowed to review the contract as a whole, even when only a partial approval is requested. When terms are found that undermine the fairness of the contract as a whole, approval should be withheld.

Another slightly adjusted policy proposal of administrative control concerns a grading scheme for the approval of contracts. The grading of the contract could provide more differentiated signals of quality to consumers; this would enable consumers to opt for lower quality should they desire to do so. It could also provide an incentive to sellers to provide standard terms of a higher quality than merely up to the level of legal substantive terms. However, as Becher explains, a consistent grading of contracts can be challenging to accomplish. Desirable terms might be business-sector specific. Weighing individual terms and developing an overall grade that is informative to consumers might also be difficult. Consumers might face difficulties in interpreting the differences in grading. When the policy instrument is too difficult to comprehend for consumers, they are not likely to base their decisions on the information that this instrument provides. As it will be very complex to evaluate and grade standard terms consistently, the proposal of a grading scheme for consumer contracts might not be advisable (Becher, 2009: 766–7).

d. *Conclusions: the assessment of administrative control over standard terms*

A pre-approval scheme for standard terms in consumer contracts is likely to have positive effects on the quality of terms. Through administrative control the level of quality in consumer standard terms can be upgraded to the quality level provided in legal substantive tests. Consumer organisations can be involved in the review process, and could request to set the benchmark even above quality level set by substantive legal tests and case law. It might however be difficult to ascertain that this quality level would correspond to consumer preferences, especially since preferences might differ across business sectors. There need to be incentives for sellers to ask for pre-approval. These incentives could consist of higher sales, when consumers respond by demanding the seal of approval when doing business. The limited success of the Israeli system and the empirical data raise doubt to whether consumers will demand approved standard terms. However, the reputational concerns of companies and other benefits they acquire from obtaining pre-approval, such as limited liability, might suffice. This policy proposal can therefore be argued to be quite promising in increasing the quality level of standard terms, and should be explored in the setting of specific legal systems.

A special remark concerns the option of partial pre-approval. The suggestion that in some contracts the efficiency of terms depends upon consumer types could hold in theory. It is however vital that the entire contract, including all options, is subject to evaluation. Consumers are not likely to assess the terms that have been left out in the pre-approval procedures. Sellers should inform the evaluation authority of their reasons why they would like to offer different terms to different consumers. When sellers can argue convincingly that it would be beneficial for both consumers and themselves to allow for different contracts to be offered to different consumers, they should be enabled to do so without losing the quality signal that they have obtained.

7.2.5. NEGOTIATED MODEL FORMS OF STANDARD CONTRACT TERMS

A last option would be to supply model forms of standard terms in consumer contracts. When these model contract forms would be the result of negotiations between consumer and business interest groups, consumers would be involved in the drafting process of standard contract terms. This policy option has the potential of improving quality of terms beyond the mere level of excluding onerous terms. It utilises the information present in both business and consumer groups to come to a real understanding about the terms in consumer contracts. Related to behavioural intervention strategies, model forms could be seen as ways to change the detrimental default that consumers base decisions on. This alternative has received some attention in scholarly and policy debate.[351] Many issues are connected to this policy proposal, including how valid consumer representation should be established and the risks of regulatory capture and anti-competitive effects. The following section will briefly discuss the main issues related to negotiated model contracts. Even though this proposal should be further assessed in actual market situations with regard to implementation details, financing, effectiveness considerations et cetera, this proposal could be argued to likely provide improvements to the quality of standard terms in consumer contracts.

a. (Negotiated) model forms of standard terms

Model forms of consumer standard terms can increase the quality of standard terms by providing an 'ideal' form that market parties should adhere to. Eisenberg suggests that legislatures should contemplate drafting standard form contracts for specific business sectors in which consumers are especially vulnerable to enhance the quality of standard terms, especially since consumers cannot be expected to discipline the market (Eisenberg, 1985: 311). Becher also suggests that a set of default terms might be proposed for specific, relatively homogeneous, industries by the administrative authority. Sellers would have to specify where they depart from the pre-drafted terms (Becher, 2009: 759–60). There are several types of model forms; they could be drafted by legislature, by regulatory agencies or by public authorities who protect the interest of consumers, such as the Consumer Ombudsman or consumer authorities.[352]

---

351 It is contemplated by the European Commission (2000: 24–5) whether this would be a valuable strategy to pursue; see also Sheldon (1974), Hondius (1983), Collins (2004), Van Boom and Kottenhagen (2006: 138), Viitanen (2007), Van Mierlo (2007) and Cafaggi (2008; 2009). This option is however not mentioned in the EC Consumer Law Compendium (2008), as is also pointed out by Van Mierlo (2007: 422).

352 It is also suggested in literature to involve the expertise of administrative agencies, law firms who are specialised in the issue, non-profit trade organisations or interest groups and associations in the drafting of these model forms. Choi and Gulati (2006: 1132) mention that law firms could draft standard terms for a group of users, which would result in a save on transaction costs and would make consistent interpretation easier. Mann (2006: 927–32) suggests using the expertise of an administrative agency, and both Davis (2006) and Choi and Gulati (2006: 1139–42) discuss the role of interest groups or trade associations in the development of standard terms for an industrial sector. Davis (2006: 1078–81) mentions that in the US trade associations play a substantial role in the production of boilerplate. This is also the case in Europe. Cafaggi (2008: 95) points to several examples where trade associations have provided model forms, such as in the insurance, banking, telecom and transport industry. Trade associations however might not be very concerned with the interests of consumers, or for that matter with society's interests in general, as is also mentioned by Davis (2006: 1091). See for a general discussion: Rakoff (2006).

One way of providing for an optional model form of consumer standard terms is by stimulating these models to be drafted in negotiations by business and consumer interest representatives. This stimulation can be regarded as co-regulation, a form of self-regulation (Grabosky and Braithwaite, 1986: 183). It corresponds to the new governance approach that is becoming more prevalent in regulation.[353] Representatives of both parties to the contract can be requested or even required to negotiate a model set of standard terms. In the case of consumer contracts, these negotiations are usually conducted between trade and consumer organisations, and some public entity (Cafaggi, 2008: 105). This strategy is currently acted out in various countries in Europe, such as the Netherlands, the Nordic countries (Norway, Sweden, Finland, and Denmark), Belgium, France, Ireland and the UK, even though it is still an underdeveloped instrument in European consumer policy (Van Mierlo, 2007: 411).[354] In the Nordic countries, besides having the right to apply for injunctions in court, the Consumer Ombudsman also negotiates about standard terms with businesses and acts as an interest representative for consumers.[355] In the Netherlands a division of the Ministry of Economic Affairs, the Social Economic Council (SER), hosts negotiations between business and consumer interest groups to draft model forms of standard terms within specific business sectors. These negotiations can result in sector-level agreements.[356]

353 See above, chapter 4, section 4.4.1e. For references to several articles that describe forms of new government, see Amir and Lobel (2008: 2128), note 84.

354 Van Mierlo (2007: 423) mentions the Netherlands, Belgium and the UK. See also Perillo (2008: 187–8, 93) for examples on standard forms that have been developed by organisations mainly in business-to-business contracts, which claim to take the interests of all stakeholders into account. He notes that consumer contracts have not been able to profit from this development, and suggests that legal institutions should fill that gap. Collins (2004: 798) however mentions that in Europe many countries have relied upon co-regulation and self-regulation to influence the content of standard terms. This regulatory strategy has been identified by the European Commission (2003: 21–3) in its Action Plan for more coherent European contract law. See for more information, EC Consumer Law Compendium (Part II C2.VI.2) and European Commission (2000: 24–5). Cafaggi (2008) extensively discusses multi-stakeholder agreements to draft consumer standard contract terms.

355 See Viitanen (2007: 86) and Cafaggi (2008: 101) who discuss the fact that Nordic consumer ombudsmen conduct these negotiations in several business sectors. Sheldon (1974: 39) describes that full ex-ante negotiations with the Swedish Consumer Ombudsman can be started on initiative of the seller. See Ramsay (2007: 211–3), Howells (2007) who discuss how the Office of Fair Trading (OFT) negotiates standard terms on behalf of consumers and also challenges terms that it deems unfair. Träger (2008: 65) mentions that negotiations are undertaken by the Irish Director of Consumer Affairs, among others. See also Cafaggi (2009: 18–9) who explains how standard terms are developed by private interest groups, such as trade associations, sometimes through negotiations.

356 This "Dutch Approach" has been discussed more in detail by Van Mierlo (2007); it is also mentioned by Van Boom and Kottenhagen (2006: 138). Van Mierlo (2007: 411) argues that the dialogue between contract parties aimed at drafting consumer standard terms is a success formula in an increasing number of sectors; therefore, this approach might serve as a best practice in the EU. See for more information: www.ser.nl/en/About_the_SER/Responsibilities/General_terms.aspx.

The effectiveness of negotiations between professional associations and consumer interest representatives, either governmental institutions or consumer associations, has varied in the countries where it has been implemented (European Commission, 2000: 24–5; Collins, 2004: 798). In France, these agreements have not had much impact, which was arguably a result of the fact that these contracts would only be valid for signatory organisations and only at a local level. In the Netherlands and Sweden however, these agreements have been highly successful: the agreements have been adopted by a multitude of businesses, resulting in a drop in court cases (Viitanen, 2007: 100). In the Netherlands, the sector-specific negotiations between professional organisations and consumer associations have resulted in many sector-level agreements, and are considered to be a very valuable approach by industry, consumer representatives and regulatory institutions.

b. Advantages of (sector-level) negotiated model form contracts

Model standard terms developed in negotiations might be quite attractive, both for society at large, sellers and consumers (Collins, 2004: 798–802). Both consumers and businesses are represented in the negotiations, which should allow for the competing interests to the contract to be taken into account in the model form. When these contracts have been negotiated under fair procedures, these terms can be expected to be fair and sensitive to the particular interests of the stakeholders. Consumers can have a say in the drafting of consumer standard terms through a representative, which should generate standard terms that correspond to consumer preferences to a larger extent than one-sided standard terms would. It would be necessary to ensure the representativeness of the parties to the contract negotiations, which could involve some technical assistance, financial and organisational help such as training to consumer organisations.[357] The level of quality in standard terms is likely to be enhanced when consumers are able to influence the content of standard term contracts. Consequently, enforcement costs of regulatory agencies and courts to guarantee that companies use fair contract terms will be lower.[358]

---

[357] See below, section f.

[358] Another advantage connected to negotiated standard terms is that, if these negotiations were to take place at a European level, these negotiated terms could be used to harmonise standard contracts in Europe. European-wide negotiations could result in a save on transaction and information costs. However, Whittaker (2006: 73) argues that the development of general standard terms for all consumer contracts would not be easy to achieve, especially at a European level. Too many parties would have to be involved; it would apply to too many business sectors and involve too many interests. Genuine collective bargaining would be extremely difficult in this setting. Also, in different Member States, different consumer issues could be at stake, or different business interests. Due to the heterogeneity of business and consumer preferences in Member States, and in business sectors for that matter, it is more efficient if model standard forms are developed within Member States, and at sector-level, as is argued by Kerber and Grundmann (2006). This argument is raised in connection to the

The model standard terms can be adjusted to the specific features of different business sectors. Consumer law is not sector specific (Cafaggi, 2008: 99); however, the desirable standard terms from the perspective of the consumer can be. Which standard term is most efficient from the combined perspective of sellers and consumers might depend on the relevant business sector. Also, not all aspects that should be considered in standard terms are the same or even similar across business sectors. Negotiated model standard terms in certain specific business sectors should be designed to incorporate all the particularities of the relevant market.

Government institutions might lack necessary information about industry cost structures and related consumer preferences regarding risk allocations. Negotiated model forms can account for the information that both businesses and consumers possess in the standard contract terms (Miller, 1985: 897–8). Information about preferences and consequences for involved parties is more likely to be brought up in discussions by the parties whom these preferences and consequences affect than by third parties.[359] Therefore, term users and parties that will actually be affected by (the invocation of) these terms will be more capable at drafting efficient contract terms themselves than a regulating agency on the behalf of these parties.[360]

c. *Incentives to use the negotiated model form contracts*

As low-quality terms are cheaper for sellers, the model form is likely to be more expensive. Costs could be partly recouped by the decrease in drafting costs that the use of the model form would effectuate. This would apply especially to small-to-medium enterprises, as contract drafting costs form a larger part of their overall costs in comparison to larger companies. These enterprises can save on transaction costs by free-riding on the drafting efforts by other parties (Davis, 2006: 1085). Business parties can also save on costs because the terms in the model standard form are less likely to be challenged in court and even if they are, these terms are more likely to hold up in court.[361] Adhering to the model

desirability of harmonisation in European private law, a discussion that falls outside the scope of this research. See also above, chapter 6, note 282.

359 As Schäfer and Leyens (2009: 110–1) argue, sellers should have an incentive to use their superior knowledge and capabilities to become engaged in enhancing contract quality.

360 See for a discussion, Mann (2006: 29–30).

361 The Dutch Consumer Authority only assesses consumer standard terms that have been drafted unilaterally; the terms that have been drafted in negotiations between consumer and business organisations are not taken up in the assessment. For the Dutch Consumer Authorities' approach to consumer standardised terms, see consuwijzer.nl/Consumententhema_s/Algemene_voorwaarden. Sheldon (1974: 39) describes that the outcome of ex-ante negotiations between the Swedish Consumer Ombudsman and sellers have no legal status as formal approval can only be obtained through procedures challenging terms at Market Court. However, as consumers do not have a legal standing in the Market Court, the approval of the Consumer Ombudsman is a good indication that these terms will not be challenged. As

form therefore provides predictability and certainty in knowing that these terms are legally valid (Collins, 2004: 802). Employing a model of standard terms can also be interpreted as a sign of consumer friendliness, a signal for consumers that the terms which are applied by this company are of higher quality than those of other companies. Reputation with the public or public goodwill, which is highly regarded by companies, provides a stimulus for adopting the model form (Sheldon, 1974: 21). The concern for maintaining a favourable image both with consumers, regulating authorities and other stakeholders can be seen as a crucial factor in effective co-regulation (Balleisen and Eisner, 2009: 131–3). As business representative organisations have agreed to these terms, companies are more likely to adopt these sets of standard terms which have been developed with also the business interest in mind, than the 'set' of standard terms drafted by legal default rules.

The attractiveness of negotiated standard terms could be enhanced in the same ways as have been discussed in the context of pre-approved standard terms.[362] The negotiation process and obtaining the rights to use the negotiated standard terms should not be too costly or require great amounts of effort on the part of individual sellers. However, negotiations can be like public goods: free-riding problems can arise when these terms are easy to acquire, and not all (business) parties who benefit from the negotiations then contribute to the costs of these negotiations. Some kind of funding scheme for these negotiations should be contemplated as the benefit to society may be large, but individual benefit to individual contributing parties may be small.

Enforcement against one-sided and onerous terms should be enhanced, which would make sellers more inclined to cooperate in a model form contract scheme.[363] Non-negotiated forms can be held as presumptively unenforceable against the consumer. Furthermore, sellers could be granted a more favourable position when they are confronted with claims against model form terms, which renders them less likely to lose a dispute when they adhere to the model term contracts. This will result in a save in legal costs. Consumers should be made aware of the fact that certain sellers adhere to negotiated terms and others do not, to stimulate consumers to shop around for negotiated contracts. Abuse of the quality signal by claiming to adhere to negotiated terms but in fact using other standard terms should be duly penalised.

Viitanen (2007: 88) describes, when the Consumer Ombudsman refuses to undertake legal action before the Market Court, a registered association looking after consumers' interests could also challenge standard terms in consumer contracts. Wilhelmsson (1993: 438–9) however argues that this occurs very rarely in practice.

362 See above, section 7.2.4b.

363 Viitanen (2007: 100) argues that one of the reasons that these negotiations have been very successful in Sweden, where sellers have been more than willing to cooperate, was that public institutions have convincingly shown their willingness to use hard law in case persuasion would fail.

d. *Correspondence to substantive requirements*

In descriptions of negotiated model forms of standard terms, regulatory institutions in particular frequently mention that these terms have to comply with necessary legal substantive requirements (as mentioned by for instance European Commission, 2003: 22). Therefore, a check of the negotiated model forms in their entirety would have to be conducted. This would increase the workload of regulatory or monitoring institutions. These institutions do not (regularly) check standard contract forms that are drawn up by individual companies in their entirety; in some cases, these institutions do respond to consumer complaints, but even then they will only assess the specific standard terms that this complaint pertains to. Especially when negotiated forms are constructed at sector-level, many negotiated forms would need to be checked with regard to their adherence to substantive requirements.

Collins however argues that the concern related to the correspondence between negotiated model forms and substantive requirements might not be justified (Collins, 2004: 800–1). Firstly, most terms that are the result of negotiations and that are therefore agreed to by consumer representatives will correspond to substantive requirements. Secondly, if all interested parties have been adequately represented, and the negotiated model form is what they agree would be a desirable risk allocation between sellers and consumers in that business sector, there is no reason to doubt this outcome even if it does not correspond to the legal requirements that are connected to the substance of the contract.[364] As has been mentioned above, substantive requirements may not have been set at an efficient level.[365] When standard term models are the result of negotiations between consumer representative organisations and business organisations, these models are more likely to consist of efficient terms than default rules drafted by policy makers. It is worth to note yet again that there might be low-quality terms, which consumers prefer to have included in contracts.[366] The reason might be that consumers can better prevent the contingency that this risk pertains to from occurring, or that they can insure themselves against that risk. Also, consumers might not want to bear the costs associated with the protection from that risk. As long as consumers have agreed to the terms in advance, and they were adequately represented, there does not seem to be much need for negotiated terms to comply with substantive requirements. In fair and adequate procedures, when negotiated terms do not meet substantive requirements, a serious policy concern should not automatically arise.

---

364 The extent to which negotiated model forms correspond to legal substantive requirements is not clear at this point; anecdotal evidence such as conversations with the Dutch Consumer Authority suggests that unfair terms might persist even in negotiated model contracts.

365 See above, chapter 6, section 6.3.1a.

366 See above, chapter 5, section 5.5.4a.

e. *Anti-competitive effects*

Besides substantive requirements, there are other legal requirements that apply to negotiated model terms. These requirements are connected to the issue of competition. A downside to industry self-regulation, and co-regulation, is that it could restrict competition (Van den Bergh, 2006: 160–2). This concern is also mentioned in the EC report on the implementation of the EC Unfair Terms Directive, where it is stated that one should "provide for and encourage the establishment of systems that encourage the negotiation and discussion of terms with the professionals (*obviously without prejudice to competition law*) (European Commission, 2000: 25, emphasis added).[367] Contractual terms and negotiated agreements over model contract forms are considered to fall within the scope of EC competition law, implying that they will be scrutinised for anti-competitive effects.[368] Especially when terms are price-related, they will be subject to strict consideration (Cafaggi, 2008: 127–31). Also in the Netherlands, the Dutch Competition Authority has been very much involved with the question which terms could be negotiated and agreed upon in the model form discussions. The Dutch Competition Authority has concluded that, in general, negotiated standard terms are not considered to be a concern with regard to anti-competitive effects, but that particular contract clauses should not be part of the negotiations.[369] Wilhelmsson describes how case law on this issue is vague. Cooperation concerning certain terms, like clauses on interest rates or certain delivery terms, may be seen as having anti-competitive effects according to case law. Cooperation concerning other terms does not necessarily have anti-competitive effects (Wilhelmsson, 2006: 68–72).

The proposal of a model form of standard terms to be used in one sector of industry has also been criticised for decreasing competition between firms. This would however only be problematic if firms compete on the basis of their standard contract terms in the first place. As is suggested by the empirical data, this kind of competition is unlikely to occur in reality for the majority of standardised contract terms.[370] If no competition in fact occurs with respect to the terms that have been negotiated, employing a model form of standard terms only stands to improve the quality of standard terms (Collins, 2004: 800–2). It is of paramount

367 See Wilhelmsson (2006: 61–3) on competition issues, arguing that even though how competition law is more suspicious than consumer law, it will allow model contract forms to be negotiated between sellers and consumers. Cafaggi (2008) also discusses the limits to negotiated standard form contracts by competition law extensively.

368 These agreements are considered to be agreements or decisions of undertakings within article 101 par. 1 of the Treaty on the Functioning of the European Union that has been in force as of 1 December 2009 (ex article 81, par. 1 of the Treaty on the Establishment of the European Community, mostly referred to as EC Treaty). The agreements described and therefore fall within the scope of EC competition law.

369 See SER (2006: 10–2).

370 See above, chapter 5, section 5.5.3b.

importance to distinguish which terms are considered by consumers in their decision which sellers to contract with, because terms that should therefore be left to the competition between sellers. Negotiated standard term agreements should therefore not aim to standardise all terms in the contract, only the ones that are not consciously included in buyer's decision making processes (Cafaggi, 2008: 110–1).

However, one anti-competitive risk remains: this model could provide a forum for businesses to meet, and to make anti-competitive arrangements other than the arrangement of standard terms in consumer contracts. This cooperation over standard terms might therefore not directly have anti-competitive effects, but can reinforce other anti-competitive measures (Wilhelmsson, 2006: 69).

f. Consumer representation

Policy strategies that aim at actually promoting the interests of consumers should require that consumer participation is ensured both at the level of policy decision making as well as at the level of enforcement. As Van den Bergh argues, consumer associations can have better information at their disposal than individual consumers do. Furthermore, representation can solve rational apathy problems. To the extent that consumer associations depend on financial contributions from consumer members, free riding could be an issue (Van den Bergh, 2008: 284–8). Consumer representation by consumer organisations would constitute a way to allow the voice of the consumer to be heard in the drafting process of standard contract forms. However, consumer participation in the EU is argued to be limited and outweighed by the influence of business interest groups (Ramsay, 2007: 19–22). Consumer representative organisations do voice consumers' interests, but their impact on politics is limited and their membership relatively small (Howells and Weatherill, 2005: 17).

Ramsay discusses how consumer organisations are faced with several problems (Ramsay, 2007: 19–22). Firstly, all consumers have a very small interest in any issue, and this interest might not be enough to get consumer organisations incentivised to take action. Secondly, consumer interests might be very diverse as the entire group of consumers is large and diverse. As has been described by Olson, a large group size which consists of heterogeneous group members complicates collective action (Olson, 1965). Striking a balance in case of conflicting interests might therefore be quite hard for consumer interest groups (Dayagi-Epstein, 2006: 231). Thirdly, consumer associations suffer from free rider issues as all consumers benefit from the efforts of these associations, but not everyone wishes to contribute. Consumer organisations in particular are faced with the concern of low resources (Dayagi-Epstein, 2006: 228). Trade associations face fewer problems in this regard, as they are likely to be better organised, have more funding, and their members have more homogeneous preferences (Gillette, 2004: 1008). Therefore, when consumers are involved in regulatory processes, the mere opportunity for consumers to be involved is not always enough to assure adequate representation of consumer interest.[371] Consumer associations should be supported by training and funding, and they should cooperate with fellow consumer associations possibly in other countries (Dayagi-Epstein, 2006: 242–7).

To make sure that consumer interest groups can adequately represent the voice of the consumer, they should be aided in their endeavours by for instance training and funding. Also, regular meetings between several consumer interest groups to share knowledge and best practices should be set up, preferably at a European level (Bourgoignie, 1987: 231–4; Dayagi-Epstein, 2006: 242–7). In some cases, public authorities might be present in legal systems that are better or at least equally able to represent the interest of consumers. In Nordic countries trade organisations negotiate with the Ombudsmen and Consumer Agencies, which is as Hondius argues a result of to the fact that consumer associations in these regions are weak (Hondius, 2006: 239). Consumer interest parties might have information advantages with regard to consumer preferences, but a Consumer Ombudsman might be a more competent and organised party. Which party would be best able to defend the interests of consumers in standard terms negotiations would depend upon the institutional arrangements and existence of (competent) consumer interest groups in the respective legal systems.[372]

A remaining issue is whether the interests of the consumer representative organisation align with the interests of the broad population of consumers, which potentially has heterogeneous interests (Van den Bergh, 2008: 293). As has been explained above, consumer organisations are argued to lobby for higher quality, perhaps at the expense of the consumer, because they are overprotective of consumers' interests and underestimate the consequences of consumer moral hazard.[373] This could be a reason to issue these model forms of standard terms as an option for sellers, instead of making them mandatory for business sectors, as will be discussed below.[374]

g. Regulatory capture

It has also been argued that negotiations between public authorities and regulated subjects are likely to be captured either by the industry which interests it should regulate, or by consumer organisations (Bates, 2002: 88–9; Gillette, 2005: 1005–12). A clear need exists to increase the understanding of how the interplay of

---

371 As discussed by Dayagi-Epstein (2006: 224–5), consumer interest groups can also suffer from problems concerning lack of legitimacy, which can be dealt with through democratic decision procedures, or other methods to make sure that consumers are satisfied with the outcomes of interest group decision making.

372 See also Van Mierlo (2007: 422–3).

373 As has been described by Van den Bergh (2008), consumer association representation can give rise to a principle-agent problem. See above, section 7.2.4b.

374 See below, section h.

interest groups and deliberative processes influences legislation and regulation (Hadfield et al., 1998: 148–150).

To limit the risk of regulatory capture, it should be made sure that these negotiations are conducted with participants who have conflicting interests, so that hidden agendas will not remain to be hidden (Cafaggi, 2008: 138). A higher number of participants will also result in the fact that the chances of one party hijacking the regulatory process are minimal. However, even when participation of as many stakeholders as possible is ensured, there is no guarantee that the contract terms that result from the negotiations are indeed the most efficient. The parties that are involved in the negotiations have their own interest in mind. They could maximise their own benefits, or externalise costs to other parties that are not included in the negotiations. For instance, consumer interest groups are often criticised of being overprotective and of asking for too much protection on behalf of consumers (Dayagi-Epstein, 2006: 230). Also, regulatory agencies are claimed to be more likely to favour consumers over sellers (Gillette, 2004: 1008). Consumer moral hazard should however explicitly be taken into account in order to counteract adverse effects of regulation; sellers are likely to be aware of this risk and should provide the necessary information. To counteract detrimental effects of conflicts of interest in individuals, Cafaggi argues that conflicts of interests in individual hidden agendas should be mandatorily disclosed. A group can also have interests that are different from the public interest. Therefore, not only should a plurality of affected actors be involved in the decision making process, but these processes should also consist of transparent procedures and a lot of deliberation in which all relevant interests are duly regarded (Cafaggi, 2006: 55–8).

h. *Optional or mandatory*

A welfare-enhancing model of standard terms might provide an effective way of stimulating the inclusion of such terms into consumer contracts. The question arises why these negotiated standard terms should not be made to mandatory to all consumer contracts conducted in the respective business sector.[375]

One answer would be that mandatory standard contract terms, even if they are differentiated by business sector, would not correspond to the regulatory approach of soft paternalism. Mandatory application of negotiated terms would in fact constitute a very far-reaching type of administrative control. Even though consumers are unlikely to consider standard terms in their decision making process, they might consider a quality signal of the standard contract as a whole. The picture is not entirely clear yet. Consumer interests are not homogeneous. Some consumers might prefer standard terms that allow for less privileges than the negotiated model form, and might opt for non-negotiated terms when given

375 In fact, Van Mierlo (2007: 414) shows that, in the Netherlands, the government is enabled by law to declare negotiated standard terms as legally binding for an entire business sector.

the choice. When negotiated model forms are mandatory, consumers can no longer opt out of the default. As has been argued above, consumer associations could be seen as being overprotective of consumers, because they lobby for a higher level of consumer protection than is deemed preferable by large groups of consumers.[376]

Furthermore, consumers might actually wish to negotiate the content of certain contract terms. Even though this might be unlikely, this possibility cannot as yet be ruled out. The negotiated terms could in these cases be of assistance to negotiating consumers, not because they are mandatorily imposed, but because they provide consumers with an anchor or reference point. Default rules, and as such model rules, tend to be sticky and have an expressive effect.[377] The default rule could be expressive in the sense that it is interpreted to be the fairest allocation of risk, simply because it is drafted in the standard term model form. Optional negotiated terms, unlike mandatory ones, do not diminish the range of available options. This allows consumers to opt for other terms if they feel confident in deviating from the default and thereby increase their welfare in their estimations.

However, in markets with consistent cognitive problems, such as markets in which the stakes for consumers are high while the learning opportunities are small, or markets in which the typical consumers are vulnerable, elderly for instance, might justify an exception to the preference for optional over mandatory application (Becher, 2009: 787–8). Mandatory application may also be preferred when the optional regime fails as a result of a lack of cooperation by sellers. As the optional model, unlike the mandatory model, can accommodate heterogeneous preferences of consumers, the first model should be generally preferred over the second. When the optional models are insufficiently effective, the mandatory model can be contemplated.

i. *Conclusion: assessment of negotiated model forms of standard terms*

In the aim to enhance the quality of standard terms, the option of negotiated model forms of standard terms can be concluded to be worthy of exploration in order to make sure this enhanced quality corresponds to actual consumer preferences. Negotiations can include consumer interests in the drafting process of standard terms. These terms are therefore likely to be of higher quality than one-sided standard terms, especially when they are allowed to differ per business sector. Enforcement costs of policing standard terms would consequently be lower, which should be balanced against the costs of the regulatory intervention. This policy intervention can be costly to set up; costs can however also be borne to some extent by participating parties, and should be considered in relation to the increase in quality of standard terms. Businesses also can gain from these

376 See above, section f, and section 7.2.4b.

377 See above, chapter 5, section 5.3.4.

negotiations, because they will save on drafting and litigation costs. The model can enhance sellers' reputation. To enhance the attractiveness of the negotiated terms, the model terms should be easily obtainable and easy to use, enforcement against unfair non-negotiated terms should be intensified, and consumers should be made aware of the quality signal that is conveyed by adherence to negotiated terms.

Negotiated terms might not all correspond to legal substantive tests. As long as consumers have been fairly represented in the negotiations, these terms are likely to be efficient even in the odd case that they do not correspond to substantive requirements. Anti-competitive effects are neither a source of serious concern, as long as the negotiations are limited to the terms that consumers do not include in their decision making process. The argument that the provided platform could allow businesses to cooperate in an anti-competitive way should be seen in relation to other platforms that already exists. Arguably, if companies want to meet and discuss, they could; online conferencing has made meeting without physically travelling to the same location quite easy. It does however remain a valid concern.

Since consumer organisations might be less well-organised than trade associations and could represent a very heterogeneous member group, some assistance to consumer organisations should be contemplated to assure fair consumer representation. Depending upon the institutional arrangements, a public authority such as the Nordic Consumer Ombudsman would be the most efficient party to include in the negotiations on behalf of consumers. Regulatory capture can be a concern; this concern is however somewhat averted by inviting both sellers and consumers to the negotiations. Procedures should be transparent and many stakeholders should be present, so that hidden agendas will not remain hidden. The negotiated model forms should ideally be an optional instrument, so that consumers could opt out from the model terms or even negotiate some terms, should they so desire. Consumers may be unlikely to do so, but as long as it has not been established that negotiated terms provide effective quality signals, mandated choice is not desirable. When the optional instrument turns out to be ineffective however, mandatorily applying the negotiated terms to the entire business sector should be contemplated.

The policy option of negotiated model forms of consumer standard terms can be argued to be most promising in the aim for improvements to the quality of standardised contract terms. One caveat should however be mentioned: when the legal system in which this policy option is contemplated is characterised by an adversarial culture, and business and consumer representatives are unlikely to ever come to an agreement with regard to standard contract terms, the policy option of negotiated model forms might be too strenuous to be effective. The previous option of administrative control over consumer standard terms might be more effective and efficient in such cases, especially when the administrative procedures employ a benchmark that is higher than the legal substantive tests.

7.3. CONCLUSIONS: PROPOSALS TO ENHANCE STANDARD TERM CONSUMER POLICY

This chapter has commented upon several policy proposals that aspire to enhance unfair terms regimes, aiming to roughly establish which policy strategies would be promising when aiming to enhance the quality of standard terms in consumer contracts.

The first type of proposals focuses on solving the signing-without-reading problem. This research concludes that this strategy is unlikely to provide to ultimate solution to unfair consumer contract term issues. Behavioural insights suggest looking beyond solving this specific problem, and for instance focus on providing a valuable information tool which allows consumers to assess the quality of terms. An example of such a tool can be provided by rating standard term forms, or providing a label which discloses the most contentious or important (from the perspective of the consumer) standard terms. As these policy tools still heavily depend on the consumer to discipline the market with respect to standard terms, some doubt can be shed on whether these proposals can really augment the quality of terms.

Other proposals argue that standard terms should be removed from consumer contracts and replaced either by a general doctrine of reasonable expectations or by forced negotiations. It would be very difficult to determine what these reasonable expectations might be, and it could even be reasonable to expect a low quality in standard terms. Forced negotiations are no viable option either, as they would increase transaction costs to such a level that consumer transactions might come to a standstill. Standard terms come with benefits for both sellers and consumers; doing away with standard terms is ill-advised. This policy strategy is not worth developing.

Expanding the scope of the fairness test and the unfair terms regime is the third policy proposal that was discussed in this chapter. Whether this policy suggestion is likely to enhance the quality of price, main subject matter or negotiated terms most efficiently or effectively remains to be seen. To the extent that the cause of low quality is misrepresentation, adverse selection, undue influence and fraud, policy instruments already exists that are aimed specifically at these causes. Also, moral hazard and a decrease in the range of available options could be a consequence of this expansion in scope. Extending the scope of the fairness test is a very general instrument which will have consequences for a large range of consumer contracts. Not in all these contracts problems with 'unfair' price, main subject matter or negotiated terms are to be expected, while costs of increased uncertainty do affect all contracts. This policy proposal fails to deal with potential underlying causes of low quality. Contracts in which the consumer might be uncertain of the price (and corresponding main subject matter) of the contract, such as fitness club, internet, telephone subscriptions and credit card services, could benefit from a behaviourally informed policy proposal.

Providing consumers with information about average use patterns could enhance consumer assessment of the contract. As a result, the quality of terms could be improved, even if the consumer is still required to discipline the market, because of improved information. The behaviourally informed proposal is better targeted at the perceived problem area and is more likely to be effective in augmenting quality than the policy proposal of substantive test scope expansion.

Fourthly, administrative control over the quality of standard terms is established to be a promising policy strategy. Standard terms, or entire forms of standard terms, could be pre-approved by some institution, which would then provide a quality seal to the contract and make sure the quality attained is at least that which is set by substantive regulation and case law. As is argued in the previous chapter, that level is currently not realised in common policy. Seller participation in the scheme could be stimulated by reducing the risk of liability and correcting free-rider problems. Consumer demand for approved standard terms could be necessary to drive this policy instrument, and therefore it would need to be carefully tested in light of empirical findings. However, theoretically, this strategy could be quite beneficial in improving the quality level of terms.

The last type of policy suggestions consists of negotiations between business and consumer representatives, which result in model forms of consumer contracts preferably at sector-level. By introducing consumer interests in the drafting process, this policy proposal stands to enhance the quality of standard terms. Businesses can also gain from this proposal by saving in drafting in litigation costs. As long as consumers have been adequately represented, the (odd yet) possible fact that these terms do not correspond to legal substantive requirements should not be a concern; neither should anti-competitive effects, as long the negotiations are limited to terms that are not considered by consumers in the decision which seller to contract with. Some assistance to consumer organisations should be contemplated to assure fair consumer representation. Transparent procedures and the representation of most to all interests should limit the risk of regulatory capture. The model terms should be optional instead of mandatory as long as the optional model has not been shown to be ineffective in raising consumer standard term quality.

To conclude, it can be argued that some policy strategies that have been discussed are capable of augmenting the quality of standardised consumer contract terms. Most promising in this regard are pre-approved standard terms and a negotiated model of standard terms. Which proposal would be more effective depends upon the respective legal regime. In a rather adversarial culture, the consensus-based approach of negotiating a model form of standard terms might not be appropriate. In this case, consumer and business organisations could be involved in lengthy and costly negotiations, possibly without any beneficial end-result. In these cases, pre-approved standard terms should be contemplated, which would ideally adhere to a benchmark that takes consumer preferences, rather than (only) the legal substantive requirements, into account. Where a consensus can be achieved between consumer and seller representatives however, the negotiated model contract terms can be a very effective way of enhancing contract quality by getting consumers involved in the drafting process, and this policy proposal should in such cases be contemplated.

CHAPTER 8

CONCLUSIONS AND RECOMMENDATIONS FOR FURTHER RESEARCH

8.1. CONCLUSIONS

To conclude this research, this chapter aims at providing an answer to the research questions that have been posed in the introduction, namely:

1. To what extent can the application of insights from behavioural economics and empirical research into economic analysis be relied upon to improve consumer policy from a social welfare perspective?
2. To what extent can consumer policy regarding standardised consumer contract terms be improved by re-assessing policy on the basis of behavioural economic insights and proposing corresponding interventions from a social welfare perspective?

After a summary of the results that have followed from the analyses conducted in this research, this chapter will also provide some recommendations for further investigation.

8.1.1. APPLICATION OF BEHAVIOURAL INSIGHTS TO CONSUMER POLICY

In the assessment of the desirability of applying behavioural insights to consumer policy, this research has first addressed the question of whether behavioural insights could justify government interventions into consumer contracts beyond the rationales that were provided by conventional economics. Secondly, it has addressed the cautions and considerations that should be taken into account when behavioural insights inform consumer protection policy; policy guidelines have been developed to account for some of these cautions and considerations.

a. *Economic and behavioural rationales for government intervention in consumer contracts*

The conditions under which government interventions in (consumer) markets are socially desirable from an economic point of view can be concluded to be the following: to correct for market failures, which are imperfect competition, public goods, externalities and information asymmetry, and to decrease transaction costs. With regard to consumer contracts, issues connected to transaction costs, information asymmetries and competition can justify government intervention. This research has focused on the first two. Transaction costs such as contracting, monitoring and enforcement costs can be decreased by the provision of enforcement mechanisms and by setting default terms in contract law. Government interventions that address the market failure of information asymmetry can provide for simple and comparable information, written in plain language, they can consist of disclosure duties or mandatory quality standards, or they can stimulate this information to be disclosed by market parties. Even though market solutions are present to counteract these market failures, there might still be a potential increase in social welfare to be obtained by government interventions. As these interventions are costly, the benefits of the intervention should outweigh the costs, and market solutions that render government intervention superfluous should be taken into account.

The next aim of this research was to establish whether behavioural insights can give implications for consumer policy that go beyond the standard economic rationales for intervention, and this research has concluded that to be the case. Behavioural literature has identified several biases and heuristics that might affect consumer decision making. These insights do not correspond to standard economic theory and the rational choice model of (consumer) behaviour. Behavioural insights such as bounded rationality and information overload, risk perception biases, self-serving biases, status quo biases, time related biases, contexts and framing, anchoring and adjustment, and bounded will-power have been discussed. However, whether behavioural insights are more accurate than rational choice at predicting consumer behaviour depends upon the specific case. Cognitive decision making might allow for dual processes, which could for example mean that one system is more rational and analytical, and the other is more affective and intuitive. Specific contexts should then be assessed to determine which decision making process is employed by consumers in this context.

Behavioural insights can have several implications for consumer policy in particular, such as a recommendation to protect consumers from their own errors, possibly even by limiting their options. Consumer interests could be harmed even in markets that are free from any traditional market failures. Even in a market that is sufficiently competitive, where no information asymmetries exist and externalities are internalised, social welfare might still stand to be increased by improving consumers' decision making process. Biases, heuristics and other notions can lead to suboptimal decision making from the perspectives of the consumer and of social welfare. Furthermore, behavioural insight challenges the effectiveness of information disclosure in aiding consumers in their decision making process. Interventions in individual decision making can debias consumers and nudge them into more rational decision making. Also, the default position of the decision can be changed to alter the outcome of the decision without changing the decision making process itself. In addition, heuristics can be employed to enhance the end-result of the decision. Which intervention strategy is more desirable should be carefully assessed, and would depend on the intrusiveness and effectiveness of the intervention, combined with the ease with which the effects of the intervention can be predicted.

b. Relying upon behavioural insights to enhance consumer policy

Behavioural insights can in many cases be argued to be more accurate in explaining and predicting describing consumer decision making. However, the assessment of the extent to which the insights from behavioural economics and empirical studies into economic analysis should inform consumer policy from a social welfare perspective has raised several concerns. This research has reviewed these concerns, but has come to the conclusion that none of these cautions and considerations prohibit welfare-enhancing behaviourally informed consumer policy. Therefore, it is concluded that it is at least theoretically possible to enhance consumer policy by the application of behavioural economic insights.

However, it is acknowledged that this conclusion will not be valid in all consumer policy issues. In some situations, rational choice is better at predicting behaviour, or the hypothesised bias cannot be shown to be detrimental to consumers with regard to the specific market. Furthermore, the behavioural intervention should not be implemented when it is too costly, when the policy is ineffective as a result of to government error, or when the policy has been devised to wrongly manipulate rather than aid consumers in their decision making. This research has identified several cautions and considerations that behaviourally informed consumer policy should take into account, in order to ascertain the beneficial welfare effects of the amended policy.

From a methodological perspective, the following cautions and considerations should be accounted for in the translation of behavioural insights into welfare-enhancing consumer policy:

- Social data should be interpreted cautiously. A clear call for prudence concerning over-generalising results from behavioural studies is put forward. The fact that a bias is found in one study, which was conducted in a laboratory setting and involved student subjects, does not automatically imply that this bias gives rise to concerns in real-life situations. Empirical studies should be undertaken as results from these studies are more easily generalised.

- Since behavioural insights and individual decision making are shown to be dependent upon contexts, contexts should be accounted for in behavioural studies. Through behavioural research the accuracy of predictions can be enhanced in specific contexts, even though psychological insights are less suited as a basis for one general paradigm. Context-specific research, theory and policy are warranted in this case.
- Conflicting biases can decrease the tractability of behavioural research. When conflicting biases can be argued to affect decision making, the issue should be cleared up preferably by empirical research as opposed to experimental studies.
- Accounting for behavioural insights could increase the complexity and analytical costs of the assessment and make the results more context-dependent. This loss in generality and parsimony could however be traded-off against increased accuracy in the cases where behavioural insights are shown to enhance predictions. As behavioural economics progresses, the analytical costs concerned with behavioural research will also decrease.

The main normative considerations for the interpretation of behavioural findings in order to improve consumer policy can be identified as follows:
- It should be assessed whether *perceived* consumer biases are detrimental for consumers *in reality*. Consumers might learn from mistakes, or they might be able to be educated by sellers and information intermediaries. Also, it should be assessed whether sellers in fact do abuse consumer biases. In cases of complex choices, which are not made on a daily basis and which hold consequences that are dreaded or that will occur mainly in the (distant) future, the government is more likely to be able to efficiently improve consumer decisions.
- Policy makers should be very aware of the difficulties connected to deciding what is in the best interests of other people, including the observation that they may be biased themselves. The reason that people decide as they do might very well be that they actually prefer this decision; consumers might also prefer being able to decide for themselves, even erroneously.
- The increased discretion allowed to policy makers and risks of manipulating consumers' decisions against their best interests are special concerns. If consumers perceive 'benign' interventions as wrongly manipulating, these interventions could have counter-productive effects.
- Paternalistic interventions can result in costs to sophisticated consumers and sellers, and risk increasing consumer dependency while deterring consumer learning. These adverse and distributional effects should be taken into account in the evaluation of some welfare-enhancing intervention.

When behavioural insights are used for the development of policy, these cautions and consideration should be considered and where possible counteracted.

This research has developed guidelines for cautious and welfare-enhancing consumer policy, such as:

- *A scientifically sound basis for policy analysis.* When a behavioural bias is argued to influence decision making to consumers' detriment, sound, preferably empirical, studies should be undertaken to provide a reliable basis for policy, the results of which should not be over-generalised.
- *Economic welfare analysis to be seen as more than rational choice.* When behavioural insights are shown to influence decision making, economic insights can and should still be included in the development of socially beneficial consumer policy.
- *Market-based analysis of consumer behaviour.* Consumer behaviour should be assessed in the markets that it relates to. The explanations and predictions for behaviour that are shown to be valid, whether they are behavioural or rational, should form the basis of the analysis. Sellers' abuse of consumer decision making should be clearly established, as well as the detrimental effects of biased behaviour, including market corrections and consumer learning.
- *Designing behavioural interventions: efficient, context-specific and heuristic-savvy.* Like any policy intervention, behaviourally informed policy should be cost-effective, it should aim at curing a clearly established issue, and it should be more efficient in this aim than other policy options, including the option of no intervention. As behavioural insights are context-dependent, behaviourally informed policy should address specific issues and refrain from providing general solutions. It should be aware of the choice architectures pertaining to the decision making process of consumers, and it should where possible take advantage of biases and heuristics to steer decision making towards welfare-enhancing options.
- *Transparent and rigorous decision making procedures for policy.* Transparent and rigorous decision making procedures, which are based upon cost-benefit analyses and allow stakeholders, experts and other interested parties to have a say in the development of policy, should guard against government error, biased policy decision making and undue discretion in or manipulation of policy. These rigorous procedures however come at a cost, and can offer no guarantee of success.

These guidelines should be a starting point for the design of behaviourally informed consumer policy interventions that aim at an improvement of consumer and social welfare. Such interventions should be based on insights from both traditional economic analysis and behavioural sciences.

8.1.2. IMPROVEMENTS OF CONSUMER POLICY REGARDING STANDARDISED CONTRACT TERMS

As has been explained above, some of the concerns that call for caution in the process of translating behavioural insights into consumer policy relate to over-generalisation and context-specificity of behavioural results, and argue that behavioural insights should not be used to inform or justify general policy recommendations. Specific consumer policy issues should be taken into account, and appropriate interventions should be developed to account for the specific context of consumer decision making. Therefore, the possible additions to consumer policy resulting from behavioural insights have been more thoroughly explored by the assessment of a specific policy issue: standard terms in consumer contracts.

With regard to the specific policy issue of standardised consumer contract terms, this research concludes that behavioural insights are able to enhance economic policy recommendations by arguing for a more limited dependence on information disclosure and consumer vigilance of standard terms in consumer contracts. This shift in policy focus is a clear addition to the economic analysis of standard terms that has resulted from the application of behavioural insights. In addition, it has been argued that these improved policy recommendations are not yet accounted for in the common core of unfair terms regimes, which thus stand to be enhanced by the application of behavioural insights. Furthermore, in the assessment of policy proposals that suggest amending unfair terms regimes, two proposals have been identified as most promising in the aim to enhance the quality of standard terms in consumer contracts: pre-approval of standard terms through administrative monitoring, and a model form of standard terms that results from negotiations between business and consumer interest groups. The strategy of solving the signing-without-reading problem does not show much potential in effectively and efficiently overcoming the market failure of information asymmetry.

a. *Economic policy recommendations*

In the assessment of the conventional economic analysis concerning standard terms, this research has shown that the quality of standard terms provided in the market is likely to be too low from the perspective of social welfare as a result of information asymmetry and adverse selection. This suggests that consumers prefer a higher quality in standard terms than the level that is being provided by sellers, even if they would have to incur the extra costs that come with providing higher quality. Market corrections are not sufficiently effective in overcoming this welfare loss. While economic insights depend mainly upon information disclosure and consumer vigilance to discipline the market and to generate efficient contract terms, behavioural economics takes a different approach.

Using behavioural insights, it can be argued that consumers are unlikely to be able to discipline the market in providing efficient standard terms, even when they are aided in this endeavour by information remedies. Biases and heuristics impair consumer decision making and consumer vigilance. Neither competition nor litigation will induce sellers to draft efficient terms in consumer contracts. The claim that low quality one-sided terms will not be invoked against consumers when this is not efficient from a social welfare perspective, cannot be supported. Social welfare therefore stands to be improved by government intervention that aims to enhance the quality of standard terms. In policy, the dependence on consumer vigilance and information duties to stimulate this vigilance is likely to be insufficient. Hence, government interventions that reach beyond the provision of information are justified if the policy aims to induce an enhancement of the quality of standard terms in consumer contracts. This shift in policy focus, which consists of arguing for a more limited dependence upon information disclosure and consumer vigilance in standard terms in consumer contracts, is a clear addition to the economic analysis of standard terms that has resulted from the application of behavioural insights.

b. Assessing the common core

Next, the common core of unfair terms regimes has been assessed to establish whether the improved behavioural recommendations can be used to enhance actual consumer policy related to standardised consumer contracts.

The assessment of the effectiveness of the common approach in unfair terms policies in enhancing the quality of standardised consumer terms has concluded that unfair terms regimes stand to be improved by the application of the behaviourally enhanced policy recommendations. First, it has been shown that policies in unfair terms regimes largely correspond to the insights of information economics. The basic principles of freedom of contract and the *laissez-faire approach* also include the freedom to make mistakes. The principles of duty to read and blanket assent also call for consumer vigilance: when the consumer assents to a transaction with undesirable terms, these terms will be held against her, as long as they meet substantive requirements. Unfair terms regimes can be argued to be highly dependent on information disclosure and consumer vigilance. The policy instrument of choice when dealing with standard terms is information disclosure. Information disclosure requires consumers to be vigilant; informed consumers, or consumers that have had the opportunity to become informed, are assumed to be able to look out for their own interests.

Secondly, even though a threshold level of quality for terms in consumer contracts is provided in unfair terms regimes, this threshold level of quality might not even be effective in truly enhancing quality. The extent to which policy employs substantive requirements as opposed to information duties is arguably small. Substantive requirements set a threshold level of quality for standard terms. This fairness level is argued to not be very high, and only able to bar very low-quality terms from consumer contracts. This research has therefore argued that the standard of unfairness, the threshold level below which consumers will not be hurt by their rational apathy, is rather low. Correspondingly, the extent to which information disclosure and consumer vigilance are required to enhance the quality of terms is quite high. The enforcement of unfair terms regimes again depends on consumer vigilance. Consumers need to be active when confronted with unfair terms. They need to know which terms are unfair, that these terms are used against them, they need to be aware of their legal rights and take action against these terms. Rational apathy concerns might be at play here, which also suggests that individual consumers should not be overly depended on to enforce unfair terms policy. These concerns have been accounted for in policy by allowing private as well as public organisations to act on behalf of consumers. However, consumer action is still regarded to be a main instigator of the enforcement of unfair terms policies. European unfair terms policies thus stand to be improved in order to enhance the quality of standardised consumer terms.

c. *Improved policy interventions*

Some policy strategies are likely to be capable to augment the quality of standardised consumer contract terms in a way that can be both effective and efficient. Solving the signing-without-problem through standardising the design of contracts, making consumers sign each page of the contract or other ways of constituting 'real' assent can be doubted with the respect of truly enabling consumers to discipline the market for standard terms. Most promising proposals that correspond to the benevolently assessed strategies are pre-approved standard terms and a negotiated model of standard terms.

Standard terms, or entire forms of standard terms, could be pre-approved by some institution, which would then attach a quality seal to the contract. When standard terms in consumer contracts are pre-approved, the quality of terms is likely to be increased, at least to the level of substantive legal requirements. The quality of the terms could further by improved by involving consumer organisations in the approval process, who might demand for an even higher quality benchmark. It would however be difficult to ascertain that this quality level corresponds to consumer preferences, especially since preferences might differ across business sectors. Seller participation in the scheme could be stimulated by reducing the risk of liability and correcting free-rider problems. Consumer demand for approved standard terms could be necessary to drive this policy instrument, and it would therefore need to be carefully tested in light of empirical findings. However, this proposal could be quite beneficial for improving quality levels of terms.

Another promising policy proposal consists of negotiations between business and consumer representatives, which result in model forms of consumer contracts preferably at sector-level. By introducing consumer interests in the drafting process, this policy proposal stands to enhance the quality of standard terms. Businesses are also to gain, because they save on drafting and litigation costs. As long as consumers have been adequately represented, the possible (but unlikely) fact that these terms do not correspond to legal substantive requirements should not be a concern; neither should anti-competitive effects, as long as the terms that negotiated are not considered by consumers in their decision which seller to contract with. Some assistance to consumer organisations should be contemplated to ensure fair consumer representation. Transparent procedures where most to all interests are represented should limit the risk of regulatory capture. The model terms should be optional instead of mandatory as long as the optional model has not been shown to be ineffective in raising consumer standard term quality.

Which proposal would be most effective in a specific legal system would depend upon the characteristics of that legal regime, and this question should therefore be more deeply assessed, taking the specificities of the relevant context into account. When the culture in this legal system is quite adversarial, the consensus-based approach of negotiating a model form of standard terms might not be appropriate. In this case, consumer and business organisations could be stuck in lengthy and costly negotiations, possibly without any beneficial end result. In these cases, pre-approved standard terms should be contemplated, which would ideally adhere to a benchmark that corresponds to consumer preferences rather than (only) to the legal substantive requirements. Where a consensus can be achieved between consumer and seller representatives however, the negotiated model contract terms can be a very effective way of enhancing contract quality by getting consumers involved in the drafting process.

This behavioural analysis related to the specific issue of consumer standardised contract terms gives an example of how behavioural insights can be used to improve consumer policy and therefore provides further support to the first conclusion of this research.

8.2. RECOMMENDATIONS FOR FURTHER RESEARCH

To conclude this research, some recommendations for further research will be provided. These recommendations refer mainly to the necessity of more extensively exploring specific legal systems, specific standard terms and specific business sectors when behavioural insights are included in consumer policy related to standardised contract terms.

8.2.1. CORRESPONDENCE BETWEEN GUIDELINES AND CONDUCTED ASSESSMENT

With regard to the guidelines, cautions and considerations that have been identified in chapter 4, it should be noticed that the assessment that has been conducted in this thesis of consumer standardised contract terms does not account fully for the identified concerns. The existing empirical studies are not entirely sufficient to serve as a basis for far-reaching policy interventions; only suggestions should be taken from the presented analysis. This implies that before these insights can be used to inform policy, further empirical studies should be conducted. A remaining issue is for instance the extent to which sellers are in fact abusing consumer standard terms. Sellers might be prevented from invoking low-quality standard terms against consumers, as is argued by some economic scholars. When reputational concerns can be shown to have such an effect, the analysis of standard terms would be improved. Again however, this argument is likely to be valid for some sellers, in some markets, but not in all markets. The relevance of this argument should be duly assessed. As has been mentioned several times in this research, it would also be vital to distinguish which terms are considered by consumers in their decision making process, and which terms they neglect. Terms that are considered by consumers can be left to competition by sellers; consumer policy should only interfere with these terms to a limited extent, if at all. Terms that are neglected however can be even substantively improved by policy.

Also, this research has reviewed the common core of unfair terms regimes. If the use of this analysis for actual policy enhancements should be contemplated, the analysis should first be re-assessed according to the specificities of the specific unfair terms regimes. The specific characteristics of legal systems, such as institutional arrangements, public consumer institutions, the strength of consumer organisations and cultural aspects such as adversarialism, should be taken up in the assessment. A related issue that should be examined in empirical studies is the effectiveness of the suggested policy proposals, such as the extent to which a pre-approved or negotiated model form of consumer contracts can serve as a signal for quality to consumers. Also, the interrelated issue of enforcement should be taken up in the assessment. Enhanced enforcement of unfair terms regimes could also increase the quality level of standard term contracts. Policy interventions should be assessed taking all other options into account.

As has been discussed above, contemplated policy interventions should take the context of consumer decision making into account; contexts have been insufficiently accounted for in this general analysis of consumer standard terms. However, the analysis that has been presented in this research can provide a sound basis for further research. The suggestions that have been developed in this analysis should not be ignored. Furthermore, this analysis can be used to identify the policy questions which are worthy of further exploration.

8.2.2. APPLICATION TO SPECIFIC STANDARD TERMS AND BUSINESS SECTORS

A further possible extension of the analysis portrayed in this research is to consider not only the general issue of standard terms, but to also assess behavioural insights related to specific standard terms, or specific contracts that are used in business sectors.

An issue that has not been explored extensively is the question of how consumers assess risks that are allocated in standard contracts other than neglecting them. Risks, as has been argued, can be both under- and over-evaluated by consumers. An assessment of consumer consideration of specific contract terms, instead of the general assessment that has been conducted in this research, could further explore consumer decision making One business sector in which this analysis would be particularly valid is the financial sector. As has been mentioned above, the analysis that has been presented with regard to standard terms is likely to be valid in the majority of standard term contracts. There might however be contracts that are properly assessed by consumers, such as mortgage contracts and consumer credit.[378] Whether this assessment corresponds more to rational predictions or to behavioural insights should be further explored. Literature on this issue is already very extensive;[379] perhaps even the analysis of consumer financial products can benefit to some extent from the analysis portrayed in this research.

In general, the assessment of standard terms would benefit from a more business sector based approach, which takes the specificities of the relevant market into account. For these sector-level analyses, the analysis portrayed in this research could provide a starting point.

---

[378] See above, chapter 5, section 5.5.5.

[379] To refer to just a few sources out of this extensive literature, see for instance: Levitin (2007), Mann (2006), Rasmussen (1998), Rosenberg (2006), Richards, Palmer and Bogdanova (2008), Littwin (2009), Bar-Gill and Warren (2008) and Evans and Wright (2009). On financial adhesion contracts in particular, see: Volante (2008) and Smith (2009). See Wright and Zywicki (2009) for a critical view of the Consumer Financial Protection Agency that is proposed by the Obama administration. Wright and Zywicki argue that this Agency will have significant unintended consequences, including but not limited to a reduction in competition, consumer choice, and availability of credit to consumers for productive uses, and that it will be an example of adverse effects of regulation while being overly bureaucratic. See also Bar-Gill (2009), Evans (2009) and Levitin (2009).

LIST OF REFERENCES

Abdellaoui, M., Barrios, C. and Wakker, P.P. (2007). Reconciling Introspective Utility with Revealed Preference: Experimental Arguments Based on Prospect Theory. *Journal of Econometrics, 138*(1), pp. 356–378.

Agarwal, S., John, C.D., Gabaix, X. and Laibson, D.I. (2007). The Age of Reason: Financial Decisions Over the Lifecycle. *NBER Working Paper no. 13191*. Available at: ideas.repec.org/p/cla/levrem/122247000000001752.html.

Akerlof, G.A. (1970). The Market for 'Lemons': Quality Uncertainty and the Market Mechanism. *Quarterly Journal of Economics, 84*(3), pp. 488–500.

Akerlof, G.A. and Shiller, R.J. (2009). *Animal Spirits: How Human Psychology Drives the Economy, and Why It Matters for Global Capitalism*. Princeton: Princeton University Press.

Alpa, G. (2008). Standard Contract Terms: The Role of the Courts and Moral Persuasion by Independent Authorities. In: H. Collins (Ed.), *Standard Contract Terms in Europe: A Basis for and a Challenge to European Contract Law*, pp. 75–91. Alphen aan den Rijn: Kluwer Law International.

Amato, C. (2008). Unfair Contract Terms in Search of Harmonization. In: H. Collins (Ed.), *Standard Contract Terms in Europe: A Basis for and a Challenge to European Contract Law*, pp. 187–199. Alphen aan den Rijn: Kluwer Law International.

Amir, O., Ariely, D., Cooke, A., Dunning, D., Epley, N., Gneezy, U., Koszegi, B., Lichtenstein, D., Mazar, N., Mullainathan, S., Prelec, D., Shafir, E. and Silva, J. (2005). Psychology, Behavioral Economics, and Public Policy. *Marketing Letters, 16*(3), pp. 443–454.

Amir, O. and Lobel, O. (2008). Stumble, Predict, Nudge: how Behavioral Economics Informs Law and Policy. *Columbia Law Review, 108*(8), pp. 2098–2138.

Ammerlaan, S. and Janssen, D. (2007). The Dutch Consumer Authority: an introduction. In: W.H. Van Boom, M.B.M. Loos (Eds.), *Collective Enforcement of Consumer law*, pp. 107–122. Groningen: Europa Law Publishing.

Aquaro, G. (2003). Enhancing the Legal Protection of the European Consumer. *European Business Law Review, 14*(4), pp. 405–413.

Ariely, D. (2009). *Predictably Irrational: Revised and expanded edition*. New York: HarperCollins.

Arlen, J.H. (1998). Comment: The Future of Behavioral Economic Analysis of Law. *Vanderbilt Law Review, 51*(6), pp. 1765–1788.

Arlen, J.H. and Talley, E.L. (2008). Introduction. In: J. H. Arlen, E. L. Talley (Eds.), *Experimental Law and Economics*, pp. ix-lxi. Cheltenham, UK: Edward Elgar Publishing.

Armbrüster, C. (2008). Standard Contract Terms and Information Rules. In: H. Collins (Ed.), *Standard Contract Terms in Europe: A Basis for and a Challenge to European Contract Law*, pp. 163–175. Alphen aan den Rijn: Kluwer Law International.

Armstrong, M. (2008). Interactions between Competition and Consumer Policy. *Competition Policy International, 4*(1), pp. 97–147.

Arrow, K.J. (1950). A Difficulty in the Concept of Social Welfare. *Journal of Political Economy, 58*(4), pp. 328–346.

Arrow, K.J. (1951). Alternative Approaches to the Theory of Choice in Risk-Taking Situations. *Econometrica, 19*(4), pp. 404–437.

Ayres, I. and Gertner, R.H. (1989). Filling Gaps in Incomplete Contracts: An Economic Theory of Default Rules. *Yale Law Journal, 99*(1), pp. 87–130.

Ayres, I. (1991). Fair Driving: Gender and Race Discrimination in Retail Car Negotiations. *Harvard Law Review, 104*(4), pp. 817–873.

Ayres, I. and Gertner, R.H. (1999). Majoritarian vs. Minoritarian Defaults. *Stanford Law Review, 51*(6), pp. 1591–1614.

Babcock, L.C., Loewenstein, G.F., Issacharoff, S. and Camerer, C.F. (1995). Biased Judgments of Fairness in Bargaining. *American Economic Review, 85*(5), pp. 1337–1343.

Babcock, L.C., Issacharoff, S. and Loewenstein, G.F. (1997). Debiasing Litigation Impasse. *SSRN eLibrary*. Available at: SSRN.com/paper=11367.

Babcock, L.C. and Loewenstein, G.F. (1997). Explaining Bargaining Impasse: The Role of Self-Serving Biases. *Journal of Economic Perspectives, 11*(1), pp. 109–126.

Baird, D.G., Gertner, R.H. and Picker, R.C. (1998). *Game Theory and the Law*. Cambridge: Harvard University Press.

Baird, D.G. (2006). The Boilerplate Puzzle. *Michigan Law Review, 104*(5), pp. 933–952.

Bakos, Y., Marotta-Wurgler, F. and Trossen, D.R. (2009). Does Anyone Read the Fine Print? Testing a Law and Economics Approach to Standard Form Contracts. *SSRN eLibrary*. Available at: SSRN.com/paper=1443256.

Balleisen, E.J. and Eisner, M. (2009). The Promise and Pitfalls of Co-Regulation: How Governments Can Draw on Private Governance for Public Purpose. In: D. Moss, J. Cisternino (Eds.), *New Perspectives on Regulation*, pp. 127–149. Cambridge: The Tobin Project.

Bar-Gill, O. (2004). Seduction by Plastic. *Northwestern University Law Review, 98*(4), pp. 1373–1434.

– (2007). Informing Consumers about Themselves. *SSRN eLibrary; New York University Law and Economics Working Papers, Paper 111*. Available at: SSRN.com/paper=1056381.

– (2008). Behavioral Economics of Consumer Contracts, the Exchange. *Minnesota Law Review, 92*(3), pp. 749–802.

Bar-Gill, O. and Warren, E. (2008). Making Credit Safer. *University of Pennsylvania Law Review, 157*(1), pp. 1–101.

Bar-Gill, O. (2009). The Consumer Financial Protection Agency: Sorting the Critiques. *Lombard Street, 1*(12), pp. 4–13.

Barnett, R.E. (2002). Consenting to Form Contracts. *Fordham Law Review, 71*(3), pp. 627–646.

Barr, M.S., Mullainathan, S. and Shafir, E. (2009). The Case for Behaviorally Informed Regulation. In: D. Moss, J. Cisternino (Eds.), *New Perspectives on Regulation*, pp. 25–61. Cambridge: The Tobin Project.

Bates, L. (2002). Administrative Regulation of Terms in Form Contracts: A Comparative Analysis of Consumer Protection. *Emory International Law Review, 16*(1), pp. 1–106.

Beale, H. and Schulte-Nölke, H. (2007). Response to the Green Paper on the Review of the Consumer Acquis. *Part of the Public Consultation on the Review of the Consumer Acquis, Held by European Commission.* Available at: ec.europa.eu/consumers/cons_int/safe_shop/acquis/responses/universitat_bielefeld.pdf.

Beale, H. (2008a). The Draft Common Frame of Reference: Mistake and Duties of Disclosure. *European Review of Contract Law, 4*(3), pp. 317–337.

– (2008b). A Law for Big Business and Competent Consumers? *ERA Forum, 2008*(9), pp. S79-S86.

Bebchuk, L.A. and Posner, R.A. (2006). One-sided contracts in competitive consumer markets. *Michigan Law Review, 104*(5), pp. 827–835.

Becher, S.I. (2007). Behavioral Science and Consumer Standard Form Contracts. *Louisiana Law Review, 68*(1), pp. 117–179.

– (2008). Asymmetric Information in Consumer Contracts: The Challenge That Is Yet to Be Met. *American Business Law Journal, 45*(4), pp. 723–774.

Becher, S.I. and Zarsky, T.Z. (2008). E-Contract Doctrine 2.0: Standard Form Contracting in the Age of Online User Participation. *Michigan Telecommunications and Technology Law Review, 14*(2), pp. 303–366.

Becher, S.I. (2009). A 'Fair Contracts' Approval Mechanism: Reconciling Consumer Contracts and Conventional Contract Law. *University of Michigan Journal of Law Reform, 42*(4), pp. 747–804.

Becher, S.I. and Unger-Aviram, E. (2009). The Law of Standard Form Contracts: Misguided Intuitions and Suggestions for Reconstruction. *DePaul Business & Commercial Law Journal, forthcoming.*

Benjamin, D.J. and Laibson, D.I. (2003). Good Policies for Bad Governments: Behavioral Political Economy. *SSRN eLibrary; Federal Reserve Bank of Boston Conference Series 48.* Available at: ssrn.com/paper=696361.

Ben-Shahar, O. (2006). Foreword. *Michigan Law Review, 104*(5), pp. 821–826.

Ben-Shahar, O. and Pottow, J.A.E. (2006). On the Stickiness of Default Rules. *Florida State University Law Review, 33*(3), pp. 651–682.

Ben-Shahar, O. (2009). The Myth of the 'Opportunity to Read' in Contract Law. *European Review of Contract Law, 5*(1), pp. 1–28.

Bernheim, B.D. and Rangel, A. (2005). Behavioural Public Economics: Welfare and Policy Analysis with Non-Standard Decision Makers. *NBER Working Paper no. 11518.* Available at: nber.org/papers/w11518.

Bernheim, B.D. and Whinston, M.D. (2008). *Microeconomics.* Boston: McGraw-Hill.

Bernitz, U. (1973). Consumer Protection and Standard Contracts. *Scandinavian Studies in Law, 17*, pp. 11–50.

– (2000). Swedish Standard Contracts Law and the EC Directive on Contract Terms. *Scandinavian Studies in Law, 39*, pp. 13–27.

Bourgoignie, T.M. (1983). *Unfair terms in consumer contracts. Legal treatment, effective implementation and final impact on the consumer.* Louvain-la-Neuve: Cabay Bruylant.

– (1987). Consumer Law and the European Community: Issues and Prospects. In: T. M. Bourgoignie, D. M. Trubek (Eds.), *Consumer Law, Common Markets and Federalism in Europe and the United States*, pp. 89–235. Berlin: Walter de Gruyter.

Brennan, T. (2005). Consumer Preference Not to Choose: Methodological and Policy Implications. *SSRN eLibrary; Resources for the Future Discussion Paper 05-51.* Available at: ssrn.com/paper=854424.

Brennan, G. (2008). Behavioural economics and public policy. Behavioural Economics and Public Policy - *Roundtable Proceedings*, pp. 131–143. Canberra: Productivity Commission.

Brooker, S. and Cullum, P. (2008). Five Steps to Consumer-Friendly Better Regulation. *Consumer Policy Review, 18*(1), pp. 4–9.

Burrows, P. and Veljanovski, C. G. (1981). *The Economic Approach to Law.* London: Butterworths.

Bussani, M. and Mattei, U. (1997). The Common Core Approach to European Private Law. *Columbia Journal of European Law, 3*(3), pp. 339–356.

Cafaggi, F. (2006). Rethinking Private Regulation in the European Regulatory Space. In: F. Cafaggi (Ed.), *Reframing self-regulation in European private Law*, pp. 3–76. Den Haag: Kluwer.

– (2008). Self-Regulation in European Contract Law. In: H. Collins (Ed.), *Standard Contract Terms in Europe: A Basis for and a Challenge to European Contract Law*, pp. 93–139. Alphen aan den Rijn: Kluwer Law International.

– (2009). Private Regulation in European Contract Law. *European University Institute Working Papers, RSCAS 2009/13.* Available at: hdl.handle.net/1814/12054.

Camerer, C.F. and Kunreuther, H. (1989). Decision processes for low probability events: Policy implications. *Journal of Policy Analysis and Management, 8*(4), pp. 565–592.

Camerer, C.F. (1999). Behavioral economics: Reunifying psychology and economics. *Proceedings of the National Academy of Sciences of the United States of America, 96*(19), pp. 10575–10577.

Camerer, C.F., Issacharoff, S., Loewenstein, G.F., O'Donoghue, T. and Rabin, M. (2003). Regulation for Conservatives: Behavioral Economics and the Case for "Asymmetric Paternalism". *University of Pennsylvania Law Review, 1151*(3), pp. 1211–1254.

Camerer, C.F. and Loewenstein, G.F. (2004). Behavioral Economics: Past, Present, Future. In: C. F. Camerer, G. F. Loewenstein and M. Rabin (Eds.), *Advances in Behavioral Economics*, pp. 3–51. Princeton: Princeton University Press.

Chaudhuri, A. (2006). *Emotion and reason in consumer behavior.* Burlington: Elsevier/Butterworth-Heinemann.

Cherednychenko, O.O. (2007). The Harmonisation of Contract Law in Europe by Means of the Horizontal Effect of Fundamental Rights? *Erasmus Law Review, 1*(1), pp. 37–57.

Choi, S.J. and Gulati, G.M. (2006). Contract as Statute. *Michigan Law Review, 104*(5), pp. 1129–1173.

Chorvat, T. and McCabe, K. (2004). The brain and the law. *Philosophical Transactions of the Royal Society B: Biological Sciences, 359*(1451), pp. 1727–1736.

Cialdini, R.B. (2003). Crafting Normative Messages to Protect the Environment. *Current Directions in Psychological Science, 12*(4), pp. 105–109.

Clive, E. (2008). An Introduction to the Academic Draft Common Frame of Reference. *2008*(9), pp. S13-S31.

Coase, R.H. (1960). The Problem of Social Cost. *Journal of Law and Economics, 3*(1), pp. 1–44.

Collins, H. (2004). The Freedom to Circulate Documents: Regulating Contracts in Europe. *European Law Journal, 10*(6), pp. 787–803.

– (2008). The Directive on Unfair Contract Terms. In: H. Collins (Ed.), *Standard Contract Terms in Europe: A Basis for and a Challenge to European Contract Law*, pp. 1–17. Alphen aan den Rijn: Kluwer Law International.

Consumentenautoriteit (2010). Benelux-onderzoek consumentenbescherming betreffende de wettelijke en commerciële garanties. Bedrijfssector consumentenelektro. *10-CB-PC-Contr(NO-012)NL-final*. Algemene Directie Controle en Bemiddeling, FOD Economie, KMO, Middenstand en Energie, België; Consumentenautoriteit, Nederland; Directie Marktregulering en Consumptie, Ministerie van Economie en Buitenlandse Handel, Luxemburg: Available at: consumentenautoriteit.nl/dsresource?objectid=28206&type=pdf.

Cooter, R.D. (1998). Expressive Law and Economics. *Journal of Legal Studies, 27*(s2), pp. 585–607.

Cooter, R.D. and Ulen, T.S. (2003). *Law and Economics*. (4th ed.) Pearson Education.

Craswell, R. (2003). Kaplow and Shavell on the Substance of Fairness. *Journal of Legal Studies, 32*(1), pp. 245–275.

Cseres, K. J. (2005). *Competition law and consumer protection*. The Hague: Kluwer Law International.

Cserne, P. (2008). Freedom of choice and paternalism in contract law: prospects and limits of an economic approach. *Dissertation*. Available at: works.bepress.com/peter_cserne/27 (abstract).

– (2009). Policy Considerations in Contract Interpretation: The Contra Proferentem Rule from a Comparative and Economic Perspective. In: G. Radhika (Ed.), *Contract Theory - Corporate Law*, pp. 66–104. Hyderabad: ICFAI University Press.

Darby, M.R. and Karni, E. (1973). Free Competition and the Optimal Amount of Fraud. *Journal of Law and Economics, 16*(1), pp. 67–88.

Davis, K.E. (2006). The Role of Nonprofits in the Production of Boilerplate. *Michigan Law Review, 104*(5), pp. 1075–1103.

Dayagi-Epstein, O. (2006). Representation of Consumer Interest By Consumer Associations - Salvation for the Masses? *Competition Law Review, 3*(2), pp. 209–249.

De Boeck, A. and Van Hoecke, M. (2008). The Interpretation of Standard Clauses in European Contract Law. In: H. Collins (Ed.), *Standard Contract Terms in Europe: A Basis for and a Challenge to European Contract Law*, pp. 201–244. Alphen aan den Rijn: Kluwer Law International.

De Booys, T.Q., Hesselink, M.W. and Mak, C. (2009). How the CFR Can Improve the Consumer Rights Directive: A Comparison between the Provisions of the Draft Common Frame of Reference and the European Commissions Proposal for a Consumer Rights Directive. *SSRN eLibrary; Centre for the Study of European Contract Law Working Paper Series no. 2009/09*. Available at: ssrn.com/paper=1492660.

De Geest, G. (2002). The Signing-Without-Reading Problem: An Analysis of the European Directive on Unfair Contract Terms. In: H. B. Schäfer, H. J. Lwowski (Eds.), *Konsequenzen wirstschaftsrechtlicher Normen, Festschrift Für Claus Ott*, pp. 213–235. Wiesbaden: Gabler.

De Hoon, M.W. (2007). Power Imbalances in Contracts: An Interdisciplinary Study on Effects of Intervention. *SSRN eLibrary*. Available at: ssrn.com/paper=985875.

Della Vigna, S. and Malmendier, U. (2004). Contract Design and Self-Control: Theory and Evidence. *Quarterly Journal of Economics, 119*(2), pp. 353–402.

– (2006). Paying Not to Go to the Gym. *American Economic Review, 96*(3), pp. 694–719.

Della Vigna, S. (2009). Psychology and Economics: Evidence from the Field. *Journal of Economic Literature, 47*(2), pp. 315–372.

Deutch, S. (1990). Control of unfair terms in consumer contracts in Israel: Law and practice. *Journal of Consumer Policy, 13*(2), pp. 181–199.

Dowling, J. M. and Chin-Fang, Y. (2007). *Modern developments in behavioral economics: social science perspectives on choice and decision making*. Singapore: World Scientific Printers.

Downs, A. (1957). *An Economic Theory of Democracy*. New York: Harper and Row.

Dworkin, G. (2005). Paternalism. *Entry in Stanford Encyclopedia of Philosophy*. Available at: plato.stanford.edu/entries/paternalism.

Easterlin, R.A. (2003). Explaining happiness. *Proceedings of the National Academy of Sciences of the United States of America, 100*(19), pp. 11176–11183.

EC Consumer Law Compendium (2008). The Consumer Acquis and it transposition in the Member States. *European Commission, Brussels*. Available at: ec.europa.eu/consumers/ rights/docs/consumer_law_compendium_comparative_analysis_en_final.pdf.

Edwards, M.A. (2007). The Law, Marketing and Behavioral Economics of Consumer Rebates. *Stanford Journal of Law, Business & Finance, 12*(2), pp. 362–424.

– (2008). The FTC and New Paternalism. *Administrative Law Review, 60*(2), pp. 323–370.

Eidenmüller, H. G. (2009). Party Autonomy, Distributive Justice and the Conclusion of Contracts in the DCFR. *European Review of Contract Law, 25*(2), pp. 109–131.

Eigen, Z.J. (2008). The Devil in the Details: The Interrelationship Among Citizenship, Rule of Law and Form-Adhesive Contracts. *Connecticut Law Review, 41*(2), pp. 381–430.

– (2009). Towards a Behavioral Theory of Contract: Experimental Evidence of Consent, Compliance, Promise and Performance. *SSRN eLibrary; CELS 2009 4th Annual Conference on Empirical Legal Studies Paper*. Available at: ssrn.com/paper=1443549.

Eisenberg, M.A. (1985). Text Anxiety. *Southern California Law Review, 59*(2), pp. 305–311.

– (1995). The Limits of Cognition and the Limits of Contract. *Stanford Law Review, 47*(2), pp. 211–259.

Ellsberg, D. (1961). Risk, Ambiguity, and the Savage Axioms. *The Quarterly Journal of Economics, 75*(4), pp. 643–669.

Ely, J.W., Jr. (2009). Whatever Happened to the Contract Clause? *SSRN eLibrary; Vanderbilt Public Law Research Paper no. 09–21; Vanderbilt Law and Economics Research Paper no. 09–26*. Available at: ssrn.com/paper=1483857.

Epstein, S. (1994). Integration of the Cognitive and the Psychodynamic Unconscious. *American Psychologist, 49*(8), pp. 709–724.

Epstein, R.A. (2006). Behavioral Economics: Human Errors and Market Corrections. *University of Chicago Law Review, 73*(1), pp. 111–132.

– (2008). Neoclassical Economics of Consumer Contracts, the Exchange. *Minnesota Law Review, 92*(3), pp. 803–835.

European Commission (2000). Report from the Commission on the Implementation of Council Directive 93/13 EEC of 5 April 1993 on Unfair Terms in Consumer Constracts. *COM(2000) 248 final*. European Commission: Brussels. Available at: ec.europa.eu/consumers/cons_int/safe_shop/unf_cont_terms/uct03_en.pdf.

– (2003). A More Coherent European Contract Law: An Action Plan. *COM (2003) 68 final*. European Commission: Brussels. Available at: eur-lex.europa.eu/LexUriServ/LexUriServ.do?uri= COM:2003:0068:FIN:EN:PDF.

– (2005). Healthier, Safer, More Confident Citizens: A Health and Consumer Policy Strategy. *COM(2005) 115 final*. European Commission: Brussels. Available at: ec.europa.eu/health/ph_overview/Documents/com_2005_0115_en.pdf.

– (2006). Green Paper on the Review of the Consumer Acquis *COM (2006) 744 final*. European Commission: Brussels. Available at: ec.europa.eu/consumers/cons_int/safe_shop/acquis/green-paper_cons_acquis_en.pdf.

– (2007). EC Consumer Policy Strategy 2007–2013. *COM(2007) 99 final*. European Commission: Brussels. Available at: ec.europa.eu/consumers/overview/cons_policy/doc/EN_99.pdf.

– (2008). Proposal for a Directive of the European Parliament and of the Council on Consumer Rights. *COM (2008) 614 final*. European Commission: Brussels. Available at: ec.europa.eu/consumers/rights/docs/COMM_PDF_COM_2008_0614_F_EN_PROPOSITION_DE_DIRECTIVE.pdf.

Evans, D.S. (2009). Consumer Protection and the Financial Crisis: An Indepth Look at the Proposal Consumer Financial Protection Agency Act of 2009. *Lombard Street, 1*(12), pp. 2–3.

Evans, D.S. and Wright, J.D. (2009). The Effect of the Consumer Financial Protection Agency Act of 2009 on Consumer Credit. *SSRN eLibrary; George Mason Law &*

Economics Research Paper no. 09–50; Loyola Consumer Law Review, Forthcoming. Available at: ssrn.com/paper=1483906.

Faure, M.G. and Van Boom, W.H. (2008). Hoe houdbaar zijn gedragsveronderstellingen in verzekeringsrecht en -economie? In: W.H. Van Boom, I. Giesen and A.J. Verheij (Eds.), *Gedrag en privaatrecht: over gedragspresumpties en gedragseffecten bij privaatrechtelijke leerstukken*, pp. 305–339. Den Haag: Boom Juridische uitgevers.

Fehr, E. and Gächter, S. (2000). Fairness and Retaliation: The Economics of Reciprocity. *Journal of Economic Perspectives, 14*(3), pp. 159–181.

Ferrante, E. (2005). Contractual Disclosure and Remedies under the Unfair Contract Terms Directive. In: G. G. Howells, A. Janssen and R. Schulze (Eds.), *Information Rights and Obligations*, pp. 115–133. Aldershot: Ashgate.

Field, C. (2008). Having one's cake and eating it too - an analysis of behavioural economics from a consumer policy perspective. Behavioural Economics and Public Policy - *Roundtable Proceedings*, pp. 89–102. Canberra: Productivity Commission.

Fischhoff, B. (1975). Hindsight is not equal to foresight: The effect of outcome knowledge on judgment under uncertainty. *Journal of Experimental Psychology: Human Perception & Performance, 1*(3), pp. 288–299.

Frey, B.S. and Stutzer, A. (2002). The Economics of Happiness. *World Economics, 3*(1), pp. 25–41.

– (2009). Should National Happiness Be Maximized? In: A. K. Dutt, B. Radcliff (Eds.), *Happiness, Economics, and Politics: Toward a Multi-Disciplinary Approach*, pp. Chapter 14. Cheltenham: Edward Elgar.

Friedman, M. (1953). *Essays in Positive Economics.* University of Chicago Press.

Frijters, P. (2008). Discussion of Shafir: A behavioural background for economic policy. Behavioural Economics and Public Policy - *Roundtable Proceedings*, pp. 27–32. Canberra: Productivity Commission.

Fudenberg, D. (2006). Advancing beyond "Advances in Behavioral Economics". *Journal of Economic Literature, 44*(3), pp. 694–711.

Garvin, L. T. (2005). Small Business and the False Dichotomies of Contract Law. *Wake Forest Law Review, 40*(1), pp. 295–388.

Gazal-Ayal, O. (1999). Economic Analysis of Unfair Terms in Standard Form Contracts. *Conference Paper European Master in Law and Economics: Hamburg, Germany.* Available at: dx.doi.org/10.1007/s10657-007-9030-x.

Gigerenzer, G., Todd, P.M. and ABC Research Group (1999). *Simple heuristics that make us smart.* Oxford: Oxford University Press.

Gillette, C.P. (2004). Rolling Contracts as an Agency Problem. *Wisconsin Law Review, 2004*(2), pp. 679–722.

– (2005). Pre-approved Contract for Internet Commerce. *Houston Law Review, 42*(4), pp. 975–1013.

– (2009). Standard Form Contracts. *SSRN eLibrary; NYU Law and Economics Research Paper no. 09–18.* Available at: ssrn.com/paper=1374990.

Gilo, D. and Porat, A. (2009). Viewing Unconscionability through a Market Lens. *SSRN eLibrary; University of Chicago Law & Economics, Olin Working Paper no. 489.* Available at: ssrn.com/paper=1493303.

Gist, M.E. (1987). Self-Efficacy: Implications for Organizational Behavior and Human Resource Management. *Academy of Management Review, 12*(3), pp. 472–485.

Glaeser, E.L. (2006). Paternalism and psychology. *University of Chicago Law Review, 73*(1), pp. 133–156.

Goldberg, V.P. (1974). Institutional Change and the Quasi-Invisible Hand. *Journal of Law and Economics, 17*(2), pp. 461–492.

Goldman, L. (1992). My Way and the Highway: The Law and Economics of Choice of Forum Clauses in Consumer Form Contracts. *Northwestern University Law Review, 86*(3), pp. 700–741.

Gozzo, P. (2005). The Strategy and the Harmonization Process within the European Legal System: Party Autonomy and Information Requirements. In: G. G. Howells, A. Janssen and R. Schulze (Eds.), *Information Rights and Obligations*, pp. 17–32. Aldershot: Ashgate.

Grabosky, P. and Braithwaite, J. (1986). *Of Manners Gentle: Enforcement Strategies of Australian Business Regulatory Agencies.* Melbourne: Oxford University Press.

Greenstone, M. (2009). Towards a Culture of Persistent Regulatory Experimentation and Evaluation. In: D. Moss, J. Cisternino (Eds.), *New Perspectives on Regulation*, pp. 111–125. Cambridge: The Tobin Project.

Grether, D.M., Schwartz, A. and Wilde, L.L. (1985). The Irrelevance of Information Overload: An Analysis of Search and Disclosure. *Southern California Law Review, 59*(2), pp. 277–304.

Grossman, S.J. (1981). Informational Role of Warranties and Private Disclosure about Product Quality, The Consumer Protection Regulation: A Conference Sponsored by the Center for the Study of the Economy and the State. *Journal of Law & Economics, 24*, pp. 461–484.

Grundmann, S., Kerber, W. and Weatherill, S. (2001). Party Autonomy and the Role of Information - An Overview. In: S. Grundmann, W. Kerber and S. Weatherill (Eds.), *Party Autonomy and the Role of Information in the Internal Market*, pp. 2–38. Berlin: De Gruyter.

Grundmann, S. (2002). Information, party autonomy and economic agents in European Contract Law. *Common Market Law Review, 39*(2), pp. 269–293.

Grüne-Yanoff, T. (2008). Old Wine In New Casks: 'Soft' Paternalism Still Violates Liberal Principles. *Working Paper Presented at Conference "Reconciling Normative and Behavioural Economics", University of East Anglia, Norwich; Currently Under Review.* Available at: mv.helsinki.fi/home/gruneyan/LiberalWelfare090127.pdf.

Guthrie, C., Rachlinski, J.J. and Wistrich, A.J. (2001). Inside the Judicial Mind. *Cornell Law Review, 86*(4), pp. 777–830.

Hadfield, G.K., Howse, R. and Trebilcock, M.J. (1998). Information-Based Principles for Rethinking Consumer Protection Policy. *Journal of Consumer Policy, 21*(2), pp. 131–169.

Hanson, J.D. and Kysar, D.A. (1999a). Taking Behavioralism Seriously: The Problem of Market Manipulation. *NYU Law Review, 74*(3), pp. 630–749.

– (1999b). Taking Behavioralism Seriously: Some Evidence of Market Manipulation. *Harvard Law Review, 112*(7), pp. 1420–1573.

– (2000). Taking Behavioralism Seriously: A Response to Market Manipulation. *Roger Williams University Law Review, 6*(31), pp. 259–392.

Harel, A. and Procaccia, Y. (2009). On the Optimal Regulation of Unread Contracts. *SSRN eLibrary*. Available at: ssrn.com/paper=1473770.

Harris Interactive (2002). 'Haggling' With Health Care Providers about Their Prices Likely to Increase Sharply as Out-Of-Pocket Costs Rise. *Health Care News, 2*(5). Available at: harrisinteractive.com/news/newsletters/healthnews/hi_healthcarenews2002vol2_iss05.pdf.

Harrison, M. (2008). Discussion of Bruno Frey: Motivation crowding theory - a new approach to behaviour. Behavioural Economics and Public Policy - *Roundtable Proceedings*, pp. 55–62. Canberra: Productivity Commission.

Hartlief, T. (2004). Freedom and Protection in Contemporary Contract Law. *Journal of Consumer Policy, 27*(3), pp. 253–267.

Hatzis, A.N. (2008). An Offer You Can't Negotiate: Some Thoughts on the Economics of Standard Form Consumer Contracts. In: H. Collins (Ed.), *Standard Contract Terms in Europe: A Basis for and a Challenge to European Contract Law*, pp. 43–56. Alphen aan den Rijn: Kluwer Law International.

Haupt, S. (2003). An Economic Analysis of Consumer Protection in Contract Law. *German Law Journal, 4*(11), pp. 1137–1164.

Heiderhoff, B. and Kenny, M. (2007). Response to the 2007 Green Paper on the Consumer Acquis. *Part of the Public Consultation on the Review of the Consumer Acquis, Held by European Commission*. Available at: ec.europa.eu/consumers/cons_int/safe_shop/acquis/responses/hamburg_univ.pdf.

Helliwell, J.F. (2006). Well-Being, Social Capital and Public Policy: What's New? *Economic Journal, 116*(510), pp. C34-C45.

Henderson, M.T. (2009). The Nanny Corporation and the Market for Paternalism. *SSRN eLibrary; University of Chicago Law & Economics, Olin Working Paper no. 456*. Available at: ssrn.com/paper=1348235.

Herrnstein, R.J., Loewenstein, G.F., Prelec, D. and Vaughan, W. (1993). Utility maximization and melioration: Internalities in individual choice. *Journal of Behavioral Decision Making, 6*, pp. 149–185.

Hesselink, M.W. (2007). Naar een (Europees) wetboek van consumentenrecht? *Nederlands Juristenblad, 2007*(14), pp. 850–857.

– (2009). The Consumer Rights Directive and the CFR: Two Worlds Apart? *European Review of Contract Law, Forthcoming*,

Hill, C.A. (2007). Anti-Anti-Anti-Paternalism. *NYU Journal of Law & Liberty, 2*(3), pp. 444–454.

Hillman, R.A. (2000). Limits of Behavioral Decision Theory in Legal Analysis: The Case of Liquidated Damages. *Cornell Law Review, 85*(3), pp. 717–738.

Hillman, R.A. and Rachlinski, J.J. (2002). Standard-Form Contracting in the Electronic Age. *New York University Law Review, 77*(2), pp. 429–495.

– (2006a). On-line Consumer Standard-Form Contracting Practices: A Survey and Discussion of Legal Implications. In: J. K. Winn (Ed.), Consumer Protection in the Age of the 'Information Economy', pp. 283–312. Aldershot: Ashgate Press.

– (2006b). Online Boilerplate: Would Mandatory Website Disclosure of E-Standard Terms Backfire? *Michigan Law Review, 104*(5), pp. 837–856.

Hillman, R.A. and Baraka, I. (2009). Warranties and Disclaimers in the Electronic Age. *Yale Journal of Law and Technology, 11*(1), pp. 1–69.

Ho, T.H., Lin, N. and Camerer, C.F. (2006). Modeling the Psychology of Consumer and Firm Behavior with Behavioral Economics. *Journal of Marketing Research, 43*(3), pp. 307–331.

Hoekstra, R. (2009). The Use and Usability of Inferential Techniques. *PhD Thesis, Rijksuniversiteit Groningen.* Available at: dissertations.ub.rug.nl/FILES/faculties/ppsw/2009/r.hoekstra/thesis.pdf.

Hondius, E.H. (1983). The legal control of unfair terms in consumer contracts: some comparative observations. In: T. M. Bourgoignie (Ed.), *Unfair terms in consumer contracts. Legal treatment, effective implementation and final impact on the consumer,* pp. 33–76. Louvain-la-Neuve: Cabay Bruylant.

– (2004). The Protection of the Weak Party in a Harmonised European Contract Law: A Synthesis. *Journal of Consumer Policy, 27*(3), pp. 245–251.

– (2006). Self-regulation in consumer matters at European level. In: F. Cafaggi (Ed.), *Reframing self-regulation in European private Law,* pp. 239–247. Den Haag: Kluwer.

Hondius, E.H. and Rijken, G.J. (2006). *Handboek Consumentenrecht.* Zutphen: Paris.

Howell, N. (2007). Catching up with consumer realities: The need for legislation prohibiting unfair terms in consumer contracts. *Australian Business Law Review, 34*(6), pp. 447–465.

Howells, G.G. (2005). The Potential and Limits of Consumer Empowerment by Information. *Journal of Law and Society, 32*(3), pp. 349–370.

Howells, G.G. and Weatherill, S. (2005). *Consumer Protection Law.* (2nd ed.). Aldershot: Ashgate.

Howells, G.G. (2007). Enforcing consumer interests by regulating agencies - the British experience; A case study of the Office of Fair Trading. In: W. H. Van Boom, M. B. M. Loos (Eds.), *Collective Enforcement of Consumer law,* pp. 65–80. Groningen: Europa Law Publishing.

Hviid, M. (2009). Too Good to be True? *CCP Newsletter, 16,* pp. 3–4.

Ibrahim, D.M. (2005). Rewriting the Law of Boilerplate Terms: Fairness, Efficiency, and a Standard Form Principle of Comparative Responsibility. *SSRN eLibrary.* Available at: No longer available (August 2009).

Incardona, R. and Poncibò, C. (2007). The average consumer, the unfair commercial practices directive, and the cognitive revolution. *Journal of Consumer Policy, 30*(1), pp. 21–38.

Issacharoff, S. (1998). Can there be a behavioral law and economics? *Vanderbilt Law Review, 51*(6), pp. 1729–1745.

Iyengar, S.S. and Lepper, M.R. (2000). When choice is demotivating: Can one desire too much of a good thing? *Journal of Personality and Social Psychology, 79*(6), pp. 995–1006.

Jacoby, J. (1984). Perspectives on Information Overload. *Journal of Consumer Research, 10*(4), pp. 432–435.

Jansen, N. (2008). The Authority of the DCFR. *SSRN eLibrary; After Common Frame of Reference - what Future for European Private Law?, H. W. Micklitz, F. Cafaggi, Eds., Forthcoming.* Available at: SSRN.com/paper=1264011.

Johnson, E.J., Hershey, J., Meszaros, J. and Kunreuther, H. (1993). Framing, Probability Distortions, and Insurance Decisions. *Journal of Risk and Uncertainty, 7*(1), pp. 35–51.

Johnston, J.S. (2006). The Return of Bargain: an Economic Theory of How Standard-Form Contracts Enable Cooperative Negotiation between Businesses and Consumers. *Michigan Law Review, 104*(5), pp. 857–898.

Jolls, C. (1998). Behavioral Economics Analysis of Redistributive Legal Rules. *Vanderbilt Law Review, 51*(6), pp. 1653–1678.

Jolls, C., Sunstein, C.R. and Thaler, R.H. (1998a). A Behavioral Approach to Law and Economics. *Stanford Law Review, 50*(5), pp. 1471–1550.

– (1998b). Theories and Tropes: A Reply to Posner and Kelman. *Stanford Law Review, 50*(5), pp. 1593–1608.

Jolls, C. and Sunstein, C.R. (2006). Debiasing through Law. *Journal of Legal Studies, 335*, pp. 199–242.

Julander, C. and Söderlund, M. (2005). Peripheral Cues in Advertising and Consumer Policy. Do physically attractive models in advertising still have an effect? In: K. G. Grunert, J. Thøgersen (Eds.), *Consumers, Policy and the Environment. A Tribute to Folke Ölander*, pp. 181–201. New York: Springer.

Kahneman, D. and Tversky, A. (1979). Prospect Theory: An Analysis of Decision under Risk. *Econometrica, 47*(2), pp. 263–291.

Kahneman, D., Knetsch, J. L. and Thaler, R. H. (1990). Experimental Tests of the Endowment Effect and the Coase Theorem. *Journal of Political Economy, 98*(6), pp. 1325.

Kahneman, D. and Tversky, A. (1996). On the Reality of Cognitive Illusions. *Psychological Review, 103*(3), pp. 582–591.

Kahneman, D. (2003). A Psychological Perspective on Economics. *American Economic Review, 93*(2), pp. 162–168.

Kanning, W.A. and Kerkmeester, H. (2004). *Economie en Recht (Economics and Law).* Leiden/Antwerpen: Stenfert Kroese.

Kaplow, L. and Shavell, S. (2002). *Fairness Versus Welfare.* Cambridge: Harvard University Press.

– (2003). Fairness versus Welfare: Notes on the Pareto Principle, Preferences, and Distributive Justice. *Journal of Legal Studies, 32*(1), pp. 331–362.

Katz, A.W. (1990). Your Terms or Mine? The Duty to Read the Fine Print in Contracts. *Rand Journal of Economics, 21*(4), pp. 518–537.

– (1998). Standard Form Contracts. In: P. Newman (Ed.), *The New Palgrave Dictionary of Economics and the Law*, pp. 502–505. Basingstoke: Palgrave MacMillan.

Keller, K.L. and Staelin, R. (1987). Effects of Quality and Quantity of Information on Decision Effectiveness. *Journal of Consumer Research, 14*(2), pp. 200–213.

Kelman, M. (1998). Behavioral Economics as Part of a Rhetorical Duet: A Response to Jolls, Sunstein, and Thaler. *Stanford Law Review, 50*(5), pp. 1577–1592.

– (2003). Law and Behavioral Science: Conceptual Overviews. *Northwestern University Law Review, 97*(2), pp. 1347–1392.

Kennedy, D. (1982). Distributive and Paternalist Motives in Contract and Tort Law, with Special Reference to Compulsory Terms and Unequal Bargaining Power. *Maryland Law Review, 41*(4), pp. 563–658.

Kerber, W. and Grundmann, S. (2006). An optional European contract law code: Advantages and disadvantages. *European Journal of Law and Economics, 21*(3), pp. 215–236.

Keske, S.E. (2010). *Group Litigation in European Competition Law. A law and economics perspective.* Antwerpen: Intersentia (forthcoming).

Kessler, F. (1943). Contracts of Adhesion-Some Thoughts about Freedom of Contract. *Columbia Law Review, 43*(5), pp. 629–642.

Klick, J. (2005). The Micro Foundations of Standard Form Contracts: Price Discrimination Vs. Behavioral Bias. *Florida State University Law Review, 32*(2), pp. 555–569.

Klick, J. and Mitchell, G. (2006). Government Regulation of Irrationality: Moral and Cognitive Hazards. *Minnesota Law Review, 90*(6), pp. 1620–1663.

Klucharev, V. and Smidts, A. (2009). Zit irrationaliteit in de mens? De neurobiologie van besluitvorming. In: W. L. Tiemeijer, C. A. Thomas and H. M. Prast (Eds.), *De menselijke beslisser; over de psychologie van keuze en gedrag. WRR-verkenning 22*, pp. 213–238. Amsterdam: WRR/Amsterdam University Press.

Knight, F.M. (1921). *Risk, Uncertainty and Profit.* Boston: Houghton Mifflin.

Kornhauser, L.A. (1976). Unconscionability in Standard Forms. *California Law Review, 64*(5), pp. 1151–1183.

Korobkin, R.B. (1998). The Status Quo Bias and Contract Default Rules. *Cornell Law Review, 83*(3), pp. 608–687.

Korobkin, R.B. and Ulen, T.S. (2000). Law and Behavioral Science: Removing the Rationality Assumption from Law and Economics. *California Law Review, 88*(4), pp. 1051–1144.

Korobkin, R.B. (2003). Bounded Rationality, Standard Form Contracts, and Unconscionability. *University of Chicago Law Review, 70*(4), pp. 1203–1295.

– (2005). Possibility and Plausibility in Law and Economics. *Florida State University Law Review, 32*(2), pp. 781–795.

– (2006). The Problems with Heuristics for Law. In: G. Gigerenzer, C. Engle (Eds.), *Heuristics and the Law*, pp. 45–60. Cambridge: MIT Press.

– (2009). Libertarian Welfarism. *California Law Review, 97*(6), pp. 1651–1685.

Kreps, D.M. (1998). Bounded Rationality. In: P. Newman (Ed.), *The New Palgrave Dictionary of Economics and the Law*, pp. 168–173. Basingstoke: Palgrave MacMillan.

Kuran, T. and Sunstein, C.R. (1999). Availability Cascades and Risk Regulation. *Stanford Law Review, 51*(4), pp. 683–768.

Lacko, J.M. and Pappalardo, J.K. (2004). The Effect of Mortgage Broker Compensation Disclosures on Consumers and Competition: A Controlled Experiment. *Federal Trade Commission Bureau of Economics Staff Report*. Available at: ftc.gov/os/2004/01/030123mortgagefullrpt.pdf.

– (2007). Improving Consumer Mortgage Disclosures: An Empirical Assessment of Current and Prototype Disclosure Forms. *Federal Trade Commission Bureau of Economics Staff Report*. Available at: ftc.gov/os/2007/06/P025505MortgageDisclosureReport.pdf.

Laibson, D. (1997). Golden Eggs and Hyperbolic Discounting. *Quarterly Journal of Economics, 112*(2), pp. 443–477.

Lando, O. (1966). Standard Contracts A Proposal and A Perspective. *Scandinavian Studies in Law, 10*, pp. 127–148.

Lane, R.E. (2000). *The Loss of Happiness in Market Democracies*. New Haven: Yale University Press.

Langevoort, D.C. (1998). Behavioral Theories of Judgment and Decision Making in Legal Scholarship: A Literature Review. *Vanderbilt Law Review, 51*, pp. 1499–1540.

Layard, R. (2005). *Happiness: Lessons from a New Science*. New York: Penguin Press.

– (2006). Happiness and Public Policy: a Challenge to the Profession. *Economic Journal, 116*(510), pp. C24-C33.

Lee, T.R., Christensen, G. and DeRosia, E. (2008). Trademarks, Consumer Psychology, and the Sophisticated Consumer. *Emory Law Journal, 57*(3), pp. 575–650.

Lee, L., Amir, O. and Ariely, D. (2009). In Search of Homo Economicus: Cognitive Noise and the Role of Emotion in Preference Consistency. *Journal of Consumer Research, 36*(2), pp. 173–187.

Leff, A.A. (1970a). Unconscionability and the Crowd: Consumers and the Common Law Tradition. *University of Pittsburgh Law Review, 31*(3), pp. 349–358.

– (1970b). Contract As Thing. *American University Law Review, 19*(2), pp. 131–157.

Levitin, A.J. (2007). All But Accurate: A Critique of the American Bankers Association's Study on Credit Card Regulation. *SSRN eLibrary*. Available at: SSRN.com/paper=1029191.

– (2009). The Consumer Financial Protection Agency. *SSRN eLibrary; Pew Financial Reform Project, Briefing Paper, no.2;* Georgetown Law and Economics Research Paper no. 1447082. Available at: SSRN.com/paper=1447082.

Levitt, S.D. and List, J.A. (2007). What Do Laboratory Experiments Measuring Social Preferences Reveal About the Real World? *Journal of Economic Perspectives, 21*(2), pp. 153–174.

Linzer, P. (2008). Implied, Inferred, and Imposed: Default Rules and Adhesion Contracts - the Need for Racial Surgery. *Pace Law Review, 28*(2), pp. 195–218.

Littwin, A.K. (2009). Testing the Substitution Hypothesis: Would Credit Card Regulation Force Low-Income Borrowers Into Less Desirable Lending Alternatives? *University of Illinois Law Review, 2009*(2), pp. 403–456.

Llewellyn, K.N. (1939). Book review on: the Standardization of Commercial Contracts in English and Continental Law, by O. Prausnitz. *Harvard Law Review, 52*(4), pp. 700–705.

– (1960). *The Common Law Tradition - Deciding Appeals.* Boston: Little, Brown and Company.

Lobel, O. (2004). The Renew Deal: The Fall of Regulation and the Rise of Governance in Contemporary Legal Thought. *Minnesota Law Review, 89*(1), pp. 342–470.

Loewenstein, G.F., O'Donoghue, T. and Rabin, M. (2003). Projection Bias in Predicting Future Utility. *Quarterly Journal of Economics, 118*(4), pp. 1209–1248.

Loewenstein, G.F. and O'Donoghue, T. (2006). "We Can Do This the Easy Way or the Hard Way": Negative Emotions, Self-Regulation and the Law. *University of Chicago Law Review, 73*(1), pp. 183–206.

Loewenstein, G.F. and Haisley, E. (2008). The Economist as Therapist: Methodological Ramifications of 'Light' Paternalism. In: A. Caplin, A. Schotter (Eds.), *Perspectives on the Future of Economics: Positive and Normative Foundations*, pp. 210–245. Oxford: Oxford University Press.

Loos, M.B.M. (2007). The Influence of European Consumer Law on General Contract Law and the Need for Spontaneous Harmonisation. *European Review of Private Law, 15*(4), pp. 515–532.

Luth, H.A. and Cseres, K.J. (2009). The DCFR and consumer protection: an economic assessment. In: P. Larouche, P. Chirico (Eds.), *Economic Analysis of the DCFR*, pp. 237–276. Munich: Sellier.

Macaulay, S. (1963). Non-Contractual Relations in Business: A Preliminary Study. *American Sociological Review, 28*(1), pp. 55–67.

Mak, C. (2008). The Constitution of a Common Frame of Reference for European Contract Law. *European Review of Contract Law, 4*(4), pp. 553–565

Mak, V. (2009). Review of the Consumer Acquis - Towards Maximum Harmonisation? *European Review of Private Law, 17*(1), pp. 55–73.

– (2010). Harmonisation through "directive-related" case law: The role of the ECJ in the development of European consumer law. *Zeitschrift Für Europäisches Privatrecht, 18*(1), pp. 129–146.

Malhotra, N.K. (1984). Reflections on the Information Overload Paradigm in Consumer Decision Making. *Journal of Consumer Research, 10*(4), pp. 436–440.

Mann, R.J. and Siebeneicher, T. (2008). Just One Click: The Reality of Internet Retail Contracting. *Columbia Law Review, 108*(4), pp. 984–1012.

Mann, R.J. (2006). 'Contracting' for Credit. *Michigan Law Review, 104*(5), pp. 899–932.

Marotta-Wurgler, F. (2007a). 'Unfair' Dispute Resolution Clauses: Much Ado About Nothing? In: O. Ben-Shahar (Ed.), *Boilerplate: Foundations of Market Contracts*, pp. 45–65. Cambridge: Cambridge University Press.

- (2007b). What's in a Standard Form Contract? An Empirical Analysis of Software License Agreements. *Journal of Empirical Legal Studies, 4*(4), pp. 677–713.
- (2008). Competition and the Quality of Standard Form Contracts: The Case of Software License Agreements. *Journal of Empirical Legal Studies, 5*(3), pp. 447–475.
- (2009). Are 'Pay Now, Terms Later' Contracts Worse for Buyers? Evidence from Software License Agreements. *Journal of Legal Studies, 38*(2), pp. 309–343.

Maugeri, M.R. (2008). The Rules Applicable When Standard Terms Are Avoided and Contracts with Inequality of Bargaining Power: Construction of a Unitary Model of Invalidity or a Plurality of Models? In: H. Collins (Ed.), *Standard Contract Terms in Europe: A Basis for and a Challenge to European Contract Law*, pp. 177–185. Alphen aan den Rijn: Kluwer Law International.

Maxeiner, J.R. (2003). Standard-Terms Contracting in the Global Electronic Age: European Alternatives. *Yale Journal of International Law, 28*(1), pp. 109–182.

McNeil, K., Nevin, J.R., Trubek, D.M. and Miller, R.E. (1979). Market Discrimination against the Poor and the Impact of Consumer Disclosure Laws: The Used Car Industry. *Law and Society Review, 13*(3), pp. 695–720.

Meyerson, M. I. (1990). Efficient Consumer Form Contract: Law and Economics Meets the Real World. *Georgia Law Review, 24*(3), pp. 583–628.

Micklitz, H.W. and Radeideh, M. (2005). CLAB Europa – The European Database on Unfair Terms in Consumer Contracts. *Journal of Consumer Policy, 28*(3), pp. 325–360.

Micklitz, H.W. (2008). Some Reflections on *Cassis de Dijon* and the Control of Unfair Contract Terms in Consumer Contracts. In: H. Collins (Ed.), *Standard Contract Terms in Europe: A Basis for and a Challenge to European Contract Law*, pp. 19–41. Alphen aan den Rijn: Kluwer Law International.

Miller, G.A. (1956). The Magical Number Seven, Plus or Minus Two: Some Limits on Our Capacity for Information Processing. *Psychological Review, 63*(2), pp. 81–97.

Miller, J.C. (1985). The FTC and Voluntary Standards: maximizing the net benefits of Self-Regulation. *Cato Journal, 4*(3), pp. 897–903.

Mulholland, J.P. (2008). Behavioural economics and the Federal Trade Commission. Behavioural Economics and Public Policy - *Roundtable Proceedings*, pp. 67–87. Canberra: Productivity Commission.

Müller, W. (1970). Residential Tenants and Their Leases: An Empirical Study. *Michigan Law Review, 69*(2), pp. 247–298.

Munier, B., Selten, R., Bouyssou, D., Bourgine, P., Day, R., Harvey, N., Hilton, D., Machina, M. J., Parker, P., Sterman, J., Weber, E., Wernerfelt, B. and Wensley, R. (1999). Bounded Rationality Modeling. *Marketing Letters, 10*(3), pp. 233–248.

Nelson, P. (1970). Information and Consumer Behaviour. *Journal of Political Economy, 78*(2), pp. 311–329.

NMa (2009). De Nederlandse Energiemarkten in 2009. Streefbeeld - Knelpunten - Maatregelen. *Energiekamer.* Nederlandse Mededingingsautoriteit: Den Haag. Available at: nma.nl/Images/Bijlage%201%20De%20Nederlandse%20energiemarkten%20in%202009_tcm16-133383.pdf.

O'Donoghue, T. and Rabin, M. (1999). Doing It Now or Later. *American Economic Review, 89*(1), pp. 103–124.

– (2003). Studying Optimal Paternalism, Illustrated by a Model of Sin Taxes. *American Economic Review, 93*(2), pp. 186–191.

– (2006). Incentives and Self-Control. In: R. Blundell, W. K. Newey and T. Persson (Eds.), *Advances in Economics and Econometrics: Theory and Applications, Ninth World Congress*, pp. 215–245. Cambridge: Cambridge University Press.

OECD (2006). Roundtable on Demand-Side Economics for Consumer Policy: Summary Report. *DSTI/CP(2006)3/FINAL*. OECD: Paris. Available at: olis.oecd.org/olis/2006doc.nsf/ ENGDIRCORPLOOK/NT00000BF6/$FILE/JT03207762.PDF.

–(2007). Roundtable on Economics for Consumer Policy: Summary Report. *DSTI/CP(2007)1/FINAL*. OECD: Paris. Available at: olis.oecd.org/olis/2007doc.nsf/ENGDIRCORPLOOK/NT00002E22/$FILE/JT03230575.PDF.

Ogus, A. (2005). Regulatory Paternalism: When is it Justified? In: K.J. Hopt, E. Wymeersch, H. Kanda and H. Baum (Eds.), *Corporate Governance in Context: Corporations, States, and Markets in Europe, Japan and the US*, pp. 303–320. Oxford: Oxford University Press.

Olson, M. (1965). *The Logic of Collective Action: Public goods and the theory of groups.* Cambridge: Harvard University Press.

O'Shea, P.M. (2005). Consumer Credit Code Disclosure: Does it Work? *Journal of Banking and Finance Law and Practice, 16*(1), pp. 5–16.

Pape, S.B. (2008). Productwaarschuwingen: psychologische lessen voor de jurist. In: W.H. Van Boom, I. Giesen and A.J. Verheij (Eds.), *Gedrag en privaatrecht: over gedragspresumpties en gedragseffecten bij privaatrechtelijke leerstukken*, pp. 245–282. Den Haag: Boom Juridische uitgevers.

Pavillon, C.M.D.S. (2006). De wisselende betekenis van de Richtlijn oneerlijke bedingen in de Nederlandse rechtsspraak: een drieluik. *Vermogensrechtelijke Analyses, 2006*(2), pp. 25–70.

Peltzman, S. (1975). The Effects of Automobile Safety Regulation. *Journal of Political Economy, 83*(4), pp. 677–725.

Perillo, J.M. (2008). Neutral Standardizing of Contracts - Keynote Address. *Pace Law Review, 28*(2), pp. 179–194.

Poncibò, C. (2007). The Challenges of EC Consumer Law. *SSRN eLibrary; EUI Working Paper Max Weber Programme No. 2007/24*. Available at: SSRN.com/paper=1028218.

Posner, R.A. (1998a). Rational Choice, Behavioral Economics, and the Law. *Stanford Law Review, 50*(5), pp. 1551–1576.

– (1998b). *Economic Analysis of Law.* (5th ed.). New York: Aspen.

– (1998c). Social Norms, Social Meaning, and Economic Analysis of Law: A Comment. *Journal of Legal Studies, 27*(s2), pp. 553–556.

Posner, E.A. (2004). Probability Errors: Some Positive and Normative Implications for Tort and Contract Law. *Supreme Court Economic Review, 11*, pp. 125–141.

– (2006). There Are No Penalty Default Rules in Contract Law. *Florida State University Law Review, 33*(3), pp. 563–588.

Priest, G.L. (1981). A Theory of the Consumer Product Warranty. *Yale Law Journal, 90*(6), pp. 1297–1352.

Productivity Commission (2008). *Behavioural Economics and Public Policy - Roundtable Proceedings*. Canberra: Productivity Commission.

Rabin, M. (2002). A Perspective on Psychology and Economics. *European Economic Review, 46*(4–5), pp. 657–685.

Rachlinski, J.J. (2000). New Law and Psychology: A Reply to Critics, Skeptics, and Cautious Supporters. *Cornell Law Review, 85*(3), pp. 739–766.

- (2003). The Uncertain Psychological Case for Paternalism. *Northwestern University Law Review, 97*(2), pp. 1165–1226.

Radin, M.J. (2006). Boilerplate Today: the Rise of Modularity and the Waning of Consent. *Michigan Law Review, 104*(5), pp. 1223–1234.

Rakoff, T.D. (1983). Contracts of Adhesion: An Essay in Reconstruction. *Harvard Law Review, 96*(6), pp. 1176–1284.

- (2006). The Law and Sociology of Boilerplate. *Michigan Law Review, 104*(5), pp. 1235–1246.

Ramsay, I. (1984). *Rationales for Intervention in the Consumer Marketplace*. London: OFT.

- (2005). From Truth in Lending to Responsible Lending. In: G.G. Howells, A. Janssen and R. Schulze (Eds.), *Information Rights and Obligations*, pp. 47–65. Aldershot: Ashgate.

- (2007). *Consumer Law and Policy*. Oxford: Hart Publishing.

Rasmussen, R.K. (1998). Behavioral Economics, the Economic Analysis Bankruptcy Law and the Pricing of Credit. *Vanderbilt Law Review, 51*(6), pp. 1679–1704.

Rawls, J. (1993). *Political Liberalism*. New York: Columbia University Press.

Repo, P., Timonen, P. and Zilliacus, K. (2009). Alternative Regulatory Cases Challenging Consumer Policy. *Journal of Consumer Policy, 32*(3), pp. 289–301.

Richards, M., Palmer, P. and Bogdanova, M. (2008). Irresponsible Lending? A Case Study of a U.K. Credit Industry Reform Initiative. *Journal of Business Ethics, 81*(3), pp. 499–512.

Rischkowsky, F. and Döring, T. (2008). Consumer Policy in a Market Economy Considerations from the Perspective of the Economics of Information, the New Institutional Economics as well as Behavioural Economics. *Journal of Consumer Policy, 31*(3), pp. 285–313.

Ritoy, I. and Baron, J. (2000). Reluctance to Vaccinate: Omission Bias and Ambiguity. In: C. R. Sunstein (Ed.), Behavioral Law and Economics, pp. 168–186. Cambridge: Cambridge University Press.

Roppo, V. (2009). From Consumer Contracts to Asymmetric Contracts: a Trend in European Contract Law? *European Review of Contract Law, 5*(3), pp. 304–349.

Rosenberg, A.S. (2006). Regulation of Unfair Bank Fees in the United States and the European Union: Current Trends and a Proposal for Reform. *SSRN eLibrary; International Association of Consumer Law Conference, Malta, March 16, 2006; Thomas Jefferson School of Law Legal Studies Research Paper no. 1028163*. Available at: ssrn.com/paper=1028163.

Ross, L. and Shestowsky, D. (2003). Contemporary Psychology's Challenges to Legal Theory and Practice. *Northwestern University Law Review, 97*(2), pp. 1081–1114.

Rubinstein, A. (1998). *Modeling Bounded Rationality.* Cambridge: MIT Press.

Rutgers, J.W. (2008). The Draft Common Frame of Reference, Public Policy, Mandatory Rules and the Welfare State. In: A. Somma (Ed.), *The Politics of the Draft Common Frame of Reference*, pp. 115–128. The Hague: Kluwer Law International.

Samuelson, P.A. (1963). Risk and Uncertainty: The Fallacy of the Law Of Large Numbers. *Scientia, 98*(4–5), pp. 108–113.

Schäfer, H.B. and Ott, C. (2004). *The Economic Analysis of Civil Law.* Cheltenham: Edward Elgar.

Schäfer, H.B. and Leyens, P. (2009). Judicial Control of Standard Terms and European Private Law. In: P. Larouche, P. Chirico (Eds.), *Economic Analysis of the DCFR*, pp. 99–121. Munich: Sellier.

Schillig, M. (2008). Inequality of Bargaining Power Versus Market for Lemons: Legal Paradigm Change and the Court of Justice's Jurisprudence on Directive 93/13 on Unfair Contract Terms. *European Law Review, 33*(3), pp. 336–358.

Schulte-Nölke, H. (2007). EC Law on the Formation of Contract - from the Common Frame of Reference to the 'Blue Button'. *European Review of Contract Law, 3*(3), pp. 332–349.

Schwartz, A. and Wilde, L. L. (1979). Intervening In Markets on the Basis of Imperfect Information: A Legal and Economic Analysis. *University of Pennsylvania Law Review, 127*(3), pp. 630–682.

– (1982). Imperfect Information, Monopolistic Competition, and Public Policy. *American Economic Review, 72*(2), pp. 18–23.

– (1983). Imperfect Information in Markets for Contract Terms: The Examples of Warranties and Security Interests. *Virginia Law Review, 69*(8), pp. 1387–1486.

Schwartz, B. (2004). *The paradox of choice: why more is less.* New York: HarperCollins.

Scott, R.E. (2000). The Limits of Behavioral Theories of Law and Social Norms. *Virginia Law Review, 86*(8), pp. 1603–1648.

SER (2006). Informatiepakket Voorwaardenoverleg. Available at: ser.nl/~/media/Files/Internet/Consumentenvoorwaarden/algemeen/200602CZInformatiePakket%20pdf.ashx.

Shafir, E. (2008). A behavioural background for economic policy. Behavioural Economics and Public Policy - *Roundtable Proceedings*, pp. 9–25. Canberra: Productivity Commission.

Shapiro, C. (1983). Consumer protection policies in the United States. *Journal of Institutional and Theoretical Economics, 139*, pp. 527–544.

Sheldon, J.E. (1974). Consumer Protection and Standard Contracts. The Swedish Experiment in Administrative Control. *American Journal of Comparative Law, 22*(1), pp. 17–70.

Shiv, B., Bechara, A., Levin, I., Alba, J., Bettman, J., Dube, L., Isen, A., Mellers, B., Smidts, A., Grant, S. and Mcgraw, A. (2005). Decision Neuroscience. *Marketing Letters, 16*(3), pp. 375–386.

Silber, N.I. (1990). Observing Reasonable Consumers: Cognitive Psychology, Consumer Behavior and Consumer Law. *Loyola Consumer Law Reporter, 2*(3), pp. 69–75.

Simon, H. A. (1957). *Models of Man, Social and Rational. Mathematical Essays on Rational Human Behavior in a Social Setting.* New York: Wiley.

– (1978). Rationality as Process and as Product of Thought. *American Economic Review, 68*(2), pp. 1–16.

Simonson, I. and Tversky, A. (1992). Choice in Context: Tradeoff Contrast and Extremeness Aversion. *Journal of Marketing Research, 29*(3), pp. 281–295.

Slawson, W.D. (1971). Standard Form Contracts and Democratic Control of Lawmaking Power. *Harvard Law Review, 84*(3), pp. 529–566.

– (1974). Mass Contracts: Lawful Fraud in California. *Southern California Law Review, 48*(1), pp. 1–55.

Slovic, P., Finucane, M.L., Peters, E. and MacGregor, D.G. (2002). Rational Actors or Rational Fools? Implications of the Affect Heuristic for Behavioral Economics. *Journal of Socio-Economics, 31*, pp. 329–342.

Smith, A. (1790). *The Theory of Moral Sentiments.* (6th ed.). London: Millar.

Smith, A. (1904). *An Inquiry into the Nature and Causes of the Wealth of Nations.* (5th ed.). London: Methuen and Co.

Smith, D.C. and Park, C.W. (1992). Choice in Context: Trade-off Contrast and Extremeness Aversion. *Journal of Marketing Research, 29*(3), pp. 296–313.

Smith, S. (2009). Reforming the Law of Adhesion Contracts: A Judicial Response to the Subprime Mortgage Crisis. *SSRN eLibrary; Marquette Law School Legal Studies Paper no. 09-34; Lewis & Clark Law Review, Forthcoming.* Available at: ssrn.com/paper=1481933.

Smits, J.M. (2008a). The Draft-Common Frame of Reference (CFR) for a European Private Law: Fit for Purpose? *Maastricht Journal of European and Comparative Law, 15*(2), pp. 145–148.

– (2008b). The Draft Common Frame of Reference, Methodological Nationalism and the Way Forward. *European Review of Contract Law, 4*(3), pp. 270–280.

Snyder, M. and Swann, W.B. (1978). Behavioral Confirmation in Social Interaction: From Social Perception to Social Reality. *Journal of Experimental Social Psychology, 14*(2), pp. 148–162.

Solan, L.M., Rosenblatt, T. and Osherson, D. (2008). False Consensus Bias in Contract Interpretation. *Columbia Law Review, 108*(5), pp. 1268–1300.

Sovern, J. (2006). Towards a New Model of Consumer Protection: The Problem of Inflated Transaction Costs. *William & Mary Law Review, 47*(6), pp. 1635–1709.

Speidel, R.E. (1970). Unconscionability, Assent and Consumer Protection. *University of Pittsburgh Law Review, 31*(3), pp. 359–376.

Stark, D.P. and Choplin, J.M. (2009). A License to Deceive: Enforcing Contractual Myths Despite Consumer Psychological Realities. *NYU Journal of Law & Business, 5*(2), pp. 617–744.

Stigler, G.J. (1961). The Economics of Information. *Journal of Political Economy, 69*(3), pp. 213–225.

Stigler, G.J. and Becker, G.S. (1977). De Gustibus Non Est Disputandum. *The American Economic Review, 67*(2), pp. 76–90.

Stiglitz, J. (2009). Regulation and Failure. In: D. Moss, J. Cisternino (Eds.), *New Perspectives on Regulation*, pp. 11–23. Cambridge: The Tobin Project.

Stolle, D.P. and Slain, A.J. (1997). Standard Form Contracts and Contract Schemas: A Preliminary Investigation of the Effects of Exculpatory Clauses on Consumers' Propensity to Sue. *Behavioral Sciences & the Law, 15*(1), pp. 83–94.

Stout, L.A. (2006). Social Norms and Other-Regarding Preferences. In: J. N. Drobak (Ed.), *Norms and the Law*, pp. 13–35. Cambridge: Cambridge University Press.

Sullivan, C.A. (2009). The Puzzling Persistence of Unenforceable Contract Terms. *Ohio State Law Journal, 70*(5), pp. 1127–1177.

Sunstein, C.R. (1996). On the Expressive Function of Law. *University of Pennsylvania Law Review, 144*(5), pp. 2021–2054.

– (1997). Behavioral analysis of law. *University of Chicago Law Review, 64*(4), pp. 1175–1195.

– (1999). Behavioral law and economics: a progress report. *American Law and Economics Review, 1*(1), pp. 115–157.

– (2001). Human Behavior and the Law of Work. *Virginia Law Review, 87*(2), pp. 205–276.

Sunstein, C.R. and Thaler, R.H. (2003). Libertarian Paternalism Is Not An Oxymoron. *University of Chicago Law Review, 70*(4), pp. 1159–1202.

Svenson, O. (1981). Are we all less risky and more skillful than our fellow drivers? *Acta Psychologica, 47*(2), pp. 143–148.

Swygert, M.I. and Yanes, K.E. (1998). A Unified Theory of Justice: The Integration of Fairness into Efficiency. *Washington Law Review, 73*(2), pp. 249–328.

Sylvan, L. (2008). Discussion papers by Mulholland and Field. Behavioural Economics and Public Policy – *Roundtable Proceedings*, pp. 103–113. Canberra: Productivity Commission.

Taylor, S.E. and Brown, J.D. (1988). Illusion and Well-being: a Social Psychological Perspective on Mental Health. *Psychological Bulletin, 103*(2), pp. 193–210.

– (1994). Positive Illusions and Well-Being Revisited. Separating Fact From Fiction. *Psychological Bulletin, 116*(1), pp. 21–27.

Terryn, E. (2008). *Bedenktijden in het consumentenrecht. Het herroepingsrecht als instrument van consumentenbescherming.* Antwerpen: Intersentia.

Thaler, R.H. (1980). Toward a positive theory of consumer choice. *Journal of Economic Behavior and Organization, 1*(1), pp. 39–60.

Thaler, R.H. and Benartzi, S. (2007). Save More Tomorrow: Using Behavioral Economics to Increase Employee Saving. *Journal of Political Economy, 112*(1), pp. 164–187.

Thaler, R.H. and Sunstein, C.R. (2008). *Nudge. Improving Decisions About Health, Wealth and Happiness.* New Haven & London: Yale University Press.

Tiemeijer, W.L. (2009). Slotbeschouwing. In: W.L. Tiemeijer, C.A. Thomas and H.M. Prast (Eds.), *De menselijke beslisser; over de psychologie van keuze en gedrag. WRR-verkenning 22*, pp. 293–312. Amsterdam: WRR/Amsterdam University Press.

Tiemeijer, W.L., Thomas, C.A. and Prast, H.M. (2009). *De menselijke beslisser; over de psychologie van keuze en gedrag.* In: W. L. Tiemeijer, C. A. Thomas and H. M. Prast (Eds.), *De menselijke beslisser; over de psychologie van keuze en gedrag. WRR-verkenning 22.* Amsterdam: WRR/Amsterdam University Press.

Träger, M. (2008). Party Autonomy and Social Justice in Member States and EC Regulation: A Survey of Theory and Practice. In: H. Collins (Ed.), *Standard Contract Terms in Europe: A Basis for and a Challenge to European Contract Law*, pp. 57–74. Alphen aan den Rijn: Kluwer Law International.

Trebilcock, M.J. and Dewees, D.N. (1981). Judicial control of standard form contracts. In: P. Burrows, C. G. Veljanovski (Eds.), *The Economic approach to law*, pp. 93–119. London: Butterworths.

Trebilcock, M.J. (1993). *The Limits of Freedom of Contract.* Cambridge: Harvard University Press.

– (2003). Rethinking Consumer Protection Policy. In: C. E. F. Rickett, T. G. W. Telfer (Eds.), *International Perspectives on Consumer Access to Justice*, pp. 68–98. Cambridge: Cambridge University Press.

Tversky, A. and Kahneman, D. (1974). Judgment under Uncertainty: Heuristics and Biases. *Science, 185*(4157), pp. 1124–1131.

– (1981). The framing of decisions and the psychology of choice. *Science, 211*(4481), pp. 453–458.

Van Bijnen, R. H. J. (2007). Contractenrecht. In: W. C. T. Weterings (Ed.), *De economische analyse van het recht*, pp. 47–69. Den Haag: Boom Juridische Uitgevers.

Van Boom, W. H. and Kottenhagen, R. J. P. (2006). De Richtlijn oneerlijke bedingen en haar plaats in het Nederlandse recht. In: F. De Ly, K. F. Haak and W. H. Van Boom (Eds.), *Eenvormig bedrijfsrecht: realiteit of utopie?*, pp. 133–154. Den Haag: Boom Juridische Uitgevers.

Van Boom, W.H. and Loos, M.B.M. (2007). *Collective Enforcement of Consumer law.* Groningen: Europa Law Publishing.

Van Boom, W.H., Giesen, I. and Verheij, A.J. (2008). Gedrag en privaatrecht: inleiding en verantwoording. In: W.H. Van Boom, I. Giesen and A.J. Verheij (Eds.), *Gedrag en privaatrecht: over gedragspresumpties en gedragseffecten bij privaatrechtelijke leerstukken*, pp. 19–48. Den Haag: Boom Juridische uitgevers.

Van Boom, W.H., Tuil, M.L. and Dijkshoorn, W. (2008). *Autonomie en paternalisme in het privaatrecht.* Den Haag: Boom Juridische uitgevers.

Van Boom, W.H. (2008). Insurance law and economics: an empirical perspective. In: M. G. Faure, F. Stephen (Eds.), *Essays in the Law and Economics of Regulation. In Honour of Anthony Ogus*, pp. 253–276. Antwerpen: Intersentia.

Van den Bergh, R.J. (1990). Economische analyse van het consumentenrecht. *Ars Aequi, 39*(10), pp. 787–793.

– (1997). Wer schützt die europäischen Verbraucher vor dem Brüsseler Verbraucherschutz? In: C. Ott, H. B. Schäfer (Eds.), *Effiziente Verhaltenssteuerung und Kooperation im Zivilrecht*, pp. 77–102. Tübingen: Mohr Siebeck.

- (1998). Subsidiairity as an Economic Demarcation Principle and the Emergence of European Private Law. *Maastricht Journal of European and Comparative Law, 5*(2), pp. 129–152.
- (2002a). Forced Harmonisation of Contract Law in Europe: Not to be continued. In: S. Grundmann, J. Stuyck (Eds.), *An Academic Greenpaper on European Contract Law*, pp. 245–264. The Hague: Kluwer Law International.
- (2002b). Towards a European Private Law: To Harmonise or not to Harmonise, that is the Question. In: H. B. Schäfer, H. J. Lwowski (Eds.), *Konsequenzen wirtschaftsrechtlicher Normen, Festschrift für Claus Ott*, pp. 327–343. Wiesbaden: Gabler.
- (2003). Competition law and consumer protection legislation. In: A. N. Hatzis (Ed.), *Economic Analysis of Law: A European Perspective*. Cheltenham: Edward Elgar.
- (2006). Toward Efficient Self-regulation in Markets for Professional Services. In: C. -. Ehlermann, I. Atanasiu (Eds.), *European Competition Law Annual 2004 - The Relationship Between Competition Law and the (Liberal) Professions*, pp. 155–176. Oxford: Hart Publishing.

Van den Bergh, R.J. and Camesasca, P.D.N. (2006). *European competition law and economics: a comparative perspective*. (2nd ed.). London: Sweet & Maxwell.

Van den Bergh, R.J. (2007). Should Consumer Protection be publicly enforced? In: W. H. Van Boom, M. B. M. Loos (Eds.), *Collective Enforcement of Consumer law*, pp. 179–203. Groningen: Europa Law Publishing.
- (2008). Enforcement of consumer law by consumer associations. In: M. G. Faure, F. Stephen (Eds.), *Essays in the Law and Economics of Regulation. In Honour of Anthony Ogus*, pp. 279–305. Antwerpen: Intersentia.

Van den Bergh, R.J. and Visscher, L.T. (2008). The Preventive Function of Collective Actions for Damages in Consumer Law. *Erasmus Law Review, 1*(2), pp. 5–30.

Van Mierlo, T. (2007). Consumer Protection on the Single Market: Self-Regulation for Dating Services. In: K. Boele-Woelki, F. W. Grosheide (Eds.), *The Future of European Contract Law, Liber Amicorum E.H. Hondius*, pp. 411–424. Alphen aan den Rijn: Kluwer Law International.

Van Wijck, P. W. and Theeuwes, J. (2000). Protection against Unfair Contracts: An Economic Analysis of European Regulation. *European Journal of Law and Economics, 9*(1), pp. 73–89.

Velthuis, O. and Noordegraaf-Eelens, L. (2009). *Op naar de volgende crisis!*. Kampen: Klement.

Viitanen, K. (2007). Enforcement of consumers' collective interests by regulatory agencies in the Nordic Countries. In: W. H. Van Boom, M. B. M. Loos (Eds.), *Collective Enforcement of Consumer law*, pp. 83–103. Groningen: Europa Law Publishing.

Volante, R. (2008). Standard Contract Terms and Financial Contracts. In: H. Collins (Ed.), *Standard Contract Terms in Europe: A Basis for and a Challenge to European Contract Law*, pp. 277–289. Alphen aan den Rijn: Kluwer Law International.

Wakker, P.P., Timmermans, D.R.M. and Machielse, I.A. (2007). The Effects of Statistical Information on Risk and Ambiguity Attitudes, and on Rational Insurance Decisions. *Management Science, 53*(11), pp. 1770–1784.

Waller, S.W. (2005). In Search of Economic Justice: Considering Competition and Consumer Protection Law. *Loyola University Chicago Law Journal, 36*(2), pp. 631–639.

Wason, P.C. (1960). On the failure to eliminate hypotheses in a conceptual task. *Quarterly Journal of Experimental Psychology, 12*(3), pp. 129–140.

Weatherill, S. (2005). *EU Consumer Law and Policy.* Cheltenham: Edward Elgar.

Weber, J. M., Malhotra, D. and Murnighan, J. K. (2005). Normal acts of irrational trust, motivated attributions, and the process of trust development. In: B. M. Staw, R. M. Kramer (Eds.), *Research in Organizational Behavior, Volume 26*, pp. 75–102. New York: Elsevier.

Weinstein, N.D. (1980). Unrealistic optimism about future life events. *Journal of Personality & Social Psychology, 39*(5), pp. 806–820.

Wendlandt, B. (2005). EC Directives for Self-Employed Commercial Agents and on Time-Sharing - Apples, Oranges and the Core of the Information Overload Problem. In: G. G. Howells, A. Janssen and R. Schulze (Eds.), *Information Rights and Obligations*, pp. 67–92. Aldershot: Ashgate.

Weterings, W.C.T. (2007). De economische analyse van het recht. In: W. C. T. Weterings (Ed.), *De economische analyse van het recht*, pp. 1–18. Den Haag: Boom Juridische Uitgevers.

White, A.M. (2009). Behavior and Contract. *Law and Inequality, 27*(1), pp. 135–179.

White, M.D. (2010). Behavioral Law and Economics: The Assault on Consent, Will, and Dignity. In: G. Gaus, C. Favor and J. Lamont (Eds.), *Essays on Philosophy, Politics & Economics: Integration & Common Research Projects.* Palo Alto: Stanford University Press (forthcoming).

Whitford, W.C. (1973). The Functions of Disclosure Regulation in Consumer Transactions. *Wisconsin Law Review, 1973*(2), pp. 400–470.

Whitman, D.G. and Rizzo, M.J. (2007). Paternalist Slopes. *NYU Journal of Law & Liberty, 2*(3), pp. 411–443.

Whittaker, S. (2006). On the Development of European Standard Contract Terms. *European Review of Contract Law, 2*(1), pp. 51–76.

Wilhelmsson, T. (1993). Control of Unfair Contract Terms and Social Values: EC and Nordic Approaches. *Journal of Consumer Policy, 16*(3–4), pp. 435–453.

– (2006). Cooperation and Competition Regarding Standard Contract Terms in Consumer Contracts. *European Business Law Review, 17*(1), pp. 51–72.

Wilhelmsson, T. and Twigg-Flesner, C. (2006). Pre-contractual information duties in the acquis communautaire. *European Review of Contract Law, 2*(4), pp. 441–470.

Wilkinson, N. (2008). *An Introduction to Behavioral Economics.* Basingstoke: Palgrave Macmillan.

Willett, C. (2005). Autonomy and Fairness: The Case of Public Statements. In: G. G. Howells, A. Janssen and R. Schulze (Eds.), *Information Rights and Obligations*, pp. 1–15. Aldershot: Ashgate.

Willett, C. (2007). *Fairness in Consumer Contracts. The Case of Unfair Terms.* Aldershot: Ashgate.

Williamson, O.E. (1981). The Economics of Organization: The Transaction Cost Approach. *American Journal of Sociology, 87*(3), pp. 548–577.

Winick, B.J. (1992). On Autonomy: Legal and Psychological perspectives. *Villanova Law Review, 37*(6), pp. 1705–1777.

Wright, J.D. (2007). Behavioral Law and Economics, Paternalism, and Consumer Contracts: An Empirical Perspective. *NYU Journal of Law & Liberty, 2*(3), pp. 470–511.

Wright, J.D. and Zywicki, T.J. (2009). Three Problematic Truths About the Consumer Financial Protection Agency Act of 2009. *Lombard Street, 1*(12), pp. 29–44.

Zak, P.J. (2004). Neuroeconomics. *Philosophical Transactions of the Royal Society B: Biological Sciences, 359*(1451), pp. 1737–1748.

Zanitelli, L.M. (2009). Default Rules and the Inevitability of Paternalism. *SSRN eLibrary*. Available at: SSRN.com/paper=1346497.

Zywicki, T.J. (2007). Evolutionary Psychology. In: D. S. Clark (Ed.), *Encyclopedia of Law and Society: American and Global Perspectives*, pp. 536–541. Thousand Oaks, California: Sage Publications.

European Studies in Law and Economics

The series *'European Studies in Law and Economics'* is devoted to further the understanding of Law and Economics in Europe. The volumes published in this series present an interdisciplinary perspective on the effects of laws on people's behaviour and on the economic system. The ample topics address a wide audience, including policy makers, legislators, economists, lawyers and judges. The series is peer-reviewed.

The series is an initiative of the PhD programme *'European Doctorate in Law and Economics'* (EDLE). The EDLE is the academic response to the increasing importance of the economic analysis of law in Europe. The programme is offered by the Universities of Bologna, Hamburg and Rotterdam in association with the Indira Gandhi Institute of Development Research, Mumbai (India). PhD students receive the unique opportunity to study law and economics in three different countries. The programme prepares economists and lawyers of high promise for an academic career in a research field of growing importance or for responsible positions in government, research organisations and international consulting firms.

The European Commission sponsors the EDLE as an excellence programme under the prestigious Erasmus Mundus scheme. For further information please visit: www.edle-phd.eu.

www.ingramcontent.com/pod-product-compliance
Ingram Content Group UK Ltd.
Pitfield, Milton Keynes, MK11 3LW, UK
UKHW051920100926
8556IPUK00021B/1284

9 789400 000865